In much of Melanesia, the process of social reproduction unfolds as a lengthy sequence of mortuary rites – feast making and gift giving through which the living publicly define their social relations with each other while at the same time commemorating the deceased. In this study Robert J. Foster constructs an ethnographic account of mortuary rites in the Tanga Islands, Papua New Guinea, placing these large-scale feasts and ceremonial exchanges in their historical context and demonstrating how the effects of participation in an expanding cash economy have allowed Tangans to conceive of the rites as "customary" in opposition to the new and foreign practices of "business." His examination synthesizes two divergent trends in Melanesian anthropology by emphasizing both the radical differences between Melanesian and Western forms of sociality and the conjunction of Melanesian and Western societies brought about by colonialism and capitalism.

To Donna & Carroll,
Some light
bedside reading

love,
John

Cambridge Studies in Social and Cultural Anthropology

96

SOCIAL REPRODUCTION AND HISTORY IN MELANESIA

Cambridge Studies in Social and Cultural Anthropology

The monograph series *Cambridge Studies in Social and Cultural Anthropology* publishes analytical ethnographies, comparative works and contributions to theory. All combine an expert and critical command of ethnography and a sophisticated engagement with current theoretical debates.

A list of books in this series will be found at the end of the volume

SOCIAL REPRODUCTION AND HISTORY IN MELANESIA

Mortuary ritual, gift exchange, and custom in the Tanga Islands

ROBERT J. FOSTER
University of Rochester

CAMBRIDGE
UNIVERSITY PRESS

Published by the Press Syndicate of the University of Cambridge
The Pitt Building, Trumpington Street, Cambridge CB2 1RP
40 West 20th Street, New York, NY 10011–4211, USA
10 Stamford Road, Oakleigh, Melbourne 3166, Australia

First published 1995

Printed in Great Britain at the University Press, Cambridge

A catalogue record for this book is available from the British Library

Library of Congress cataloguing in publication data
Foster, Robert John, 1957–
Social reproduction and history in Melanesia: mortuary ritual, gift exchange, and
custom in the Tanga Islands / Robert J. Foster.
    p.   cm. – (Cambridge studies in social and cultural anthropology: 96)
Revision of the author's thesis (Ph.D.) – University of Chicago, 1988.
Includes bibliographical references and index.
ISBN 0 521 48030 2 (hardback). ISBN 0 521 48332 8 (paperback).
1. Tanga (Papua New Guinea people).
2. Tanga (Papua New Guinea people) – Funeral customs and rites.
3. Ceremonial exchange – Papua New Guinea.
I. Title. II. Series.
DU740.42.F67   1995
995.3–dc20   94–30846   CIP

ISBN 0 521 48030 2 hardback
ISBN 0 521 48332 8 paperback

Contents

Illustrations

Maps

Tables

Preface

On February 1, 1992, I returned to Tanga for five weeks. My welcome was both casual and dramatic: casual inasmuch as my position in local social relations was already given, dramatic inasmuch as that place required public definition before anything else could happen. It had been more than six years since I had lived there from about April, 1984 to July, 1985.

Partui Bonaventura, my friend, host, and patron, led the group of mostly men who met me at the airstrip. I recognized Negut, Tikot, Netang, Bingfiu, and Kiapsel – all of whom happily recognized me as fatter than they had remembered. Among them was Nancy, the tall seven-year-old daughter of my friend and collaborator, Somanil Funil. Nancy was born the day before I first arrived in Tanga; Somanil subsequently named her after my wife. Nancy was a toddler who preferred to be carried when I had last seen her – her growth measured the time that had passed.

Partui instructed me to stop at the parish tradestore and to purchase a 25 kilogram bag of rice and several tins of mackerel. He had a plan. We all climbed into Piskot's rusty Toyota pickup truck, miraculously still running, and drove slowly to Taonsip at the eastern end of Boang Island.

At Partui's hamlet, more greetings – this time from local men and women gathered inside and outside the men's house. Soon Partui called me into his house, where my old room had been readied. He explained the situation. Somanil and Timir, whom I had not yet greeted, were at Somanil's hamlet, preparing a feast to which we would repair as soon as the rain let up. I was to put on a black shirt and a black *laplap*, and wear an old filthy baseball cap. As I did so, we rehearsed the brief speech I would make to Somanil.

The walk from Partui's hamlet to Somanil's was no more than one hundred yards. Off to the left was the large neighborhood cemetery. Tinaluklukar, Somanil's mother, whom I too called mother, was buried there. She had died after I left Tanga, not long after my own mother had died unexpectedly in Staten Island. My eyes filled with tears at the memories, as had the eyes of Tinaluklukar's old sisters, Tingkauisi and Imbusil, when they saw me again.

We delivered to Somanil two cooked pigs: one from Nancy, for bringing me to her father, the other from Partui, for allowing me to see Tinaluklukar's grave. I presented the rice, tinned fish, and some coins to Somanil, and informed him of my mourning: I was not here when our mother died, and I was not able to help Somanil organize the necessary feasts. My voice cracked. Somanil, in turn, presented me with a one kina coin, acknowledged my help, and removed my black clothing and dirty cap. We then sat down, ate, and began to catch up with each other. Within two hours of landing, I was once again engaged in a flow of sociality conditioned by the exigencies of "finishing" the dead: my filial relationship to Tinaluklukar, and thus to all her relatives, had been evinced and acted upon.

The position that I came to occupy in the flow of Tangan sociality enabled and limited what I came to understand and what I failed to understand. Some comments are in order, perhaps more for Tangan than non-Tangan readers.

I slept in Partui's hamlet, Mokatilistunglo, on the night of my arrival in 1984 and remained there for the duration of my stay in Tanga. Many Tangans later told me that it seemed to them as if I had gone directly and intentionally to Mokatilistunglo, indeed, as if I had kin there. But my itinerary was determined only by a chance encounter with Nebutikorofi, who volunteered to introduce me to people in the part of the island where his mother's and father's relatives reside (see Foster 1988).

Partui was the leader or big man (*kaltu dok*) of Solsol lineage of clan Korofi. He was then a not yet remarried widower who slept in a house made of fiber-board with a corrugated iron roof, built during the early 1960s for Ngamnabo – an aged big man and prominent figure in F. L. S. Bell's pre-World War II ethnography of Tanga. I soon moved into a small bush-material house that we had constructed next door.

For the next month, Partui and Somanil, a Solsol lineage man of about my age, introduced me to their various relatives and friends in Taonsip and elsewhere. They helped me collect basic information on social organization and begin work on the local language. Although I became somewhat proficient at understanding the language, my speaking ability never became impressive. I did most of my research in Melanesian pidgin, in which almost all New Irelanders are fluent, or through the mediation of an interpreter, usually Somanil, who became familiar with my ethnographic project.

It was from my position in the network of relations that enmeshed the men and women of Solsol lineage that I conducted my daily inquiries. Accordingly, my view of Tangan sociality is a particularly situated view. I learned the system of kinship through the various affinal and paternal ties to Solsol lineage. Likewise, I learned firsthand the details of preparing and executing a mortuary sequence by participating in the sequence hosted by Solsol lineage during my stay. My main informants and fastest friends were all residents of Taonsip. I did not visit western Boang as much as I would have liked and consequently I never learned in detail the internal organization and history of the clans which occupy this area. Nor did I do extensive interviewing and participant observation in the cluster of hamlets located near the Mission complex and airstrip at Amfar.

I would disagree with Tangans who find the following account Taonsip-centric. Instead, I maintain that the account given here is of general validity for the Tanga Islands, though I recognize that life is not lived exactly the same in all parts of the islands. In Amfar, for example, there seemed to be a different rhythm to activity, a pace conditioned by the presence of the tradestore, church, hospital, and other arenas for social interaction. In the outlying islands of Lif, Tefa, and Malendok, which I visited only for a total of two weeks, this is even more the case; these islands, sparsely populated and without vehicular roads, clearly constituted a periphery to central Boang. Nonetheless, Tangans recognize no local differences in the practice of mortuary ritual, and indeed people from various parts of the islands participate in each other's rites. The topics of mortuary ritual, gift exchange, and custom addressed in this book, I contend, do not require extended consideration of intra-island variations.

Other Tangans, and non-Tangans too, might find this account too silent on issues of gender. My wife, Nancy Foster, spent the last six months with me in Tanga. The two of us lived in Partui's house while Partui moved into my house, an arrangement that suited all of us. Nancy befriended many women and accompanied them in their daily routines. Her presence afforded me some access to the non-public world of women; but her presence also closed that world to me by establishing in the eyes of many Tangans a gendered division of labor for our inquiries. Much of the information reported in this book was gathered from men; similarly, the focus of the book (and the accompanying plates) on the publicly drama-tized aspects of mortuary rites highlights the activities of men rather than women.

Finally, some specialist readers might wish that more sustained com-parisons were made in this book with recent ethnographies of New Ireland. I have tried to indicate connections, where space allowed, between my interpretations and data, and those of other New Ireland ethnographers, particularly Roy Wagner and Brenda Clay. Although not explicitly a regional comparison, this book nevertheless complements existing New Ireland ethnography inasmuch as the paramount concerns of New Irelanders with "finishing" and "replacing" the dead have shaped that ethnography.

Acknowledgments

This book is a revised version of my doctoral thesis (Foster 1988), the research for which was funded by the US Department of Education (Fulbright-Hays Doctoral Dissertation Research Abroad Grant No. 600–83–008510) and the National Science Foundation (Doctoral Dissertation Research Grant No. BNS–8312747). Two brief trips to Tanga in 1992 (one for a week during the polling period of the national elections) were made financially possible by the Australian–American Educational Foundation, the American Council of Learned Societies, and the University of Rochester.

I thank the New Ireland Provincial Government for its generous permission to conduct field research and for its advocacy of the value of anthropological studies. I have received help in facilitating my work at various times from: C. S. Rangatan, Esikiel Waisale, Ephraim Apelis, and Ben Kamil.

During my trips to Papua New Guinea, I was affiliated with the Institute of Papua New Guinea Studies (now the Cultural Studies Division of the National Research Institute). I thank the Institute, especially its past directors, Professor Andrew Strathern and Dr. Jacob Simet, for advice and aid in securing research permits. A number of other institutions kindly allowed me access to their resources. I thank the library staffs of the Institute for Applied Social and Economic Research, the New Guinea Collection of the University of Papua New Guinea, and the National Archives of Papua New Guinea. I also thank Father Superior Norbert Birkman of the Catholic Mission at Vunapope, East New Britain, for allowing me to use the Mission library.

I thank Nancy Munn for her intellectual support and example over the years. At various stages, this book has benefited from comments made by

Terence Turner, Marshall Sahlins, Jane Fajans, Scott MacWilliam, Deborah Gewertz, Anthony Carter, Aletta Biersack, and two anonymous readers for Cambridge University Press. I also owe a debt of gratitude to F. L. S. Bell for the leads his work provided me in my own fieldwork.

Revisions of the manuscript were begun during a stay at the Research School of Pacific Studies, Australian National University. I thank Professor James Fox and the entire staff of the Department of Anthropology for their warm hospitality and the use of their resources. I thank Margaret Tyrie for preparing the kinship figures used in this book and Marilyn Anderson for printing plate 1.

I thank the American Anthropological Association, the Royal Anthropological Institute, and Oceania Publications for kind permission to use in this book sections from my previous published articles.

On the road from fieldwork to thesis to book, I have accumulated as souvenirs more personal debts of more kinds than I can enumerate, much less repay. I wish to single out Roy Wagner and Phil Lewis for their interest and pre-field guidance. The late Professor Peter Lawrence gave me his time and consideration, as did Dr. J. Specht of The Australian Museum. The staff of the Rare Books Collection of the Fisher Library, University of Sydney, helped me in consulting the fieldnotes of F. L. S. Bell and arranged for me to reproduce by permission Bell's photograph of Ngamnabo and Bitlik. Dick Bryant, Deane Fergie, and Chris Morgan offered unselfish hospitality in Sydney and Canberra on the trip back to the USA in 1985.

In Port Moresby, three people sustained me with their companionship and intellectual stimulation: James and Achsah Carrier, and Scott Mac-William. I thank them for their generosity and friendship. Numerous other individuals made life easier by showing concern for me and interest in my research: Peter Larmour, Herb Thompson, Marc Schiltz, Lisette Josephides and, on my 1992 trips, Mark Busse and Wari Iamu.

In Rabaul, Blaise Sumsuma and Mark Nebau and their families opened their homes to me and made me welcome in every way. I warmly thank them for their uncompromising hospitality. *Kone aro sing gam.* In 1992, Tom Barker and Marta Rohatynskyj kindly took me into their home.

Ben Kamil first helped me orient myself in Kavieng. Later, Roger Dixon assisted me immensely by introducing me to his wife's nephew, Nebutikorofi, who in turn introduced me to the people of Taonsip in the eastern end of Boang. I thank them all for their hospitality and confidence.

Ben Topikol of Muliama invited me to stay in his home and made possible a brief reconnaissance in southern New Ireland. I gratefully acknowledge the assistance he and his family gave me.

In Namatanai, I sometimes stayed with Aladin Sakias, who also opened his home to me without hesitation. Thanks are due as well to Fr. Joe Gloexner of St. Martin's Parish for his hospitality and advice.

I owe a great debt to the Catholic Mission in Tanga and, in particular, to Fr. Leon Weissenberger for permitting me to consult St. Boniface Parish records and to use parish resources and facilities when needed. I also thank the entire staff of Sisters at the Mission for their thoughtful gifts of fresh bread.

My greatest debt, of course, is to the people of Tanga, who showed me numerous kindnesses and accepted me wherever I went among them. All of the people of Taonsip with whom I lived deserve my gratitude. I must thank first of all Partui Bonaventura, for taking a chance on taking me in and then never reneging on his offer. Somanil Funil, my companion and colleague, made much of my work possible through his ethnographic attitude. I am grateful for his friendship and for the material care given me by him, his late mother Tinaluklukar and wife Salome, and by Partui and his wife Likot. The men and women of Solsol lineage, *tanga tuaklik ma tang'indung*, and their spouses and children all shared with me their project of building a commemorative men's house. I thank them all for making me feel at home, especially Negut, Timir, Timfaim, Tingkausi, Nekwit, Fabian, Sebastian, Kiapsel, and Kapsa. I thank Tomai and Piskot for making the service of their trucks available to me, and Parbil, Pangang, Netang, and Fumpas for gifts of *sugka*, fish, *brus*, and food. I thank the late Manilbau for showing me what *kastam* means to Tangans. I thank all those who hosted me on excursions away from Taonsip, especially August Paptabil of Lif, Bulu of Fangwel, and Siaronatui and Beno of Fonli. I thank all of the families who participated in the household income survey, including the families of Bakok, Tading, Tikot, Nefu, Kiaptes, and Neof. Many other people invited me to their feasts, shared their stories with me, answered my questions, asked me their questions, offered me drinks, betel nut, tobacco, and conversation. They all participate inextricably in this text. *A ti sangkifeni gam. Kone aro sigit.*

My wife Nancy sustained me with copious correspondence when we were apart; she assisted me as a colleague when we lived together in Tanga; and she has supplied constant critical appreciation and uncritical sympathy in writing this book. I dedicate it to her.

Glossary

Note on orthography

In spelling Tangga words, I have used with some modification the orthography developed by Mihalic (1971) for Melanesian Pidgin (Tok Pisin) (cf. Capell 1977; Maurer 1966). The orthography is convenient; it is not phonemically complete.

Vowels:

a   as in "calm"; e.g., *fat*
e   as in "bed"; e.g., *en*
    as in "hey"; e.g., *male*
i   as in "hit"; e.g., *pirpir*
    as in "machine"; e.g., *bif*
o   as in "hot"; e.g., *kong kuen*
    as in "or"; e.g., *mor*
    as in "snow"; e.g., *bo*
u   as in "bum"; e.g., *gumgum*
    as in "tulip"; e.g., *lulu*

Diphthongs:

ai   as in "find"; e.g., *kaik*
au (ao) as in "mouth"; e.g., *taufi*
oi   as in "oil"; e.g., *poiem*

Consonants:

b d f g k l m n ng p r s t w   Pronounced as in English, except:

g   is always hard, as in "get"; at the end of a word it becomes more like a /k/ sound; e.g., *fasuigk* (Bell's spelling, which I retain)

ng   one sound, as in "singer"
r   is flapped
w   sometimes interchanged with a /v/ sound

Selective glossary
Bia: Men's house
Bif: Funeral house, commemorative men's house
Bo: Pig
Do: Emblem, marker
En: To eat, consume; a feast
En tike: "Eat everything," feast in which all food must be consumed at
   the site of the feast
Fang: Nurture, care; particularly, paternal nurture; cf. *fangte*, to adopt,
   to look after
Farop: To finish, complete, bring to an end; said of the deceased,
   memories of the deceased, and obligations to the deceased
Fasuigk: Redistribution of pigs made during major mortuary feasts
Fat: Hard, rooted; stone; generic name for shell discs (*am fat*)
Fel: Generic name for house; traditional Quonset style funeral house
Fen: To feed, to give, to cause to eat (*fa-en*)
Fil: To buy; *fil fifin*, brideprice ("to buy a young woman")
Fimfil: Temporary men's house
Finailim: Sign, omen, foreshadowing
Fumbarat: Cluster of children, family, ancestral line
Funmat: Matriclan
Furis: Dramatic skit or monologue that accompanies certain mortuary
   feasts
Kaltu: Human being, man; *Kaltu dok*, big man
Kemetas: Valuable small red shell discs strung on lengths of twine and
   used in a variety of exchanges; *mis* in Tok Pisin
Kilis: To replace; *kilis asa*, to replace (change) a name
Kinaf: Short form of the reference term for cross-cousin; *fat kinaf*,
   "bound cross-cousins," the relationship between two intermarrying
   lineages
Laplap (*Tok Pisin*): a waistcloth, a loincloth
Lulu: To buy; *lulu am bo*, payment for the pigs, an important
   transaction that climaxes major mortuary feasts
Male: place, hamlet; *waranmale*, origin place (*asples* in Tok Pisin)
Mangat: Baked packets of scraped yam mixed with shredded coconut
   meat

Mapu: To stink, rot

Matambia: Matrilineage, "eye" of the men's house

Mor: Compensatory meal fed to collective work parties

Mui: Power, strength; syn. *mia*

Palang: Garden in full bearing

Pief: Ashes, sites formerly occupied by lineage big men

Pilis: To replace; *pilis lo iau*, my replacement (e.g., said by a man of his younger brother)

Sangkulung: To grieve; sorrow

Sangsang: To think, to feel; *sangfi*: to remember; *sangkifeni*: to forget

So puek: To bring or deliver a pig as a contribution to another lineage's feast

Tafu: Space, slot; *kep tafu*, to take the place of (said of an heir)

Tam en: Dietary restrictions, assumed as part of mourning procedures by the affinal and paternal relatives of the deceased

Tang: Purse, personal basket used to carry tobacco and betel nut chewing paraphernalia

Tara: Spirits, associated with particular pieces of the landscape and particular lineages (*masalai* in Tok Pisin)

Tinge: To buy; *ting bo*, to buy the pigs, describes the payment of one *tintol* for each pig donated to a lineage's supply for redistribution at *fasuigk*

Tintol: Type of shell disc (*am fat*) most often used in all exchange transactions

Tu: Bone; true; ridge post of a men's house; *tutor*, a carved ridge post

Warangus: Basket of food given to those designated to contribute and receive a large pig at the culminating feast of the mortuary sequence; literally, "base/source of the food heap" (*gus*)

Warantang: The largest and most valuable type of shell disc (*am fat*), a lineage heirloom which never circulates in exchange; literally, "base of the basket" (*tang*) in which shell discs were once stored

1

Introduction: history, alterity, and a new (Melanesian) anthropology

Soon after F. L. S. Bell, anthropologist and librarian, returned to Sydney from his fieldwork in Tanga, he told the readers of *Oceania* that: "With these people death is the leit-motif of their culture and their mortuary rites, which last for years and have endless social repercussions, are undoubtedly the most culturally satisfying and sustaining elements in the native life" (1934:291). Fifty years later, when I arrived to begin my fieldwork, Tangans themselves seemed to echo Bell's claim in glossing their mortuary rites with the word *kastam* – Tok Pisin (Melanesian pidgin) for "custom" or "tradition." I heard the echo frequently, in part because I inevitably elicited it with my own inquiries into "culture," and in part because the people with whom I lived most closely were themselves preoccupied with the garden making, pig raising, debt reckoning, song rehearsing, and myriad other doings associated with hosting a sequence of mortuary rites. But no matter how much these doings resembled the doings that Bell wrote about fifty years earlier, Bell did not describe *kastam*. For there is neither evidence to suggest nor reason to suppose that in 1934 Tangans imagined or labelled what they were doing as "customary" or "traditional."

The gloss of "custom" is a paradox, a claim about historical continuity expressed in a creolized form that bespeaks historical change. It is a paradox that raises a familiar question about the relationship between continuity and change, structure and process: how do things stay the same as they change, and change as they stay the same? This is a question of social reproduction and social transformation, of how people continuously produce their social relations amidst circumstances that they cannot always anticipate but must nevertheless engage. It is a question, moreover, that has received increasing attention with the conceptual shift

1

toward "a time-oriented anthropology" (Moore 1986), an anthropology preoccupied with events, processes, and history.

Throughout island Melanesia, mortuary rites define the privileged site of social reproduction, the ensemble of activities through which people secure the conditions for their future existence. Mortuary rites in Tanga, a cluster of small islands off the east coast of New Ireland, are no exception. Death regularly triggers a series of feasts, sponsored by the deceased's matrilineal relatives, which accompany the wake over and burial of the corpse and the commencement of mourning observances for the living. The series climaxes but does not terminate years later with exchanges of wealth made in connection with the construction of a new men's house. In the process, feast makers constitute and display themselves as a discrete social entity, what anthropologists have long called a lineage. These feasts and exchanges, the collective action that brings them to pass, and the changing historical circumstances of that action, are the main subjects of this book.

The Tok Pisin gloss of "custom" (*kastam*) that Tangans put on mortuary practices suggests both historical continuity and historical change. Other glosses, rendered in the local dialect, suggest a different apprehension of unbroken temporal continuity amidst the incessant changes wrought by death. In particular, Tangans speak of mortuary practices as the means for "finishing" (*farop*) and "replacing" (*pilis*) dead matrilineal relatives. What sort of analysis is required to encompass the significance and interrelationship of these three different glosses? How, in other words, is it possible to relate the contemporary status of mortuary practices as custom or tradition to their locally perceived effects of ensuring matrilineal succession?

The answer that I present in this book requires juxtaposing two different analytical approaches that have emerged in Melanesian studies during the last decade. One of these approaches, which I call the New Melanesian Ethnography (after Josephides 1991), highlights fundamental differences between Melanesian and Western presuppositions about social reality; that is, it argues for the recognition of radical alterity, of cultural differences on a scale, say, of the Dumontian distinction between homo hierarchicus and homo aequalis. In so doing, it constructs an opposition between Us and Them in order to criticize a mode of anthropological inquiry unselfconsciously predicated upon Our presuppositions. The other approach, the New Melanesian History, highlights similarities between Melanesian and Western social realities, similarities generated out of shared histories of colonialism and commerce. In so doing, it deconstructs dichotomies between Us and Them in order to criticize a mode of anthropological inquiry that emphasizes (even essentializes) the otherness of the Other and de-emphasizes the contingent effects of time (history) and power (colonial and capitalist domination).

These two approaches, regardless of their common stance against ethnocentrism, have developed in tension with each other. This tension goes far beyond the obvious and inevitable disjunction between generalizing comparative exercises, on the one hand, and particularizing historical accounts, on the other. At stake is nothing less than what defines the legitimate practice of anthropological description. For example, New Melanesian Historians such as Thomas (1991), Carrier (1992a, 1992b) and Gewertz and Errington (1991b), renewing Said's critique in *Orientalism* (1978), have questioned whether anthropology ought to be or need be "a discourse of alterity, a way of writing in which us/them distinctions are central, and which necessarily distances the people studied from ourselves" (Thomas 1991:3). They eschew the attempt to explicate alternate cultural orders or social logics or any such unitary, organic conception of "other cultures" – what Thomas (1991:3) not unfairly characterizes as a project of endlessly elaborating on dense metaphors, key symbols, concepts of the person and agency, and indigenous views of time and history. Instead they urge anthropologists, Melanesianists especially, to destabilize the discourse of alterity with an affirmation of shared history, "the manifold and problematic engagements of various classes of Europeans, North Americans, or Australians with various colonized peoples, and the equally asymmetrical contacts and combats between Third World nation-states and tribal peoples within their borders . . ." (Thomas 1991:3). They thus call attention to the relationships between us and them, "those sociohistorical forces of systemic connection, those forces which *articulate* between, and *shape*, our lives and theirs in a world system" (Gewertz and Errington 1991b:81).

By contrast, the New Melanesian Ethnographers have self-consciously embraced the Us/Them opposition as a useful and, more importantly, a *necessary* analytic device for anthropological inquiry. Their methodological argument has been made most forcefully by Marilyn Strathern in *The Gender of the Gift* (1988), although earlier adumbrated by Roy Wagner in his essay, *The Invention of Culture* (1975). Strathern claims that "the strategy of an us/them divide" neither suggests "that Melanesian societies can be presented in a timeless, monolithic way" nor implies "some fixity in their state-of-being which renders them objects of knowledge"

(1988:16). Instead, she argues, the strategy intentionally makes explicit "the practice of anthropological description itself, which creates its own context in which ideas drawn from different social origins are kept distinct by reference to those origins. Creating a kind of mirror-imagery gives a form to *our thoughts* about the differences" (1988:16–17, emphasis mine). In other words, the strategy of an Us/Them mirror imagery addresses the inescapable human condition that "our thoughts come already formed, that we think through images" (1988:16). The strategy exposes anthropological exegesis – indeed, all exegetical activity – as creative analogy: "an effort to create a world parallel to the perceived world in an expressive medium (writing) that sets down its own conditions of intelligibility" (Strathern 1988:17). Accordingly, then, the challenge of the New Melanesian Ethnography is to achieve critical awareness in deploying the images or metaphors (i.e., heuristics such as the too-familiar contrast between "gifts" and "commodities") that form our thoughts about how others think or might think about themselves. Not surprisingly, then, in a pointed response to Thomas, Strathern (1993:93) insists that attention to historical change will not "destabilise the idea of stable cultures" as long as anthropologists fail to relativize their concepts, that is, to explicate the assumptions entailed in the images, metaphors, constructs, and vocabulary *we* use to describe how other people conceptualize what *they* are or were doing.

Laid side by side like this, the perspectives of the New Melanesian History and the New Melanesian Ethnography easily accommodate each other; one certainly does not preclude the other. Keesing and Jolly (1992), in their epilogue to a volume of papers advancing the arguments of the New Melanesian History, draw the same conclusion. Although they question the very category of "Melanesia," and advocate "a more serious engagement with the transformations of the colonial period and the predicaments of the present," they do not regard an anthropology of Melanesia (qualifying quotation marks removed) to be impossible:

We regard it as a quite legitimate anthropological enterprise to explore the human diversity of Melanesia. Indeed, as Marilyn Strathern (1988) has brilliantly shown, in examining that diversity we can interrogate our own assumptions and categories, subjecting Western conceptual systems to deconstructive scrutiny.

(Keesing and Jolly 1992:241)

I agree, but I also wish to enlarge their observation. For if there is to be a New Melanesian Anthropology, then it must regard both the New Melanesian History and the New Melanesian Ethnography not only as legitimate anthropological enterprises, but also as inseparable anthropological enterprises. In other words, the New Melanesian History and the New Melanesian Ethnography *must* provide frames of reference for each other. My claim is that only anthropological practice premised upon such a juxtaposition of frames of reference is in a position to apprehend the specific terms upon which Melanesians themselves premise their own actions. For the frames of reference in terms of which Melanesians act are separate in their historical and cultural origins, as the New Melanesian Ethnography would keep them, but conjoined in ways that inform how people think about, talk about, and do what they are doing in the present, as the New Melanesian History would stress. A New Melanesian Anthropology, then, must begin with the recognition that Melanesians understand themselves and act in terms – sometimes oppositional, sometimes syncretic – conditioned by the continuing encounter between agencies of (post)colonial states, capitalism, and Christianity, on one side, and highly localized practices for making meaning, on the other (see, for example, White 1991).

In this book, I demonstrate my claims about a New Melanesian Anthropology by arguing that *we* require both "historical" and "ethnographic" approaches in order to understand how Tangans understand mortuary rites as the means of social reproduction. A Tangan speaker might use the gloss of "custom" to describe mortuary rites in one situation and that of "replacement" in another; in this sense, the glosses are alternatives. Each gloss, however, conditions the meaning of the other; the connotations of one gloss furnish the background to the connotations of the other gloss. Both sets of connotations must be apprehended in order to register the significance of either one. But while the Tok Pisin gloss of *kastam* moves anthropological description in the direction of a history of colonial capitalism, the Tangga (see chapter 2, footnote 9) gloss of *pilis* moves anthropological description in the direction of an elaboration of local conceptions of personhood and agency (not to mention dense metaphors and key symbols). Consequently, the juxtaposition of "historical" and "ethnographic" approaches is necessary for placing local understandings of mortuary practices in the context of supralocal (global) political economic circumstances *and* vice versa. To do one without doing the other would be either to deny the links between Tangan mortuary rites and a larger world of social practices or to pretend that these links are the only frame of reference in which Tangans undertake mortuary rites. In other words, Tangan social reproduction must be regarded as collective action conditioned by changing circumstances of both endogenous and exogenous origins. It is the particular conjunction of these circumstances in 1984–85, the period of my main fieldwork, that I describe and analyze in this book.

The New Melanesian History draws upon arguments consolidated in the merger of history and anthropology during the 1980s (Cohn 1981). It endorses the wisdom of opening up ethnography to history, that is, of extending the context of ethnographic analysis beyond the space of "the village" and the time(lessness) of "the present." It uses the resulting awareness of regional and temporal variation as a corrective for naive essentialism, subverting ethnographic representations that ascribe to people authentic ontologies or mentalities which reproduce themselves inevitably, inexorably – beyond the influence of shifting social and economic conditions. At the same time, the New Melanesian History raises questions about the notion of society as a "sealed unit" of study, about the "very existence of a set of people, relationships, and practices sufficiently stable to justify being called 'a society'" (Carrier 1992a:19). As Carrier correctly asks: "After all, if what the people of X village do turns out to be historically fluid, malleable, then what are we to understand by the notion of X society or X culture?" (1992a:19).

These questions call attention to the long history of Western expansion and colonization in island Melanesia. Particularly relevant to my analysis of Tangan mortuary practices are the attempts of New Melanesian Historians to relate local situations to the development of a transnational web of capitalist social relations. I refer specifically to some recent subtle efforts to treat such ur-Melanesian practices as gift exchange and initiation rites as emergent products rather than resilient survivals of ongoing engagements with wage-labor, international tourism, and capital accumulation (e.g., Carrier and Carrier 1989; Gewertz and Errington 1991a; see also Gregory 1980). To this same end, I embed an ethnographic analysis of Tangan mortuary feasting and exchange in a history of "commoditization," the always variable and sometimes forcible process by which local people and their products enter into wider relations of commodity production and consumption. This strategy allows me to address the question of how Tangan mortuary practices both changed and did not change during the colonial and immediate postcolonial periods. It is through such a strategy, moreover, that I am able to trace the emergence of *kastam* as a Tangan cultural category.

There is convenience in beginning my interpretation of mortuary practices with the gloss of *kastam*: it more or less delimits the main object of analysis in this book. But there is also a point to be made: the mortuary practices that I observed in 1984–85 had acquired their coherence *as an object* – a set or domain of activities – only as the result of specific historical circumstances. I recount these circumstances through a chronology of commoditization that also traces the emergence of *kastam* as an explicit cultural category. This account yields yet another case of the "invention of tradition" in the Pacific (Linnekin 1990). My purpose, however, is not one of demystifying putative traditions. What I draw out of the Tangan case is its insistence that the objectification of "culture" and hence *heightened* cultural self-consciousness need not emerge only in circumstances of confrontation with an external (usually colonial) other (cf. Keesing 1992; Keesing and Tonkinson 1982; Thomas 1992a).[1] Nor, the case suggests, does cultural objectification depend upon the machinations of official elite cultural producers purveying romanticized (and generic) notions of the traditional past (cf. Keesing 1989; Philibert 1986). Instead, cultural objectification can occur as an aspect of transformations in local political economic relations. In Tanga, such a transformation entailed the generation of a categorical opposition between *kastam* and *bisnis*, the latter term denoting petty commodity production in the form of cash cropping. The emergence of this opposition, I argue, reconfigured the field of cultural categories in terms of which mortuary practices are locally undertaken and given meaning. My analysis of the cultural premises and social dynamics of Tangan mortuary rites starts from this recognition.

More than a century of entanglement between Tangans and a web of transnational capitalist social relations has transformed the practice of mortuary rites. What was arguably once an undifferentiated field of practice has now become divided conceptually and to a large extent practically into distinct domains such as *kastam* and *bisnis* (see Otto 1990). Nevertheless, a comparison of my description of Tangan mortuary rites in 1984–85 with the description composed by F. L. S. Bell after his fieldwork in 1933 suggests that the observable forms of mortuary feasting and ceremonial exchange have remained fairly constant. That is, the sequence of feasting and exchange, the overt symbolism of mortuary performances, and most of all the central place of the rites in public social life do not appear to have altered radically.

This combination of continuity and change invites explanation. There is, of course, no need to presume that modification let alone elimination of mortuary rites would necessarily occur (say, as a consequence of "modernization"). But there is equally no need to assume any continuity to ritual practices, especially given the manifest changes in the categorization of these practices. The issue then is to account for neither change nor continuity, but rather to account for the *specific combination* of continuity and change in Tangan mortuary practices. How?

Answering this question requires some conceptualization of what mortuary practices accomplish. In Tanga, I suggest, power (*mui*) is made manifest in mortuary ritual. But this is not the political power to command others so much as the potency to formulate collective identities, specifically, matrilineal identities or matrilineages (*matambia*). That is, mortuary ritual is the practical locus for social reproduction, the privileged site for producing and fixing, again and again, social identities and relations imagined as preconditions for future action (see Damon and Wagner 1989). It is this intermittent public process that Tangans gloss as "finishing" and "replacing" the dead.

In order to address the historical question of continuity and change, then, it is necessary to grasp how the production and reproduction of matrilineal identities and relations were organized in 1984–85. I therefore move from an historical account of Tangan mortuary practices to an ahistorical account of their processual structure. For, as I will propose in the conclusion, it was this structured process of social (re)production, in articulation with capitalist social practices, that precipitated a practical insulation of *kastam* from *bisnis*. And it is this insulation, in turn, which has apparently both conserved the symbolic form of mortuary practices and given them a set of connotations wholly unlike those attached to the mortuary practices that Bell observed in 1933.

It is through the propositions of the New Melanesian Ethnography that I attempt to outline the structure and effects of Tangan mortuary practices. Like the New Melanesian History, the New Melanesian Ethnography questions the notion of "society," but it does so through a model of "Melanesian" personhood and agency constructed in dialectical opposition to a model of "Western" personhood and agency. The strategy involved is one of sophisticated, self-conscious essentialism, the purpose of which is to enable a reconceptualization of "the social order" in terms other than those of relationships between "individuals" and between "individuals" and "groups."[2] Put differently, the conceptual aim of the New Melanesian Ethnography is to displace the static, morphological notion of "society" with the alternative notion of "sociality," the dual processes of constituting social relationships and precipitating social identities.[3]

At the center of the model of Melanesian personhood lies the notion of "composite persons," persons understood as nodes in a given matrix of relations. This notion mirrors its counterpart in the Western model, the notion of "individuals." Developed most fully by Strathern (1988), this key contrast has been formulated succinctly in relation to Orokaiva ideas by Iteanu, who derives it from Dumont:

> Among the Orokaiva, men and women, whom we call persons, are not seen as having been created differently or as being different in kind from the rest of the universe. For them, there is no special, universal category of individuals possessing unique, shared characteristics and placed above and in opposition to things. Consequently, society is not conceived of as being composed of an ensemble of such individuals, nor is there an ontological relation of identity between any two persons. Persons only exist because they are caught up in a network of relations ...
>
> *(1990:40)*

This sort of mirror imaging has consequences, as the New Melanesian Ethnography would expect, for the way in which *we* describe what *we* take to be Melanesian notions of personhood. Neither the term "group" nor "individual" can be used to denote a preconstituted empirical entity, the irreducibly self-evident elements of "social structure." Similarly, as Iteanu remarks about the Orokaiva, "the notion of 'being a relation' takes the place of our idea of 'having' relations, in the sense of possession."

> When we say that men "have" social relations, we imply that men as such exist apart from their relations and that their "possession" of these relations is in some sense secondary. Precisely the opposite is true in Orokaiva logic.
>
> *(1990:41)*

The strategy of an Us/Them contrast, as Keesing and Jolly allowed, thus subjects certain assumptions of sociological inquiry, including its lexicon, to "deconstructive scrutiny."

Mosko's summary of Strathern's position extracts from the notion of composite persons the implications for conceptualizing agency:

> ... each Melanesian person is a composite formed of relations with a plurality of other persons. The relations comprising any one person have or compose a history in the sense of a record of others' prior contributions. By the same token, the relations of which a person is composed constitute so many capacities for action, and so every person can be said to have a future. But in acting as agents themselves, persons externalize the parts or relations of which they are, or until then have been, composed. By acting, in other words, persons are "*de*composed." As agents in this sense, persons evince and anticipate the knowledge or recognition of their internal composition and capacities in the responses of others. Thus

decomposing and externalizing their parts, relations, or capacities, persons stimulate one another to action and reaction.

(1992:702)

In other words, the notion of composite persons implies a notion of agency as "activation," that is, the activation or evincement of relations which compose the person (see Clay 1992). This notion of agency inverts that of autonomous self-determination associated with the concept of free and discrete individuals. Whereas composite persons conventionally act in terms of their relations, individuals act with reference to themselves as bounded entities, that is, individuals act as their own cause (Strathern 1988).

This model of Melanesian personhood and agency opens up the possibilities explored in this book for thinking anew about exchange and exchange-value. Exchange is conceived not as a means for making debts and credits – though it is surely this – but rather as the action whereby persons make themselves known (i.e., externalize "their internal composition") in the responses they elicit from others. Likewise, exchange-value is conceived not as the measure of the things exchanged – a ratio of congealed labor, a determination of relative utility – but rather as the specific relationship between persons that the exchange of things evinces (see Foster 1990a). Exchange-value, in other words, refers to the double relation between persons and things as terms that define each other's significance. Like the New Melanesian Ethnography as a whole, then, this particular conceptualization of exchange and exchange-value exposes and dislodges some of the presuppositions of what Strathern (1988) calls the "commodity metaphor" – unspoken assumptions about Commodity Transactions that threaten to infiltrate Our understandings of what We describe as Gift Exchange.

Strathern furthermore notes that relationships between composite persons rest on two different grounds: interdependency and difference; and shared identity – Iteanu's "relations of identity." Exchange, as social action for making relationships known, can assert difference or similarity, or both simultaneously. This last possibility is especially a feature of collective action such as the ceremonial exchanges that are a staple of Melanesian ethnography. Collective action of this sort brings together disparate composite persons and "de-pluralizes" them or makes them "homologues of one another" (Strathern 1988:13). In so doing, composite or plural persons are conceptualized and represented as a "collective individual," what the model of Western personhood would recognize as a "group." In doing so, however, exchange agents enact a paradox. For the

construction of a collective individual, of shared identity within a group
of individuals, denies or eclipses the relationality between composite
persons that provides the moral basis of everyday (non-ceremonial, non-
collective) social action. That is, the construction of collective individuals
as bounded and discrete groups intimates autonomy rather than interdependency, separation rather than relationality. Such intimations are
acts of power, power understood not as domination, but as the capacity
to transcend sociality. Nevertheless, the entire project of constructing
collective individuals presupposes interdependency and relationality, i.e.,
reciprocal relations that allow exchange agents to take turns at constructing collective individuality and autonomy for each other. Hence the
paradox.

My interpretation of the two glosses "finishing" (*farop*) and
"replacing" (*pilis*) the dead draws on the model of personhood, agency,
and exchange informing the New Melanesian Ethnography. For my
analysis works within a set of propositions that do not take for granted
autonomous individuals (or groups of individuals) acting as their own
cause. Accordingly, I treat Tangan mortuary practices as a form of
collective action that constructs collective individuals – matrilineages, in
this case – out of composite persons. That is, I treat mortuary rites as the
practical means for constructing relations of shared identity, relations
which are not otherwise presumed. The practical catalyst in this process
of construction is the action of giving, an action that effectively evinces or
makes known the specific relations in terms of which persons are acting.
Giving, in the context of mortuary feasts, evinces the relations between
hosts and guests through comparison, that is, by qualifying each party
with attributes relative to the other. The action of giving, in other words,
effects a comparative evaluation of the parties involved. I regard feast
giving, then, as a form of collective action that qualifies a set of particular
persons as *a group of like individuals*. This qualification is the condition
for "replacing" the dead with living likenesses, and thus displacing or
"finishing" the dead.

In short, I suggest that "finishing" and "replacing" the dead describes
for Tangans a unitary process of things and persons continually taking
the place of other things and persons. On the one hand, the idiom of
"taking the place" (*kep tafu*) describes for Tangans the succession of a
deceased MB by his ZS. Appropriately, Tangans refer to the ZS as the
"replacement" (*pilis*) of the MB, and likewise to a younger brother as the
"replacement" of his elder brother. On the other hand, Tangans view the
exchanges of objects accompanying mortuary feasting as acts of

"replacement." That is, Tangans describe the long-term identical exchanges between affinal and paternal relatives in the same terms as they describe lineage succession – as "replacement" (*pilis*). It is my contention that these reciprocal exchanges are the instrument and expression of achieving lineage succession – the non-reciprocal substitution of the living for the dead. Exchange practices thus function as elements in a regenerative, cyclical process – the means for reproducing definite social relations and identities over time (see Weiner 1976).

To adopt the New Melanesian Ethnography's perspective on sociality – the creation and maintenance of relationships – is to expose presuppositions about "society" as an aggregate of "groups," themselves in turn an aggregate of "individuals." But it also forces clarification of what we mean by the term "social reproduction." For social reproduction cannot be grasped from this perspective in Durkheimian terms of the efforts of "Society," imagined as a corporate whole, to preserve its integrity and cohesion in the face of the mortality of its "individual" parts. To do so in the Tangan case would be to conflate indigenous understandings of "replacement" and "finishing" with analytical ones. For what Tangans make of their mortuary practices sometimes recalls the postulates of Durkheimian sociology. How, then, are we to understand Tangan social reproduction if not as a defensive process for consolidating the property of corporate descent groups and thus ensuring the continuity of these groups?

In this book, I treat social reproduction as the process, achieved in and through mortuary rites, by which agents fix the form – make the form visible – of relationships conceived of as basic to their definition as persons. More specifically, I treat mortuary rites as an instance of deliberate collective action through which agents define relations of similarity among themselves – bound themselves as a group – by differentiating themselves from other persons likewise grouped as similar to each other. The outcome of this concerted activity is what might be called Tangan social organization, the historically given framework within which agents construct their relations to each other. While the collective action that produces this framework is contingent – variable in its efficacy, timing, and scale – the ideal and motivation of this action are less so. Tangan sociality is not a directionless flow, but rather a process guided by the goal of producing social relations in a definite form, a form locally conceived to enable people to give and receive life. This form of relations, I argue, is dyadic. It precipitates (or "elicits," in Wagner's term) two groups that confront each other as both the source and result of each other's well being (cf. Wagner 1986a). These groups are "matrilineages" (*matambia*), paired through intermarriage, which exchange paternal nurture between them and so effectively father each other's children.

What is gained by juxtaposing the New Melanesian History with the New Melanesian Ethnography? How does each approach, used as a frame of reference for the other, point to its own limitations and potentials? And what does this juxtaposition indicate about the direction of a New Melanesian Anthropology?

Most anthropologists, I think and hope, accept the main point of the New Melanesian Historians that to produce ethnographic descriptions of Melanesian people without acknowledging the engagement of these people with colonialism, Christian missionization, and capitalist markets is politically and intellectually irresponsible. But it does not follow from this acceptance that all ethnographic description must foreground this engagement as the lodestar of Melanesian social life. Indeed, to do so would risk indulging just the sort of ethnocentrism that the New Melanesian Ethnography sets itself against, namely, the presupposition that Melanesian history and culture must be construed in relation to agents and agencies *originating elsewhere*. Or, more bluntly, it would risk a historical ethnography "inspired by the principle that 'there must be a white man behind every brown'" (Sahlins 1993:5, quoting Shineberg 1967:214).

This risk is particularly great for anthropologists like myself who seek to connect their accounts of local situations to a history of "commoditization"; for the very word conjures ideas of an abstract but overwhelming "force" that shapes world history. Consider, in this regard, the remarks of Eric Wolf in one of the basic texts of the new anthropological history, *Europe and the People Without History* (1982). Wolf criticizes the separation of "ethnohistory" from "real" history on the grounds that the subject of these two kinds of history is actually the same: "The more ethnohistory we know, the more clearly 'their' history and 'our' history emerge as part of the same history" (1982:19). The methodological problem, then, becomes one of conceptualizing the "common process" or "common dynamic" that organizes this one and the same history (Wolf 1982:19). For Wolf, the answer lies in a version of world systems theory modified to include consideration of the various "peripheral" micropopulations habitually studied by anthropologists – "their modes of existence before European expansion and the advent of capitalism, and of the manner in which these modes were penetrated, subordinated, destroyed, or absorbed, first by the growing market and subsequently by industrial capitalism" (1982:23). Such an approach, Wolf proposes, serves the ostensibly democratic purpose of representing Them as well as Us as "participants in the same historical trajectory" (1982:23).

Surely it is not too contentious to ask if the cost of thus recovering one history for both Us and Them is unjustifiably high: the reduction of other (Other?) histories and other agencies to the effects of and responses to Western imperialism. Marshall Sahlins's droll observation is apposite: "The 'peoples without history' finally acquire one, but it is a tale of victimization, deprivation, and transformation, turning their cultures likewise into adulterated goods" (1992:16; see also 1988, 1993). And equally surely, it is unnecessary to adopt the perspective of the New Melanesian Ethnography in order to see things in this light. Sahlins, for example, most certainly has not, despite his own rhetorical predilections for wholesale contrasts between the West and the Rest. The New Melanesian Ethnographers, however, like Sahlins, clearly illuminate the direction in which the New Melanesian History must keep moving in order to avoid allying itself with Wolf's vision, namely, away from the equation of colonial history with the history of the colonizers (Sahlins 1993:13). But toward what?

For Sahlins, the answer lies in recognizing that people always and everywhere "respond to what has been inflicted on them by devising on their own heritage, acting according to their own categories, logics, understandings" (1993:18). For Strathern (1990), the answer requires going beyond this recognition, itself premised upon the conventional Western view that subjects appropriate/interpret/assimilate objects (events) to contexts (structures), and wondering about the very premises of "Melanesian history" entailed in the model of Melanesian personhood and agency. Could it be, for example, that neither the uniqueness of the event nor the laying out of events in sequence are presuppositions that oriented Melanesians in their encounters with Europeans (Strathern 1990)? Could it be that "their" history will look nothing like "ours" (Wagner 1991b:344–345)? For both Sahlins and Strathern, then, the New Melanesian History must be tempered by steadfast awareness of cultural difference and of the means people, including anthropologists, use to represent cultural difference.

By the same token, juxtaposition with the New Melanesian History enables critical appreciation of the New Melanesian Ethnography, particularly of the limitations inherent in the New Melanesian Ethnography's approach to social action. As Josephides (1991:159) has noted, in treating action as the process whereby relations and meanings are "evinced" or "made visible," the New Melanesian Ethnography tends to equate action with enactment, the instantiation in practice of patterns of sociality given to the actors (and already identified by the ethnographer). This tendency follows in part from the critique of Western assumptions that treat "individuals" as primordial facts and the relations "between" individuals as artificial secondary creations. For the claim, advanced by radical contrast, that Melanesians regard relations (or "relationality") as natural has a corollary: that action can only be known by its effects in eliciting relations and meanings already given, even if given *in potentia*. In other words, the contingency of action is formulated in a limited way, namely, as whether or not action makes itself known through its effects.

The historical account that frames this book is a means of restoring another sort of contingency (and temporality) to action. For, among other things, it makes it clear that the meanings and relations evinced in mortuary practices in 1984 were not those evinced fifty years earlier. It also makes it clear that these changes cannot be accounted for solely in terms of a process of symbolic innovation whereby actors exploit or improvise upon the metaphorical possibilities of prevailing relations and meanings (Wagner 1975, 1986b). The status of mortuary practices as *kastam* in 1984 was not latent in Tangan sociality, but rather generated in definite historical circumstances out of the articulation of this sociality with the exigencies of commodity production and exchange. Accordingly, the collective action of contemporary mortuary feasting must be recognized as the contingent product of a particular history, a history of attempts by local agents to shape the consequences of commoditization. The New Melanesian Ethnography, then, must be tempered with an awareness of what even Sahlins grudgingly acknowledges as "strictly functional demands to production for the market, adaptations that reach deeply into the indigenous society" and as "foreign meanings and economic dispositions [that] come across the beach, along with the foreign goods" (1993:14). Or, put in more methodological terms, the New Melanesian History serves the New Melanesian Ethnography as a constant reminder that the postulated radical separation between Us and Them is just that – a postulate or analytic fiction (see Strathern 1988:17).

The New Melanesian Anthropology born of the encounter between the New Melanesian Ethnography and the New Melanesian History thus acknowledges, like much anthropological inquiry in the 1990s, that historical research is integral to cultural interpretation. But the New Melanesian Anthropology modifies this new orthodoxy and prevents it from becoming a practice of particularistic accounts by attempting to revise an older orthodoxy, namely, that anthropological inquiry is fundamentally comparative. This revision entails not only the methodological challenge of explicating the assumptions upon which We regard Them as different, but also the ethnographic challenge of accounting for similarities and differences in the ways our sociality and theirs have become historically entangled. That is, the New Melanesian Anthropology responds to Herskovits's (1956:141) old plea for a "*comparative study of cultures within a given historic stream*," a study based not on the comparison of geographically delimited, clearly separable societies, but on the comparison of "acculturative change" and "cultural dynamics," or of what I recast here as changes in the practices of social reproduction.

If the recovery of history is rapidly becoming a familiar feature of ethnographic description, not so the project of comparative history (but see Thomas 1991). Yet comparative history is precisely one of the results yielded by bringing the New Melanesian History into contact with the New Melanesian Ethnography. For such a coupling prompts the question of whether or not one can identify similarities and differences in the ways in which Melanesian sociality becomes articulated with the exigencies of commodity production and exchange. And this question, in turn, enables consideration of how differences in endogenous sociality – differences internal to "Melanesia" – explain differences in the effects created by circumstances of exogenous origin. Accordingly, I turn in the conclusion of this book to comparative social reproduction, that is, to comparing the ways in which Melanesians create and recreate their social relations and identities amidst circumstances inflected by practices of production for and exchange in capitalist markets. The result is a complication, but not an undoing, of the ideal binary contrast between Melanesian and Western types of social reproduction.

I give the name "replication" to the type of social reproduction effected through Tangan mortuary practices. The ideal outcome of replication is the conservation of social relations or, put otherwise, the construction of non-hierarchical, complementary relations in a form that is constant and enduring. Replication is implemented and underpinned by a kind of exchange practice that is itself replicative in nature and which I call (after the literature) identical exchange. Identical exchange involves delayed transfers of identical objects or replicas, that is, the exchange of two large male live pigs for two large male live pigs, one small shell disc for one small shell disc, and so forth. Exact reciprocation – no more, no less, in kind only – is the rule of identical exchange. It is this type of social reproduction, I argue, that is indigenously understood as "finishing" and "replacing" the dead.

The identical exchange practices that make replication possible operate according to a logic of "keeping-while-giving" (Weiner 1985, 1992) and emphasize the return of valuables previously put into circulation. For the parties involved, the *realization* rather than the content of the exchange is at issue inasmuch as the content is given axiomatically. Accordingly, identical exchange is hedged around by various strategies for limiting and controlling the circulation of objects.

I contend that identical exchange is a particular method for creating or evincing relationship, one that can be specified further through contrast with exchange practices typical of several Highland societies (cf. Godelier 1986; Strathern and Godelier 1991). These latter exchanges – large-scale, ceremonial distributions such as Enga *tee* or Melpa *moka* – operate according to a logic of dispersal and emphasize increments in the quantity of valuables put into circulation. Melanesian ethnography has come to identify these exchanges with the undertakings of entrepreneurial big men and the dynamics of a prestige economy. My concern, however, is to correlate these exchanges with the type of social reproduction that they underpin and implement. I call this type "multiplication." Its ideal outcome is the expansion of social relations, or the construction of social relations in a form that measures these relations as more or less extensive.

My point in developing a broad ideal typical contrast between replication and multiplication is to furnish the means for returning to the question of continuity and change in Tangan mortuary practices. I conclude the book by asking how a particular form of social reproduction, Tangan replication, conditioned its own transformation in the historical encounter with practices of commodity production and exchange. The contrast between replication and multiplication facilitates speculation about how the process of commoditization has taken different trajectories in different Melanesian societies.

My argument is that one of the conditions for sustaining a form of social reproduction grounded in identical exchange is the sealing off of key social relations from the hierarchizing effects of commoditization. In Tanga, the disjunction between *kastam* and *bisnis* accomplished this "sealing off." *Kastam* in Tanga entails the deliberate attempt to preserve an arena for the social constitution of positively valued relations and identities, an arena conceptually and practically insulated from *bisnis*, the activities of petty commodity production. By contrast, multiplication, the form of social reproduction grounded in incremental exchanges, encourages a conjunction between *kastam* and *bisnis*.[4] The pressures generated by multiplication continually to disburse (and disperse) valuables, for instance, makes money a much-sought-after resource. The deployment of money in exchange practices gives them a hybrid (even "postmodern") appearance: money, trucks, and tradestore items circulate alongside of pigs and pearlshells.

This comparative discussion thus relocates the synchronic analysis of Tangan mortuary feasting and ceremonial exchange within the context of historical circumstances. It is an implication of my analysis that such relocations are particularly necessary for the interpretation of social practices that the practitioners themselves call "custom" or "tradition." But it is more of a demonstrated conclusion that the glosses of Tangan mortuary practices – not only "custom," but "finishing" and "replacing" too – cannot be adequately registered otherwise.

A brief final question: What, if anything, does the juxtaposition of the New Melanesian History and the New Melanesian Ethnography imply for bending the conventions of ethnographic narrative?

The general responses to this question are correlates of the respective critiques of the New Melanesian History and the New Melanesian Ethnography. On the one hand, a New Melanesian Anthropology must not edit out the elements that connect the people it represents to a contingent present in a world that extends beyond the village. And here I refer not only to apparently discordant items of material culture, matter as seemingly out of place as the empty sack of Kellogg's wholewheat biscuits fastened to the headdress of the unidentified Wabag man whose image appears in the film, *First Contact*. I refer also to the institutions of postcolonial states (schools, patrol posts, elections) and the mundane practices of capitalism (wage-labor, cash cropping, retail trade). On the other hand, a New Melanesian Anthropology must make explicit its own assumptions about what it takes to be Melanesian assumptions. Achieving this sort of explicitness will not come through narcissistic introspection, but only through self-conscious modelling of a dialectical opposition between Us and Them.

The particular responses to this question – responses about narrative genre and style – do not greatly concern me here, though I readily admit their importance (see Keesing and Jolly 1992). This book is not an experimental piece of writing, let alone an anxious self-reflexive one; it is neither montage nor collage; it is not autobiography. But it is what

Marcus and Cushman (1982:63) refer to as a "composite text," one in which the presentation of ethnographic detail shares textual space with other kinds of writing, specifically, historical narrative and typological comparison. In other words, I circumscribe ethnographic details with ideas and data originating – maybe more obviously than usual – from sources besides my own first-hand fieldwork; my aim is to describe Tangan mortuary rites as a means for theorizing about gift exchange and social reproduction.

Accordingly, I do try to innovate on one narrative convention, namely, the old ploy of embedding synchronic ethnographic description in a temporal context by appending chapters on Historical Background and Social Change to each end of the book. I have organized this book as a similar sort of sandwich, placing an analysis of the structure and symbolism of Tangan mortuary rites between discussions of the mortuary rites as historically conditioned social practices. That is, I begin by treating mortuary rites as "custom," locating them in the context of the historical circumstances of colonization and capitalist expansion, on the one hand, and of the changing social organization of matriliny, on the other. This strategy engages the concerns and follows the leads of the New Melanesian History. I then treat mortuary rites as social action that "finishes" and "replaces" the dead; in other words, I locate mortuary rites in the context of local conceptions and practices of social reproduction. That is, I engage the concerns and use the model of the New Melanesian Ethnography. It is at this point in the book that I describe and analyze the sequence of feasts and exchanges as a coherent set of procedures. I conclude the book by developing the ideal typical contrast between replication and multiplication as two types of social reproduction, and by arguing that the exigencies of these two different types of social reproduction have differently conditioned the process of commoditization. In other words, I synthesize the concerns and insights of the New Melanesian History and the New Melanesian Ethnography in an exercise of comparative cultural history. I suggest that this exercise illustrates one, but only one, possibility of the New Melanesian Anthropology coming into being.

In chapter 2, I trace the emergence of an explicit indigenous categorization of mortuary rites as "custom" or "tradition" (*kastam*). The narrative unfolds as an account of commoditization, the process whereby social relations become increasingly engaged with and transformed by the exigencies of commodity production and exchange. The chapter ends with a profile of the material inequalities entrained by the consolidation of the household as the unit of commodity production and exchange. In chapter 3, I speak of "matrilineages" and I delineate a "social structure." I do this mainly in order to outline the framework of social relations and identities which agents create in mortuary rites and which, in turn, conditions the creation of relations and identities. But I also attempt to show how the emergent categorical opposition between *kastam* and *bisnis* ("business," or cash cropping) maps on to tensions within a matrilineal social organization exacerbated by the effects of commoditization.

In chapter 4, I describe and summarize the sequence of feasts and exchanges initiated by a death and climaxed years later by the construction of a new men's house. I indicate the various arrangements that feast sponsors must make in order to ensure a successful outcome: the management of pigs and pig debts; the provision of sufficient food supplies; the cooperation of supporters; the preparation of song and dance performances. I emphasize the indigenous conceptualization of the mortuary sequence as a fragile process of image construction. For, I argue, mortuary rites consist in the foreshadowing, revelation and final realization of images projected at various feasts in the sequence. The process of image construction gives feast sponsors temporary control over what other people know while at the same time demonstrating the power of the sponsors to effect their own publicized intentions. To the extent, moreover, that the images constructed induce responses from others, the process also displays and "finishes" the relational personhood of the deceased and exhibits the capacity of feast sponsors to draw others into a project of collective self-definition.

Chapters 5, 6, and 7 analyze the sequence of mortuary rites in terms developed by the New Melanesian Ethnographers, especially Marilyn Strathern (1988). I also draw on the works of Annette Weiner (1980, 1985) and Nancy Munn (1983, 1986) in furthering my interpretation of Tangan feast giving and exchange as reproductive, value-creating practices. In chapter 5, I discuss Tangan conceptualizations of lineage succession as "replacement." I also discuss the way in which Tangans imagine long-term identical exchanges between lineages to be the *sine qua non* of "replacement." Chapter 6 begins by confronting two questions raised by the fact of exchanges in which the parties involved give and receive identical objects ("replicas"). How does one determine the value of the objects exchanged? How does one determine the value for the exchangers of the objects transacted? My answer lies in thinking of exchange as metaphorical juxtaposition, and therefore taking seriously the qualitative properties of exchange objects. In the case of Tangan mortuary exchanges, this strategy allows me to articulate an immanent conceptual contrast between consumption and perdurance that orients a wide range of ordinary social practices. It is in terms of this basic contrast, I argue, that feast sponsors define collective identities for themselves in the image of an enduring matrilineal group.

Chapter 7 synthesizes elements of the previous two by re-presenting the mortuary sequence as the process through which agents do three related things: (1) construct themselves as a collective individual, that is, a bounded group of similar people; (2) qualify this collective individual as enduring and transcendent; and (3) fix and publicly display this identity as one to be known by others. Giving, of feasts in general and of food in particular, is the action that accomplishes these things. I conclude the chapter by discussing a myth of the origin of pigs that expresses the complementarity between consumption and perdurance and proposes, I argue, this complementarity as the source of both life and death.

Chapter 8 concludes the book with a discussion of social reproduction and *kastam* in comparative perspective, thus connecting the ethnographic particulars of Tangan mortuary rites both to the ethnography of New Guinea Highlands exchange systems and to broader questions about different trajectories of social change within Melanesia.

I

MORTUARY RITES AS *KASTAM*

2

Commoditization and the emergence of *kastam*

On the morning of April Fools' Day, 1984 – the first full day after my arrival on Boang Island – Rafael Dingkelmale (or Tading) explained to me in Tok Pisin that "the basis of custom is death" (*olgeta kastam i kamap antap long man i dai*). Two generations ago, Tading would have had neither interest in nor means for making this statement. Such is the implication, at least, of my understanding of custom (*kastam*) as a cultural category that assumed its definition only recently. Other ethnographers have drawn similar conclusions from their experiences elsewhere in New Ireland. Phil Lewis (personal communication) claimed that during his first fieldwork among Notsi speakers in the early 1950s, he never encountered the word *kastam*. By the time of his second fieldwork in 1970, the word occurred regularly in everyday speech. Brenda Clay likewise noted a growth of interest on the part of Mandak speakers in practices they labelled *kastam* between the time of her first fieldwork (1970) and second fieldwork (1979–80). She attributed this change to the explicit policy of the New Ireland Provincial Government in encouraging the revitalization of local traditions.[1]

The word *kastam*, as Tangans used it in 1984–85, derived its connotations from categorical oppositions with other Tok Pisin terms that identified distinct domains of activity: *lo* or *gavman* ("law" or "government"), *lotu* ("church" or "Christianity"), and *bisnis* ("business" or "commercial enterprise," distinguishable from wage-labor [*wokmani*]).[2] In order, then, to account for the historical emergence of *kastam* as a cultural category, it is necessary to account for the emergence of the taxonomic contrasts that determine its significance. This exercise, which I undertake in this and the next chapter, demonstrates how *kastam* came to refer specifically to the mortuary feasts and exchanges

25

through which collective matrilineal identities (or "matrilineages") are produced.

I argue that the particular opposition between *kastam* and *bisnis* proved critical in engendering this outcome. Unlike much of the recent literature on the processes of cultural objectification in Melanesia, I emphasize neither the stimulus of colonial encounters (Keesing and Tonkinson 1982; Thomas 1992a, 1992b) nor the effects of postcolonial state policy (Philibert 1986; MacClancy 1982; Babadzan 1988; LiPuma and Meltzoff 1990; Lindstrom 1990a). Instead, I argue that *kastam* only gradually acquired its meaning by coming to articulate a set of evolving conflicts and contradictions in daily life. These conflicts were and still are rooted in the progressive "commoditization" of Tangan social relations.[3]

Commoditization refers to the process by which a society dominated by the production of use-values – whether for immediate consumption or for circulation in long-distance trade and ceremonial exchange – becomes over time increasingly constituted by relations of commodity production and exchange.[4] That is, commoditization implies the way in which commodity relations become incorporated into cycles of social reproduction as necessary conditions for sustaining socially defined standards of living: "on one side, the production of commodities as means of exchange to acquire elements of necessary consumption, on the other side the incorporation of commodities in the cycle of reproduction as items of productive consumption (e.g., tools, seeds, fertilisers), and individual consumption (e.g., food, clothing, building materials, kerosene, domestic utensils)" (Bernstein 1979:425).[5] Bernstein points out that what is significant in this process is the *necessity* of incorporating commodity relations, *not* the relative amount of resources (such as labor time or land) expended in these relations:

Simple quantitative measures which might show, say, that only 20 percent of labour-time or 20 percent of land is devoted to commodity production, are misleading if they imply that the household is still basically a 'subsistence' unit (in the narrow sense of use-value production for direct consumption), and for this reason is only marginally involved with commodity relations and can therefore easily withdraw from them.

(1979:426)

This observation is especially pertinent in rural Papua New Guinea, where often the limited extent of commodity production indicates not resilient traditional economies, but rather labor reserve areas in which the principal commodity produced is labor power itself (see, for example, Carrier and Carrier 1989; Morauta 1985).

The process of commoditization is neither uniform nor universal in the actual forms that it assumes; nor is it inexorable. A variety of empirical circumstances, including the organization of pre-capitalist production, the interventions of colonial and ex-colonial states, and the booms and busts of speculative market cycles, all give the process definite shape under definite historical conditions. The overall tendency of the process, however, is toward an "intensification" of commodity relations: "At the level of household economy the intensification of commodity relations refers to the degree to which the reproduction cycle is realized through the production and exchange of commodities" (Bernstein 1979:429). For example, the regular satisfaction of food requirements through cash purchases characterizes more intense commodity relations than does the satisfaction of these needs through agricultural or other production. The concept of "intensification," moreover, implies relative differentiation in the process of commoditization not only *between* societies, but also *within* a specific society. For example, one can distinguish between households that reproduce themselves through exchange of labor power for wages and households that reproduce themselves through family labor and the sale of cash crops. That is, intensification, in addition to extending commodity relations, internally differentiates a society along previously undrawn lines, viz., according to the relations of commodity production. Or, put otherwise, intensification implies a qualitative transformation of social relations as well as a quantitative increase in the degree to which social relations are commoditized.

The intensification of commodity relations, as Grossman (1984) documents in a case study of commodity production in the New Guinea Highlands, proportionately undermines the autonomy of rural households, that is, their "capability of reallocating their labour time dependent upon the importance and parameters of a number of exogenous variables (e.g., international prices and Government policy)" (Thompson and Mac-William 1992:5); and, I might add, dependent upon the importance and parameters of undertaking mortuary feasts, ceremonial exchanges, initiation rites, and so forth. In other words, what often passes for and justifies itself as Development – increased market involvement through cattle projects, coffee growing, copra processing, and so on – involves a surrender by rural communities to state and/or market agencies of control over the technical and social arrangements of resource use and production (see Grossman 1984:14–16). At the same time, these rural communities must contend with the local ecological effects of intensified commodity relations – not only the spectacularly disastrous consequences of large-scale mining and logging projects, but also the less visible environmental alterations that follow upon the exploitation of new plants and/or animals.

After first providing a brief introduction to the islands and islanders of Tanga, I propose a periodization of Tangan history based upon changes in the form and intensity of the commodity relations in which Tangans have become enmeshed. While the process of commoditization has refigured and continues to refigure Tangan social life, it has not done so in the generic image of bourgeois society.[6] Instead, I argue, the process has defined the household as the locus of commodity relations or *bisnis*, and the matrilineage, almost by default, as the unit of non-commodity relations. According to this ideological distinction, the lineage, and not the household, is the proper point of reference with regard to mortuary feasting or *kastam*. In other words, household-based cash cropping or *bisnis* came to be defined as a domain of activity separate from and even antithetical to *kastam*; *kastam*, in turn, became defined as the proper domain of big man-activity, a domain taken up by the performance of mortuary rites held to commemorate deceased matrilineal relatives. Accordingly, the self-reflexive process of externalizing "culture" as *kastam* must be seen as one aspect of an overall transformation of Tangan society – a transformation motivated by the intensification of and qualitative change in the way Tangans engaged in commodity relations of production and exchange. It is this quiet, continuous process of commoditization rather than a noisy confrontation with colonizers and/or the postcolonial state that has conditioned the genesis both of the Tangan category of *kastam* and of the particular lived experience to which this category gives discursive form.

Tanga and Tangans: a background

Four islands together with several uninhabited islets comprise the Tanga Islands (maps 1 and 2). The group lies roughly fifty five sea miles east of Namatanai, the district headquarters of southern New Ireland Province. Boang, where 75 percent of the resident population lives (5,083 in 1990, New Ireland Provincial Government 1992), is a crescent-shaped coral island some six miles long and three miles wide at its widest point. The island measures about 10.4 square miles or approximately 6,656 acres of easy terrain (PR NAM 8/1958–59).[7] An extensive plateau rises 200 feet from the beach plain and ends in steep cliffs that drop directly into the sea on the north shore of the island. Vehicular roads, some paved with coral and others simple bush tracks, provide access to almost all areas of the

Map 1   New Ireland and the Gazelle Peninsula

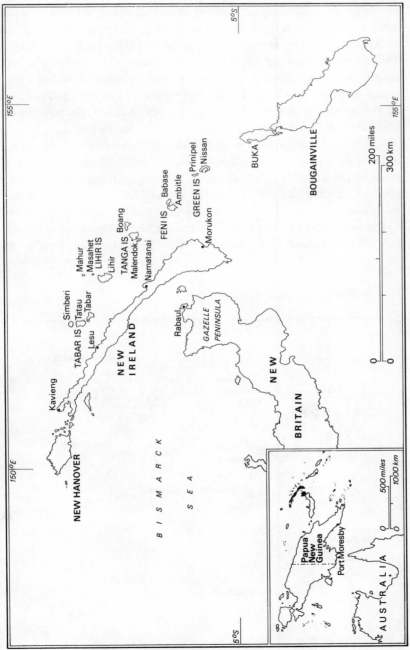

island. The Roman Catholic Mission (Sacred Heart) maintains a complex of buildings, including a well-stocked tradestore, infirmary, church, school, and staff residences at Amfar. During the period of my fieldwork, an American missionary resided at Amfar and supervised mission affairs. Twice a week, weather permitting, Talair flights connected the Amfar airstrip with Namatanai and Rabaul, the urban center to which Tangans orient themselves.[8] Consequently, Boang is the economic and social hub of the group, a center relative to the peripheral volcanic islands of Malendok, Lif, and Tefa.

Malendok is larger than Boang, with approximately 13.5 square miles or 8,640 acres, but also much more rugged and difficult to traverse. The peak of the island reaches about 1,200 feet. 15.6 percent (795) of the resident population lives scattered in hamlets built close to the shores of the island.

The remainder of the population resides on the two smaller islands of Lif (196 or 3.8 percent) and Tefa (143 or 2.8 percent) which together make

Map 2   The Tanga Islands

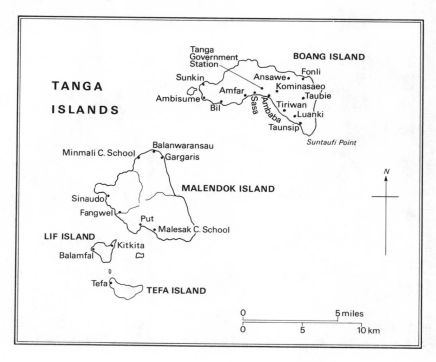

up about 1.7 square miles or 1,088 acres. A narrow channel across which one can walk at low tide separates Lif from Tefa. Dugout canoes (*wang*) link Lif and Tefa to Malendok. The four-mile-wide channel between Boang and Malendok, however, requires a speedboat for crossing and even then only when the prevailing winds allow passage on the open sea. Ocean-going plank canoes (*mon*), not being made in 1984–85, were used in the past for such voyages.

Every section of the islands bears numerous names. On Boang, district-level names (e.g., Lop, Sungkin) are generally known by everyone, though in my experience used less than the names of the principal school and church districts: Amfar, Fonli, and Taonsip. Hamlet names are known and used by neighbors, especially the names of those hamlets used both now and in the colonial period to designate census units (domiciles). Names of particular patches of land, often uninhabited though perhaps occupied in the past, are known only to lineage members and in some cases not by all lineage members. Such names do not seem to constitute secret knowledge; rather, infrequent use simply restricts the extent to which the names become known.

Residents of the eastern plateau of Boang refer to Amfar and the lower lying western end of the island as "the beach" (*kin*). When at Amfar, these residents refer to their hamlet areas as "on top" (*iat*) and when returning exhort each other "to climb" (*kenek*). (Patrol reports likewise refer to the two local government council wards on Boang as the "beach" ward and the "top" ward.) Boang people in general refer to Lif, Tefa, and Malendok as *am bit* ("the islands"), while "islanders" refer to Boang as Tanga. Tangans refer to mainland New Ireland, its mountainous spine visible on clear days, as *male dok* ("the big place"). Finally, Tangans visiting or resident in Rabaul sometimes refer to their homeland, the Tanga Islands, as "the beach" (*kin*).

Tangans speak a language of the Patpatar-Tolai subgroup of Austronesian languages (Beaumont 1976). Beaumont (1976), Maurer (1966) and others refer to the language as "Tangga." Oddly, this is the only word in the language in which the *ngg* sound occurs.[9] A dialect of the Tangga language is spoken in the Feni or Anir Islands (Anir dialect) southeast of Tanga (map 1). Tangans, particularly residents of eastern Boang, Lif, and Tefa, maintain close ties with Anir islanders, with whom they intermarry and ally themselves in hosting mortuary feasts. Many, but not all, of the clans localized in Tanga (chapter 3) are represented on Feni.[10] Another dialect (Maket) is spoken in three villages on the east coast of the southern New Ireland mainland: Sena, Warangansau, and Muliama. Tangans also maintain connections with these villages, but contacts seem to have attenuated somewhat with the demise of inter-island canoe voyages. Nonetheless, Tangans fully recognize their kinship with these villagers and some men, when prompted, speculated that Tangans originally migrated from Muliama and the southern New Ireland region of Siar.

Comprehensive social and economic ties as well as the linguistic ties within the Patpatar-Tolai subgroup link the Tanga Islands into a regional culture that extends through southern New Ireland to the Duke of York Islands and the Gazelle Peninsula. Archaeological analysis as well as the early accounts of Parkinson (n.d.) and Bell (1950) suggest the previous existence of an inter-island trade network connecting the off-shore islands of New Ireland (Tabar, Lihir, Tanga, Anir) to each other, to the New Ireland mainland, and to Nissan and Buka in the northern Solomons (map 3). Each island group produced some specialized item – pigment, canoes, shell valuables, pigs, clay pipes – for distribution "through a

Map 3   Reconstructed inter-island trade network

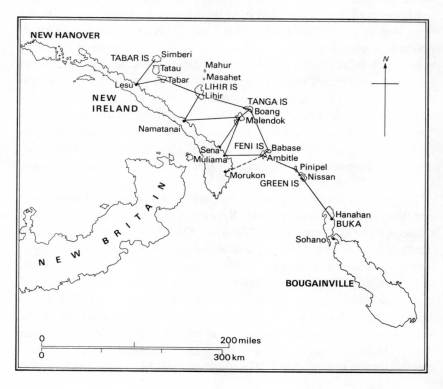

series of inter-locking short trading voyages, each between two neigh-boring areas" (Kaplan 1976:80). Kaplan dates trade between Buka and Nissan to AD 500 and proposes that "by A.D. 1000–1200 this trade might have involved parts of southern New Ireland" (1976:86). Organized inter-island trading no longer occurred in 1984–85, but individuals from Lihir sometimes travelled to Tanga to trade strung shell disc valuables (*kemetas*) for pigs, while Tangans visiting relatives in Anir invariably returned with ochre used as pigment (*puk boiam*) and betel nut. Indi-viduals arrange such trips by either chartering speedboats or buying passage on one of the coastal vessels that sporadically service the local copra industry. On important occasions, I was told, Tangan feast givers might charter a boat (for example, a Catholic Mission ship) to transport guests from Anir.

Rabaul focuses the interests of inhabitants of the area by virtue of its central place in the regional economy. Tangan smallholders who sell directly to the Copra Marketing Board (as well as the Catholic Mission, Tanga's largest single exporter of copra in 1984–85) prefer to send their product to Rabaul rather than to the sub-depot at Namatanai which offers slightly lower prices. Rabaul is the source of almost all consumer goods, especially those purchased by local entrepreneurs: copra bags, stocks for tradestores, beer, benzene, and pickup trucks. The orientation of Tangans to Rabaul continues practices initiated in German colonial times when all of New Ireland was administered from Rabaul and the majority of contract laborers were employed there. The Catholic Mission likewise maintains its regional headquarters in the Rabaul area and Tangans who work for or receive training through the Mission usually spend some time there. Seriously ill islanders seek treatment in the Catholic Mission hospital at Vunapope. And, of course, Rabaul serves as the nearest urban job market for Tangans seeking wage labor off the islands. The population of Tangans working in Rabaul at any one time thus plays host to the numerous visitors who frequent the town on business (selling copra) or for pleasure (visiting relatives). In effect, the Tanga Islands for all practical purposes comprise an economic satellite of Rabaul. Although Tangans elect a member to the New Ireland House of Assembly, and for political and administrative purposes Tangans fall under the jurisdiction of New Ireland Province, Rabaul possesses more tangible reality for Tangans than Kavieng (the capital of New Ireland Province). This geographic schism of political and economic practice perhaps reinforces an indigenous distinction between *lo* (government, regulations, taxes) and *bisnis* (business, commercial activities).

The regional culture of south-central New Ireland and the Gazelle Peninsula also derives from a shared repertoire of song and dance performances, many of which originate from the Rabaul area. Tolai and Duke of York people reputedly export various "power practices" or magic, including potent forms of love magic (*malera, mindal*), performance magic (*buai*; cf. Nachman 1978) and the distinctive *tumbuan* complex, a men's secret society (see Errington 1974).[11] *Tumbuan* occur as far north in New Ireland as the Usen Barok area north of Namatanai; informants dated their appearance on Tanga to just after World War II. Mortuary feasting, the elaboration of which also gives the area a common identity, provides the pre-eminent occasions for undertaking these activities and exhibiting them to guests who later introduce them to their own local communities. Tangans, for example, regularly stage *singsing* (combination song/dance performances) in the Tolai, Lihir, and Sursurunga (southern New Ireland) languages. Both the sense and reference of the lyrics often remain inaccessible to the performers, for whom the meaning of the songs inheres mainly in their being sung (chapter 4).

What ultimately distinguishes Tanga from the rest of New Ireland, and indeed most of Papua New Guinea, is a demographic rather than cultural or socioeconomic feature. The National Statistic Office of Papua New Guinea (1983) records the total population of Tanga in 1979 as 3,982 of which 3,661 resided locally at the time of the census. Of the resident population, 2,563 people lived on Boang, leaving just under 2.6 acres of land (not all of which is arable) per head.[12] Given that provincial government figures from the 1990 census indicate that the resident population was around 5,000 people, and that about 75 percent or 3,750 people resided on Boang, this figure could be lower than two acres per head. With much of this land taken up by permanent plantings of coconuts, the pressure on gardening land generated by population size is among the most extreme in all of rural Papua New Guinea (King and Ranck 1982).

The population of the islands grew vigorously during the late Australian colonial era after apparently overcoming the depopulation crisis that many areas of New Ireland underwent in the first third of the century (table 1). The steady and startling growth of the Boang population through the 1950s and 1960s can be attributed in large measure to the health services provided by the Catholic Mission at Amfar. By the mid-1950s the great majority of births on Boang took place at the mission infirmary. By the late fifties, the population boom invariably received mention in patrol reports. A move to resettle some of the Boang population on the New Ireland mainland began in the late 1960s. At least

Table 1. *Tanga Islands population estimates, 1914–84*

Year	Boang	Other islands	Total resident pop. (unless indicated)	Source
1914			1,241 + est.1,000	RTNG 21/22[a]
1921			1,040	RTNG 21/22
1922			947	RTNG 22/23
1923			1,008	RTNG 23/24
1925			1,663	RTNG 24/25
1930			1,628	RTNG 30/31
1933	1,200	500	1,700	Bell (1935a)
1936			1,741	RTNG 36/37
1939			1,778	RTNG 39/40
1949			1,752	PR21 49/50[b]
1950			1,878	PR21 49/50
1953	1,513	527	2,030	PR1 53/54
1958	1,788	538	2,326	PR3 58/59
1963	2,060	619	2,679	LTC Exhb. M[c]
1964	2,168	667	2,835	PR5 65/66
1970	2,534	818	3,352	PR10 69/70
1975			3,818	PR21 74/75
1979	2,563		3,982 (total)	NSO (1983)[d]
1984			4,859 (total)	PC 1984[e]
1990			5,083	NIPG 1990[f]

Notes: [a] RTNG: Annual Report on the Administration of the Territory of New Guinea
[b] PR: Patrol Reports, Namatanai Sub-District
[c] LTC: Land Titles Commission, Exhibit M, Tanga Land Investigation 1963
[d] NSO: National Statistics Office (1983)
[e] PC: Personal communication. Field counts from 1984 census.
[f] NIPG: New Ireland Provincial Government. Preliminary figures from 1990 census.

twenty-eight household heads, mainly from the congested eastern end of Boang (Taonsip, Luangki and Fonli), expressed interest in the scheme, but the initiative withered before bearing any results. In 1984, Tangans were quite aware of the land shortage and its manifestation in endless land disputes. No immediate solution to the problem, however, in the form of either provincial government policy or individual decisions to emigrate, seemed close at hand.

The relentless population increase on Boang, along with the exigencies of petty commodity production, render the contemporary Tangan economy one of developing internal inequalities and external dependence. But the current household-based form of copra production marks only the latest phase in the history of Tangan political economy. This history can be divided into four phases, each of which describes a different articulation (and hence constitution) of Tangan political economic practice with transnational capital. Roughly speaking, the historical process of commoditization first took the primary form of contract labor and then the form of cash cropping. In each phase, moreover, Tangan big men (*kaltu dok*) insinuated themselves as mediators into the process of subsuming Tangan labor power to transnational capital, whether such capital appeared in the concrete guise of plantation recruiters or of the Copra Marketing Board. The transition to the latest phase in Tangan political economy was marked by the disengagement of big men from privileged control of the commodity economy. This disengagement, precipitated by the collapse of the postwar cooperative copra societies, can be coordinated with the emergence of *kastam* as a discrete cultural category. Incarnate in big men, *kastam* burst upon the Tangan scene as the realm of indigenous activity definitively separate from the activity of alien white men, namely, the exchange of commodities for cash which came to be known as *bisnis* ("business").

Phase one: the pre-colonial labor trade
The journal of William Dampier, who sailed by the Tanga Group in 1700, records the first known contact of Tangans with European explorers. Several canoes came off "Cave's Island" (Boang) toward Dampier's vessel and signalled him to come ashore. When the vessel found anchorage, some Tangan men boarded:

> At this time 3 of the Natives came aboard: I gave each of them a Knife, a Looking-Glass, and a String of Beads. I shew'd them Pumpkins and Coco-nut shells, and made Signs to them to bring some aboard, and had presently 3 Coco-nuts out of one of the Canoes. I shew'd them Nut-megs and by their Signs I guess'd they had some on the Island. I also shew'd them some Gold-Dust, which they seem'd to know, and call'd out Maneel, Maneel, and pointed towards the Land.

> *(Dampier 1906:530)*

Evidently the three men were eager for Dampier to come ashore, though for what reason remains unclear. Their exhortation of "*Manil, Manil*" ("Peace, Peace"), however, recalls the conventional (but ambiguous) salutation issued in order to soothe the recipient of a gift pig (chapter 6). Dampier regarded the words as "Signs of Friendship" and in any event concluded the encounter without incident.

Bougainville sailed the eastern coast of New Ireland in 1768, (re)naming Anir, Tanga, and Lihir after his principal officers Bournand, D'Oraison, and DuBouchage. Other explorers followed in the last quarter of the century and in July 1812, Captain Abraham Bristow definitively charted Boang (Day's Island) (Jack-Hinton 1972). Undoubtedly Tangans sporadically encountered a variety of merchants, whalers, *bêche-de-mer* fishermen, and geographers through the first part of the nineteenth century.[13] But intense contact with the inhabitants of the area probably did not begin before the region became one of the most prized destinations of recruiters for Queensland sugar plantations.

German recruiters operated in the Bismarck Archipelago in the early 1880s, trafficking New Irelanders off to DHPG[14] plantations in Samoa, possibly after Wesleyan mission outstations had accustomed certain groups to visitors (Docker 1970:170).[15] The demands of the growing Queensland sugar industry quickened the pace of recruiting considerably. A general rush to the Bismarcks in the spring of 1883 followed when the Fijian recruiter *Lord of the Isles* successfully seduced a shipload of northern New Irelanders already familiar with the German trader Eduard Hernsheim. In April of 1883, five vessels combined to obtain 528 laborers from the west coast of New Ireland (Docker 1970:179). Their success entrained another rush in July 1883, this time to the islands off New Ireland's east coast: Anir, Tanga, and Lihir.

Two months later, John Bird of Coomera hired ten Tangans, signed to three-year contracts, who had arrived in Brisbane on the *Jessie Kelly* (Docker 1970:215). The newcomers did not fare well, however, as this unfortunately worded account makes clear:

He [Bird] could see that they were inclined to be edgy, needing delicate handling, and went to some trouble to make them feel at home. But one day a gun exploded behind a standing group of them and they took off like startled rabbits to find some burrow in the distant scrub. By the time they were retaken many weeks later a higher authority had decided that they should forthwith be returned to the islands ...

(Docker 1970:215; see also Corris 1968:95)

Desperate escape was by no means an uncommon response among New Guinea recruits who deserted in large numbers upon learning the length of the term that they were expected to work. In addition, mortality rates among New Ireland and New Britain recruits soared to such a height that by the end of 1883 plantation managers issued reports discouraging recruiting in these areas. By 1884 the death rate for the entire Melanesian population varied between 13 percent and 23 percent from district to district (Corris 1968:94–96) and 14.8 percent overall (Firth 1976:51). And at least six New Irelanders who remained in the colony until 1887 –

perhaps some of them Tangans returned that year on the *Para* by Rannie (1912:286) – contracted venereal disease.

In all, some 368 Tangans arrived in Queensland, most of them before May 1884, when the Premier of Queensland, S. W. Griffith, "announced that because of the high death rate he had given orders to all government agents that no more recruits were to be taken from New Ireland and New Britain, 'as the natives were totally unfit for the work, and only came to the colony to die'" (Corris 1968:95).[16] Tangans were involved in one of the scandalous voyages which led to the establishment of a Royal Commission in December 1884 and to the closing of all New Guinea waters to recruiting the following year. On that occasion, the *Heath*, a Burns Philp vessel, returned to Mackay in May 1884 with 89 New Ireland recruits with whom no one could communicate.[17] Inquiries disclosed that:

... the government agent, Duffield, had not supervised the recruiting from an accompanying boat as was the rule; that the recruiting boat went ashore heavily armed; that the meat carried by the ship had been putrid; and that the ship had carried more recruits than she had capacity for.

(Corris 1968:93)

The recruits, confined aboard ship during the investigation, grew sick; fifty of the eighty-nine developed scurvy and the government health officer predicted that 80 percent of them would die unless action was taken immediately. In the end, the government supplied each of the natives with "a warm shirt and a pair of trousers" and packed them homewards in July aboard the *Heath*, under William Wawn (Corris 1968: 93).

Wawn's histrionic description of the landing at Boang mentions some of the items that were slowly becoming familiar consumption goods for Tangans:

Before we sailed from Mackay, the sub-immigration agent of that port had provided the ship with a quantity of "trade," which was to be distributed amongst the "rejected" islanders when they were landed at their homes. Each of them now received his or her "whack" before getting into the boats, consisting of beads, tobacco, pipes, calico of divers hues and patterns, tin pannikins and billies, fish-lines and hooks, tomahawks and knives, etc., etc., etc. Clothing and blankets were provided by the ship.

In the boats they were quiet enough, but, as soon as they got on shore, what an uproar and commotion! They shouted, yelled, screamed, danced and ran about like a parcel of lunatics. Off came every stitch of clothing, every man and woman stripping as bare as the day they were born. Their countrymen and countrywomen appeared in hundreds, and, no doubt, made a good haul, for in all directions, men and boys were continually rushing off to the bush with some article or another – a brightly flashing knife or billy, or a yard or two of red or yellow calico. I expect that the "stay-at-homes" got more out of the Queensland Government that day than did those for whom the "trade" had been really intended.

(1973:342–343)

However exaggerated, this account no doubt renders something of the attractiveness of the "trade" to Tangans. In 1984, several men discussing the time of "pulling boys" *(tate boi)* explained this attractiveness in terms of the scarcity of steel axes on Boang. They claimed that one man, Pultaufi, stole an axe from a visiting ship and fled overboard, chased by bullets. These first axes, the men continued, were loaned on a daily basis by their owners to people who presented small amounts of food for the privilege. Regardless of its accuracy, the story invites speculation about the impact that steel tools and rifles (until their ban in 1884 by the Queensland Government) probably bore upon island communities. The initial unequal distribution of such weapons/tools might have promoted the careers of particular big men or otherwise realigned power relations (see Foster 1987:63).

Douglas Rannie's account of the *Heron*'s voyage in April 1884 to the off-shore islands of New Ireland likewise affords a glimpse of how the local inhabitants perceived recruiting. At Green Island (Nissan), Rannie (the government agent) sensed an inclination to emigrate on the part of the younger men. Older men, however, a few of whom had worked in Samoa, opposed their juniors. The latent tension erupted when a number of youths dashed toward the boats returning to the *Heron*. Some of the older men intercepted them and "armed with bows and arrows, formed themselves into a guard between us and the bush to prevent any runaways" (Rannie 1912:45). Eventually, the ship left empty-handed. The incident suggests, among other things, the disruption recruiting created for local political economies which functioned in part through control over bachelors by senior men. By constantly removing young single men from the population, recruiters deprived local big men of labor, while at the same time providing young men with otherwise unavailable avenues to prestige and distinction. The standoff at Green Island physically displayed the medial role senior big men would come to play in the evolving colonial economy of labor recruiting.

At St. John's Island (Anir), the inhabitants enthusiastically greeted Rannie. On the beach, the recruiters exhibited their presents to anyone who would sign on:

These consisted of about a fathom of fancy print stuff, on which was placed a looking-glass, a tomahawk, a large knife with eighteen inch blade, a small knife,

three or four pounds of tobacco, half a dozen clay pipes, and a few glass beads.
(Rannie 1912:47)

About twenty islanders accepted these bundles and, after handing them to friends, stepped into the ship's boats. When, however, the boats headed back to the *Heron* in order to get more "trade," the recruits all at once stood up and dived overboard, swimming underwater to the shore. Though frustrated, Rannie restrained the boat's crew from firing upon the escapees and from returning to recapture them. The trick, evidently a response as organized as that of the Nissan elders, nicely illustrates the irregular and tenuous integration of local communities by recruiters into the labor trade at this stage. With the curtailment of the abuses of blackbirding during the 1870s, in many cases islanders signed on or not *as it pleased them*. At the same time, however, the boldness of the trick perhaps testifies to the desires that trade goods excited in their consumers.[18]

When the *Heron* hove alongside the Caen Islands (Tanga), an interpreter ("Mungish, *alias* English") informed Rannie that several islanders wished to go to Queensland. Mungish himself had made the trip, but he had been returned with one or two other Tangans as unfit upon arrival. A swarm of women flocked to the boats, desirous – according to Mungish – to join male relatives who had departed on previous vessels. Significantly, the mate recruited a sixty-year-old "chief," Ambulull, who had heard much of Queensland and wished to follow his men there. Ambulull took with him a wife and a dozen of his men. While supervising all this, Rannie watched an old man deposit a large basket in one of the boats. Upon inspection, Rannie discovered two human heads:

The interpreter told me they were the heads of a young man and woman who wanted to run away and go to Queensland. The young woman was the property of the old man. The previous night the two eloped and hid in the bush to watch for a chance to get away in our boats. The old fellow stalked them in the early morning, and taking them by surprise speared them both. Cutting their heads off, he brought them with him as tokens of his prowess.
(Rannie 1912:52)

The macabre jest recalls the senior/junior confrontation on Nissan and, without putting too much faith in Mungish's "translation," hints that control over women and/or labor might have been the focus of this conflict. I submit this proposal on the ground that much of the contemporary capacity of big men to organize a work party depends upon their control over the means of bride price: shell valuables called *am fat* (see chapters 3 and 6).

In the end, after relatively unsuccessful visits to Lihir and Tabar, the *Heron* returned to Tanga and picked up thirty-three more volunteers, bringing the total number of Tangans recruited to seventy-three. Inexplicably, while the islanders of Nissan, Anir and Lihir by this time all demurred from emigration, Tangans apparently continued to engage the labor traders as willing recruits. Nevertheless, Rannie's voyage quite possibly might have been the last of the Queensland recruiters before the closure of these waters became effective.

Much more than the sporadic encounters with passing vessels, the Queensland labor trade accelerated and extended the process of commoditization. The vehicle for this expansion was the injection of commodities into local economies and the instigation of new consumer needs satisfiable only through the exchange of labor. As Bernstein might put it, the local production of "use-values" – food, shell discs, canoes, and so on – continued, though not just as before. That is, "use-values" continued to be produced rather than replaced by commodities acquired through exchanges that linked Tangans with an expanding mode of capitalist production. But this does not imply that local economies remained autonomous subsistence units marginally engaged in capitalist relations. The growing use of steel axes in garden production and, perhaps, in warfare, established conditions which could not be reproduced outside commodity relations. Likewise, the use of calico and glass, items less far reaching in their consequences than steel tools, created needs that could only find satisfaction through the exchange of labor. Thus the labor trade commenced the reorganization of social reproduction not so much through a "'superimposition' (of capitalist exchange relations on pre-capitalist forms of production)" (Bernstein 1979:426), but through the generalization (or insinuation) of needs which impel participation in commodity relations. In this regard, it is important to keep in mind that although the labor trade originated in practices more akin to kidnapping than trade, the viability of the project ultimately "required the substantial consent of all concerned" (Scarr 1967:139, quoted in Firth 1976:52).

By the same token, the very tenuousness in 1884 of New Guinea islanders' participation in commodity relations derived from conditions that allowed islanders to determine their own needs. Islanders effectively retained control over the relationship with recruiters by simply deciding for (or struggling among[19]) themselves whether or not to sign on, as the examples of the Nissan elders and the Anir tricksters demonstrate. The ever-increasing regulation of the trade by the Queensland government and the public prosecution of the worst offenders denied to recruiters the superiority of arms. As a result, local decisions on the part of concerned elders or men who were satisfied with their current supply of "trade" dictated the flow of cheap labor to the Queensland sugar industry. From the point of view of Queensland planters, then, the New Guinea labor trade of 1883–84 was a massive flop, an expensive adventure that instead of resolving the "labor problem" only exacerbated difficulties. From a global perspective, however, the labor trade effectively and irreversibly articulated New Ireland economies with the wider colonial economy and through the instigation of new (reproductive) needs set the preconditions of the following phase of commoditization.

Phase two: "systematic labour mobilisation," 1884–1945

From annexation in late 1884 until 1899, German New Guinea fell under the administration of the New Guinea Company, "a speculative venture which was forced into the plantation business after the thousands of German settlers whom it had expected to rush to the colony failed to materialize" (Firth 1976:52). Firth maintains that recruiting during this period, mostly conducted in the Bismarck Archipelago, essentially continued the tradition of the Queensland labor trade in which recruits signed on for three years "as it suited them" (1976:53). New Irelanders comprised a large percentage of these recruits and though precise figures are unavailable, it is certain that Tangans were among them. From 1887–1903, 1,716 contract laborers recruited in the "islands east of New Ireland" (Anir, Tanga, Lihir) registered at Kokopo, the German administrative capital. Four hundred and two of these recruits died during the same period (Firth 1982:178–9).

By the mid-1890s, New Irelanders expressed clear preferences for work in the Gazelle Peninsula. They resisted, sometimes violently, recruiters contracting for the killing fields of Kaiser Wilhelmsland (mainland New Guinea), then infamous for its 40 percent mortality rate (Firth 1976:53). Firth stresses the political independence of most of German New Guinea and virtually all of New Ireland at the close of the century:

Most New Guineans remained independent of the foreigners in 1899, and saw work on contract as a matter of their own choice. People on the southeast coast of New Ireland, for example, told Governor Rudolf von Bennigsen in 1900 that none of them was available to sign on because the village was at war; and on Lihir Island he was asked why villagers should go to the plantations when they had plenty to eat at home.

(1976:54)

In other words, until the close of the century Tangans most likely determined their own engagement in commodity relations, *at least* with respect to the extent and timing of such engagements. With transfer of the colony to the *Reich* in April 1899, irregular and unpredictable recruiting in the style of the labor trade gave way to a "systematic labour mobilisation" (Firth 1976:52).

In Bernstein's (oversimplified) terms (1979:424), the German colonial government began to dismantle "natural economies" based on the "simple reproduction" of locally produced use-values by creating the social conditions of commodity production. The means employed by colonial states to this end typically include:

> ... the imposition of taxes necessitating sources of cash income, the use of forced labor in public works (creating the infrastructure necessary to the establishment of colonial administration and the enforcement of 'law and order'), frequently an initial use of coercion in the recruitment of labor for production enterprises ... and ... the imposition of cash-crop production on the peasantry.
>
> *(Bernstein 1979:424)*

The German government first began to extend its apparatus of rule beyond Kokopo by setting up permanent government stations in outlying areas. One district officer and thirty native police established a station at Namatanai in central New Ireland in August 1904. Soon afterwards, a visit by the Japanese trader and sometime government employee Isokide Komine officially brought the Tanga Islands under German administrative influence (Foster 1987). Komine persuaded Boang islanders to collect and destroy their weapons and ordered a huge feast to be held at Amfar (originally cleared for the occasion) to mark the event. In addition, Komine appointed *luluai* or government representatives to act as the local agents of German rule (see below). These *luluai* accompanied Komine to Namatanai in order "to get the law," as Warasau of clan Korofi, a very old man who died in 1985, once put it to me. The genesis of the contemporary Tangan category of *lo* – rules, regulations, and restrictions emanating from an absentee government – lies in Komine's eradication of warfare and cannibalism.

From the time of Komine's visit until the end of German and Australian military rule in 1922, direct government intervention in Tangan affairs appears to have been slight, probably because of the remoteness of the islands and chronic shortages of appropriate government vessels. A head tax was introduced to certain parts of the colony in 1907 as an alternative to the forced labor already made statutory in 1903 (Firth 1976:58). But it is unclear whether Tanga was ever declared a "taxation area" or if labor conscription ever took place in the absence of regular patrols. For the two years after its founding, Namatanai Station apparently extended its control mainly to coastal villages to the north and south, imposing road-building duties and suppressing warfare between coastal and inland groups. The 1911–12 Annual Report notes that: "The southern island groups, Lihir, Tanga and Anir, are entirely peaceful and have for a long time been more or less in contact with the Namatanai Station." However, the report admits that because of poor communications "the administration has not been able to play a more active role here" (Sack and Clark 1979:337–8).

Nonetheless, it is virtually certain that recruiting for plantation labor continued unabated, for the German administration never confined recruiting to "controlled" areas (Rowley 1958:115). New Ireland and its environs sustained the German plantation economy until 1913 despite the depopulation suspected by administrators and recruiters alike. And, moreover, New Ireland exported "female laborers, household servants and concubines" in large numbers (Firth 1982:125):

Half of the New Guinea Islanders employed by the Germans up to 1903 were New Irelanders. Virtually all women in the workforce were New Irelanders: in the three years 1905 to 1907, for example, recruiters took 475 women from New Ireland to the Gazelle Peninsula and Madang. One-seventh of the entire population of New Ireland was working for the expatriates in 1913, and a German official thought that even a system of universal labour conscription would hardly have added to the number of workers.

(Firth 1976:60–1)

Firth's conclusion that contract work had become a familiar, if not wholly welcome, part of New Ireland life seems unavoidable. Whether the extent of indenture on Tanga approached that of the heavily recruited areas of the northern New Ireland mainland remains uncertain. By 1903, though, the famous ethnologist Parkinson, disappointed in his efforts to obtain Tangan masks as carefully executed as his earlier specimens, could write:

I was told that the older people who knew how to make them [masks] were dead, and the younger ones, who for the most part hire themselves out on distant plantations, have no opportunities for learning the arts of their forefathers.

(n.d.:522)

The evidently rapid disappearance of past customs moved Parkinson to assert that "the population is moribund" (n.d.:524).

An important element in the recruitment of labor throughout the colony and in the general routinization of commodity relations were the local "chiefs" or *luluai* designated by the colonial government (plate 1). The German colonial government furthered the institution of commodity relations through the agency of *luluai*, often but not always men of influence (sometimes retired warriors) in local communities:

Luluais were from the first responsible for the maintenance of roads and bridges in the village areas ... At one time they seem to have had responsibility for the collection of head tax where it was imposed, and to have been allowed to retain ten percent of what they collected. The *luluai* had to arrange for the presence of the fit adult males for forced labour, and, after the introduction of taxation, for labour in lieu of tax.

(Rowley 1958:217)

The Australian military administration and later the civil administration continued the *luluai* system in many respects unchanged, especially with respect to recruiting. Under the Germans, a system of bonuses encouraged *luluai* and other influential village elders to induce young men to sign on. The Australians recognized and regulated the practice:

In 1922 the value of the presents that might be given to chiefs as a bonus for inducing natives to recruit was limited to "a sum ranging from 10s to £1 according to the length of the service of the recruit"; it was not until 1932 that such payments to chiefs were prohibited altogether, and not until 1933 that native officials were forbidden to accompany or assist recruiters.

(Mair 1970:181)

In addition, New Guinea law exempted indentured laborers and village officials from payment of head tax.[20] The system of indirect rule put in place thus functioned not only to invent "chiefs," but also to provide "chiefs" with access to cash and goods without requiring the "chiefs" to leave the village. What were the effects of these circumstances on local social affairs? How did the direct linkage effected by *luluai* between the colonial economy and village sociopolitical life manifest itself in the activities of these *luluai*?

A specifically Tangan reply to these questions emerges from an examination of the careers of two such men, Kiapsel and Imbaul. Both men worked in Queensland and upon their return to Boang introduced several innovations in Tangan lifestyles. Kiapsel, in an act of reinscription worthy of Bougainville, renamed his area of Boang "Townsville." Tangan pronunciation eventually changed the name to Taonsip and this remains the name by which Tangans refer to the eastern portion of Boang. In addition, Kiapsel modified the design of Tangan plank canoes (*mon*) by adding sails in order to match more closely the sailing ships he had seen in Australia (the name Kiapsel means in Tok Pisin "captain of a sailing ship"). When Komine arrived to pacify the islands in 1905–6, both Kiapsel and Imbaul served as his interpreter and assistants. Eyewitness accounts of the event feature the two men as instrumental in effecting Komine's project. Accounts also state that Komine appointed both men among the first *luluai* of Boang (Foster 1987).

By the time the anthropologist F. L. S. Bell arrived on Boang in 1933, Kiapsel, who had died about ten years earlier, had achieved legendary status:

> Kiapsel was a real autocrat. No other leader within his clan *fung Korofi*, dared organize any rite or feast or economic activity without first submitting his plans to Kiapsel. He performed no physical work whatever. His throne was the food display bench found in every settlement. Seated thereon, he issued his orders to his fellow clansmen and they were quickly carried out.
>
> *(Bell 1955:284)*[21]

Bell never attributed Kiapsel's status to his position as "paramount *luluai.*"[22] However, Bell (1955:28) noted among the available sources of individual prestige participation in the men's secret society called *Sokopana*. Elsewhere, Bell recorded his being told that after Komine's peacemaking visit, Komine:

> ... took with him to Namatanai several of the more important men of the island, among them being two by name Kiapsel and Baul. Both of these men, during their stay in New Ireland, became friendly with Misikilliman, an influential native leader from Nokon near Cape Matamtamberan. They were initiated by this man into the secrets of a tamberan [spirit] society which flourished in that district of New Ireland, and on their return to Tanga proceeded to hold meetings of this society and to initiate new members.
>
> *(1935b:314)*

In the hands of influential big men, *Sokopana* once provided an important avenue to the acquisition of numerous shell valuables, the media of marriage payments, funeral feasts, and sundry compensations.[23] Bell reports that in some cases initiates paid to the society leader (*kabin pindik*) as many as six shell discs (*am fat*) and three fathoms of strung shells (*kemetas*) as well as several pigs – nearly the amount of a marriage payment. Control over the supply of these valuables enabled big men to control the services of others, especially young bachelors seeking a sponsor for their marriage payments.

I suggest that *Sokopana* be regarded as one of a number of means created or embraced by Tangan men with the advent of German and later Australian administration for establishing and enlarging themselves as big men. Such means became increasingly important with the suppression of fighting and cannibalism and the disruption of relations between seniors and juniors brought about by contract labor. This suggestion would explain the importation of Sokopana and perhaps also Kiapsel's desire, communicated to Fr. Neuhaus by people on Lihir, to send a Catholic priest to the Tanga Islands (Neuhaus 1925:328).

Another means apparently seized upon by big men was the practice of declaring a child taboo. A big man might so designate his sister's child or own child or grandchild by sponsoring feasts which brought in large amounts of shell valuables (see Bell 1936). By subjecting the child to long periods of seclusion and preferential treatment, the rites also secured for the child concerned (*dafal* if female, *tamnon* if male) a degree of lifelong superior status. Timanmale of Am Funanil lineage, clan Korofi, informed me that Kiapsel had thus tabooed him at birth.[24] The ceremony was also witnessed on the island of Lif by the Administrator of New Guinea during a tour of inspection in September 1927. One of the two girls in seclusion was the daughter of the *luluai* (RTNG 1927–28:83). Bell (1936:87) also reported that although he never witnessed the proceedings, *dafal* rites had been sponsored recently by Kepgas of Boang and Nepur of Tefa. Kepgas, according to a postwar report, was the *luluai* of Taubie Village, appointed approximately in 1932 (PR NAM 8 1958/59). Thus, all the available evidence suggests the active involvement of big men-*luluai* in *Sokopana* and *dafal* rites, practices that explicitly engendered both social hierarchy and the threatening autonomy of big men. Indeed, my friend and host Partui attributed the retrenchment of *dafal* rites in Tanga not only to the expense entailed, but also to the jealousy (*balfaun*) such projects provoke. Partui underlined his opinion by informing me that his own sister had died soon after emerging from *dafal* seclusion, the victim of a sore on her leg caused by sorcery.

The organization and sponsorship of *Sokopana* and *dafal* (and of feasts in general) demands a workforce, substantial amounts of food, and numerous pigs. *Luluai* were strategically placed to convert the cash and "trade" accrued from labor recruiting into these resources. Accounts of Komine's mission demonstrate how Kiapsel and Imbaul, capitalizing on their ability to act as Komine's translators, controlled the distribution of goods brought by Komine as peace offerings. Tangan informants claimed that returning laborers likewise submitted their boxes of trade goods to their big men who then arranged a feast, the highlight of which was the opening of the box and the distribution of its contents. Some informants, moreover, maintained that big men exploited their positions as *luluai* by paying the head tax of their followers in return for pigs to be used in competitive feasting.

The only patrol report known to have survived World War II is extremely suggestive on this count. During tax collection, the author of the report remarks, many men short of cash resorted to borrowing. On Boang, one scene recurred again and again:

The natives of practically all these places were very short of cash and many natives had no money at all. The deportee SumSuma together with a few other natives eventually financed all those who were short of cash.

(PR NAM1/1934–35)

Though not a *luluai*, "the deportee" Sumsuma was a man of great influence on Tanga, bitterly familiar with European ways. He organized the 1929 Rabaul strike, the first ever collective protest of New Guinea workers, and received a jail term of three years for his efforts (Gammage 1975; RTNG 1928/29). His return to Tanga helped initiate a new phase of

Plate 1   Ngamnabo, with *luluai* cap, and Bitlik, 1933

commodity relations (see below), but also renewed his participation in the local politics of feast giving. The role he played in one particular bout of pig exchanges furnishes more circumstantial evidence of the conjunction effected by *luluai* and other big men between the commodity relations of labor exchange and the less commoditized relations of ceremonial pig exchanges.[25]

Bell's ethnography describes an impressive ceremonial life in the Tanga Islands of 1933 that, I submit, recalls the efflorescence of ceremony documented by Salisbury (1962) among the Siane in the years following pacification. A decidedly competitive flavor spiked large-scale prestations of live pigs. Bell (1947a) recorded in useful detail one such exchange (*arel sigit*) that continued for twelve days between September 30 and October 11, 1933. The *arel sigit* pitted against each other two groups opposed along lines of longstanding marriage and warfare alliances (see chapter 3). One coalition apparently attempted to overwhelm the other with a prestation of fifty-eight live pigs that required immediate and exact (as to size) reciprocation. The challenged coalition overcame the affront by mobilizing the combined resources of a number of men, some of whom Bell fortunately recorded by name. Subsequent patrol reports reveal that of the dozen men identified by Bell as clan or clan sub-section (lineage) leaders, at least three were *luluai*.[26] Three other *luluai* contributed pigs to the *arel* along with one whom, according to one report, Komine had appointed as *luluai* but who deferred because of lameness to a younger brother. The challenging coalition as a whole was led predominantly by Sumsuma himself, who left undisguised his intentions to humiliate the leader of the opposite coalition, the *luluai* Buktom.

The precise means by which *luluai* or other big men might use their positions and resources to sponsor or contribute to such feasts remain matters of informed speculation.[27] Nonetheless, the *arel sigit* attended by Bell can be usefully contrasted with the feasts organized by Tangans in 1984–85. First of all, Tangans never to my knowledge engaged in the exchange of live mature pigs. All pigs contributed to a feast were cooked before their redistribution by feast sponsors. Secondly, although feasts retained a competitive dimension, this aspect of practice was not as pronounced as in the *arel sigit* recorded above. Individual men might "test" (*traim* in Tok Pisin) a host by unexpectedly contributing large pigs, or working power (*mui*) in spells, but on no occasion did I witness organized, public competition. Finally, the scale of feasts in 1984–85 was much smaller than that of the 1933 *arel sigit*, over the course of which at least twenty-eight pigs were cooked in addition to the more than one hundred exchanged alive. While twenty-five cooked pigs were distributed at the 1985 feast (*arer sigit*) reported in chapter 4, smaller distributions were not uncommon.

I suggest that the combination of pacification and new forms of stratification brought on by colonization increased the scope of competitive feasting during the interwar years. Perhaps strengthened by their control of comparatively scarce goods – cash and "trade" – big men incorporated a prestige economy into the dynamics of mortuary feasting. In other words, commodity relations enabled a reorganization of the social relations of feasting. Big men did not incorporate *commodities per se* into feasting, as happened in other parts of Melanesia, but rather used commodities to restructure the production and exchange of pigs and vegetable food. The *arel sigit* of October 1933, I argue, must be understood as the product of such practices.

Through the 1920s and 1930s, then, the Tanga Islands constituted a labor reserve within the colonial economy. Of sixteen men of whom I inquired whose birthdates could be estimated at 1920 or earlier, fourteen had worked for a minimum of three years as contract laborers. One man travelled as far as the New Guinea mainland (Salamaua) and another visited Australia, but most found employment in Rabaul on plantations, with the Catholic Mission at Vunapope, or with Chinese traders in New Ireland. The trend continued into World War II, during which the Japanese removed about 150 Tangan men for gardening work and for the construction of an airport at Kavieng (PR NAM 13/1944–45).[28] Other men reportedly worked various jobs for Allied forces in the Solomon and Nissan Islands. Thirty-seven other men were recruited by the Australian military administration (ANGAU) in March 1945 for short stints of restoration work on the New Ireland mainland (PR NAM 13/1944–45). On October 30, 1945, the Australian civil government cancelled all labor contracts made with natives by the Army (Mair 1970:205). The announcement effectively ended an era of Tangan labor history, for after the war the interest of Tangans shifted emphatically to copra production. Labor migration continued, but on the basis of casual employment instead of contract indenture. Simultaneously, it appears, at least some Tangan big men attempted to extend their enhanced authority to the nascent local copra industry.

Phase three: copra and coops
Quite possibly, Tangans entered the trade in *bêche-de-mer*, tortoise and conch shell, and copra as early as the end of the first decade of the

twentieth century. Opportunities to transact would have been presented by itinerant Chinese traders, whose number in the Bismarck Archipelago grew with the overall increase in Chinese immigration after 1907 (Biskup 1970:95ff).[29] By 1914, an area on the east coast of southern New Ireland had been opened up for Chinese settlement (Biskup 1970:98). Chinese traders, who frequently combined commerce with interests in recruitment of labor and small plantations, were active in the Namatanai District to the extent that in 1913 the station officer complained of their falsifying tax statements (Biskup 1970:101). Whether such traders visited the Tanga group for purposes other than recruiting cannot be determined from written sources.[30] In October 1924, when P.K. Neuhaus installed five Catholic Tolai catechists on the various islands of the group, he noticed an abandoned tradestore on Nekin (an islet between Lif and Tefa) that had been run by a Chinese trader (Neuhaus 1925). The observation supports Biskup's claim that Chinese traders "settled in out-of-the-way villages where trading opportunities were negligible" and underlines the incisive comment of a contemporary observer, Karl Sapper, who said that the Chinese:

... play the role of cultural pioneers and often prepare the soil for large European enterprise, by slowly acquainting the natives with the way of life of the foreign immigrants, *and by accustoming them with trade and new needs.*

(quoted in Biskup 1970:102; emphasis added)

Just as Wesleyan outstations and the pioneer posts of traders like Hernsheim once conditioned local populations for the labor trade, so the activities of peripatetic Chinese traders probably laid the groundwork for simple commodity production in the form of a copra industry.

At the close of the 1920s, no regular trade in copra had been organized in the Tanga group. During his inspection tour of the Territory in 1929, the Administrator remarked that at Tanga:

... it was ascertained that the natives had sufficient coco-nuts to produce copra, but that there was no trader in the vicinity who could purchase it. I instructed the District Officer to approach persons on the mainland opposite to Tanga, with a view to finding a possible trader to whom the natives could dispose of their surplus.

(RTNG 1929/30:122)

This situation changed significantly in 1933 with the arrival of Chin Pak, who purchased land near Amfar on Boang for the establishment of a coconut plantation (variously referred to as Angfa, Sunmiul, and Amfa in patrol reports).[31] Chin Pak reputedly bought green (unsmoked) copra from local residents whom he also employed to work the plantation. In 1938, land on the west coast of Malendok was surveyed for the establishment of Put plantation by W. R. Carpenter and Co.[32] At the same time, apparently, acreage on the east coast of Malendok was set aside to create Nonu plantation, though the area remained uncleared until 1956. The two plantations, eventually acquired by the New Guinea Co. Ltd., are referred to as Putnonu in postwar patrol reports. Together they comprise over 1,000 acres, nearly ten times more acreage than Chin Pak's plantation. Although I cannot verify whether Putnonu plantation purchased local copra before 1953, I am certain that until his removal by the Japanese in 1942, Chin Pak provided Tangans with a source of cash and trade goods. In a small but significant way, the establishment of Angfa plantation made the Tanga Islands a site for the regular production of commodities other than labor. This transition from the production of labor to the production of copra opened the third phase in the commoditization of Tangan society.

It would be a mistake, however, to attribute this shift solely to the presence of Chin Pak at Amfar. Upon completion of his jail term, Sumsuma returned to Boang in 1932 and soon afterwards planted a large grove of coconut palms in the Waranmale section of the island (Gammage 1975). At least one older man, Malnge of Balantengkalok hamlet, claimed that other men followed Sumsuma's example. Malnge recalled thus how he and his father were perhaps the first to plant coconuts in the Lop section of Boang. Presumably, by the time ANGAU reestablished contact with Tangans at the beginning of 1945, a number of smallholders must have been in control of a significant number of mature palms.

Five years later, however, a patrol officer wrote that the native copra industry lay dormant despite a keen interest in copra sales and an abundance of coconut groves (PR NAM 21/1949–50). The officer observed that only Angfa plantation bought copra and that arguments continually erupted between the natives and the buyer, an "aged Chinese," most likely Chin Pak or his brother, Chin Him. Tangans complained about the unfairness of the price paid for their copra (15 shillings per bag of dried copra).[33] An earlier patrol report (PR NAM 4/1947) reflected a similar sensitivity to "fair exchange" on the part of Malendok residents who, eager to work on the soon-to-be-opened Put plantation, held meetings to determine the wages to be sought from their employer. The 1950 report also noted that many Tangans had obtained licenses to trade copra, but that irregular shipping to the district market in Rabaul posed difficulties for the routinization of copra production. The twin problems of limited access to the Rabaul market and unfair trade arrangements at home receive mention in patrol reports throughout the 1950s. Tangans themselves attempted to overcome these restrictions on their copra production through the formation of copra societies geared to the purchase of a locally owned vessel.[34] Such a vessel, it was felt, would substantially reduce the cost of copra production and increase local control of marketing arrangements.

From about 1953 on, annual patrol reports record the tangible evidence of the growing copra industry:

There is a great deal of money circulating in the area and most natives own a large quantity of manufactured goods. There are a large number of bicycles on Boang, and it appears to be the intention of every male on the island to own one in time.

(PR NAM 5/1952–53)

Manufactured goods also included galvanized iron for roofing and water tanks (PR NAM 4/1954–55). This flow of commodities into Tanga perhaps stimulated more the general desire to obtain a vessel. In March 1953, the patrol officer C. A. J. Symons recorded a request on the part of "one clan," which had accumulated £600 in a bank account, for assistance in both instituting a cooperative society and securing a pinnace to ship copra directly to Rabaul. Two unidentified "leaders" were taken to Rabaul to discuss the issue with the Assistant Registrar of Co-ops. Three years later, a registered cooperative society still had not been set up and patrol officers persisted in requests for a survey of the islands by a cooperatives officer. In the interim, however, the formation of two indigenously organized societies exacerbated the contradiction between activities that would come to be categorized as "*bisnis*" and "*kastam*."

Sometime during 1952, two copra marketing societies emerged under the leadership of Sumsuma and Wasman, respectively. Dissatisfied with Chin Pak's price of £1 15s per bag, the two groups coalesced around the goal of obtaining transport for the direct sale of copra in Rabaul. In August of 1953, Sumsuma enlisted the aid of D. P. Farley, a private trader who had taken up a trading allotment lease near Sungkin in western Boang. Farley appears to have been one of several Europeans who during the postwar period purchased copra or shell from Tangans and sold tradestore items. Farley helped Sumsuma, along with two other leaders of the group (Dokasaris and Pongnauf), to buy a jeep and trailer in Rabaul. Wasman's group, by this time in quasi-competition with Sumsuma's society, acquired a jeep and trailer the following year for £450 from Chin Pak in Rabaul. Sumsuma's group responded by contributing 1,200 bags of copra toward the purchase of the M.V. *Venus* which, with contributions from Farley and another European, was purchased in November 1955 from Frank Chow of Rabaul. Sometime in 1958, Wasman's group acquired a 38-foot work boat, the M.V. *Tanga*, for the sum of £3,600.

From 1956 onwards, patrol reports register a number of irregularities about the operation of the two copra societies, particularly concerning Farley's participation in the affairs of Sumsuma's group. Not until September of 1957 did Sumsuma's group obtain legal registration as the Boang Island Advancement Society (BIAS). BIAS remained for the duration of its existence an independent society unsupervised by the Cooperatives Section. Early in 1958, the M.V. *Venus* was wrecked on the reef at Sungkin. In November of that year, the patrol officer heard complaints against Sumsuma and Wasman and recorded that copra production had declined because "... workmen who do the collecting and processing have not been getting paid" (PR NAM 3/1958–59). He concluded his report by advocating an extended visit on the part of some patrol officer "to set up both these ventures on a decent footing and see that the contributors to these ventures get a square deal." The following year, Cadet Patrol Officer R.W. Hallahan took up residence on Boang for 107 days in order to install an effective bookkeeping system for Sumsuma's society and to investigate Farley's activities. Administrative concern over the £2,300 debt of the BIAS for repairs on the *Venus* also prompted this unusual patrol.

Hallahan's detailed report (PR NAM 8/1958–59) provides some account of the internal organization of the copra societies, especially of the social relations of copra production. The report begins with Hallahan's major finding:

The unfortunate part of the story is that the majority of the coconut trees on Boang are owned by a limited number of "big men" who employ the rest of the men and women to work for them. *Over the past four to five years these people have received little or no reward for their work* and this is the main cause of the present apathy (original emphasis).

Hallahan noted, for example, that Sumsuma's BIAS consisted of "... thirty six coconut owners and some two hundred and eighty other men and women (owning few or no coconuts) who work for these 'big men' on two or three days each week." The executive committeemen of the society, as well as most of the coconut owners, represented the most senior generation. Five of the eight executives, moreover, were either *luluai* or *tultul* (assistants to the *luluai*), that is, government appointees who functioned as part of the system of indirect rule that the Australian colonial regime inherited from the Germans. And, as was the case from the inception of the *luluai* system, *luluai* and *tultul* often held positions of leadership within their own lineages (see PR NAM 5/1955–56). Likewise, Wasman's group included "only eighteen important coconut owners and one-hundred-and-eighty other men and women who own few or no coconuts at all." Hallahan observed about Wasman and Male, the vice-president of the group, that: "Both of these men have built themselves large and ornate native materials houses, employ house servants and in other ways try to ape the plantation manager." According to an earlier report, Wasman had married a second wife in 1958 and had leased the *Tanga* to a "half-caste" without the consent of society members (PR NAM 3/1958–59).

In short, the evidence of Hallahan's account and other patrol reports – admittedly partial in both senses – suggests the continuing local refiguration of the colonial economy in terms of big-man politics. Senior big men, sometimes *luluai* and *tultul* already empowered to organize native labor for government purposes, apparently commanded a workforce of younger men and women to process copra from palms owned by these big men. Monopoly ownership derived in part from the simple fact that senior men had planted the palms that were first to mature (see chapter 3 for local concepts of tenure). Thus Hallahan remarked that several young men had started their own plantations but the palms had not yet come into bearing. Holding the organization of work together, then, was the authority of big men, on the one hand, and a generalized feeling that locally owned vessels were necessary for overall prosperity, on the other. Although Hallahan characterized this latter desire as a "'boat belief' movement," his own report makes it clear that the only alternative to locally controlled transport was fleecing at the hands of foreign traders.

What remains unclear is how big men distributed and consumed the proceeds of copra sales. That is, did the control over copra production exercised by big men and senior men carry over into mortuary feasting, as in the case of the *arel sigit* described above? Or were the proceeds of copra sales largely spent on imported food items for household consumption, as seemed to be the case by 1969 and certainly was the case in 1984 (see below)? All that can be inferred reasonably from the patrol reports, which resolve a complex situation into the simple terms of "owners" and "workers," is that senior men, in their synthetic role of *luluai*/big man/ coconut owner, dominated much of the Boang copra industry throughout the 1950s. In some parts of Boang, however, and in the islands of Lif,

Tefa, and Malendok, many copra producers remained unaffiliated with a copra society. These producers sold directly to Angfa Plantation or to Putnonu Plantation at a price varying from £2 to £2/5/- per bag. The extent of big-man influence in these areas is difficult to assess, but all patrol reports indicate that, as with the societies, coconuts lay largely in the hands of a small number of men. Nonetheless, it seems that these men used family labor rather than (non)wage labor to produce copra. Apparently marketing independently of each other, these producers exemplified the form of production to which almost all Tangans turned in the 1960s.

In 1960, the *Venus* was sold and the BIAS shareholders decided to distribute the proceeds of the sale as well as accrued proceeds from copra sales on a proportionate basis. Although a reserve fund of £800 was maintained, the society seemed to function thereafter on a greatly reduced scale. When patrol reports next mention the BIAS, in 1967, it is only to note its gradual dissolution:

Since then [1960], however, owing to conflicting loyalties and disputes of one kind or another, sections of the community have been breaking away from the society and forming their own copra groups ... This has left the society with a sadly depleted list of membership ...

(PR NAM 20/1966–67)

Similarly, Wasman's group seems to have disbanded by the mid-1960s. The M.V. *Tanga*, like the *Venus*, fell into disrepair and apparently generated burdensome debts for Wasman and his group.

While patrol reports suggest that the difficulties surrounding the *Venus* and *Tanga* contributed mightily to the collapse of the copra societies, at least part of the cause lies, I argue, in the transformation of the social relations of copra production during the 1960s. On the one hand, disputes among major producers over the policy of copra groups appears to have stymied collective undertakings. No single producer could effectively hold together a group of his peers. By 1968, most of the larger producers (about thirty) maintained their own accounts with the Copra Marketing Board in Rabaul to which they shipped their copra directly by commercial freighters. On the other hand, the younger men who furnished large producers with labor in the 1950s were able to harvest palms in the 1960s which they themselves had planted. In 1958, Hallahan had counted 46,005 mature palms in the Tanga group with another 18,648 not yet bearing. By 1970, a patrol report cited Department of Agriculture, Stock and Fisheries estimates of 120,000 mature palms and 80,000 immature palms throughout the group (PR NAM 10/1969–70). This massive expansion of plantings enabled many more individuals to obtain income from copra sales. Small producers sold copra by the pound to local traders or to the plantations. These circumstances, combined with others discussed below, precipitated a local copra economy in which individual households replaced cooperative societies as the significant units of production. This development signalled the retreat of big men from the copra industry and the establishment in practice of the discrete domains of *kastam* and *bisnis*.

Phase four: household atomism and the emergence of *kastam*

The intensification of commodity relations entrained by expanded copra production altered the social relations of production originally associated with the copra societies. Explicit though uneasy hierarchy between big men and their followers yielded to a general state of household autonomy (though hardly household equality; see below). At least three factors can be identified in this shift: the demise of the system of village officials; the ill-fated government scheme of land demarcation; and the direct entry of the Catholic Mission into the administration of the Tangan economy. Together these factors precipitated the form of household production that I observed in 1984–85.

After about 1965, several patrol officers remarked that the system of village officials (*luluai* and *tultul*) had broken down. Having lost control over the channels of labor recruiting after the war, and having lost with the demise of the "cooperative" societies control over copra production, *luluai* no longer exerted a pervasive influence over commerce. Leaders who had consolidated their positions before the war died or became senile, their successors unable to wield effective authority over the first generation of school-educated, business-wise men.[35] Infrequent patrols to the Tanga group and the abeyance of the head tax from 1965 to 1970 left Tangans with an accurate impression of the Administration as merely "a licensing and policing authority" (PR NAM 3/1967–68). The growing importance of the Catholic Mission (see below) also diminished the dependence of Tangans on the government, and hence on its local representatives, for social services.

Finally, in early 1969, the Tanga Islands formally became part of the Namatanai Local Government Council – one of the last groups in the Namatanai sub-district to do so. Elections were held for three councillors in April. Boang Islanders voted into their two ward positions schoolteachers employed by the Catholic Mission. Their choice signalled the decisive dissociation of the role of big man from the realm of "government" or "law" (*gavman* or *lo*). This change was not lost on colonial administrators, who complained of the ineffectiveness of these councillors in the months following their election. District Commissioners and patrol officers alike attributed this situation mainly to the councillors' vested interests in and full-time employment by the Mission. At least one patrol officer, however, observed that:

The old village officials retain most authority on Tanga due mainly to the ineffectiveness of the Councillors. None of the three councillors on Tanga at present held authority either by Administration nomination or by clan hereditory system [*sic*] prior to the Council elections ...

(PR NAM 10/1970–71)

Out of the decomposition of the role of the big man (*kaltu dok*) thus sedimented the separate statuses of *bisnisman* (businessman) and *kaunsel* (councillor). Categorically, this creation of new roles corresponded to the emerging distinctions among *kastam*, *bisnis*, and *lo*; each domain had its own representative (*lotu* had its representative as well, the foreign missionary [*Pater*] and local catechists [*katekis*]). Thus, I suggest, the emergence of *kastam* as an explicit cultural category can be traced approximately to the redefinition of big-man status that occurred during the 1960s. Both the practice of big men and the conduct of *kastam* described and analyzed in subsequent chapters demand appreciation in this light. Although in many ways mortuary rites have remained remarkably resistant to change – much of what Bell observed in 1933 could be observed in 1984 – the entire political economic context of these rites has changed significantly. The singular identification of big men with *kastam*, discussed in chapter 3, grew out of a previously undifferentiated field of social practice, constituted by the comprehensive activities of men like Kiapsel and Sumsuma, that recognized no distinctions between *kastam* and *bisnis*, or between *kastam* and *lo*.

In retrospect, the administrative laments about ineffective leadership seem ironic if not paradoxical inasmuch as major administrative efforts throughout the 1960s furthered an overall policy of "individualization" (Fingleton 1984:158). Nowhere was this policy more apparent and potentially revolutionary than in the area of land law. Fingleton argues that administrative dismay at the failure of various postwar cooperative ventures – plantations, copra societies, and so on – led to an attempt to strengthen "individual interests in land, at the expense of group-based interests" (1984:156). To this end, the Land Tenure Conversion Act of 1963 enabled the registration of individual titles in land, a presumed prerequisite for economic development.[36] In order to determine and recognize registration interests in customary land, the Land Titles Commission (LTC) created a number of local "Demarcation Committees" to assist in the work. The LTC convened two such committees on Boang in October of 1966, and another two committees for Malendok/Tefa the following year. Records of the LTC, unfortunately incomplete, suggest that demarcation on Boang proceeded at an almost frenzied pace. By September 1969, 1,347 blocks of land had been marked by the two Boang committees alone – this on an island of about 10.4 square miles. Little more than a year later, however, the committees existed in name only as the entire land scheme had distinguished itself as, in the words of one District Commissioner, "a massive great flop" (PR NAM 3/1970–71).

Despite the failure of the land conversion policy, the activity of the demarcation committees contributed to the drift in the social relations of production on Tanga toward household autonomy. The scale of demarcation suggests that the committees parcelled blocks of land for individual households and not for clans or lineages. Such a move would agree with the interpretation of land law that Jessep found among Barok demarcation committeemen in central New Ireland: ". . . government wanted people to think of the *famili* (family) and not just of their *bisnis* (New Ireland Pidgin: here, lineage)" (1980a:121). Besides the difficulties such an interpretation entailed for a system of matrilineal tenure (see chapter 3), one political consequence of demarcation was the further reduction of the influence of local leaders. For by removing the management of land from the hands of lineage elders and by usurping the authority to settle land disputes, the demarcation committees and the LTC threatened to extract land from its dynamic context of kinship and alliance. In other words, big men stood to lose yet another of the means of creating and manipulating social relationships. Instead of a fluid system of tenure conditioned by the requirements of cross-lineage kin relations, the possibility of independent and inflexible household tenure intruded itself into Tangan affairs. Every household head would be a big man on his half acre of land, and every household would in large measure maintain and reproduce itself through its own engagement in relations of commodity production and exchange.

The story of land demarcation in the Tanga Group also reveals the extent to which the Catholic Mission had evolved into the effective focus of economic life in the islands. Since 1933, the mission had been administered mainly by Fr. Heinrich Maurer, a man fluent in Tangan language and familiar with Tangan conventions. During Maurer's tenure, the Mission provided schooling and health services to local residents.[37] Several informants claimed, however, that Maurer discouraged business enterprises and maintained a protective attitude toward his parishioners with regard to their involvement in the cash economy. For example,

Maurer reportedly bartered trade goods for local produce rather than establish a tradestore under the auspices of the Mission.

Whatever Maurer's policy toward cash dealings, the projects of his American successor, Fr. Hager, indicated an attitude that one Namatanai Assistant District Commissioner called "progressive" (PRNAM 3/1967–68). Another ADC characterized Father Hager soon after the latter's departure in 1969 as "a young energetic priest who involved himself in every facet of life on Tanga and was always a spur for development" (PR NAM 12/1968–69).[38] Thus, in May 1966, W.J. Read, then Acting Senior Commissioner of the LTC, solicited Fr. Hager's assistance in setting up the demarcation committees (LTCR 75–01). Fr. Hager apparently agreed and actively supervised the work of these committees, including participation in the resolution of land disputes brought before the committees. In addition, Fr. Hager's activities seem to have encompassed copra marketing, banking, and tradestore operation.[39] Although patrol reports are silent on the details of these operations, the following remark by the ADC in 1971 registers the extent of Mission activity:

> There is no doubt that the Mission is the dominant force in the islands. Most facets of life revolve around the Mission, viz:- shipping, banking, copra marketing, road transport, education, health, postal services, etc., etc. Indeed, Mission power is so pervasive that I believe that the Tanga people are on the verge of some kind of repudiation of the Mission.
>
> *(PR NAM 11/1970–71)*

In the event, no such repudiation occurred. Rather, the Mission continued to furnish Tangan smallholders with the secure and convenient marketing outlet sought since World War II. One patrol officer commented in early 1970:

> There are approximately 24 copra numbers [accounts] owned by the more energetic producers. The other producers sell to local traders, of which Father P. Vavro and Mr. P. Chan [of Amfar Plantation] are the biggest. Local producers pay quite heavily for the privilege of not having to worry about marketing details. The Catholic Mission buys copra for [AUS]$6 per bag at the wharf, as does the manager of Amfa Plantation. The only vehicles now present on the island are owned by these two purchasers. Father Vavro charges one bag of copra per 8–10 bag load from the Top Ward [Taonsip] to the wharf, a maximum distance of five miles, while Mr. Chan charges $4 for the same. Other purchasers in the area have varied copra prices, but their activities are often limited through lack of capital.
>
> *(PR NAM 10/1969–70)*

My intention in citing this lengthy quote is not to contend that the Mission exploited Tangans, but simply to suggest how Mission involvement in the local copra industry limited the expansive activities of big men and entrepreneurs. For copra smallholders, the Mission provided not only immediate cash payments for small amounts, but also a sales outlet detached from kin relations and local political considerations. That is, direct sales to the Mission or plantation meant access to cash unmediated by extra-household social relationships. The support given to the Mission activity in copra marketing, I submit, thus reflected and advanced the detachment of *bisnis* from the control of big men. In addition, the large amounts of cash passing through the parish office enabled the Mission to extend its provision of social services, thus further enlarging its role in Tangan social life.

This state of affairs continued into the 1980s, perhaps accelerated by the closing of Amfar Plantation in the late 1970s. While many local traders operated in 1984–85, buying green copra by the pound and shipping their produce by commercial freighter to the CMB in Rabaul, and while several individuals or small group ventures completely controlled transport on Boang with several pickup trucks, the Catholic Mission remained a potent economic force. As the major buyer of copra and the major seller of consumer commodities (see below), the Mission linked the households of numerous Tangans into relations of commodity exchange. In effect, the central position of the Mission in the organization of commodity relations on Tanga grew out of and reinforced the autonomy of households in copra production.

Not surprisingly, the emergence of *kastam* and *bisnis* as explicit cultural categories during the 1960s refigured the older category of *lotu*, "church" or "Christianity." One man, for instance, criticized the missionary in 1985 for devoting too much time to *bisnis* and not enough time to *lotu*.[40] Not only did this man implicitly perceive the two as discrete activities, he also suggested their potential antagonism to each other. The complaint, however, was based less on some conceptual distinction between mundane enterprise and otherworldly concerns than on the man's opinion that the Mission effectively hampered locally directed development. His criticism underlines the extent to which Tangans regard the practical domains of *lo*, *lotu*, *kastam*, and *bisnis* as separate and ideally non-overlapping. This tendency gains its fullest expression in the opposition between *bisnis* and *kastam*, which I discuss further in the next chapter.

Conclusion: "the simple reproduction 'squeeze'"
Although particular historical and cultural contingencies conditioned the form in which commodity relations became increasingly intensified for

Table 2. *Tangan copra production, 1962–85*

Year	Tons	Kilograms	Source
1962	360 (est.)		PR 8/1961–62
1967/68	475 (est.)		PR 9/1968–69
1970	420 (est.)		PR 3/1970–71
1974	600 (est.)		Area Study/Tanga Census Div.
1978		149,670[a]	
1979		209,670	
1980		207,351	
1981		268,929	
1982		307,680	
1983		123,812[b]	
1984		353,636	
1985[c]		226,597	

Note: [a] The figures for 1978–85 are for Tanga parish copra production *only*, that is, for copra purchased by the Mission. Fr. Leon Wiessenberger generously provided me with these figures. The total amount of copra shipped from the Tanga group is *greater* than that indicated during these years.
[b] 1982–83 was a drought year in the Tanga Islands, the effects of which are registered in the drastic decline in production.
[c] 1985 figures are for January to June only.

Tangans, the effects of this process can be summarized under Bernstein's general characterization of the "simple reproduction 'squeeze'" (1979:427). Put simply, the simple reproduction squeeze identifies a situation in which peasant households encounter more and more difficulty in maintaining or increasing the supply of commodities necessary for the reproduction of prevailing levels of consumption and production. Bernstein lists as factors contributing to the squeeze: "exhaustion of both land and labor"; "rural 'development' schemes which encourage or impose more expensive means of production"; and "deteriorating terms of exchange for peasant commodities" (1979:427). (The second of these factors is notably irrelevant to the Tangan case.) In addition to these pressures, all of which are directly exerted by the exigencies of commodity relations, one must add for the Tangan case the condition of population growth. Taken together, these circumstances effectively regulate household production in the absence of any state agency undertaking its direct organization.

To the extent that it can be determined, copra production in the Tanga group increased dramatically from 1962 to 1985 (see table 2). New plantings continued through the 1960s, moving one patrol officer to note that:

... although their [Tangan] earnings are good, the standard of living is not of a corresponding order. This is due mainly to a severe land shortage as most arable land is under economic cultivation. Therefore little is left for gardening. Some even try to plant food crops in their coconut groves. Consequently most money earned is spent on buying trade store foods.

(PR NAM 3/1970–71)

A previous patrol officer vaguely but suggestively recorded a similar impression:

It was stated by Mr. P. Chan, who manages Amfa Plantation, that at the trade store he operates, he sells a considerable quantity of tinned fish and meat, although rice is the commodity most in demand. Large amounts of rice are also sold from the Mission trade store at Amfa.

(PR NAM 10/1969–70)

In 1984, the Mission store *alone* sold 49.995 tonnes of rice at a price of K21,887.50, and an additional K22,000 worth of tinned fish, tinned meat, and biscuits.[41] In all, the Mission tradestore had an income of K163,727.79, an amount that exceeded the total paid by the Mission to copra smallholders (copra expenditure) by more than K50,000 (see table 3).

The overall situation is clear. Large sums of money from a variety of sources – copra income, remittances, wage labor – have become necessary in order to supply the population with consumer commodities, especially food. Many factors condition this situation, including Tangan tastes and preferences for rice and tinned fish, and the consumption needs of teachers, nurses, and Mission staff without access to gardens. Unarguably, however, the scale of imported food consumption measures the degree to which subsistence gardening fails to meet the subsistence needs of the growing population. The exhaustion of arable land by coconut holdings (and consequent reduction of fallow periods on available arable land) has led to a dependence on commodity foods typical of the simple reproduction squeeze.

The tightness of this squeeze is evident when the Tanga Parish Copra Production figures are placed in the context of fluctuating market prices for copra (see table 3). Regardless of changes in the price of copra, the income of the Mission tradestore grew every year from 1978 to 1984. In 1982, the year of a severe drought, tradestore consumption topped K100,000 while the bottom dropped out of the copra market. The combination of climatic and market variability demonstrated to Tangans the vulnerability of their position in a system of intensified commodity relations. Despite the discouragingly low price for copra, Tangans apparently

Table 3. *Tanga Mission (St. Boniface Parish) copra and tradestore income, 1978–85*

Year	Copra prod. (kgs)	Copra income[a]	Copra expend.[a]	Store income[a]	Avg. price per tonne[a]
1978	149,670	NA	NA	NA	214.74
1979	209,670	68,686.56	48,565.03	56,191.12	300.34
1980	207,351	56,145.22	41,726.92	59,178.94	235.95
1981	268,929	61,342.89	47,771.28	69,609.54	210.27
1982	307,680	58,128.31	46,318.42	100,340.24	169.66
1983	123,812	29,995.45	23,458.82	113,754.68	192.42
1984	353,636	139,213.10	109,561.87	163,727.79	391.06
1985[b]	226,597	NA	NA	NA	351.76[b]

Note: [a] Figures in PNG Kina (K1.00 = US$ 1.10 in 1984–85).
[b] Figures for the first six months of 1985 only.

increased their production over the 1981 total by 50,000 kilograms.[42] Thus, in order to maintain existing levels of consumption – an unsuccessful attempt by most accounts of the drought – Tangans resorted to a quantitative intensification of commodity relations. Interestingly, the recovery of gardens in 1984–85, coincident with a boom in the copra market, led not to a reduction of production but rather to further quantitative intensification. Population growth and the progressive deterioration of gardening land fuel the vicious cycle, the net effect of which is an overall reduction in the standard of living (consumption), an increase in the cost of commodity and non-commodity production (gauged in labor time and returns to labor), or both.

I emphasize the qualification of "overall" in the scenario outlined here, for individual households experience the effects of commoditization differently. That is, one result of the intensification of commodity relations in Tangan society has been the differentiation of households on the novel basis of their ability to enter into commodity relations. Bernstein distinguishes, in this regard, "poor" peasants who must exchange their labor power on a regular basis in order to reproduce (the landless or rural proletariat); "middle" peasants who reproduce mainly through nonwage labor and land; and "rich" peasants who accumulate sufficiently to purchase the labor power of others (that is, the class of people Tangans call *bisnisman*). On Boang, such differentiation is not readily visible in terms of the distribution of expensive consumer items such as vehicles or European-style houses. Nevertheless, households do differ in their cash incomes and thus in the amount of cash available for commodity purchases. A survey of

Table 4. *Copra income for sixteen Taonsip households, January–June 1985*

Household No.	Size[a]		No. of copra sales	Copra income[b]
	A	C		
1	4	4	3	166.95
2	2	5	0	0.00
3	3	7	6	207.60
4	2	4	6	266.45
5	2	2	3	200.00
6	3	3	2	141.60
7	2	3	7	362.20
8	2	1	2	145.00
9	2	2	12	437.40
10	2	2	2	400.00
11	2	7	15	248.30
12	2	5	4	156.37
13	5	3	8	400.06
14	2	5	5	299.95
15	2	3	9	350.15
16	2	1	4	150.00

Note: [a] A = number of adults; C = number of children.
[b] Figures in PNG Kina (K1.00 = US$ 1.10 in 1984–85).

household incomes for sixteen households in Taonsip during the first six months of 1985 revealed significant differences in income from copra, the primary source of cash earnings (see table 4). These differences translate in practice into variations in the ownership of kerosene lamps, aluminum pots, special clothing, and other personal items. That is, for the most part Tangan households comprise a "middle" peasantry of which the individual constituents vary in terms of levels of consumption. Inequalities in consumption, based mainly on the unequal distribution of coconut palms, assume their greatest significance during the annual "hungry time" when purchases of rice must supplement the uncertain supply of available garden produce.

Several "rich" peasants resided on Tanga in 1984–85, but their *bisnis* activities were not always regular. Men might purchase green copra for several weeks and then desist while other men began to buy. Similarly, tradestores might operate for several weeks and then fold after one or two shipments of inventory were sold out. Only the Mission offered Tangans a permanent source of commodity exchange.

At the other end of the spectrum, few households seemed reduced to the status of rural proletariat. Household No. 2 of the income survey, however, had achieved this condition temporarily. I say temporarily because the possibility remained of gaining access to coconuts through the future marriages of younger household members.

In short, class differentiation among households had by no means crystallized and hardened. Nevertheless, the long-term outlook for households on Boang appeared bleak in 1985.[43] The population continued to grow while coconut holdings had reached the limits of their expansion. Labor migration for all but the highly educated was not a viable option in the retrenched national economy of the 1980s. With literally no room for "rich" peasants to accumulate agrarian capital, further differentiation among households promised to enlarge the class of "poor" peasants while progressively impoverishing the "middle" peasantry. Yet, the outcome is undecided, for strategies ranging from political action to resettlement and partial withdrawal from commodity relations remain unexplored. Commoditization, in Tanga as elsewhere, describes an open-ended, contingent process and not a teleology in which the terminus is known in advance.

3

Kastam, *bisnis*, and matriliny

The historical emergence of the household as the locus of commodity production and consumption, or *bisnis*, entailed an ideological association of mortuary rites, or *kastam*, with matrilineal identity. According to this ideal, men and women genealogically related to each other through women comprise the personnel that undertake the project of hosting mortuary feasts for their deceased kin. That is, with regard to *kastam*, the lineage appears as an enduring, self-replacing, solidary group of enates[1] under the successive leadership of senior mother's brothers or big men (*kaltu dok*).

The ideal, of course, must not be taken uncritically. It is appropriate to ask, for example, whether it is genealogical prescription or the project of mortuary feasting itself that defines the matrilineage (*matambia*) (cf. Sahlins 1985:27). For the "groupiness" of Tangan matrilineages becomes salient mainly if not only in the context of performing mortuary rites. That is, enates initiate collective action and consequently make themselves appear as a matrilineage almost solely in connection with hosting mortuary feasts and constructing commemorative men's houses. Hence, the term *matambia* might alternatively be glossed as "men's house [*bia*] coalition" rather than "matrilineage," thereby obviating the latter term's connotation of "corporate descent group."

In order to deepen our understanding of what is at stake in the taxonomic opposition between *kastam* and *bisnis*, it is therefore necessary to open a discussion of Tangan matriliny. In this chapter I accordingly describe a variety of elements that enter into the definition of matrilineal identities and matrilineages – marriage strategies, residential arrangements, and land tenure. In so doing, I also trace the structure of social relations and identities that agents draw upon, create, and transform in the mortuary rites described in subsequent chapters.

Clan identities and intimations of moiety

While the definition of the matrilineage is always subject to revision through the performance of mortuary rites, matriclan (*funmat*) identities are not; they are axiomatic or "given," immutably fixed at birth. People with the same clan identity consider themselves to be descended from a single ancestress (though it is never relevant to demonstrate this descent) and use kin terms appropriate to enatic relatives in addressing and referring to each other (see table 5). Marriage and/or sexual relations with someone of the same clan identity are considered incestuous (*mumu*). The public sanction for incestuous sexual relations is a reciprocal exchange of pigs, referred to as "rectifying the lineage" (*fakausi matam funbaratam*), between the illicitly conjoined lineages of the offenders.[2] Undiscovered instances of incestuous intercourse might be revealed when an offender falls ill during or immediately after a visit to Anir, the residence of a particular *masalai* ("spirit"; see below) that attacks transgressors. (Genealogies that I collected show only one incident of incestuous marriage between spouses with the same lineage identity; some informants claimed that recent marriages had occurred in which the spouses shared a clan Filimat identity.) The brother/sister relationship remains the most circumscribed of all relationships, characterized by name avoidance and avoidance of all physical contact.

Shared clan identity also implies a common totem animal (*do*, "emblem," or *man*, "bird") with which no special observances are associated.[3] But despite the deictic and exogamic functions of clan identity, "clans" act as corporate groups in no salient context. I witnessed collaboration among several lineage leaders of clan Tasik on the occasion of one death and another instance in which a clan Korofi lineage leader organized members of other Korofi lineages to abrogate mourning taboos assumed by the leader's BW's lineage. Each of these events, however, seemed to be orchestrated specifically by the relevant lineage leaders. Matters of death, marriage, and land tenure, in particular, impinge upon enates who recognize a shared lineage (*matambia*) identity rather than clan (*funmat*) identity.

Tangans distinguish by name twelve matriclan identities (see table 6); people with the same identity tend to live in the same area. If a "clan" is defined statistically as the aggregate of people who share the same clan identity, then it can be said that 75 percent of the membership of most Tangan clans resides on Boang. Two clans (Pen, Tunaman), however, have a majority of their members resident on Malendok, and one clan (Tulefaleng) on Lif. Approximately 40 percent of clan Firfir comprises a

Table 5. *Terms of reference for a male speaker with partial list of genealogical specifications*

	Term[a]	Genealogical specifications
1.	*fengong*	FF, FFB, FM, FMZ, WZH, SS, SD
2.	*tibung*	MM, MMZ
3.	*tibuk tamat*	MF, MZH
4.	*koktamat*	MMB, ZDS[b]
5.	*tabung*[c]	F, MZH, MMBS, MFZS
6.	*indung*[c]	M, MZ, FBW, BW
7.	*kewaklik*	MB, ZS
8.	*ianang*	FZ, FZH, MBW, WF, WM, DH, ZSW
9.	*kamlang*	WMB, ZDH
10.	*tuaklik*	B, FB, FBS, MZS, BS
11.	*fefneklik*	Z, MZD, FBD, BD
12.	*ang kingkaf*	MBD, MBDD, FZD, FZDD
13.	*ifaklik*	MBS, FZS, WB, ZH
14.	*kek wok*	W, MBD, MBDD, FZD, FZDD
15.	*kiang kaik*	S
16.	*kek fangkafik*	D
17.	*awang*	SW
18.	*kewakfifinlik*	ZD
19.	*tibuklik*	DS
20.	*tibukfifinlik*	DD
21.	*nebik*	infant boy (still suckling)
22.	*intaklik*	infant girl (still suckling)
23.	*kaik*	young boy
24.	*ang kafik*	young girl
25.	*an sakanguam*	teenage boy
26.	*fifin*	nubile girl
27.	*kaltu*	man (parent)
28.	*fatina*	woman (parent)
29.	*matuk*	mature man (grandparent)
30.	*wok*	mature woman (grandparent)
31.	*matuk saksak/ matuk lamlam*	senile man

[a] Terms for a female speaker are listed in Foster 1988. All terms are given in the first person singular possessive form except nos. 21–31, which are the same for both male and female speakers. All terms can be used in address, except in cases of relationships where teknonyms are used (B/Z; WB/ZH) and/or the relationship term is avoided altogether (MB/ZS).

[b] These relationships are more appropriately labelled MBMB and ZSZS, a practice I follow in the text. In the table I follow the conventions of social anthropology.

[c] The terms for M and F are different words in their second and third person possessive forms: *indung/tinam/tina* and *tabung/temam/tema*. All other terms differ only in the form of the infixed or suffixed personal pronoun or in the form of the prefixed particle (see Capell 1977).

Table 6. *Census of Tangan "clans"*

Clan (*funmat*)	Totem (*do* or *man*)	Total population in 1963[a]	Total population in 1979[b]
Korofi	*Porot* (chicken)	194 (6.89)	274
Tasik	*Kosor* (sea eagle)	282 (10.02)	399
Filimat	*Ang Kika* (parrot)	1,002 (35.60)	1,418
Fasambo	*Bo* (pig)	466 (16.55)	659
Ku	*Am Bal* (pigeon)	307 (10.91)	434
Firfir	*Am Pul* (dog)	68 (2.42)	96
Eski	*Am Bin* (bird)	41 (1.46)	58
Fale	*An Teoteo* (kingfisher)	83 (2.95)	117
Tulefaleng	*Tagau* (sea hawk)	56 (1.99)	79
Tunaman	*Ang Kel* (chough)	270 (9.59)	382
Pulim	*Am Bek* (flying fox)	6 (0.21)	8[c]
Pen	*Ang Kut* (rat)	40 (1.42)	57
Waf[d]	*Borokilu* (dove)	–	–
	Total	2,815	3,981

[a] Source: Land Titles Commission, Exhibit M, Tanga Land Investigation.
[b] Source: National Statistics Office. *Provincial Data Systems, New Ireland Province* (Port Moresby, 1983), p. 83. The total population is that recorded in the 1980 census; the figures for each clan are based on extrapolations from the 1963 figures.
[c] This extrapolation is significantly inaccurate. In 1985, clan Pulim numbered only two men.
[d] This clan, recorded by Bell, was defunct by 1963. It was apparently localized on Tefa.

single lineage (likewise understood as the aggregate of people who at a given moment share a lineage identity) with members resident on Tefa and Lif (see table 7). Clans Tasik and Korofi occupy the eastern end of Boang, and Fasambo and Filimat the western end of the island. Lineages of clans Filimat, Ku, and Fale are settled in the central-eastern areas of the island.[4]

Clans vary greatly in size (see table 6). The largest clan, Filimat, whose members reside on all four inhabited islands of the Tanga group, makes up more than a third of the total population. Fasambo, the second largest clan and traditional marriage partner of Filimat (see below), comprises over 16 percent of the population. By contrast, the smallest clan, Pulim, bordered on extinction in 1985 with a membership of only two adult men.

The relatively large size of Filimat and Fasambo as well as their traditional marriage alliance suggests the possibility of a previous or presently submerged dual organization. Unlike nearby south-central

mainland New Ireland groups (Wagner 1986a; Albert 1987a), Tangan
clans do not divide into exogamous moieties (usually referred to in Tok
Pisin as "*bik pisin*" [sea eagle] and "*smol pisin*" [fish hawk]). Tangans
whom I asked denied that clans could be segregated into moieties at all.
As Tikot of clan Tasik (An Ififkin lineage) forcefully put it: "*Tanga i no
bruk!*" ("Tanga is not split!"). Marriages do not reflect a pattern of moiety
exogamy; with some exceptions (listed below), examples of marriages
between spouses with any two clan identities can be adduced. Nonetheless, informants agreed that marriages between members of certain clans
were less preferable than other marriages, and that certain clans were
recognized as traditional allies with whom marriage was discouraged.
These preferences, statistically real, match those provided by Bell in his
reconstruction of warfare on Tanga, one of the few instances in which he
addressed the question of Tangan social structure. Broadly speaking,
intermarrying clans, which Bell identified as clans hostile to each other,
are contiguously located (1935a:255). On Boang, the five largest clans
form three intermarrying pairs, each pair associated with a particular part
of the island. Both informant statements and marriage statistics readily
identify the pairs: Filimat/Fasambo (western Boang), Filimat/Ku (central
Boang), Korofi/Tasik (eastern Boang).

By contrast, clans that regard themselves as allies *and* as less suitable
for marriage do not occupy contiguous land: Korofi/Ku; Korofi/
Fasambo; Firfir/Eski/Ku. Allies found their relationship on the basis of
either patrilateral or matrilateral ties, and in both cases liken their
relationship to "brotherhood." For example, the alliance on Boang
during 1984–85 of clans Firfir, Eski, and Ku was explained to me as
deriving from their interrelationship as "children of one father" (*fat tualik*
– "bound brothers").[5] This relationship differs from ties obtaining
between several other clans in which "brotherhood" is conceived of as
siblingship between children of the same mother. Accordingly, there is a
definite prohibition on marriage between members of these latter clans:
Korofi/Pen; Tasik/Fale; Tasik/Tulefaleng (however, Fale can marry Tulefaleng).[6]

In sum, although no overarching moiety organization links all Tangan
clans in a single scheme, both regular marriage preferences and
"brotherly" support relationships intimate the presence of dual organization.[7] Significantly, marriage and patrilateral siblingship recall the
double principle of affinity and paternity that defines mainland New
Ireland moieties: each exogamous matrimoiety is at once the father and
paternal offspring (source and product) of the other moiety (cf. Wagner

Table 7. *Percentage (and number) of clan members by locale, 1963*

Clan	Boang	Malendok	Lif	Tefa	Other[a]
Filimat	80.44 (806)	14.00 (140)	2.20 (22)	1.80 (18)	1.60 (16)
Fasambo	76.39 (356)	9.87 (46)	2.19 (13)	3.65 (17)	7.30 (34)
Korofi	82.99 (161)	0.52 (1)	11.34 (22)	1.03 (2)	4.12 (8)
Tasik	80.85 (228)	3.90 (11)	2.13 (6)	–	13.12 (37)
Ku	93.16 (286)	1.30 (4)	2.61 (8)	0.33 (1)	2.61 (8)
Firfir	35.29 (24)	7.35 (5)	16.18 (11)	16.18 (11)	25.00 (17)[b]
Eski	100 (41)	–	–	–	–
Fale	78.31 (65)	8.43 (7)	9.64 (8)	–	3.61 (3)
Pulim	66.66 (4)	–	–	–	33.33 (2)
Tulefaleng	3.57 (2)	1.79 (1)	94.64 (54)	–	–
Tunaman	32.22 (87)	48.90 (138)	7.41 (20)	5.19 (14)	4.07 (11)
Pen	–	100 (40)	–	–	–
Total	73.18 (2,060)	13.96 (393)	5.79 (163)	2.24 (63)	4.83 (136)

Source: Land Titles Commission, Exhibit M, Tanga Land Investigation.
Note: I suggest that extrapolations from these percentages would provide an accurate profile of the disposition of clan members in 1984–85 with the one exception of the category "other." In 1979, 321 Tangans, or nearly 9 percent of the population, were away from the islands at the time of the census.
[a] The category "other" includes people residing in or visiting Anir as well as people working, schooling, or visiting in Rabaul, on mainland New Ireland, and on mainland New Guinea.
[b] The large percentage of clan Firfir members in the category of "other" is accounted for by the descendants of one woman who married a non-indigene and migrated from the island. These people were included in the list of people with active land rights compiled by the Land Titles Commission.

1986a). I shall examine this issue of moiety-like relations in later discussing the "cross-cousin" (*fat kinaf*) bond between a pair of lineages.

Lineages, men's houses, big men

Tangans differentiate people who share a single clan identity on the basis of lineage identities (*matambia*). Most clans (in the statistical sense defined above) consist of several lineages (in the same statistical sense) ranging from a low of one or two (Pulim, Eski, Firfir) to a high of ten (Fasambo) or more than fifteen (Filimat). Lineages of Boang-based clans average in size from forty-five to sixty men, women, and children, though lineages in decline might be much smaller.[8] Each lineage is referred to by the name of a "base/origin site" (*waranmale*; *asples* in Tok Pisin) located on that lineage's land. Often, but not necessarily, the site is associated with one or more of the following: a former or current men's house; a cemetery (*matmat* in Tok Pisin; *an inof* [ossuary]; see chapter 4); or the residence of the lineage leader. Lineages might be referred to by more than one name, the names designating in some cases not only customary sites for men's houses (see below), but also constituent "lines" (*fumbarat*; *lain* in Tok Pisin) within a lineage.[9]

No overarching genealogical framework links all the lineages within a clan, nor do Tangans rank the "composite" lineages of a clan according to seniority or any other such criterion. By contrast, Tangans expect that they can trace genealogical relations among members of a lineage. Tracing relations in practice proves quite possible in smaller lineages which consist of a set of siblings and the children and grandchildren of the female siblings. In larger lineages, however, enatic relations cannot always be traced. In the Solsol/Seber lineage of clan Korofi, for example, it was necessary to ascend six generations from an adult ego in order to connect the three recognized Boang-based lines of the lineage. However, relations established through marriage (patrilateral consanguinity) effectively linked all the lines within the generations of living members (see figure 1 and below for more on patrilateral consanguinity).

Genealogical knowledge tends to be lateral rather than vertical: the farther up (or "back"?) one goes, the greater the chance that both lineage men who were not leaders and the husbands of lineage women are forgotten. Genealogical knowledge of enatic ties is usually deeper than that of patrilateral ties. Most people, for example, could provide the names of their MM, and certain men could be counted on for more extensive information, particularly lineage leaders and men who had contact with the land demarcation committees of the 1960s.

Whatever the degree to which lineage members can state genealogical connections between themselves, it would be a misapprehension of Tangan ideas of sociality to regard the lineage as a genealogically defined group. The word for lineage, *matambia*, literally means "eye of the men's house." In this context, *mata* – the widely distributed Austronesian word – could mean "cluster," as in *matangku*, a cluster of coconuts piled at the base of a palm. The idea expressed would be something like a "men's house (*bia*) cluster" or a coalition of people associated with a men's house. Alternatively, the word might refer to the area just in front of the men's house (the "eye") where cooked pigs are carved for distribution at feasts. Both of these glosses stress the connection between the lineage and its men's house.[10] In practice, a lineage is a group of people that constructs a men's house and holds feasts at that men's house. In other

Table 8. *Lineages of two eastern Boang clans, 1984–85*

Clan Korofi	Clan Tasik
Solsol/Seber	Am Pel/Piklingkamu
An Siko	Taunakel
Sukeobum[a]	Taubo
Lofe	Matansal[d]
Am Funanil[b]	Matangkerem
Enalubun[c]	Fintim
	An Ififkin/Piklinmale
	Nesnum[e]

[a] Sukeobum lineage had recently split off from An Siko lineage; genealogical ties could easily be traced between the two. However, in 1985, each group had its own men's house.

[b] Am Funanil lineage numbered three adult men on Boang Island. Other female members were claimed, but their genealogy was disputed. The future of the lineage and its land holdings was not certain in 1985.

[c] Enalubun lineage was in decline in 1963, when its membership included only seven men and two women (one of childbearing age) according to Land Titles Commission genealogies. In 1984, the lineage was defunct on Boang. One man, however, the DS of Suguguk or Lutnampok, the last big man of Enalubun, married a woman from Anir said to be his MFMZDD. This marriage, it was claimed, would validate the DS's rights to his MF's land and continue the lineage on Boang.

[d] A dispute over the location of a new men's house opened a latent rift between the Matansal and Taubo groups; each group erected its own men's house in 1986.

[e] Members of Nesnum and An Ififkin lineages recognize their close genealogical relationship; the two groups, however, did not cooperate with each other in 1985. Nesnum lineage built a small men's house to use as a meeting site in 1984; it was not part of a mortuary sequence. An Ififkin lineage had no men's house in 1985.

words, the lineage is a performatively rather than genealogically defined unit. This is not to say that simply by participating in the construction of a men's house one becomes a member of a lineage. Rather, active participation defines the current constituency of a lineage. The close relationship between a men's house (*bia*) and a matrilineage (*matambia*) marks the construction of men's houses as the practical locus for the formation and reformation of lineages. Thus, the number of lineages "in" a clan is by no means fixed, but instead always subject to addition or subtraction through processes of lumping and splitting effected by the pragmatic necessities of men's house construction (see table 8).

A men's house condenses into a potent symbol important aspects of the ideal of lineage identity (plate 2). Unlike men's houses in mainland New Ireland societies, which remain associated with a particular hamlet site (a lineage's residential land within a village), Tangan men's houses are rebuilt on different sites.[11] One man explained that men's houses follow big men. That is, men's houses are rebuilt at the former residential sites, called *pief* ("ashes"), of deceased big men whom a lineage "finishes" as part of a mortuary sequence that culminates in the construction of a new men's house (chapter 4). The "spirits" (*malafua*) of these big men are thought to lend support to the project. These residential sites, in turn, are often origin/base sites of the lineage. Ideally, men's houses are built only at these recognized sites, such that each new men's house rises upon a site once occupied by a men's house. One man explained to me that the necessity for men's houses to circulate or move accounts for the resistance of Tangans to roof men's houses with corrugated iron. The impermanence of the structure, its need for constant renewal, is thus a definitive quality. In their cyclical movement, men's houses recapitulate the past of a lineage – its past personnel and their projects – and thereby assert an ideal of lineage continuity, that is, the identity of the lineage as a group that perdures through time.

The same assertion of continuity is expressed differently by the pig jaws (*an sengel*) which line the rafters of every men's house. Whenever a lineage hosts a feast, the jawbones of cooked pigs presented to recipients must be removed and left with the hosts. These jawbones accumulate over the

Plate 2   Timir working on the roof of the new men's house at Seber, 1985

years and visibly measure the capacity of both specific big men and the lineage in general to give feasts. The "temporary men's house" (*am fimfil*; see chapter 4) of Solsol lineage, for example, contained 283 *an sengel* in 1984. According to some informants, some or all of these jawbones might be burned at a feast to "finish" the big man (or men) under whose supervision the connected feasts were conducted. The present big man then renews the process of collecting *an sengel* by installing the new jawbones from the "finishing" feast. Men's houses thus epitomize all at once the productive capacity (past feasts) and the reproductive capacity (the continuation of activities initiated by successfully "finished" deceased members) of the lineage. The relationship among men's houses, mortuary feasting, and lineage succession will be examined in detail in Part II.

Although big men coordinate consensus about the feasts that a lineage hosts, they do not achieve this through the entrepreneurial skills typically associated with big manship (Sahlins 1963). Big men are, above all, *lineage* leaders. Each lineage is generally associated with a single leader, often the most senior male.[12] Some lineages have more than one recognized big man, each often the senior male of his particular line. Big men manage the resources of the lineage rather than a network of egocentric relationships. These resources include the labor of lineage members – especially that of unmarried males dependent to some degree upon the support of their lineage leaders in assembling a marriage payment – and the network of support and affinal relations linking various lineages rather than individual big men. Nor do big men exercise the measure of personal independence associated with big manship in some mainland New Ireland societies (Clay 1986; Albert 1987a). For example, big men neither "own" men's houses nor can they deed men's houses to their own children as among the Usen Barok (Wagner 1986a). Even transfers of temporary use rights in land are subject to the approval of a big man's lineage mates. Of course, big men vary among themselves in oratorical skills, knowledge of power uses (see chapter 7) and, as younger Tangans would say, "style." In the past, polygyny and military prowess also distinguished big men. Nevertheless, and this is my point, big men lack status apart from their lineage. The concept of big manship derives its meaning from the context and practice of lineage succession, not from local ideas about singular personalities.

Like other New Ireland big men, Tangan *kaltu dok* do validate their leadership through successful feast giving. These feasts – Tangan *kastam* – invariably form part of the mortuary sequence that "finishes" (*farop*) the dead. As a result, the identity of big men is inseparably bound up with the idea of succession or "replacement" (*kep tafu*) of the deceased. Lineage leaders are sometimes even formally "invested" during such feasts with presentations or displays of lineage heirlooms (Bell 1955:283). The practico-symbolic triad of big man, men's house, and mortuary feasts accordingly permits each of the three to signify both the other two and the continuous identity of the lineage. Big men, I argue then, can be understood as preeminent mother's brothers, the idiom and instrument through which a lineage figures its own succession.

In this regard, Tangan big men vary a theme recognizable in other New Ireland societies (Clay 1986:284–285; 1992). By realizing their ascendancy in the context of mortuary feasts, big men effectively "remove power from its human manifestations and ally it to a broader sense of potency beyond any individual effectiveness" (Clay 1986:283). That is, the power (*mui*) which big men make manifest is not merely that of individual achievement and competition, itself ephemeral, but rather a power apart from any one individual. As I suggest in chapter 7, this power connotes the legacy of the ancestors, the immunity to dissipation realized in the continual lineage succession enacted through mortuary feasting. Thus, as one informant explained, the lineage can be thought of as the "emblem" (*do*, the word glossed above as "totem") of a deceased big man:

Ngamnabo i dai pinis bifo. Tasol inap today mipela matambia long Solsol i stap iet. Oraet, long mining bilong dispela hap tok do bai i stret olsem, matambia na Solsol i do Ngamnabo.

Ngamnabo [a famous big man] died long ago. Yet today Solsol lineage [Ngamnabo's lineage] remains. This is the meaning of the word *do*: Solsol lineage is the emblem of Ngamnabo.

Like the "totem," the enduring emblem of immutable clan identity, the lineage itself is the "emblem" (*do*) of the deceased big men through whose agency the lineage is continually reproduced.

Marriage and the *fat kinaf* relationship

Lineage succession, and indeed the lineage itself, cannot be understood apart from the concentrated relationships of intermarriage that bind together pairs of lineages. Tangans speak of matrilineages as interrelated by reciprocal exchanges of paternal care (*fang*) bestowed upon the children of one lineage by men of other lineages. Maternal ties thus furnish an invariable background against which the variability of paternal ties can be plotted. Unlike enatic relations, which are fixed at birth, these

paternal-exchange relations require constant attention for their maintenance. This cultural emphasis on rendering paternal care, a pronounced
feature of New Ireland sociality (see, for example, Wagner 1986a; Clay
1986; Jessep 1987), establishes patrilateral consanguinity as a pervasive
principle of relationship within and between lineages. Much as Kelly
(1977) demonstrated for the Etoro, the kinds of relatedness created
through "filiative" ties – that is, relations of consanguinity engendered by
marriage – effectively condition the composition and "boundaries" of the
lineage.

Although Tangans speak of marriage alliances in terms of clan identities (see above), they practically define the relationship by acting upon a
stated preference for both men and women to marry back into their
father's matrilineage. Two lineages so linked regard each other as "bound
cross-cousins" (*fat kinaf*). *Fat* (literally, "stone") denotes "fastness" and
kinaf is the short form of the reciprocal relationship term for opposite-sex
cross-cousin (*ang kingkaf*). Marriage with one's actual *kingkaf* is not
allowed on the grounds that the two share "one blood" (*wan blut* in Tok
Pisin; see chapter 5) (but see Bell 1935c:183). An almost textbook joking
relationship obtains between *kingkaf*, typified by the mutual invasion of
each other's purses for betel nut and tobacco. However, marriage with the
actual FZDD/FZDS or MBDD/MBDS (the two are categorically identi-
cal [i.e., *kingkaf*]; and they are actually identical if the *fat kinaf* relationship operates over the long run) is not only allowed, but also stated as a
preference, though I learned of no instances of such marriages. The
preference states not so much a desire for the union of two particular
relationship categories as for the renewal of the relationship between two
matrilineages.

It follows then that it is the set of relationships that compose persons, as
the New Melanesian Ethnography would have it, that are at issue in
arranging marriages. For example, Partui made this reply to my inquiry
about whether a young man named Kiapsel, whose father was of a Tasik
lineage, had married in accordance with *fat kinaf* relations:

Kiapsel married as follows. His sister married into clan Filimat at Warangue. So,
Kiapsel reciprocated (*bekim* in Tok Pisin) and married the sister of his brother-in-
law. He reciprocated his sister; he didn't marry according to *fat kinaf*.

In other words, the marriage of the brother reciprocated the marriage of
the sister and thus extended the relationship between the two lineages, but
the marriage did *not* reciprocate the marriage of Kiapsel's own father.
Although this marriage involved a lineage not related as *fat kinaf*, the

principle of reciprocating marriages is precisely the same as that motivating the *fat kinaf* relationship. Hence the possibility of developing new *fat kinaf* relationships through appropriate marriages.

In the same way, while both demography and individual taste often preclude marriage back into ego's father's lineage, marriages of ego's lineage mates serve to revitalize the *fat kinaf* relationship with ego's father's lineage. A lineage then can be thought of as a pool of eligible partners whose marriages continue generalized and longstanding relations with various *kinaf* relatives.[13]

The Solsol lineage of clan Korofi sustained *kinaf* relations with several other lineages, mostly of clan Tasik but also with at least one lineage of clan Filimat (Taubie). Genealogies reveal that intermarriage with Tasik lineages extends back as far as the genealogies themselves. However, as Partui's reply suggests, such relations can be created by reciprocating unprecedented marriages. Conversely, disputes and/or demographics might cause relations to languish unrenewed by current marriages. The formation and maintenance of *kinaf* relations is one of the main concerns of Tangan big men, who try to guide the marriage choices of lineage bachelors. According to one senior man, a lineage endeavors as a unit not to multiply its marriages with a single matrilineage, but rather to sustain ties with a number of lineages.[14] Occurrences of more than two brothers or sisters marrying into the same lineage are not frequent, though cases of a brother/sister pair marrying in this way (as in the example of Kiapsel) are more common. The importance of such ties for mobilizing support in mortuary feasting will become obvious in later chapters. Strategically speaking, a lineage and its leader attempt constantly to vivify established *kinaf* relations and, when possible and apparently worthwhile, to initiate new relations.

The repeated intermarriage entailed by *kinaf* relations generates several effects, the most salient of which is the consolidation of lines within a lineage. This effect can be represented in genealogical terms. Genealogical aging of the lineage increases the consanguinal distance among enates and potentially introduces structural weakness into the framework of descent relations. Put simply, the component lines of a lineage become "less related." To the extent that members of each of these lines continue to marry into the same lineage, relatedness can be augmented by affinal ties. For example, in the situation illustrated in figure 1, the marriage of Partui (A) to his classificatory MBD directly connected the Seber line to the Mokatilistunglo line. The marriage was of political significance inasmuch as Partui, the current lineage leader, married the daughter of Malafua (B), his predecessor as lineage leader. Thus, the marriage effectively mediated the transfer of lineage leadership from one line to another.

Similarly, the marriage of Funil (1) and his brother to classificatory sisters of two different lines had the effect of directly linking enatic relatives whose closest link through women is the MMMM. This tie too was of political consequence, for lineage leadership was left uncertain after the death of Ngamnabo (E), a big man of island-wide reputation, a former paramount *luluai* and a renowned feast giver. The two more closely related lines of Seber and Mokatilistunglo together sponsored feasts and raised a men's house under the tutelage of Malafua. At the same time, the Solsol line worked under the direction of Pampok and Pampol (C and D). The lineage was close to splitting permanently and, in fact, the separate men's houses of the two lines performatively stated as much. At the urging of Funil, however, an important lineage leader in his own right and head catechist at the Catholic Mission, the three lines reunited upon the deaths of Malafua, Pampok, and Pampol. Funil directed his wife and eldest son to follow the lead of Partui, Malafua's son-in-law and nephew. Timir (F), the senior male of the Solsol line, is now formally recognized as the *sekan* (Tok Pisin for "second") to Partui, that is, Partui's assistant and heir apparent.

Fig. 1   Ancestral lines within Solsol/Seber lineage

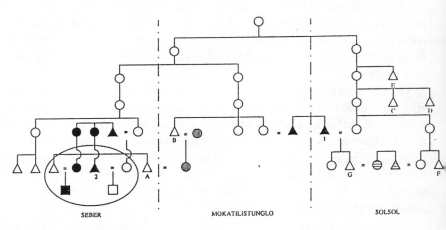

SEBER   MOKATILISTUNGLO   SOLSOL

○, △ =   Solsol/Seber Lineage
●, ▲ =   Matansal Lineage (Clan Tasik)
◍, ▲ =   Fintim Lineage (Clan Tasik)
⊖, △ =   An Ififkin Lineage (Clan Tasik)

The relatedness set up by the marriage of Funil and his brother differed importantly, however, from that predicated upon Partui's marriage. For the marriage of Funil and his brother not only reestablished links between divergent lines, but also established patrilateral consanguinity *within* their children's lineage. The children of Funil and his brother are related both as lineage brothers (matrilateral siblingship) and as children of one father (*fat tualik*, children of men of the same lineage; see footnote 5) and hence as patrilateral siblings. This observation allows us to see better how the *fat kinaf* relationship functions and how Tangans conceive the relationship to function in creating interlineage relations. For Tangans, the *fat kinaf* relationship connotes not affinity or intermarriage, but rather paternity. Two lineages confront each other, much like moieties for the Usen Barok (Wagner 1986a), as both the paternal progeny and paternal inceptors of each other. The idiom of paternity eclipses that of affinity, expressed in the use of the relationship term *kiang kaik* ("my son") as a substitute for the harsher affinal term (*ifaklik* – "my WB") whenever possible.[15] Thus, the *fat kinaf* relationship consolidates relationships within and between lineages according to the one principle of patrilateral consanguinity (for example, in figure 1, the marriage of Timir's sister to the brother of Somanil's [G] wife).

The importance of *kinaf* relations in consolidating and defining the lineage is matched by their equal importance in precipitating lineage splitting. Figure 1 again illustrates a relevant example. The death of Funil (1) entrained a dispute between Funil's lineage and that of his children over the disposition of Funil's inheritable property: shell wealth, a bicycle, and money presumably accrued from his salary as head catechist. Funil had previously constructed a European-style, cement-floored, fiberboard house on his children's land, thus ensuring its transfer to his wife and children upon his death. The dispute, eventually resolved, strained relations with Funil's lineage, led by Kamdamut (2), the husband of Partui's sister and classificatory brother of Partui's brother's wife. Both Partui's sister and his brother were, in 1984, living on land owned by Kamdamut's lineage.

During a mortuary sequence sponsored by the people with whom I lived, resentment grew on the part of several Solsol lineage members (Solsol lineage was hosting the event) that Partui's brother, sister, and her children, some of them grown but unmarried men, were not actively participating in the affair. One man, the husband of a Solsol woman of the Mokatilistunglo line, asserted to me that Partui's brother, Nebait, wished the Seber line to form a distinct lineage. He attributed this desire to bad feelings between both his wife and her sister, on the one hand, and Nebait, on the other. At the same time, Kamdamut's lineage announced plans to erect a men's house of its own, tacitly competing with the Solsol project and diverting the pig resources of Solsol lineage by calling in two outstanding debts. Although the issue never received public airing, and in the end Partui and his siblings buried their grievances, the general feeling at the time was that Partui's WH, father to his sister's children, encouraged the dissension.

The case, which I present from the interested perspective of some Solsol lineage members, shows how *kinaf* relations can condition the decomposition as well as consolidation of interlineage relations. Genealogical aging specified the point of lineage splitting while the exigencies of the *kinaf* relation provided the catalyst. The affinal tie between Nebait and Kamdamut, and the patrilateral ties between their children, circumscribed a nucleus of coresident supporters (see figure 1) who, for different reasons, considered the redefinition of lineage boundaries in their interest. For such a split would mean that the reproductive core of the new lineage – its childbearing women – would be the children of Kamdamut, whose influence over his sons was already a matter of concern to their MB, Partui.[16] Thus, whereas Funil was said to have supported the reconsolidation of the matrilineage, the perception in 1985 was that Kamdamut's hold over his children and sister's children (Nebait's sons and daughters) promoted lineage dissension. The situation demonstrates the indirect and contingent, but no less real way in which the interplay of maternal and paternal relationships that join *kinaf* variably affects the definition and solidarity of the matrilineage.

Residence, settlement, land tenure
The case of Solsol lineage's averted split points to the role of residence in social life. Lineages consist of a number of families (*fumbarat*) that typically consist of a man, his wife, and their unmarried children. Elderly parents, widowed or not, unmarried siblings, and married children might also live together with the family in a single named hamlet (*male*). Married women of a lineage generally reside on their husband's land in accordance with standard expectations. Instances of patrivirilocality and uxorilocality, however, are not uncommon (see below). Upon the death of her husband, a woman generally takes up residence with her children on land of their *matambia*. As with most things Tangan, this generalization expresses a tendency and not a rule (cf. Jessep 1987).

Most Tangans do not live in villages of the sort characteristic of mainland New Ireland, but instead occupy clearly demarcated hamlets scattered across the islands. Smaller hamlets contain one or two dwellings for sleeping and cooking (*felungkur*); large hamlets contain several such dwellings (one per couple) and perhaps a men's house in which young bachelors sometimes sleep.[17] This seems to approximate the aboriginal settlement pattern (see Bell 1953). During the colonial period, large multi-dwelling villages ("camps") were mandated by patrol officers, according to older informants. And indeed patrol reports characteristically complain of the preference of Boang people to live dispersed near gardens rather than in villages more convenient for census taking and tax collecting. No evidence remains of such villages except along the beach near the Boang mission station. But it would be a mistake to attribute the contemporary pattern of dispersed settlement to the persistence of tradition. It is more likely an effect of the household atomization discussed in the previous chapter, that is, an effect of the efforts of men to settle close to stands of coconut palms that they and they alone control.

Ideally, all the families headed by lineage men (*ian tun fumbarat* or *matamfumbarat*) reside in nearby hamlets on lineage land. Big men almost invariably reside on their lineage land in order to manage the men's house and its connected feasts. Inmarried women and their children, along with resident lineage women such as "returned" widows and unmarried girls, furnish necessary labor for such undertakings.[18] Outmarried women often return home to participate, but they provide a less reliable source of labor. This accounts for Partui's claim that a lineage leader prefers his sisters and nieces to marry locally. Given the preference for marriage into clans that live contiguously, most marriages are in fact local. More generally, a big man desires the residence of his brothers and their children on lineage land not only for their labor, but also for the facility of planning lineage affairs and monitoring the relations with other lineages that men anchor. Thus on one occasion Partui made this point by contrasting the lineage with a branch, noting that if everyone "sits in one place" the lineage will not break.

Some older men told me about a former settlement pattern, perhaps idealized, in which residential hamlets clustered about a men's house site. One man thus referred to *felungkur* as "watch houses" of the men's house (*fel na tutu en bia*), the place where food is cooked for presentation to visitors and guests. In turn, lineage-owned bush (*mok*) surrounded the hamlets and furnished land for gardens to produce food for men's house feasting.[19] Men frequently told me that they resided on sites that were formerly used for gardening. Hamlet sites could be found in the center of

Boang in areas that were alleged to be once unclaimed tracts of virgin bush exploited by local residents for bamboo. This situation derives from a combination of factors, including continued increases in population size, the desire of men to live near their stands of coconuts, and the pressure generated by permanent coconut groves that reduce the amount of land available for shifting horticulture.

Lineages are the recognized titleholders in land, though it is not infrequent that discrete territories of lineages of the same clan are contiguous. Male and female lineage members enjoy birth rights to reside and garden on lineage land, the boundaries of which are vaguely marked by natural features such as cliffs and large trees. In general, the boundaries remain vague until disputes prompt the parties concerned to define the borders. Likewise, land tenure is less a set of context-invariable rules and more an aspect of ongoing social process. Matrilineal inheritance gives overall direction to this process, but ties of affinity and paternity also influence the disposition of land and use rights to land (see below; cf. Jessep 1987).

A lineage's land contains a number of *ples masalai* (Tok Pisin – "spirit places") which can be of three kinds. *Sun longan* are small stretches of bush between or near hamlets on which huge, ancient trees grow. *Sun tara* are larger stretches of relatively uncleared bush, full of stones and exposed tree roots, thought to be "truly *tara*" (in the Taonsip area, two such places are Sukeobum and Waranmale). *Tara* designates one of two major classes of *masalai*, form-changing manifestations of power (*mui*) associated with a variety of familiars. One man, Pamfir of clan Filimat, explained to me that *tara* was of the bush while *madas*, the other class of *masalai*, was of the beach or sea. Thus, while *tara* familiars tend to be stones, caves, large trees, and other oddities of the landscape, *madas* familiars are primarily large banded sea eels (*maomao*) and, perhaps, sharks that occupy certain stretches of water, e.g., beneath certain cliffs.[20]

Particular features of the landscape that are *tara* – mounds of earth, queerly shaped roots, protruding rocks – are called *matamfunmat* ("eye of the clan"), the third kind of spirit place. Every lineage ideally has its own *matamfunmat*, each of which is named. Netang of clan Filimat claimed that *tara* "watch over" (*fangte*) the hamlets and personnel of the lineage.[21] Similarly, Pamfir claimed that a man might plant ginger along with the seeds of *ngasngas* (a creeper) as a way of manipulating or "working" *madas*, of formulating *madas* into particular objects or actions. If someone comes to find a piece of food with which to poison the planter, the *madas* (ginger) will retrieve the food. Unlike some *masalai* they do not cause sickness, but a lineage's *tara* smell sickness and might attach themselves to the skin of sick men and women. However, they can be removed by blowing appropriately bespelled lime powder (*kabeng*) on the victim. In general, *tara* and *madas* stand in a tutelary relationship to their associated lineage and inform a lineage's identity along with its men's house.

Despite their function as markers of *matambia* identity, *matamfunmat* do not usually validate claims to land as they do among other New Ireland groups (Jessep 1980b). Disputes over land, which had become endemic by 1984, are resolved through a procedure called *tet* (cf. *pantetet*, a story associated with observable "marks" or "traces," as opposed to *pansoksok*, a story with no such marks or traces). *Tet* is the process of recounting past instances of residence on or use of the disputed land, a genealogical reckoning aimed at discovering the identity of the first man or woman (*an tumlam* – "ancestor") who occupied the land. Claims to land are thus validated through demonstrations of previous use, not through mythological charter. The most potent demonstrations of land use establish the presence of a former men's house or matrilineage ossuary (*an inof*). These conventions render contemporary burials potential flashpoints for disputes over land (see chapter 4).

At some point during a *tet*, it is expected that the source of the dispute will be revealed as a transfer of land out of the control of the owning lineage. The mechanism for such transfers itself reveals the effects of the *fat kinaf* relationship on land tenure. Upon the death of a man, his widow and children usually relocate to their lineage land at the conclusion of the initial burial feasting (see chapter 4). Frequently, however, men arrange for one or more of their children to remain on the land after their death. Such an arrangement is generally recognized as a man's right, just as it is recognized as a son's right to harvest coconut palms planted with and by his father after the latter's death. The man's children, in turn, secure the approval of their patrilateral relatives by contributing vegetable food and cooked pigs to the projects of their father's lineage. This may take the form of a prestation called *marmaris na male* that might comprise a cooked pig and a small amount of cash. Upon the death of the child(ren), however, the father's lineage resumes its control of the land and coconuts; the original man's grandchildren must move to their own maternal ground. When this resumption fails to occur, and when the owning lineage contends that no further arrangements were made, disputes develop.

One recognized way of obviating this problem is for a man to marry a paternal *kingkaf* (FZD, FZDD), in which case his children are the rightful heirs to the land and its above-ground improvements. Such a marriage gives an intergenerational dimension to the transfer of paternal nurture (*fang*) inasmuch as alternate generations of children of two different matrilineages grow up (or are grown up) on the same land (see chapter 7). In these cases marriages *must* be with a FZD/FZDD of the father's *lineage* and not merely of the father's clan. I learned of one case (table 8, note c) in which a man who resided on the land of his MF (his M was still living) arranged to marry into his MF's lineage. Because this lineage was almost defunct on Boang (the man's MF was the lineage's last big man), however, the man had to find a wife from a line of the lineage localized on Anir. This marriage was presumed to cement his claims to the land of his MF.

Another way of sidestepping the expectations of matrilineal inheritance is for either the father or the child(ren) to purchase outright the land in question from the father's lineage. Such purchases seem to have occurred mostly in the 1960s and 1970s and by the time of my fieldwork almost every lineage felt a need for land and consequently refused to sell land.[22] (It remains to be seen, moreover, whether past purchases will not themselves be renegotiated upon the deaths of the parties involved.) In one instance, however, a man preparing such a payment to his father's lineage (of clan Fale on Boang) contemplated a price of two pigs, five shell discs (*tintol*), two lengths of strung shells (*kemetas*), and 1,000 kina (PNGK1.00 = US$1.10 in 1984) for a chunk of residential and gardening land that also included coconuts that his father had planted. This man explained to me that he intended the land for his own lineage nephews (of clan Ku) and not for his children (he himself had married into his father's clan Fale). He would instruct his lineage to allow one child to remain after his death, but to exercise control of the land upon the death of this child. In another instance, a man purchased a tract of land from his lineage on which he had built with his only child and her husband a large, permanent European-style house. He planned to transfer the land to his daughter and her children upon his death.

A variety of land transfers and transfers in use rights occur in the context of mortuary feasting. For example, I observed on one occasion the outright purchase of a residential site by a lineage which had constructed a men's house there. According to members of this lineage (Ang Kirkir lineage of clan Firfir on Boang), their ancestors once had possessed ample land in the eastern end of Boang. A former big man (Pasam), however, allegedly sold this land when it appeared that the lineage was headed for extinction.[23] Consequently, all members of Firfir on Boang in 1984–85 resided and gardened on the land of various *kinaf*-related lineages. The purchase of the site (called Ang Kirkir, "pebbly" or "stony" place) from their classificatory MBS (two men of the land-owning lineage) took place during a feast to mark the refurbishing of the roof of the Firfir men's house.

At another feast, made to mark the construction of a men's house, the two cooked pigs that were distributed each concerned interests in land. One pig was presented by the host lineage to a man, Bingfiu, of a *kinaf* lineage, in order to terminate the latter's claim to harvest coconuts on the host lineage's land. Bingfiu's father was the son of a man of the host lineage and Bingfiu had followed his father in harvesting the coconuts of his FF on his FF's land. The prestation of the pig, along with one shell disc (*tintol*) and some coins, reclaimed the coconuts for the host lineage (cf. Weiner 1976 on Trobriand *sagali* prestations).

The second pig, along with two kina, was presented by a man of the host lineage, Neuk, to a man, Bakok, of another lineage of the same clan in order to secure ownership rights to a piece of residential land to which both men had claims. Neuk informed me that he had previously given Bakok a large shell disc (*an simpendalu*) for the same purpose.

These examples demonstrate how Tangan land tenure involves besides matrilineal inheritance a variety of negotiable practices for defining and redefining specific rights to residence, gardening, and coconut harvesting, usually among lineages related as *kinaf*. On this view, FZD marriage as a way of mediating patrilineal inheritance – of which Bell noted several cases in 1933 – must be seen not as an exception to the rule of matrilineal inheritance, but as a recognized feature of interlineage relations (Bell 1953:44–45). Likewise, the transfer of land rights effected by prestations of pigs and shell valuables must be regarded as consistent with the mutual support characteristic of *kinaf* relations. This is not to say that such practices are not in their current form historical products. Bell, for example, attributed to pacification the effect of breaking up previously contiguous tracts of land claimed by lineages of a single clan. He noted both that the cessation of hostilities permitted allies and affines to establish settlements on the land of other lineages, and many instances of "fruit bearing trees being planted by members of one clan in the soil of another, the former being generally though not necessarily related by marriage" (1953:45). Indeed, Bell predicted that "with the passage of time, this tendency to settle on land belonging by tradition to another clan will spread and so further complicate the land ownership situation" (1953:31).

Clearly, pacification affected the ways in which Tangans used and defined rights to land. The postwar rush to plant coconuts combined with subsequent attempts at land demarcation equally affected the practice of land tenure, perhaps enabling the incorporation of transfers such as Neuk's within the familiar context of feasting and pig/shell prestations. The point is, however, that such circumstances impinged upon a set of practices in which transfer of rights in land outside the matriline already had a recognized place (cf. Jessep 1987). For the practice of allowing children of the lineage to remain on lineage land, or to harvest fruit-bearing trees, simply continues the relationship of nurturance (*fang*) between father and child(ren). Rather than viewing the presence of affines and allies on lineage land as the incursion of "foreign" settlements into lineage holdings, I suggest that such fluidity was always an aspect of Tangan social organization. Nevertheless, I concur with Bell's assessment that such fluidity is also the source of complication of Tangan land tenure. The articulation of this system with the world economy through cash cropping, and the cash sale of land, have left the islands, particularly crowded Boang, awash in land disputes. At the core of these disputes frequently lies the opposition between *bisnis* and *kastam,* to which I now return, which summarizes in abbreviated form some of the developing tensions of Tangan sociality.

Household inequality: *bisnis* versus *kastam*
Besides the strategies of FZD marriage and land purchases, men often planted coconuts on their children's land during and after the 1960s in order to avoid subsequent problems over inheritance. Similarly, several men with whom I spoke explained their uxorilocal residence as a way of maintaining a hamlet site which their children could inherit directly. Both of these practices suggest an important way in which the household or "family" (*fumbarat*) is potentially disjunct from and opposed to the matrilineage (*matambia*). The household and not the lineage is the unit responsible for producing and marketing copra. Usually a man, his wife, and their children collect the nuts and together split them open and extract the meat. (Unmarried siblings as well as teenaged matrilineal relatives of either spouse sometimes assist and often receive cash remuneration.)[24] This same household unit of production also consumes the cash income derived from copra sales. As a result, inequalities in the distribution of coconuts give rise to inequalities among households that are uneasily masked by the image of lineage solidarity projected in mortuary feasting (*kastam*).

Whereas any lineage member is entitled to reside and garden on lineage land, rights to harvest coconut palms derive primarily from particular egocentric relations. That is, individual men of a lineage own specific palms, planted by themselves, by their fathers or by their actual MBs.[25] Brothers might alternate harvesting a particular grove or each sibling might harvest only specific stands of palms. A man might allow his ZS, or in some cases his FZS (if a man is "bossing" trees ultimately destined for his father's lineage), to harvest a crop upon request, but rights to the trees remain vested in individuals and not in lineages. This generalization applies not only to coconut palms but also to other cultivated trees including areca palms and banana trees.[26] Bell's observation still retained its relevance in 1984: "With regard to cultivated trees, the person who plants a tree thereby obtains exclusive rights to the products of that tree. In addition, he is recognized as having the right to cut it down or dispose of it as he wills" (1953:45).

This situation, combined with an overall shortage of garden land that has prompted a virtual ban on new coconut plantings, discriminates both generally and particularly. In general, coconut tenure discriminates against younger families which, lacking opportunities for new plantings, must depend upon the holdings of their elders. Specifically, the situation discriminates against lineages with relatively large memberships and relatively small land holdings. More specifically, the pattern of coconut palm inheritance disfavors men whose fathers and/or mothers' brothers, for whatever reasons, never planted extensive holdings and consequently left nothing for their children and nephews to exploit. It is this last sort of discrimination that introduces inequality among households *within* the lineage. For example, table 9 illustrates differences in copra income over a six-month period among six households of roughly similar size headed by classificatory brothers of a single lineage.

The head of Household 2, a man in his forties, reported that he had no coconuts of his own planted by his father or by his mother's brother; nuts that he himself had planted a few years earlier were not yet mature and in any case were not doing too well. His wife belongs to a lineage itself pressed for land and he harvested no coconuts by virtue of her and her children's rights. Instead, the man depended upon sporadic wage income from work done for various local entrepreneurs as his primary source of cash income.

By contrast, the head of Household 3 harvested palms planted on his own land by his father; palms planted on his wife's land by his WMB; palms planted on his father's land by his father; and even palms planted

Table 9. *Intralineage differences in household income, Jan.–June 1985*

Household no.	Est. copra income (PNG kina)	Remittance income (PNG kina)
1	166.95	300.00
2	–	–
3	207.60	–
4	266.45	–
5	200.00	–
6	141.60	

by his MBMB (*koktamat*) on his MBMBW's land. The extreme difference between the incomes of the two households indicates both how the production of cash income engages egocentric and not lineage relations and how the lineage itself does not function as a redistributor of cash income. Morauta has documented this same situation in Kukipi village (Gulf Province) where an overall household equality in subsistence production "is modified towards greater inequality by all other forms of income" (1984:124). Moreover, inter-household transfers – the often assumed "traditional" support network of kinship reciprocity – do not redistribute income to the neediest households (precisely because the neediest households are incapable of maintaining their position in a system of *reciprocal* transfers). Similarly, in Tanga, copra income is consumed by the producing household with little or no transfer outside the household apart from occasional payments to non-household members who assist in copra production.[27] In Kukipi, however, the main source of cash income is remittances from migrant laborers. This source of income was secondary to cash cropping in Tanga in 1984–85, but nonetheless a significant factor in exacerbating household inequality. For example, during the first half of 1985, Household 1 reported an income of K300 from a remittance sent by the household head's unmarried younger brother, a teacher working in another province. This single remittance amounted to nearly double the household's copra income for the first half of the year.

Lineage members often express generalized expectations of partaking of remittances, while fathers regard remittances as filial recognition of paternal care and resent the demands of their children's lineage. Because of their less defined nature as a source of income, then, remittances become the focus of disputes among lineage members and *kinaf* that expose the latent tensions of household inequality created by copra sales.

Ordinarily, these tensions remain unremarked upon though naggingly present in the differential consumption of rice and tinned fish, tea and sugar, kerosene for lamps and biscuits for children. Such inequality heightens further the culturally defined ambiguities of consumption and non-consumption (see chapters 6 and 7).

The sorts of tensions described here are not uncommon in matrilineal systems; but that is not my point. My point is to suggest how these tensions have become inflected in the context of commoditization outlined in the last chapter. In this context, the household becomes conceptually married to *bisnis*: household enterprise in particular and cash transactions in general. Reciprocally, because *bisnis* is a household or family concern, both *bisnis* and family (*famili* in Tok Pisin; *fumbarat*) become conceptually assimilated to patrilineality and opposed to the matrilineage. The matrilineage, in turn, emerges as the practical unit not of *bisnis* but of *kastam*. Such are the coordinates of a discussion which Tangan men sometimes carried on among themselves during local meetings. On one occasion, for instance, Partui replied to some men who argued for a shift to patrilineality (Tok Pisin – *bihainim papa*) as a way of resolving problems over land and coconut inheritance by asking them who would look after the men's house.[28] His rhetorical rebuttal countered the appeal to *bisnis* with an appeal to *kastam*, epitomized by the condensed symbol of the men's house, index of both matrilineage and "finished" matrilineage members. In speaking so, Partui also highlighted the disjunction between big men (*kaltu dok*) and businessmen brought about in the previous generation. If as a big man Partui could not meld *bisnis* and *kastam* as did his predecessors, then at least he attempted to maintain the integrity of *kastam* and lineage and their priority over *bisnis* and family/household.

By the same logic, the household or family becomes through its association with *bisnis* conceptually synonymous with restricted consumption. The household is not only the unit of material production on a daily basis but also the definitive locus of salient consumption. This salience (if not conspicuousness; see chapter 7) derives in large measure from the expenditure of almost all cash income on coveted consumables. *Kastam*, on the other hand, connotes for Tangans non-monetary consumption, the "free" distribution, as one man put it, of garden produce and pork at feasts made to "finish" the dead of a lineage.[29] Consumption through feasting sustains or extends relations; household consumption contracts or involutes relations.

From another perspective, though, *kastam* opposes *bisnis* as non-consumption to consumption (*kastam*:*bisnis*::non-consumption:consumption). For through *kastam*, the successful hosting of feasts, a lineage gives food *to others* for *their* consumption. In the event, the lineage "finishes" its own deceased and accumulates shell valuables necessary for participation in the mortuary feasts of related lineages and in making marriage payments.[30] Put differently, *kastam* denotes that aspect of social reproduction in which the lineage and not the household is most directly implicated and featured.

What ultimately distinguishes *bisnis* from *kastam*, then, is not that one is monetized and the other is not, but rather the duration and form of the social relations that each activity implies. The household or family is a particular and temporary realization of the enduring bonds (*fat kinaf*) between enduring lineages. Although obviously critical to the sustenance of these bonds, and indeed to the physical sustenance of individual Tangans, the family amounts to an assemblage of people without fixed form from one generation to the next. Families instantiate specific permanent *kinaf* alliances but themselves change their composition over time, despite tendencies toward consistent FZD/S marriage. What persists beyond and beside the family in an ideally unchanging form is the lineage, the building block of the cross-cousin (*fat kinaf*) relationship.[31]

Such is the ideology of *kastam* (for in practice *kastam* can function to create discontinuities, as when enates define themselves as two discrete lineages through the construction of separate men's houses). Through *kastam*, not *bisnis*, feast givers both pragmatically achieve lineage succession and reproduce the lineage as a unit. Through *kastam*, that is, feast givers make the present and future reality of the lineage continuous with its past incarnations. Such is the process of "finishing" and "replacing" the dead, to which I now turn in earnest.

II

MORTUARY RITES AS "FINISHING" AND "REPLACING" THE DEAD

4

Finishing the dead: an outline of Tangan mortuary feasts and exchanges

Melanesian mortuary rites – which usually entail lengthy series of exchanges and feasts that regulate the production and distribution of pigs, vegetable food, and material wealth – singularly exemplify Mauss's (1967) famous "total social phenomenon." Ethnographers of New Ireland, in particular, have long been told as much. Hortense Powdermaker, for example, reports a conversation with some old Lesu men about the intricate sculptures (*malanggan*) that her servants were packing for shipment:

> I had explained that they [the sculptures] would be carefully housed [in a museum], and that "my people," who had never seen these *malanggans*, would then know about them. After my explanation the old men very seriously urged me to tell these people who would look at the *malanggans* that they were not just carved, painted pieces of wood, but that I must make the people understand all the work and wealth that had gone into the making of them – the large taro crops, the many pigs, all the *tsera* [shell currency], the cooking for the feast, and other essentials of the rites. These, said the old men of Lesu, are the important things to remember about *malanggans*.
>
> *(Powdermaker 1933:318–19)*

Powdermaker's informants effectively, perhaps presciently, warned her against fetishizing the carvings. They insisted that the significance of *malanggans* is bound up with their production and display in the context of commemorative feasting for deceased matrilineage members. Their admonition rightly called attention to the functional importance of Melanesian mortuary rites for coordinating a multiplicity of social activities.

Following Powdermaker, ethnographers of New Ireland have continued to describe mortuary rites as the primary locus of political,

95

aesthetic, and economic activity (e.g., Billings and Peterson 1967; Küchler 1987, 1988; Lewis 1969) and to represent mortuary rites as practices that engage pervasive cultural concerns and impart to social life its distinctive shape and rhythm (e.g., Wagner 1986a; Clay 1986; Albert 1987a). I too follow customary procedure, then, in focusing here on the sequence of Tangan mortuary feasts and exchanges. My purpose is to outline the processual structure of mortuary feasting and to sketch some typical features of feasts, such as the public display and distribution of food and pigs. But I cannot overemphasize that while no performance of mortuary feasts is totally unique and unprecedented, every performance remains in important respects an improvisation upon an open set of generalized procedures. Feasting is sequential, but the sequence does not occur automatically; the accomplishment and outcome of every performance is problematic. Various considerations and circumstances affect the timing and scale of feasts: the capacity of the hosts to raise fat pigs and grow heaps of yams; unexpected deaths of relatives that channel previously allocated resources in unforeseen directions; outstanding exchange obligations that other feast makers – not always friendly – recall at inopportune moments. Mortuary feasting, in other words, is a contingent and flexible practice, the emergent product of temporally contextualized social action.

The outline of feasts and exchanges presented here obscures their inherent contingency, that is, their status as "joint action."[1] Elsewhere (Foster 1988) I have attempted to highlight this contingency through a detailed accounting of one particular mortuary sequence performed by Solsol lineage members with whom I lived during my fieldwork. My specific aim there was to take seriously Bourdieu's (1977) suggestion that exchange be understood as strategic practice rather than as rule-governed conduct. My more general aim was to communicate a sense of the Maussian "totalness" of Tangan mortuary rites. Accordingly, my ethnographic description took the form of a long story – a dense narrative of particular names, dates, and places, interrupted by digressions on gardening, pig husbandry, and other sundry matters. Along the way, I tried to illustrate with concrete examples a range of variations upon the generalized procedures of Tangan mortuary rites.

Although I often draw in this chapter upon my previous account of the Solsol lineage mortuary sequence, my aim, and hence the form of my narrative description, are different. My guiding concern is to define an ethnographic frame of reference within which to analyze sequential mortuary feasting as an instrument of social reproduction or, in Tangan terms, of "replacing" and "finishing" the dead. I accordingly provide a synoptic account of the various feasts and exchanges that follow upon death and that comprise the entire sequence of mortuary rites. I thus render temporally contextualized action in the highly schematic forms of tabular summaries and recipe-like instructions that characterize ethnographic accounts of complex Melanesian mortuary rites (see, for example, Damon and Wagner 1989). Put differently, my account is of precisely the sort that a New Melanesian Historian would criticize as "out of time." I openly sin against the new orthodoxy of privileging practice over structure – processual or otherwise. But my sin, at least, is one of commission. My explicitly limited intention is to summarize the whole sequence of feasts and exchanges as a prelude to interpreting the glosses that Tangans themselves put on their mortuary practices. In this chapter I gloss their gloss of "finishing." In the next chapter, I do likewise, but more concertedly, for the gloss of "replacement."

The mortuary sequence, phase one: death, burial, and mourning
The sequence of mortuary feasts and exchanges can be divided into two phases, recognized by Tangans as distinct and separable.[2] I will review in turn the feasts and exchanges associated with each phase. Phase one involves the disposal of the corpse and the routines of mourning; it commences when the death of an adult becomes imminent, or immediately upon sudden or accidental deaths (table 10). Phase two, which may last up to ten years, involves the construction of a new men's house and the large-scale feasts and exchanges that collectively "finish" one or more of the host lineage's deceased members.

"Finishing" (*farop*) minimally connotes two different processes: dispelling the sadness and worry evoked by particular deaths, and fulfilling the obligation of a lineage to commemorate periodically all of its recently deceased members.[3] In this latter sense, "finishing" implies an act of remembrance undertaken in order to enable forgetting, a forgetting of the debts that survive the deceased (Battaglia 1992; see below). Understood in terms of the New Melanesian Ethnography's model of personhood and agency, "finishing" also implies a final activation or evincement of the internal relations that composed the deceased person. These relations are objectified not only in the taboos assumed by mourners, but also in the exchanges and displays of wealth occasioned by sequential mortuary feasting, which function "as temporary memorials, culturally inscribing social relationships as an ephemeral coherence 'located' in the particular person being honored in his or her physical absence" (Battaglia 1992:4).

Table 10. *Synopsis of feasts of death and burial*

Name of feast	Description
En turan kaltu i filis	Feast held when a sick individual is near to death
Kis fakut	Feast held while the body of the deceased is waked in the men's house (*en tike* – "eat everything"); pig(s) presented to members of the deceased's lineage only
Morapup/Mor na minet	Feast in connection with burial; mourning taboos assumed by affines/*kinaf* of the deceased
Pam bi na pokta'ng kinit	Evening vegetable meal eaten in the men's house where the deceased was waked by supporters (*kinaf*) of the deceased's lineage; also designates weekly community-wide distributions that last until the feast of *moratineng*
En mapu'ng kinit	Feast held three days after burial; *en tike* feast for men and boys only; lineage of deceased consumes "stink of the corpse"
Tau uk su in makos	Feast to call the widow/er (*makos*) from confinement; abrogation of some or all mourning taboos
Moratineng	Feast to compensate women who cried for the deceased; abrogation of remaining mourning taboos; promises made to initiate *pok bif*

Publicly exhibited as a set of observable social relationships, the deceased is "finished" as the material traces of these relationships disappear from public view.

The people arranging and participating in the mortuary feasts fall mainly into two unnamed categories: the lineage of the deceased and everybody else. Everybody else refers mainly to the affinal and paternal relations (*kinaf*) of the deceased. Given the cross-cousin pattern (*fat kinaf*) of marriage, affines tend to be paternal relatives.[4] For a man, of course, his children necessarily fall into the affinal category. The lineage of the deceased may cooperate with other lineages of the same clan, representatives of which sometimes fulfil roles assigned to the deceased's lineage at various points in the proceedings. Similarly, the cooperation of *kinaf* is ideally expected and their particular wishes about funeral arrangements are usually respected (say, if a recognized big man wishes to bury his wife on *his* matrilineage's land). There is rarely any question, however, that the lineage of the deceased is in charge of the disposal of its dead and ultimately responsible for hosting subsequent feasts. The deceased's men's house is almost always the site of all mortuary events.

Most deaths on Tanga follow a period of illness ranging from twenty-four hours to several months. On two observed occasions, elderly men who felt their death at hand asked to be removed from either their own house or the parish hospital and taken to the men's house of their lineage. Generally, a body will be brought to the deceased's men's house to be waked if the man or woman did not in fact die there. This delivery is simply the most dramatic instance of the return of all the deceased's personal possessions to the deceased's own lineage members. Over the course of the mortuary sequence, various artefacts of the deceased, dispersed among the persons comprising the deceased's "relational personhood" are both exhibited and concentrated at the deceased's men's house. These artefacts include not only inert reminders of the deceased – a walking stick or photograph – but also persons related (and indebted) to the deceased by the deceased's "hard work" (*fang*), such as a man's children, friends, and allies. That is, the relational personhood of the deceased is publicly reconstituted and displayed as the necessary pre-requisite for its final deconstitution – its "finishing" as an active node in a matrix of living social relations (cf. Battaglia 1990).

The disposition of a body may in some cases be a matter for negotiation between the two main categories of people immediately concerned. In one case, Pangang, the father of a young man, Tabunima, who died suddenly while working on the New Ireland mainland, requested that his son's body be brought first to the men's house of his (Pangang's) lineage. From there, Pangang and his lineage's supporters returned the body to the deceased's own men's house. Should the circumstances of death strain relations between the lineages concerned, funeral arrangements may become the vehicle for expressing ill feelings. Likewise, should a death involve a lineage whose internal relations are strained, arguments over the site of the waking may develop among the various lines (*fumbarat*) within the lineage.

The location of the grave is also potentially a matter of contention, especially given the extent of land disputes, which render burials as particularly strong statements about ownership of land. In the past, lineages maintained ossuaries (*an inof*) wherein were deposited the bones of lineage members after their display at mortuary feasts (see below). Claims that a lineage ossuary exists on a particular piece of land figure in contemporary land disputes. Most lineages now maintain small areas for the burial of their members (Tangans use the Kuanua/Tok Pisin term *matmat*, meaning "cemetery"). Some lineages, however, especially in the Taonsip area of Boang, bury their dead in large cemeteries that in principle belong to no single lineage. These cemeteries, maintained by community labor, seem to have been initiated within the last fifty years by the pre-council *luluai*.[5] In at least two instances, the bodies of elderly big men, past *luluai* and last of the important post-war leaders, were buried immediately adjacent to their men's houses. An individual may express his or her wishes (*singsingle*, which Tangans gloss in English as "promise") about burial before death. In one case of which I am aware, a deceased man's reported wishes to be buried in the cemetery of his children were allegedly disregarded by his lineage. Both in ideal and in practice, the lineage of the deceased exercises ultimate authority over the funeral and burial of its dead.

En turan kaltu i filis ("eating together with the sick man")

When an individual's death is imminent, his or her lineage may organize a small feast (sometimes at the request of the dying person) referred to as *en turan* ("to eat together"). The occasion marks the start of a person's public transition from life to death. Lineage leaders sometimes use the occasion to announce their intentions to forego certain funeral feasts and "rubbish" the deceased (see below). Similar feasts are held when a person recovers from severe illness, thus celebrating a reversal of the transition from life to death.

News of a death spreads quickly and soon men and women arrive in small groups at the hamlet where the body of the deceased lies. Close relatives and friends of the deceased, predominantly women, surround the bier in the center of the men's house. Throughout the day, more women enter the men's house and approach the body. Some of the newcomers squeeze onto the bier; others crouch nearby and, covering their faces with their hands or forearms, begin to wail. The women already seated inside thereupon begin a new round of keening. After one group of arrivals has finished crying, they take seats in the men's house and smoke tobacco and chew betel nut while awaiting the next contingent. Men may also enter the men's house, but most tend to mill about outside, quietly talking and chewing betel nut. The male members of the deceased's lineage, consulting with the deceased's affines, busy themselves with immediate arrangements: finding an old canoe to be cut into a coffin; collecting money to purchase rice and tinned fish for feeding the assembled guests; finding one of Boang's few pickup trucks to transport the food; digging the grave. The women of the deceased's lineage who are not occupied inside the men's house and the wives of lineage men collect firewood, prepare fires for boiling the rice, and borrow plates with which to serve the visitors.

At least one decision will have been reached and put into effect before any guests arrive, namely, whether or not the deceased's lineage will accept contributions of pigs or rice from other lineages, including the affinal lineage of the deceased. If the host lineage decides to refuse contributions, which would have to be reciprocated at some future time, then arriving guests will silently observe markers in the form of five-feet-high forked poles planted in the ground at the mouths of paths leading into the hamlet (specific examples are called *an ulau*; the genus of markers is called *ang gumgum*). Tied to the forks, an empty plastic one kilogram rice bag and the jawbone of a pig symbolize the unwelcome prestations. This decision might generate vigorous protest and even aggressive disregard, especially from the *kinaf* of the deceased.

The *ang gumgum* increase speculation, rife the moment a death is reported, as to the funeral plans of the deceased's lineage. One strategy not infrequently followed is to "rubbish" the deceased. Rubbishing means burial without any of the associated feasts or, more specifically, without any consumption of pork. Those responsible for funeral arrangements may decide to rubbish the deceased for several reasons, including a shortage of pigs and/or vegetable food or because the deceased expressed a wish that there be no burial feasting.[6] Their decision may be only temporary; that is, they will begin the cycle of feasts as soon as an adequate supply of food becomes available.

Should a lineage intend to carry out the various burial feasts with the assistance of others, groups of men might arrive with pigs for presentation to the deceased's lineage. The pigs, tied to carrying poles, are brought into the hamlet along with baskets of green coconuts, betel nut, and raw tubers. The pig is put down and the donor steps forward. Placing his left foot on the pig he addresses a representative of the deceased's lineage: "*Bo aiam, tuaklik*" ("Your pig, my brother"), indicating his relation to the representative of the receiving lineage. The pig and food are carried away and become the concern of the deceased's lineage, which might decide to use the animal for immediate burial feasts or to save it for subsequent affairs related to this death. Various clan mates, *kinaf*, and other relatives may contribute pigs.

Kis fakut ("sit and be silent")

Friends and relatives gather at the hamlet where the body is being waked and stay overnight. A body generally remains in the men's house overnight, though should a man die during the night, he may be buried the following afternoon; there is no hard and fast rule about the duration of a wake. The deceased's lineage provides food during the evening, which is generally the time for *kis fakut*, the first distribution of pork associated with the death. The pig slaughtered may be one of the deceased's, one of the deceased's lineage member's, or one of the pigs contributed by supporters. Before being distributed for consumption, however, the pig should be presented to a member, usually male, of the deceased's lineage. The cooked pig, having been removed from the earth oven in which it is baked whole, is picked up by several men, who put the rump of the pig to the mouth of the recipient, who squats before them. The recipient takes the first bite (*ngaungau na bo*) and the pig is thereby recognized as his gift. This is the procedure at all feasts. A recipient of such a pig will ordinarily distribute the pork to others, who will thus become indebted to the pig recipient; the recipient himself will receive the head and the entrails of the pig.[7] At *kis fakut*, however, the pig, including the head, frequently is cut into small pieces and distributed to all in attendance, including women, who must consume the entire pig and are forbidden from taking away any of the pork. The term *kis fakut* is thus often used as a synonym for "eat everything" (*en tike*), a procedure followed in other contexts as well (see below).

Morapup or *mor na minet* ("compensatory meal for the grave" or "compensatory meal for the corpse")[8]

The burial service, generally conducted in Tok Pisin by a local catechist, follows the conventions of the Roman Catholic Church. The body, resting in a coffin fashioned from an old canoe, is carried out of the men's house by several men; this task, as well as digging the grave, is performed largely by whoever happens to be present, not by any specific category of kin. *Morapup* or *mor na minet* may be held at the men's house of the deceased immediately following the burial.[9] I observed such a feast only once, despite it often being reported as part of the ideal sequence of burial feasts. Either at this time, or sometime before the body is buried, the surviving spouse and other affinal/paternal relatives (*kinaf*) of the deceased declare and assume various mourning taboos, mostly dietary restrictions (*tam en*) on eating pork (*bo*), yam (*buk*), and rice. A mourner assuming such taboos will indicate this by wearing around his or her wrists and/or ankles knotted bands made of a tough vine called *an asem*, once used to lash together the planks of ocean-going canoes. Each of these bands represents one of the taboos: *pan tam en bo* ("band for taboo on eating pig"), *pan tam en buk* ("band for taboo on eating yams"), and so forth. Mourners wear the bands until formally relieved of their obligations at a subsequent feast. Mourners usually also blacken their foreheads with a solution made from charcoal and coconut oil (*kus mikit*), a practice known as *an du* ("blackness").

Those who assume mourning taboos present small amounts of money (from ten toea to two kina), live pigs or shell valuables to the lineage of the deceased. When the deceased's lineage, at its own discretion, removes the mourning taboos, these payments are reciprocated precisely. The size of the payment varies with the stringency of the taboos assumed. On the occasion of Tabunima's death, Pangang assumed a taboo on all garden work and on fishing as well as numerous dietary restrictions. He blackened his body from head to toe (including his hair), wore a black loincloth and neither shaved his face nor cut his hair. After naming each taboo, coins were handed from representatives of Pangang's lineage to Tabunima's actual and classificatory MBs. When finished, one of Pangang's classificatory brothers, Neanan, withdrew from his basket a shell disc (*am fat*) with an attached string of smaller ground shells (*kemetas*), which he gave to the big man of Tabunima's lineage. Neanan then led Pangang into the men's house, to which Pangang was confined until his son's lineage relieved him of this "sacrifice" (Tangans use the English word in this context).

The same procedure, minus the taboos on work and fishing, was repeated for Tabunima's MBD (whom the deceased would address as either *kek wok*, "my wife," or *ang kingkaf*, "my *kinaf*") and she was led into the men's house. Many more people, classificatory affines/patrilateral relatives, pledged "sacrifices" at this time; written lists of taboos were either read or presented to Tabunima's lineage along with ten-toea coins for each taboo. On this occasion, moreover, Tabunima's mother was also confined to the men's house. Should a child predecease his or her parents, both parents confine themselves to the men's house. No shell valuables, however, were given to her lineage for this; her confinement was the responsibility of her own lineage. Confinement now lasts for two to three weeks; in the past, confinement lasted for a longer period (see Bell 1937).

Pam bi na pokta'ng kinit ("vegetable meal behind/following the corpse")

The practice of sleeping in the men's house of the deceased, begun during the night the body was waked there, continues for several weeks after the burial. Some affinal relatives of the deceased are confined to the men's

house, while others may go about their normal routines during the day
but sleep in the men's house at night. Friends, neighbors, and members
of the deceased's lineage frequently visit the men's house at night to
socialize. In this sense, their gathering repeats the one prompted by *en
turan*, but without the physical presence of the deceased.[10] All who con-
gregate are served a vegetable meal of yams, *mami* (a species of Dioscorea), or taro with greens in coconut cream referred to as *pam bi na
pokta'ng kinit*.

   Pam bi na pokta'ng kinit also refers to larger community-wide distributions of vegetable food that might follow upon burial. About ten days
after a death, the lineage of the deceased and its supporters assemble
baskets (*dik*) of food, each containing drinking coconuts, some thirty to
forty *mangat* (oven-baked packets of scraped yam mixed with shredded
coconut) and about thirty betel nuts. These are distributed at a small
evening feast, sometimes along with cooked pigs, to various men and
women related to the lineage of the deceased. These recipients collect
their baskets and redistribute the contents to the men and women assembled for the event. Those who receive *pam bi* baskets are obligated to
reciprocate them soon at a time determined by the leaders of the lineage
of the deceased.

   Several community-wide distributions of *pam bi na pokta'ng kinit* followed the death of Tabunima. About one dozen *pam bi* baskets were
distributed by a member of Tabunima's clan Tasik acting in conjunction
with the leader of Tabunima's lineage (Matangkerem). These baskets
were given to representatives of the various lineages of clan Tasik as well
as to "children" of the men (*kinaf*) of clan Tasik. The distributor
announced that the *pam bi* baskets were to be reciprocated the following
Sunday evening.

   At the next distribution, the reciprocated baskets were given *in toto* to
a member of Tabunima's lineage, who in turn redistributed the baskets
to various individuals and announced the following Saturday as the time
for reciprocation. The reciprocated baskets were then presented to the
elder brother of Tabunima's father, who likewise redistributed them and
called for a return seven days hence. On the next occasion, the baskets
were presented to an elderly and respected big man of clan Tasik, who
redistributed them to various Tasik lineages along with a pig that he formally presented to his ZSZS (*koktamat*), a teenage boy. Some baskets
were again presented to the now adult "children" of deceased Tasik men.
The pig was cut into small pieces and distributed to the assembled guests
along with some of the contents of the *pam bi* baskets. The final *pam bi*

distribution occurred about ten weeks later as part of the larger *mora-tineng* feast (see below).

Like the *pam bi* eaten in the men's house where a corpse is waked, the community-wide distributions are considered to be food to feed those related to the deceased, that is, people who comprised the deceased's relational personhood. Tabunima's lineage leaders used the occasions to define and display publicly his and their *fat kinaf* relations to other lineages as well as to affirm the brotherhood of lineages within clan Tasik. As with almost all aspects of mortuary rites, the degree to which a lineage wishes to elaborate upon *pam bi* distributions remains open to nego-tiation. Indeed, *pam bi* distributions by no means form a necessary part of all mortuary sequences.

En mapu'ng kinit ("eat the stink of the corpse")

Ideally three, but often four or five days after the burial, *en mapu'ng kinit* occurs. This feast is always regarded as made by *and* for the matrilineage of the deceased. The size of the feast varies; I witnessed distributions ranging from one to three pigs. The pig(s) consumed must be formally presented to a male member of the deceased's lineage. I saw pigs pre-sented to ZSZS (*koktamat*), ZS (*koalik* or *kewalik*) and, in the case of a deceased woman, the son (*kaik*) of the deceased. This action marks the pig recipient as in charge of the specific distribution of the pork and the consumption of food in general. After the food has been distributed, this man will stand in view of all the guests and eat some of the pork, a signal that others may commence eating. (More than one person may receive pigs at a feast; usually the person receiving the largest pig will publicly "eat first" [*en kulkul*].) The rationale behind designating a member of the deceased's lineage, one informant explained, lies in the explicit metapho-rical equation of the pig with the rotting corpse (*mapu'ng kinit*). The privilege and obligation of consuming the deceased falls to the deceased's own male lineage mates.

Only men attend *en mapu'ng kinit*, to which they are formally invited (*fatil*), and all of the pork and food must be entirely finished (*en tike* – "eat everything") at the hamlet of the feast. When the men's house is occupied by the widow/er (*makos*) of the deceased and/or others who may be observing seclusion taboos, the feast takes place beneath a specially constructed awning in front of the men's house. The pig is distributed as at any other feast (chapter 6); recipients of choice pieces incur obligations to reciprocate at a future *en mapu'ng kinit* hosted by their own lineage. As at other "eat everything" feasts, the first sitting of men gives way to a second, who come to finish the remainder of the unconsumed food. Small boys often accompany their elders and participate lustily. Women and girls do not eat.

Tau uk su in makos ("calling out the widow/er")

Following *en mapu'ng kinit*, the lineage of the deceased begins to plan the feasts at which the mourning taboos assumed by its various affinal/ patrilateral relatives are abrogated. This may be done progressively or all at once at *moratineng*, the feast in which the women who wailed over the deceased are compensated for their crying (*tineng*) (see below). For example, Tabunima's lineage arranged a feast to end the most severe taboos assumed by Tabunima's father and MBD one week after hosting *en mapu'ng kinit*. The main purpose of this rite was to call the mourners out of the men's house (*tau uk su in makos*) and end their period of confinement.[11] The rite requires exact reciprocation to the patrilateral/ affinal relatives of the various payments of money, pigs, and shell wealth that originally established this period of confinement and taboo. Tabunima's parents, however, continued living in the men's house until the feast of *moratineng* some ten weeks later. Certain taboos on fishing and on the consumption of pork as well as the prescription for blackening the forehead were also maintained until *moratineng*.

Moratineng ("meal for the crying")

Moratineng denotes for Tangans a large-scale women's feast, at which the lineage of the deceased compensates all the local women who wailed over the body during the wake and funeral. Sometimes a reversal of the usual seating plan at feasts occurs with the women occupying the men's house and receiving their pork distribution therein while the men sit about the edges of the hamlet. Several cooked pigs are generally reserved for exclusive distribution to the women. These pigs, moreover, are given to particular women. Although men invariably cut up the pig and often suggest to whom pieces should be given, the women themselves frequently deliver pork sections to other women, establishing and repaying debts in the same fashion as the men. These debts are, like those of the men, debts between lineages and *not* between individuals (see chapter 6). Nevertheless, *moratineng* is one of the few occasions on which women publicly play a role in pork distributions; and for individual women, as for men, giving and receiving a choice piece of meat creates prestige.

Both the timing and form of *moratineng* are the most variable of the feasts comprising phase one of the mortuary sequence. This is due to the extensive preparations involved in assembling the necessary supplies of food and pigs as well as to the pivotal position of *moratineng* in the mortuary sequence. On the one hand, *moratineng* ends the string of feasts initiated by the death of a single individual. Consequently, the feast often involves the final removal of mourning restrictions on diet, dress, and demeanor. Similarly, the final distribution of *pam bi* baskets occurs at *moratineng*, thus terminating a practice that began during the wake of the deceased. On the other hand, *moratineng* opens the phase of the mortuary sequence directed toward building a new men's house (*pok bif*), which may be held for a single individual but which often "finishes" several recently deceased members of a lineage. For instance, at *moratineng* held for a Boang man who died on Anir, where he resided with his wife, a large pig was presented by the host lineage leader to his brother, thereby committing the latter to organize *pok bif* for the deceased at some future time.[12]

Moratineng potentially transforms the mortuary sequence from a series of events focused on a particular death into a collective effort concerned with "finishing" the collective dead of a lineage. This transformation slowly crystallized during the week preceding Tabunima's *moratineng* when, nearly every evening, lineage mates and various other relatives and friends gathered at Tabunima's men's house to sing *an u-a*. *An u-a* are lullaby-like songs sung dolefully and softly, punctuated with a drawn-out "u-a" (ooohhhhhh-aaahhhhhh). Mothers sing *an u-a* to soothe infants and thus Tangans regard the lullabies as appropriate for collective performance on the occasion of the death of a young man or woman. (No food distribution is associated with these performances which generally get under way following the early evening meal.) These lullabies sometimes express the sentiments of those surviving the deceased:[13]

Cry now – he's gone.
What am I going to do, where can I see him?

Mauna, you have abandoned me here.
I wait and look for you to come.
I stand wearily, I cry.
I sit and I cry, looking for you to come.
I cannot see your face here at Tanga.
I sit and grieve for you, my sister's son.
Ooooohhh-ahhhh.

I am very sorry, my nephew Mauna.
I did not think that something would happen to you.

I am confused.
I cry myself to death.
The men here have poisoned my nephew;
He has left me among you.
Ooooohhh-ahhhh.

Often, however, *an u-a* recall events involving big men long deceased, as in the following song sung during one of the evening sessions at Tabunima's men's house:

Hey, my friend, what are you doing?
You are not eating or drinking well.
Take pity on me, I cry for you.
Ngamnabo, you worry because of them.
They deceived you and they shout hurrah.

This *u-a* refers to a wartime incident in which Ngamnabo, the former paramount *luluai*, was brought before the Japanese on charges manufactured by his rivals on Tanga.[14] Like the first *an u-a*, this song expresses and evokes the sentiment of "worry" accompanying specific deaths, especially by means of the lugubrious words *sangkulung* ("worry"), *tineng* ("crying"), and *mariau* ("pity," "sympathy"). The point to be noted here is simply that the lullaby also evokes events and actors from the past and in so doing merges the individual death with other deaths or, in other words, elides the reality of an actual individual death with a collective representation of death and loss. This merging indicates a shift in emphasis from the recent loss of the particular deceased, and thus the particular relations composing the person of the deceased, to the future work of preparing *pok bif* for the deceased of the lineage as an internally undifferentiated *group*. This shift entails another transformation: the host lineage transforms itself from primary consumers, as at *kis fakut* and *en mapu'ng kinit*, to primary givers (see chapter 7). In finally abrogating the mourning taboos of its *kinaf*, the host lineage redefines its *kinaf* as consumers and itself as givers, that is, as feast givers. Thus, *moratineng*, by discharging the host lineage's obligations to outsiders who participated in the immediate funeral rites, anticipates the fulfilment of the lineage's obligation to "finish" and "replace" its own deceased members.

The mortuary sequence, phase two: building a commemorative men's house

The feast of *moratineng* introduces "building the commemorative men's house" (*pok bif*), the phase of the mortuary sequence concerned with the

Table 11. *Synopsis of feasts connected with constructing a men's house*[a]

Name of feast	Description
En pao-et palang	Occasion of the first harvest from a new garden used to announce a lineage's intentions of starting *pok bif*; taboos on various resources instated; *warangus* basket(s) presented
Fapang mor	Feast made to mark completion of all gardens planted to provide food for subsequent feasts; more *warangus* baskets presented; pig debts called in (*fakawit*)
	[When gardens are ready, a lineage begins construction of the new men's house. Some or all of the stages of construction are accompanied by *mor* for workers or feasts (*en*) for both workers and non-workers: clearing the site, raising the ridgepole, erecting the walls, etc. There is tremendous variation in the strategies pursued by different lineages.]
Papte bia	*Mor* ("eat everything" style) for lashing sago-leaf tiles to the roof of the men's house; this feast is never omitted. *Fasuigk* distribution of pigs
Bot	Night time dance held on the eve of *en bala'm bia*; food might or might not be provided for guests
En bala'm bia	First feast held inside the new men's house; always occurs the day after *papte bia*. More *warangus* baskets revealed. Recipients "buy" their pigs with shell discs (*lulu am bo*)
	[At this point, a lineage again might host feasts in conjunction with remaining construction tasks: putting the ridgesheet in place, completing the walls, etc. Such feasts also vary in their scale and frequency of occurrence.]
Saf bala'm bia	"Sweeping the inside of the *bia*"; vegetable tubers brought from garden and arranged in an impressive heap (*gus*) inside the men's house; this process occurs for two or three weeks prior to *arer sigit*
En fafas	Small feast or *mor* held in connection with preparation of *mangat* for *arer sigit*; *fasuigk* distribution of pigs; held day before *arer sigit*
Arer sigit	"The final feast"; feast that commemorates completion of the men's house. Final number of *warangus* baskets revealed. Large-scale payment (*lulu*). Dance performances (*binian*) presented by commissioned leaders of other lineages
En tura'n iu	"Feast concerning the spears"; feast that commemorates the burning or burial of personal effects of the deceased (spear, purse, walking stick, etc.) which had been stored in the men's house since the time of burial. Might occur up to twenty years after the death of an individual.

Note: [a] This list is not meant to be definitive; variation in the timing and number of and occasions for feasts is common. Compare the schedule of feasts in Bell (1937).

construction of men's houses and the one most closely identified by Tangans with *kastam* (see table 11). Whether or not a feast accompanies every step of construction, as is the ideal, feasts associated with *pok bif* occasion all other public exchanges. Thus, for example, a groom must wait until his lineage (or in some instances the bride's lineage) undertakes *pok bif* before his mother's brother or father can publicly make a marriage payment. In providing the context for almost all public exchanges, *pok bif* furnishes the framework and timetable of Tangan sociality.

Pok bif takes shape as a series of unfolding revelations about what is to come. Through the concrete activity of hosting mortuary feasts, lineages demonstrate their capacity to realize advertised intentions, thereby redefining their position in a nexus of social relations and reiterating performatively their capacity to sustain and reproduce that position. From this perspective, *pok bif* comprises a definite series of communications, predominantly non-verbal, that publicize a lineage's intentions or "plans" (*enfinawer*).[15] The master trope of *pok bif* is foreshadowing. Each feast contains within it "signs" (*finailim*) both of the progress of the preparations for the "final feast" (*arer sigit*) and of the size and scale of the final feast. These signs include actions such as the presentation of specially marked baskets of food to men designated as major pig recipients at the final feast; the performance of brief dramatic dialogues which, in their veiled verbal content, suggest the significance of the feast and anticipate future feasting; the distribution of various material tokens (also called *finailim*) either to call in debts for pigs or to invite participation in various feast-related activities. Some of these signs, standard visual props, communicate relatively unambiguously the intent of the hosts; other signs, particularly the dramatic dialogues, though equally conventional, retain a degree of ambiguity and hence admit the possibility of dissemblance.

Throughout the sequence, changes in the form or number of signs progressively modify the image of the final feast being projected by the host lineage. I use the word "image" to denote a composite representation actively constructed by feast givers from a repertoire of signs (*finailim*). Signs function as omens or auguries inasmuch as they presage or point to future activity. For example, the cry of a bird in the depths of the night is a sign that someone is about to die. In their capacity to foreshadow, signs differ from "emblems" or "totems" (*do*; see chapter 3) which imply nothing about future practice. In addition, many of the signs deployed throughout the feast sequence are iconic in character, that is, they model in their sensuous material qualities aspects of the future activity that they presage.[16] For example, a feast organizer distributes small lengths of a bushcreeper to representatives of various lineages as an invitation to help lash the roof of the men's house, a procedure in which men use the bushcreeper as rope. Or, similarly, a feast organizer distributes betel nuts to representatives of lineages which owe pigs to the host lineage; the ripeness of the nut corresponds to the approximate time at which the debt will be called in while the size of the nut corresponds to the size of the pig expected by the feast host. The qualitative immediacy of the icon communicates intention wordlessly. That is, the deployment of signs by the hosts of a feast ideally requires no further commentary. Spectators apprehend the projected image of the final feast as it is gradually revealed to them by the feast organizers.

Through such a process, actors not only construct images of future events, but also draw the future into the present. Conceived as such, the successful sequence necessarily culminates in a *realization* of previous foreshadowing, in an event that effectively makes real its own prefigured image and pragmatically validates past projections of that image. Not unlike a teleology, but different in that its telos undergoes constant alteration, *pok bif* as process is never absolutely given. The host lineage commits itself beforehand neither to the specific shape that the final feast will assume (i.e., its scale and elaborateness) nor even to the certainty of the event coming to pass. In this regard, then, the actual accomplishment of the mortuary sequence, the realization of the final feast, constitutes the measure of its success. The final feast amounts to a display of power, that is, a display of the capacity to formulate or fix a collective identity and to make that identity publicly known (see chapter 7). Such realizations complete "the passage from the highest probability to absolute certainty" (Bourdieu 1977:9), the qualitative leap that finally overcomes any lingering uncertainty as to the outcome of the mortuary sequence.

Pok bif is thus a twofold transformational process. In terms of mood, *pok bif* transforms the worry and grief (*sangkulung*) of an individual's death into the celebration and happiness (*laes*) surrounding the collective "finishing" of a lineage's deceased. The same transformation can be stated as the movement from "remembering" (*sangfi*) the deceased, the experience of which moves individuals to tears, to "forgetting" (*sangkifeni*) the deceased (cf. Thune 1980; Munn 1986; Battaglia 1990). "Forgetting" does not imply indifference or callousness, but rather the liberation, attained through *pok bif*, of having fulfilled obligations to deceased lineage members. Thereafter a lineage relaxes its efforts to remember or commemorate and instead allows the process of forgetting, thought in any case to be inevitable, to take its course. Put otherwise, remembering becomes thereafter a particular and personal affair rather than a general and collective one.

The correlate of this transformation in mood is the redefinition of the lineage as an autonomous social unit capable of hosting feasts, meeting its own obligations to the dead and, most importantly, of "replacing" its deceased (especially its big men). *Pok bif* functions as the activity and expression of transforming loss and expenditure into replacement. The central exchanges of pigs for shells, analyzed in subsequent chapters, effect the "replacement" of deceased lineage members. This complex process, predicated on the social construction of the host lineage as feast givers, lies at the heart of *pok bif*.

Am fimfil ("promissory men's house")

The *pok bif* phase of the mortuary sequence, which does not follow upon every death, itself includes two distinct stages which together may last over ten years. Each stage involves the construction of a men's house. The first structure, called *am fimfil*, is regarded as merely a "temporary" or "promissory" men's house that indicates a lineage's intention to construct a "true" men's house (*bif*) at a later date. Its construction is associated with one or more feasts, the scale of which is generally smaller than that of feasts associated with "true" men's houses.

The death of an individual, especially a big man, or the physical deterioration of an old men's house may prompt the construction of an *am fimfil*. At an accompanying feast, the host lineage's big man distributes cooked pigs in a procedure called *fil taufi* ("to buy a big man") that obliges recipients to raise pigs for the future *pok bif*.[17] The site of the future men's house might also be indicated at this time.

In constructing an *am fimfil*, builders often join the bamboo strips (*an as marer*) used to construct the roof frame into bunches of four or five in order to publicize intentions of initiating *pok bif* in as many years. Men's houses, like public calendars, measure Tangan social time, materially testifying to past sequences of *pok bif* and stating pledges of future sequences. *Am fimfil* allow visitors to speculate silently on the various stages of preparation which lineages might occupy with regard to pig and garden resources. In the extent of their disrepair, men's houses indicate imminent collective activity or unmet obligations and unavailable feast resources. Men's houses thus communicate intentions and hence actively construct or anticipate the future in the present (see Munn 1983).[18]

En pao-et palang ("first fruits of the garden feast")

En pao-et palang (sometimes called *kalmu*) designates a first-fruits feast after the completion of which gardens (*palang*, the garden in full bearing) may be harvested. *En pao-et palang* are not mandatory; lineage leaders create the occasion as an opportunity to announce their intentions to commence *pok bif* presently. *En pao-et palang* take place from late April to June when most yam gardens come into full bearing. These events open the season of men's house-related feasts when yams are plentiful (*bing tao'n mas/bing kausi*, "good time") that lasts until January of the following year when food stores run low and seed yams have been replanted (*kis piklim faim*, "time of sitting under our work," *bing im fitol*, "time of hunger").

During the *en pao-et palang*, the presentation of a special basket of food (*warangus*) might be made by the host lineage to mark a particular individual as someone who will receive a large pig at the culminating feast of the impending *pok bif*. Similarly, the host lineage might publicize the institution of a taboo on all betel palms growing on lineage land by displaying forked poles (*an ulau*) with a sprig of betel palm and a pig jaw fastened to the crotch of each pole. The pig jaws metonymically communicate the penalty for transgressing the prohibition on harvesting betel nut, namely, the presentation of a cooked pig. Both the *warangus* and *an ulau* are notices to big men of other lineages that outstanding debts of pigs are about to be recalled; they are signs that anticipate the actions they set in motion.

Vegetable food is the essential basis of mortuary feasting, and Tangans, despite their island habitat, imagine themselves as gardeners. Gardening constitutes the ideal typical work (*faim*) for both men and women. Every married couple makes a garden, and gardening together makes a man and woman a married couple. Each spouse brings to the marriage a separate supply of seed tubers, grows the tubers in separate plots, and stores the harvested tubers separately inside the garden storehouse.[19] Within extended households that include a senior couple and the family of one (or more) of their married children, each couple will maintain a separate garden. Similarly, widows and widowers often maintain their own gardens. The capacity to garden, and hence to feed oneself and others, demonstrates both personal autonomy and social viability.[20] Only children, unmarried youths, and the very elderly depend upon the gardens of others for their food.

The primary garden furnishes mainly yams (*buk* or *sinam*; Dioscorea alata) and *mami* (called *kaukau* or *inen* in Tangga; Dioscorea esculenta) as well as some taro (*pas*) (plate 3). Yam/*mami* gardens , which supply feast food, epitomize gardens for Tangans; sweet potato and "Chinese taro" (*singapor* in Tok Pisin) appear in feasts only as inferior substitutes for yams. Supplementary gardens of *singapor* and sweet potato, often made at the borders of the primary yam garden, do not conform to the orderly layout used for yam gardens.[21] Yams complement (*gemgem*) pork as do few other root crops. Indeed, the annual "hungry time" refers as much to an absence of yams and *mami* as to a relative lack of food.

A couple and their immediate family (children and unmarried siblings) provide most of the labor for almost all stages of gardening unless their garden is intended for *pok bif*. Gardens made for *pok bif* receive labor assistance from the leaders of the host lineage who assemble work crews composed of various lineage members, *kinaf*, and other allies. Nonetheless, each garden remains the responsibility of a single man and his wife after the major tasks of clearing, fencing, groundbreaking, and planting have been accomplished collectively.

Work parties invariably undertake the strenuous task of ground breaking (*susup*). Gangs of men, friends, relatives, and neighbors of the garden owners, fashion digging sticks (*waswas*) from branches four to five feet long of various hardwood trees. The men methodically dig rows of holes,

Plate 3   Women peeling yams for distribution at a mortuary feast, Bulam, 1984

crossing the garden from one side to the other and back again. At times the young men let out high-pitched yelps, the pace of work quickens and the sweaty, whooping gang charges furiously across the garden. When a garden is intended for *pok bif*, a certain license (*am pilumbo*) prevails and frequently the whooping leads to upsetting garden fences, displacing section markers, and wildly digging holes ("like pigs") beyond the borders of the garden. The garden owner must witness this "play" (*soro*) without complaint. In addition, a compensatory meal (*mor*) must be supplied to the workers by the sponsors. The last and most elaborate of these meals, which is attended by invited guests as well as workers, is called *fapang mor*; it is made to mark the completion of preparatory garden work for the upcoming *pok bif*.

Fapang mor ("compensatory meal for making open")

Fapang mor, much like a first-fruits feast, advertises a lineage's progress in the mortuary sequence, but *fapang mor* reveals more of a lineage's plans to outsiders. Most obviously, *fapang mor* indicates the point at which the lineage stands with respect to the gardening schedule that determines the timing of feasts. More importantly, however, *fapang mor* occasions another presentation of *warangus* baskets that identify future pig recipients at the final feast of *pok bif*. It also occasions the distribution of betelnuts to representatives of lineages expected to settle pig debts with the host lineage. In this sense, Partui described *fapang mor* as the "start" of *pok bif*, the revelation of specific details about the lineage's particular intentions for realizing the mortuary sequence.

The *fapang mor* hosted by Solsol lineage in February 1985 illustrates some of the typical features of Tangan feasts. While the junior Solsol men butchered and cooked the pigs, and the women baked packets of *mangat* and other tubers, men from invited lineages broke the ground in the last two remaining gardens made to provide food at upcoming feasts. When all was ready, a display of cooked food was arranged outside the men's house at which the feast was held. Food displays at feasts, whether constructed inside the men's house or immediately outside, assume a standardized form. Several coconut fronds, completely overlaid by banana leaves, protect the food from direct contact with the ground. Drinking coconuts (*kuen*) placed side by side atop the banana leaves comprise a roughly rectangular platform which, covered in turn with banana leaves, supports several layers of cooked vegetable food (*gus*). The bottom layers contain *mangat* bundles or sometimes oven-baked *mami*. Top layers contain the large, variously shaped large yams (*buk*) that Tangans prize as the pre-eminent vegetable food. Men build the display, if constructed inside the men's house, around the central ridge post, which thus appears to grow out of the middle of the pile. Displays composed outside in front of the men's house may center on a length of bamboo thrust into the ground, clusters of betel nut hanging from the trimmed shoots of the central stalk. Pigs may be arranged together on one side of the food or in groups on either side. Sometimes the arrangement separates pigs designated for consumption by men from those designated for women, but sometimes the number of pigs necessitates their being heaped atop one another so as not to obstruct the entrances to the men's house.

I could discover no name for this visual display other than *gus*; nor am I able to analyze the display in local symbolic terms. Indeed, most inform- ants, in apparent fits of practical reason, explained the purpose of the display as economizing the space within the men's house in order that guests might occupy the benches and yet leave room for their hosts to distribute the food (figure 2; plate 4).[22] What is important to note, however, is that at all feasts the food is never simply removed from the oven and distributed, but rather carefully gathered together, publicly displayed and only thereafter individually apportioned among the guests.

Plate 4   Food and betel nut displayed inside the men's house at Am Fungkalu, 1984

These displays momentarily materialize the social (exchange) relations focused on the deceased person(s) before dissolving or "finishing" this focus in the ensuing disassembly and distribution of the food pile (cf. Battaglia 1992).

At the Solsol *fapang mor*, workers arriving from the gardens and guests coming from nearby saw five cooked pigs flanking the layers of food, three to one side and two to the other side. Guests generally sit themselves in clusters around the periphery of the hamlet, men invariably sitting apart from women. The male guests for this *fapang mor* outnumbered the women approximately three to one, as is common at Tangan feasts. Nonetheless, a group of Solsol women and inmarried wives set out formally to invite a number of women from neighboring hamlets. Partui and Timir, the feast organizers, meanwhile invited some of the senior men to sit inside the old men's house. A familiar scene ensued in which the guest demurs and protests that someone else be given this honor while the host insists until, half jokingly, he grabs the guest by the arm or hand and leads him inside the men's house. With as many men as possible seated inside the men's house, the remaining men settled onto the trunks of betel palms set in the shade while the women clustered on the other side of the hamlet beneath the eaves of the nearby cookhouse (*felungkur*).

On the heels of a pregnant pause, four Solsol lineage brothers began a dramatic skit (*am furis*). Negut, feigning impatience, loudly asked the whereabouts of Timir. Partui did likewise. Negut shouted "Timir! Timir!" and Timir answered with a yelp from the bush bordering the hamlet. Within seconds, Timir entered the hamlet shouldering an axe and five forked poles (*an ulau*), a section of betel nut vine attached to each:

Fig. 2   Floor plan of a typical men's house (*bia*)

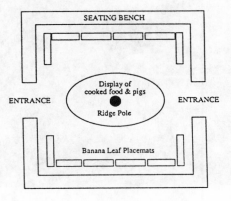

Timir: "Who placed these *gumgum* taboos preventing me from clearing the bush?"

Negut: "Don't you know? That bush is taboo. You can't work your garden there."

Timir: "You didn't tell me."

Kiaplang: "You two can't argue! There is a *komiti* [committee member] here to take care of you two."

Partui: "Don't you two recognize these *gumgum*? I recognize them. This one here belongs to Kiapun [saying this Partui took one of the *an ulau* and planted it in the ground]. This is Parbil's [Partui again planted an *an ulau*]. This belongs to Eric [repeat planting]. And two of them are mine."

Partui's statement concluded the skit, the point of which was publicly to transfer the *an ulau* to the named recipients, who thus became obliged to place restrictions on their betel nut and *pao* nut (*galip* in Tok Pisin; Canarium spp.) groves in expectation of contributing these delicacies to the impending *pok bif*. Each recipient, including Partui, would remove the *an ulau* and stand it up at his own hamlet. The skit also alluded to the bush at Seber, site of the projected men's house and taboo (*mapek*) since 1981, the clearing of which comprised the next step in the *pok bif* sequence.

Four of the five pigs distributed went to the supporters of the upcoming *pok bif*, including two men married to Solsol women who had planted

Plate 5   Food distribution at site cleared for a new men's house, Seber, 1985

gardens to supply future feasts (plate 5). Following the distribution of pigs, Partui sat down just inside the doorway of the men's house. Timir then presented him with three *warangus* baskets, placing each basket on the ground at Partui's feet and handing to Partui a ten-toea coin for each basket. Partui initiated a prayer which, mumbled in Tangga, precedes eating at all feasts. He then took a banana from one basket and, taking a bite, returned to Timir a ten-toea coin from his own supply. This was repeated for the other two baskets and allowed the assembled guests to commence eating. Against a background of quiet munching, Partui asked: "Why did you give me three baskets? I'll give some to my friends. One to Kiapun. Finish my portion. One to Parbil. And I'll keep this one." Thus Partui revealed that in addition to himself, Kiapun (the leader of Partui's paternal lineage and "child" [DS] of Ngamnabo, the deceased Solsol big man) and Parbil (Partui's WZH and Timir's FZS) would receive large pigs at *pok bif* and in turn support the feasting with food, labor, and pigs.

Warangus baskets contain a choice selection of various feast foods, but no pork, and generally grow in size proportionate to the scale of the feast as the *pok bif* sequence progresses. The baskets designate pig recipients who also agree to support the effort of *pok bif* with gifts of pigs, food, labor, and administrative advice. *Warangus* presentations are thus similar to the procedure of "buying a big man" (*fil taufi*) enacted at the construction of promissory men's houses. Both Parbil and Kiapun were pledged to repay debts incurred previously in similar circumstances at mortuary feasts sponsored by their own respective lineages.

Closely related to the exhibition of *warangus* baskets is the distribution of *fawit* ("to hook" or "to pull in") betel nut. While the guests were still eating, Partui stood and walked to the center of the hamlet where he called the names of three men to whose lineages Solsol lineage had rendered support in the past. Each man or his representative received a green betel nut that symbolized a pig owed to Solsol lineage. The size of each nut indicated roughly the size of the pig; ripe red nuts connote debts due sooner than those symbolized by the more common green nuts. Each recipient's lineage was thus "hooked" or "pulled" into the Solsol *pok bif* and obliged to contribute a pig at one of the upcoming feasts.[23] Partui also announced that anyone of the recipients unclear about the debt referred to by the betel nut should inquire. In fact, all three of the recipients inquired about their betel nuts. Tangans keep no records of pig debts, written or otherwise, and thus creditors must discuss their claims with debtors reminding the latter of the circumstances which initiated the debt. Given that the debts of deceased persons fall to their surviving enates, such discussions often occur when debts to be collected are many years old.

Like the *warangus* baskets, the *fawit* betel nuts work as public signs that tacitly reveal more of the organization and scale of upcoming feasts to the assembled guests. For the host lineage, then, the challenge of feasting becomes one of *realization*, that is, realizing the image both anticipated and constructed in the public display of *warangus* baskets and *fawit* betel nuts.

The feast of *fapang mor* closes the period of *pok bif* preparatory to the actual construction of the men's house. Bell's ethnography suggests that it is only over the past fifty years that the building of men's houses has been integrated into the mortuary sequence. Previously, men's house construction depended upon the decision of a lineage leader to renovate an old structure or to build anew. The leader simply organized his lineage's men, women, and children into a building team and erected the structure. Purely local in character, the enterprise required no more than the necessary compensatory meal for the workers.[24] Quite separate from the construction of the men's house was the mortuary sequence that culminated in the construction of a funeral house called *fel* (the generic Tangan word for "house"), impressively long Quonset-style buildings (see Bell 1949b:323–4).

By 1985, men's houses (*bia*) had almost completely supplanted *fel* in the mortuary sequence.[25] The rites described by Bell as being associated with *fel* have been transposed in whole or in part to the construction of men's houses. Two older informants accounted for this change by characterizing the latter as "easier to work." Feasts associated with *fel*, they claimed, required extensive cooperation among affines and *kinaf* as well as many pigs. Men's houses, on the other hand, which in the past did not "come up atop a man who died," could be built by a single man. Contemporary men's houses, the two men argued, represent a "short cut," a recent importation from Uris in the Sursurunga area of south-central New Ireland, whereby an individual may "work *kastam*" (*tel kastam*) on the strength of his own pig herd. This "short cut" is perhaps the cause and consequence of what many informants perceived as an explosion of men's houses. Several men complained that not only were new men's houses rising on sites that were previously unoccupied bush, but also that the scale of men's house feasting had undergone noticeable reduction due to the contraction of cooperative kin relations (i.e., *kinaf* relations). All of this can be related, albeit speculatively, to the decline of authoritative big men and the growth of population and land disputes discussed in chapters 2 and 3.

Nevertheless, the basic form of the contemporary men's house fits Bell's description: "a single story structure with a beaten earth floor, built on a rectangular plan and consisting of a single undivided room" (1949b:321). Nor have the dimensions of the structure changed appreciably, with a relatively consistent width of about fifteen feet and a length that varies with the purpose of the men's house and the pretensions of its builders.[26] A ridged roof, approximately ten feet high in the center and thatched with tiles made of sago palm leaves, extends beyond the walls to form two-foot eaves at the sides and similar sized gabled canopies at the front and back ends.[27] Now as then, the orientation of the men's house within a hamlet, usually but not always that occupied by the lineage leader, follows no specific cosmographic determination.

The actual construction of the men's house is no less an improvisatory process than the sequence of mortuary feasts as a whole. Contemporary men's houses vary in a number of minor architectural details that express the idiosyncratic "style" of their builders, such the shape of the windows or the inclusion of a carved ridge post (which requires prestations of pigs by the person donating the post). Similarly, although Tangan big men can articulate an ideal of marking every stage of men's house construction with the consumption of pork, the ideal is rarely realized in practice. It is a matter of variation whether or not feasts are organized in conjuction with each addition to the men's house – the wall posts, walls, ridge posts, ridge pole, roof, and so forth. All of these details recall the numerous details of feasts in general, which may be elaborated, simplified or transformed at the discretion of the host lineage. They define an area in which innovation and creativity find acceptable public outlets, in which through collective action a lineage distinguishes itself from other lineages and from its own past efforts by realizing the physical structure with which others verbally and conceptually identify its builders.

The construction of the Solsol men's house in 1985 commenced with the public removal of a taboo (*mapek*) that had been placed on the construction site several years earlier, thus allowing the site to be cleared. Several contingents of supporters contributed pigs and foods to Solsol lineage for making a feast on this occasion. While some members of the assembled group prepared the food and cooked the pigs, others began the work of clearing the site of scrub, bush, and saplings. The organization of work resembled that in clearing gardens with the men chopping down the growth and the women collecting the debris into piles for burning. These activities occasioned another bout of licensed play in which the women workers chased and seized Solsol women, men and their wives. The victims were led or carried to the piles of debris, thrown thereupon and buried beneath layers of dirt, vines, and scrub. Throughout the remaining construction process, similar bursts of aggressive play occurred.

These episodes mark the mood of *pok bif* as one of celebration in distinct contrast to the somber tones of the immediate rites of death. The *pok bif* sequence progressively diminishes a lineage's collective grief, transforming grief into collective celebration by "finishing" the *necessity* to remember (*sangfi*) the dead. The transformation of grief into celebration mirrors the step-by-step construction of the men's house, the two processes coordinated and administered under the direction of the host lineage's leader(s). In other words, the transformation is effected as a controlled multi-stage process, a continuation of the mourning process, in which changes transpire in a series of measured steps instead of all at once. During the construction process, as during the mourning process, lineage leaders initiate taboos that must be observed by everyone involved in the work: hats must not be worn inside the men's house; workers must leave their personal baskets outside the men's house; chewing betel nut and smoking tobacco are forbidden inside the men's house. All of these taboos are lifted at subsequent points in the mortuary sequence.

Various steps in the construction process might or might not precipitate a compensatory meal or even a more elaborate feast: laying the foundation (*warambof*); setting up the wall posts (*am bubis*); fastening split bamboo panels to the wall posts. Sometimes all the food must be consumed on the spot; at other times guests are permitted to remove uneaten portions of pork and other foods to their own hamlets. During this time, too, work might or might not begin on the creation of a carved ridge post (*tutor*), commissioned by the host lineage or one of its supporters for a subsequent formal presentation. Feast organizers follow no formula or orthopraxy in these proceedings, but rather improvise upon a set of guiding premises.

Almost always, however, positioning the rafters (*an as pilulu*) and raising the ridgepole (*an singluf*) occasion a feast. Bringing the ridgepole from the site where it was cut to the site of the Solsol men's house sparked aggressive play similar in form to other such outbursts. One group of men and a few senior Solsol women, faces streaked with lime, forearms and buttocks covered with Cordyline leaves (*ang gaf*), waited at the site for a second group carrying the long, thick ridgepole, itself draped with various ornamental leaves.[28] As the second group entered the hamlet, the first group, whooping, rushed to meet it, each person grabbing the ridgepole wherever possible. A vertical tug of war ensued in which the first group tried to drag the ridgepole downwards while the original carriers struggled to keep it aloft. After one or two minutes of tussling, the participants eased their opposition and carefully lowered the ridgepole to the ground. The two groups then set about raising the ridgepole to rest atop temporary bamboo ridge posts and lashing the rafters to the wall plate (*an is an balo*) at one end and to the ridgepole at the other. With this work, the frame of the roof, to which sago-leaf tiles would be lashed, began to take shape. More importantly, the stage had been set for the first of two major feasts that punctuate if not climax the entire mortuary sequence.

Mor na papte bia ("compensatory meal for roofing the men's house")

On the day before a new men's house is roofed, the host lineage takes delivery of pigs contributed by parties either repaying debts or spontaneously offering support for the host lineage. These pigs are consumed in association with roofing the men's house.

Bringing a pig (*so puek*) to the feast of another lineage is a matter of standard procedure. Distant shouts (*kau-un*) alert the waiting recipients to the approach of the contributing party. The recipients, who may or may not decorate themselves with lime, red ochre, and various leaf decorations, prepare for the ritualized greeting (*butbut*). The approaching party enters the cleared hamlet and pauses, still holding a pig or pigs slung on a carrying pole, baskets of tubers, green coconuts, and sometimes clusters of betel nut. A man, sometimes two or three, from the host group then steps forward to meet them. Solidly planting his right foot, the man lunges forward with his left, pounding his left heel into the ground and rocking back and forth by flexing his left knee. With his right hand he gestures menacingly with either a spear (*iu* or *sum bo*) or ceremonial axe (*asok*), both of which nowadays constitute part of a matrilineage's patrimony. Timir generally played this role at the *so puek* for the Solsol men's house, confronting the contributors with shouts of "*Aiang! Aiang! Aiang!*" ("Mine! Mine! Mine!") or "*Siaro! Siaro! Siaro!*" ("Peace! Calm! Peace!").[29] At the conclusion of his display, the visitors would lay their contribution at his feet. Sometimes the leader of the visiting party would touch his foot to the pig and speak simply "*Bo aiam*" ("Your pig"). Timir ended the scene by placing coins (*ting bo*) on the various items brought by the visitors, though not on the pigs which would be acknowledged later (see below). The guests collected the coins as well as a cluster of betel nut hospitably proffered (*tugum*) by one of the Solsol men. Meanwhile, the slit gong sounded a special signal (*sif m'bo*) that announces in its beats the number and sex of the pig or pigs delivered. Dallying for a few minutes to chat and chew betel nut, the visitors soon uttered salutations and left.

Also on the day before roofing, the host lineage's leaders will dispatch small pieces of tough vine (*sung kis*), used as a rope for lashing sago tiles to the roof frame, to several other lineage leaders. These wordless invitations will elicit on the next day a party of men who set about their task by first splitting long bamboo rods into three-quarter-inch-wide strips (*fauis felof*). Some of the strips (*am fos marer*) are lashed parallel to the braces, others (*an as marer*) are passed over the ridgepole and lashed perpendicular to the *am fos marer* to form the frame (*felof*) for the thatching. Still other strips are placed criss-cross across the rafters to form a diamond patterned (*an lis*) open latticework designed to rest atop the sago-tile thatching. For the Solsol men's house, this work was accomplished by handing the strips up to Timir who, perched on the ridgepole, was the only individual permitted to climb on top of the unfinished men's house. Timir's appearance on the roof wordlessly announced his identity as the lineage member who later would ceremonially stand on the roof of the men's house (see below). It also visually reiterated a taboo on promiscuously "stepping over" (*kau*) the various component parts of the structure.[30]

A makeshift scaffolding (*kai-iauau*) of betel palm trunks is erected inside the men's house. The invited workers stand on this platform as they lash the tiles to the rafters; it is later removed and refashioned into temporary benches that seat the workers inside the men's house for the ensuing compensatory meal. At this time, the various restrictions on smoking, chewing betel nut, and bringing personal baskets inside the men's house will be lifted. A brief skit (*am furis*) often precedes the actual consumption of the food. At the Solsol men's house, Timir climbed a bamboo ladder placed at the back end of the men's house and walked across the length of the ridgepole to the front end. Partui, standing on the ground below, looked up to Timir and asked: "What do you expect? Do you think that there is a big man here to talk with you? Come down!" Timir silently descended the ladder, repositioned at the front of the men's house, on the command ("*Om pu!*") that concludes all *am furis* of this type. Abbreviated versions of this style of *am furis* frequently invoke the image of a hamlet devoid of all its big men in order to communicate the memorial purpose of *pok bif* and the need for lineage succession (see Clay 1992). The same image of the empty hamlet – the space waiting to be filled

– appears in many of the *u-a* sung in the aftermath of an individual's death.

As many of the workers and spectators – men only – as can be accommodated are invited inside the men's house to consume the compensatory meal. Once the guests are seated, lineage leaders often drape items of shell wealth from the crossties at either end of the men's house. This action, not uncommon in such situations, wordlessly signifies that the meal is of the "eat everything" type and no food will be permitted to leave the confines of the men's house. Men therefore eat their fill and surrender their seats to a second sitting of workers waiting outside. Before so doing, however, one of the guests leads the others in a choral chant known as *mai*. The chant climaxes with all the men responding in unison three times to the solo exhortations of the singer. Each time the response grows louder until finally culminating in the high-pitched whoops (*kau-un*) that mark other aspects of feasting. Host lineages interpret the chanting (*tut mai*) as a sign that the guests have satiated themselves and guests generally regard the *mai* as an incumbent part of feasting etiquette.

Fasuigk ("redistribution of pigs")

Fasuigk refers to the distribution of pigs collected by a host lineage, including any pigs supplied by members of the host lineage. *Fasuigk* invariably takes place in late afternoon on the day before the distributed pigs are to be cooked. Usually, *fasuigk* occurs on the day of roofing the men's house, just after the men finish eating. Likewise, the feast called *en bala'm bia* ("feast inside the men's house"), at which the distributed pigs are cooked, carved, and redistributed in pieces, usually takes place on the next day (see below). *Fasuigk* distributions, however, also occur in other contexts, such as prior to the final *pok bif* feast or prior to a large *moratineng* feast.[31]

Fasuigk distributions conform to an apparently longstanding procedure (see Bell 1949b:342) regardless of the context of the event. All of the pigs to be distributed (*ti*), still tightly tied to the carrying poles (*au bo*) on which they were brought to the new men's house, are arranged in a straight line. The line extends from the "eye" or "front" (*mata*) of the men's house outward to the edge of the cleared hamlet site. Makeshift posts (*tam*) of bamboo or wood are thrust into the ground at 4 to 5 feet intervals and the pigs placed on the ground between the posts with their heads pointing toward the men's house. The largest pig (*paklu'm bia*, "head of the men's house" or *waram pan sinol*, "base of the banana leaf serving plate") is placed closest to the men's house; the remaining pigs

Plate 6   Pigs lined in size order for *fasuigk* at Am Fungkalu, 1984

stretch away from the men's house in size order; the line ends with the smallest pig. A small distribution may include fewer than ten pigs arranged in this fashion while a major *fasuigk*, such as at a final feast, may result in a line that stretches one hundred fifty feet and includes twenty-five or more pigs.

Once the pigs have been secured by lashing the end of each carrying pole to a post, the process of *ting bo* begins. Tangans gloss *tinge* in Tok Pisin as "*baim*," so that *ting bo* (or *sage bo*) connotes "buying pigs" from various contributors in the same way that placing 10- and 20-toea coins on baskets of coconuts and betel nut "buys" these items (I discuss Tangan words for exchange transactions in the next chapter). The man who walked (or will walk) on the roof of the men's house stands at the head of the line of pigs, holding in his right hand a spear, ceremonial axe or some other such lineage heirloom. While the slit gong sounds in the background, the man trots counter-clockwise around the line of pigs, holding aloft the spear. After one full circuit, returning him to the head of the line, a lineage mate gives the man a shell disc (*tintol*) which he takes with his left hand. As the slit gong resumes its signal, the man again circles the line of pigs displaying aloft both the spear and the shell disc.[32] Instead of completing the circuit, however, the man rounds the far post and on his return nimbly hops over one of the pigs (plate 7), depositing as he does so

Plate 7 Timir leaping over a pig and displaying a shell valuable (*tintol*) during *fasuigk* at Seber, 1985

the shell disc on top of or next to the pig. The man again takes a disc from the lineage supply and repeats the process, but not in any particular order, sometimes dropping a disc on the fifth pig, then the seventh, then the third and so on. The size of the pig is correlated to the size of the shell disc, large pigs receiving large discs, and so forth. The process continues until all of the pigs have been "bought," though in certain circumstances some pigs do not require payment. After the last shell disc has been deposited, the various pig contributors or their representatives step forward to collect the shell matched with their pig.[33]

At this point, control over the total array of pigs officially passes to the host lineage, the leader(s) of which begin to redistribute them. Accompanied by big men of supporting lineages, the leader stands at the head of the line holding a number of *sinaf* (midribs of sago palm used as broom bristles). After some deliberation, the leader or one of his assistants calls the name of the pig recipient and offhandedly flips the *sinaf* either on to the pig or toward the named recipient. Sometimes the recipient comes forward to accept the *sinaf* directly. This procedure, beginning at the head of the line, is repeated for each of the pigs. While some decisions have been taken earlier, others seem to emerge only after a quick review of outstanding debts or intelligent strategies for initiating new debts. Significantly, redistribution means not that new recipients can carry off their live pig, but rather that they must butcher and cook their pig for piecemeal distribution at the feast on the following day. Recipients may either cook the pigs on the morrow at the site of the men's house or remove their pig to their own hamlet, returning the next day with the cooked pig. Thus *fasuigk* distributions often end with small parties of youths moving in the shadows of dusk, scouring the nearby area for the requisite firewood.

At the Solsol *fasuigk*, some of the people who contributed pigs at *so puek* received in turn other pigs, a not uncommon practice referred to as *bili bo* ("to exchange pigs"). In this sort of redistribution, the unspoken goal is to bequeath contributors with a redistributed pig of the same or slightly larger size than the pig originally contributed. For example, the contributor of the pig fourth in line (and, roughly, in size) received the pig first in line; the contributor of pig number 5 received pig number 4; the contributors of pigs numbers 7, 13, and 14 received pigs numbers 2, 10, and 12, respectively. (The ability to match pigs in this way defines a successful *fasuigk* and, by implication, a big man capable of managing feasts.) Other recipients of *sinaf* included representatives of lineages to which Solsol lineage owed pigs, and several men and women whose lineages assumed new debts to Solsol lineage.

Bot ("dance around the slit gong")

Bot (Tok Pisin; *bel* in Tangga) refers to the night-time revelry that celebrates the roofing of the men's house and preludes the first feast convened therein (*en bala'm bia*). The distinctive feature of *bot* performances, common throughout New Ireland, is the "promenade about the sounding *garamut* [slit gong/*gamti*] by radial lines of slow stepping singers" (Wagner 1986a:202). In Tanga, these lines comprise four or five individuals, usually of the same gender, who shuffle step counterclockwise around a slit gong beaten by some man skilled in the art. *Bot* occur almost always on the night preceding *en bala'm bia* and also on the night preceding the final feast of the *pok bif* sequence; they last until dawn. In some instances, *bot* performances take place each of several nights running before a feast, growing in size and intensity as the feast day draws nearer. The songs sung on such occasions contain words not only in Tangga, but in the languages of Lihir, Siar, and in Tok Pisin. Singers rarely claim to know (*parfat*) the meaning of the words, at least in the sense that they can offer translations. But almost all men, women, and children understand (*onge*, "hear") the lyrics in the sense that they can sing them with stylish fervor and exuberant appreciation.[34]

On the night prior to a feast, men and women from the host lineage seek out individuals who either contributed or were given pigs at *fasuigk*. Spotting their quarry in the procession around the slit gong, they slap burning flares to unsuspecting heads. Standard refrains narrate the action: "Tonight we cook you, tomorrow we cook your pigs" or "Tonight we smell your hair burning, tomorrow we smell the [singed] hair of your pigs." Frequently, the field of potential targets expands to include the lineage mates, then relatives of pig contributors and recipients until, eventually, the hosts themselves suffer harassment from stray flares wielded by mischievous old women. In the shadows of such agitation, male informants claimed, various guests make assignations for sexual encounters. Reportedly, sexual restrictions loosen temporarily in keeping with the overall boisterousness of the night.

The songs sung at the *bot* for the Solsol men's house illustrate an important aspect of "finishing" the dead. They were not taken from the standard repertoire (known generally by all adult men and women), but rather a set of compositions especially selected for the occasion. Weeks prior to the *bot*, Partui had convened members and certain affiliates of Solsol lineage in order that a senior Solsol woman might instruct them in singing. The songs to be learned were originally sung by Tangan men, including a deceased Solsol leader (Nerau), who worked for the Australian colonial government as crewmen in the 1920s. These men travelled not only throughout the Mandated Trust Territory of New Guinea, but also to Sydney. The songs, composed in a typical pastiche of Tangan, Tok Pisin, English, and unidentifiable New Ireland languages, record the adventures of these men in their travels. This particular song alludes to romantic contests waged by means of love magic (*pupulu, malera*):

My work is hot from *pupulu*.
My work is hot from *malera*.
I challenged the Tangan boys, *malera* in Rabaul.
A short man challenged me with *malera*.
I heard my heart pound like a machine last night.

Another song features Nerau, whom Tangans remember as having starred in a soccer game played against Australian naval personnel at Balmain in Sydney:

I'm on the road at Balmain
Eeee anaoi mari i anoi mari
Indurung sorry friends at Balmain
Cheers at Kokotu
The people ui usot mariou
Nerau was number one at playing ball at Balmain

A similar song pictures Nerau as a skillful navigator, while a companion piece recalls the seasickness of Nesik, a long deceased clan Korofi man from An Siko lineage:

My mates, sorry my friend, have lost me.
Nesik vomited at the helm.
What the hell, me alone at the wheel.
Hey brothers, so what if I'm green [inexperienced].
I'll try to steer the ship close to the lighthouse at Townsville.

Together, these songs enhanced the commemorative quality of *pok bif* while simultaneously creating the playful atmosphere of *bot*, an atmosphere congruent with the playfulness of the images evoked by the songs. Overall, the Solsol *bot* exemplified well the sense in which the sadness and worry (*sangkulung*) of the immediate rites of death gradually give way to the relative levity and happiness (*laes*) of *pok bif*. These particular songs, moreover, illustrate the way in which feast organizers bend the flexible conventions of *pok bif* – in this case, the standard performance of *bot* – into highly innovative and distinctive shapes.

The manner in which Solsol men and women learned the *bot* songs amounted to no less than the flip side of my experience in seeking to transcribe the songs (see footnote 34). Tingkarangis, the senior Solsol woman who alone could sing the songs "from memory," sang them over and over for the assembled group. Gradually, individuals joined in for a phrase or two, hesitantly marrying their voices to that of hers. As the evening sessions progressed, more individuals joined their voices in more places until everyone sang all of the phrases. In effect, individuals imitated with their voices the sounds that Tingkarangis made. No one seemingly memorized the words of the songs, which informants were unable to reproduce outside the context of singing. Rather, individuals initially mimicked Tingkarangis, adjusting their voices to fit the template she projected. Thereafter, the ensemble relied upon their own collective efforts to realize the songs in speech; in order to generate the songs it was necessary to recreate the context of collective singing. As with so much of Tangan social life, "practical mastery is transmitted in practice, in its practical state, without attaining the level of discourse" (Bourdieu 1977:87). The process of transmission, then, is one of "example and imitation," a mimetic procedure completely consistent with the predominantly non-verbal character of communications that constitute the *pok bif* sequence.[35]

Songs, stories, dances, and other performances (including the rites of secret societies) do not survive their realizations in practice as photographs, texts or other objectified forms. They lead precarious existences that require periodic realizations for survival; that is, practice alone realizes them in any apprehensible form. Likewise, the memories (*sangfi*) of the dead commemorated in song require periodic objective realization for their survival. *Pok bif finally* realizes or "finishes" the memories of their MBs and MBMBs held by the senior members of host lineages. That is, *pok bif* formally "finishes" the memories of those MBs and MBMBs as lineage members to whom current lineage members are beholden. At the same time, this senior generation's performance of *pok bif* presents a practical model against which, in time, junior generations of ZSs and ZSZSs will measure their efforts to "finish" memories of newly deceased MBs and MBMBs. The realization of *pok bif* hence entails the imitative procedures that ensure its future existence. Realization is simultaneously inculcation.

En bala'm bia ("feast inside of the men's house")
En bala'm bia is the first "feast" (*en*, as opposed to *mor* or some combination of the two) held inside the newly thatched men's house. All of the

pigs distributed at *fasuigk* are cooked for distribution along with the vegetable food taken in at *so puek* and supplied by the host lineage. (Recipients
of pigs at *fasuigk* are responsible only for cooking their pigs.) The vegetable food served at the feast is prepared by women of the host lineage,
wives of lineage men, and other female supporters; women invariably take
charge of all aspects of cooking root crops.[36] The women frequently inter-
rupt their chore with bouts of horseplay. They dump baskets or hurl hand-
fuls of peelings at a variety of people, including the members, children,
and even toddling grandchildren of the host lineage and anyone contributing or receiving a pig at the feast. As at almost all Tangan feasts, hours of
preparation precipitate an event that often requires less than thirty
minutes to run its course. Guests enter the site close to the time that the
dramatic *am furis* begins, often lingering on the way to a feast to synchron-
ize their arrival precisely. After the main event of the feast, the prestation
of shell wealth called *lulu am bo* (see below), the guests await only the frenzied distribution of food. Because *en bala'm bia* is never an "eat everything" affair, guests ordinarily conserve their portions for taking away.
Having sat through a perfunctory prayer, the obligatory "first bite"
presentation, and a polite period of waiting capped by a round of *mai*
chants, the gathering disperses almost as quickly as it coalesced.

Plate 8   The late Manilbau, seated, watches as shell valuables are laid at the
feet of his ZS, Negat, during *lulu am bo* at Bulam, 1984

The *am furis* on this occasion invariably involves a male representative of the host lineage, decorated with lineage heirlooms, climbing to the roof of the men's house and walking across the ridgepole. This role usually falls to one or more of the actual ZS or ZSZS of the deceased man or men being "finished." As he moves slowly forward, a chorus of lineage men (sometimes women, sometimes men and women of paternally related lineages) sings on the ground below, occasionally pausing to speak with the boy or man on the roof. (The image enacted in this performance is perhaps the most potent and compelling effect of mortuary rites; its meaning will be explored more fully in subsequent chapters.)

Immediately upon descending, the man or boy receives *lulu am bo* (plate 8). *Lulu am bo* ("*baim pik*" in Tok Pisin) is the counterpart of *fasuigk*. Those who received broom bristles (*sinaf*) at *fasuigk* come forth to make a prestation for the pigs which were redistributed to them. Men or women individually and separately approach the person receiving *lulu*, who often sits on an upturned slit gong, holding their prestation above their heads for all to see (cf. the photo in Bell 1935d:100). The prestation – ideally shell discs, less ideally, cash – is placed at the feet of the seated recipient. The separate prestations accumulate until, when no more donors come forth, the recipient quietly collects the total *lulu* and carries it off.

Generally, the recipient of a small to mid-size pig presents a single disc; sometimes a two-kina note will be offered instead, although hosts may announce at *fasuigk* that they will not accept cash in lieu of shell discs. Larger pigs may require a proportionately larger payment, with the largest pigs sometimes entailing payments of five discs, one strand of smaller strung discs and a small amount of cash (5 or 10 kina) "on top." In such cases, an individual will stand before the seated man and remove the shells from his basket, placing them carefully on the ground one by one. *Lulu am bo* occurs without commentary or speeches made by either hosts or guests; assembled onlookers look on, silently noting the size and manner of payments made.[37] The intense yet guarded interest taken on the part of the spectators underlines the significance of *lulu* which, I will later suggest, models in its form the core meanings of mortuary feasting.

The completion of *lulu* entrains the slapdash work of distributing the food to the assembled multitude (large feasts may attract several hundred guests). Invited men enter the men's house while various lineage members and affiliates disassemble the food display (*gus*) for apportionment. The pigs are carried out to the front of the men's house where their various recipients supervise the carving and distribution of pork pieces. Pieces of pigs received by women are normally distributed to women, but men alone carve the pig and in general men determine to whom the pieces will be presented.

At the Solsol *en bala'm bia*, the *warangus* baskets were exhibited at this point in the proceedings. Six baskets were revealed, that is, three more men were identified as recipients of large pigs to be distributed at the final feast (*arer sigit*). The size of the baskets and the share of the food each contained were also larger than on previous occasions. Thus, coordinate with the architectural progress of the men's house, the hosts of the Solsol *pok bif* further constructed the yet to be realized image of the "final feast." Through the exhibition of *warangus* baskets, moreover, the hosts imagined not only the size and scale of future pig distributions, but also the expanding network of support underpinning their efforts. In this sense, as I will also suggest later, the construction of a men's house becomes the means for explicating or making visible the structure and function of socially reproductive relationships.

The sequence of events leading up to the final feast, like the *pok bif* sequence as a whole, varies in timing and elaboration. Several tasks necessary to complete the physical structure of the men's house remain after *en bala'm bia*. For example, a ridge sheet (*pungin*) made from the leaves of Cycas palms (*am bebe*) must be laid over the ridgepoles, and the end wall panels must be fastened and perhaps decorated with painted designs. These tasks are carried out according to no fixed schedule; they may or may not require collective work teams and collective feasting.

As part of their preparations, host lineage leaders usually commission dance performances (*binian*; *singsing* in Tok Pisin) from other lineage leaders to be performed at *arer sigit*.[38] Acceptance of such a commission obligates the host lineage to furnish likewise a dance performance at future feasts of other lineages. The procedure described to me for publicly making these arrangements involves the presentation of Cordyline leaves by a man of the host lineage to the man from whose lineage the *singsing* is requested. This procedure did not occur at the Solsol *en bala'm bia*, though several informants mentioned this feast as the appropriate time for presenting *tanget*. Partui, when queried, assured me that the prestation would occur at the time of *saf bala'm bia*.

Saf bala'm bia ("to sweep the inside of the men's house")

Saf bala'm bia refers, according to Bell, to a rite in which the female relatives of the deceased clean the inside of the funeral house. During my own fieldwork, I witnessed no feast or any such rite that bore the name.

One informant explained *saf bala'm bia* as an occasion that marks the completion of all construction work; hence, the site has been swept clean of all remaining debris. After *saf bala'm bia*, the food for distribution at the final feast is brought inside the men's house (*fakale gus*). *Fakale gus* often lasts for several weeks prior to the final feast as workers load the harvest of various gardens made for *pok bif* into the men's house.

Throughout, the hosts keep track of the amount of food by a special system of accounting (see Foster 1988 for a description of this system). Baskets of tubers are brought into the men's house and their contents added to a mound (*gus*) that slowly grows around the ridge post(s). A running total of tubers gives feast organizers an idea of their resources, but in no precise way, despite the fact that the total indicates a precise number of tubers. That is, feast organizers do not calculate, for example, the number of tubers per guest. Instead, on the basis of past experience, organizers can assess the adequacy of their food resources. Similarly, numerical units provide standard measurements of support. Partui once mentioned that he expected one *atis* (800 *mami* or 200 yams [*buk* or *sinam*]) from each of the supporters who had undertaken to make gardens for the Solsol *pok bif*. At large feasts, ten *atis* (*pali n'atis*) of tubers may be distributed. In a letter in which he described the final feast for the Solsol men's house, Partui claimed that the food display added up to *"olsem 1000 over"* (approximately more than 10 *atis*) and measured "four feet high, five feet wide and twelve feet long," rising to the neck of the life-sized figure carved into the central ridge post. While this amount of food might be characterized as exceptionally large, displays composed of five to ten *atis* are common.

Arer sigit ("final inspection" or "last look")
Arer sigit reproduces essentially the same pattern of activities as *en bala'm bia*.[39] Like *en bala'm bia*, *arer sigit* proceeds the preparation of *mangat*, the distribution of pigs at *fasuigk* and at least one night given over to the conviviality of *bot*. During the *am furis*, the ZS or ZSZS of the deceased walks across the ridgepole of the men's house, decorated with some of the lineage's shell heirlooms (in the past, the ZS carried with him the skull of a deceased MB). Wealth prestations (*lulu am bo*) – substantially larger in proportion to the scale of the feast – also focus the attention of guests.

At the final feast, each recipient of a *warangus* basket donates a pig as large as the one that he himself receives from the host lineage. These large pigs are referred to with the phrase "I come inside to eat my pig" (*uflek usi ak bo*). In addition, *warangus* recipients contribute a smaller pig that the host lineage adds to the supply of pigs distributed at *fasuigk*. These smaller pigs are referred to with the figurative phrases "plant the leg pig" (*so kekem bo*), "organ meat and leafy green mixture of the pig" (*mida na bo*), and "I help you/indebt you" (*an sue o*). These smaller pigs are regarded as extra assistance rendered to the host lineage; the smaller pig is represented as accompanying support for the larger pig. So, for example, a father who gives a pig to his son to present along with the son's own pig to the son's enates might say "I plant my leg your pig" (*a so kekeng keo bo*).

Other minor elaborations enlarge the scale of the festivities. For example, a specially constructed three-sided enclosure (*raut*) made by standing four-foot lengths of bamboo side by side accommodated a large percentage of the female guests at one feast. More generally, the use of a specially decorated ladder (*an sup*) instead of a plain length of bamboo (*an tumal*) for ascending to the roof visually marks the completion of the men's house. *An sup* often take the form of long, festooned poles of bamboo, the thin tapered end of which, weighted with free hanging-flowers or ornaments, droops languorously over the roof of the men's house.[40]

Only at *arer sigit*, however, do line dances (*binian*) provide a third focus for attention for guests.[41] Men often used the Tok Pisin phrase "*lukluk singsing*" ("to watch the dancing") as shorthand for *arer sigit*, as in the sentence: "Around Christmas we will hold *arer sigit*/watch the dances at Seber."[42] The sentence not only indicates the date of *arer sigit*, but also asserts the image-oriented nature of the dances which, rehearsed for weeks in secrecy, are fully revealed (*fanangsio*) only at the final feast.

At the final feast for a small funeral house or *fel* at Warankeng, the dance group remained secluded during the feast preparations. Small whooping sounds intermittently emanated from the nearby bush and punctuated the gurgle of noise in the hamlet. When all the food and cooked pigs had been placed inside the *fel* and the guests had seated themselves, the main organizer of the feast impatiently pounded a slit gong to summon the dancers. At last the group approached, preceded by the sound of throbbing hourglass drums (*kundu*). Forty decorated men and boys paraded into the hamlet singing. The aroma of their heavily perfumed bodies immediately suffused the air. Several members of the group let forth puffs of smoke from their mouths, though no source (e.g., a concealed cigarette) was apparent.[43] Aligned in four columns, ten deep, the group arrayed and displayed itself in front of the new *fel* before beginning its performance.[44] The capacity of the dance group to engage the attention and admiration of the guests extends the capacity of the feast organizers to construct and realize an image for public consumption. In effect, the premiere of the dancers signifies the final revelation of the prefigured feast; the dance performance typifies the more general process of revelation. The hold that a proficient line dance exerts over the eyes, ears, and noses of the guests engenders in immediate sensuous experience the acknowledgment by the guests of the realized intentions of the hosts.

For the hosts, a successful final feast means well-crafted skits, vibrant line dances that incite envy (*balfaun*), and, above all, overabundance of food. Partui wrote in a letter to me of the final feast Solsol lineage hosted after I had left Tanga:

Food rotted in the hamlet. People threw away pieces of pork. Only the dogs ate them. Food went bad. Neamut collected bits of food and fed them to his pigs.

On one level, the statement reflects the status competition entailed in hosting feasts. On a deeper level, however, the description – however stereotyped – intimates transcendence, not only of the more palpable physical demands of hunger, but also of the less sensible constraints of time. *Arer sigit* finally realizes the visions and images projected over years of planning. Unlike the prefiguring signs of *warangus* baskets and "promissory" men's houses, the realized *final* (*sigit*) feast alludes to no additional future revelation. In this sense, the very realization of the feast measures its own success. "Simultaneity-along-time" (Anderson 1983) – the almost millennial collapse into the present of the future anticipated in the past – is achieved. The event condenses the past while temporarily transcending future constraints, to wit, the future deaths that ineluctably will necessitate resuming the sequence.

Finishing the dead

Arer sigit marks the completion of the men's house and climaxes, but does not conclude, the mortuary sequence. Bell (1937:329) identified in his table of funeral ceremonies two rites of "final disposal" which followed a complete repetition "on a less pretentious scale" of all the feasts and *mor* from *fapang mor* to *arer sigit*. The first rite, held after the second *arel sigit* (itself held three to four years after the first *arel sigit*), involved "a small feast of close relatives which accompanies the removal of the skull from the funeral house and its burial at the base of a taboo coconut palm" (Bell 1937:329). Schlaginhaufen's (1908) account of his brief visit to Boang suggests that the skull itself mattered much less than the feasts for finishing the dead. A local leader gladly presented Schlaginhaufen with a skull at the latter's request, but only one, on the grounds that the others required further feasting.

The second rite, *en tura'n iu n'kinit* ("feast concerning the spear of the deceased"), might "not occur for twenty years after the death of the person commemorated, but ... it is an essential part of the funeral ceremonies" (Bell 1937:329). Finishing the dead means not only disposing of the deceased's physical remains but also of his or her personal possessions. At *en tura'n iu* not only the spear but any other personal effects of the deceased – baskets, lime gourds, clubs – were burned.

The procedure reported by Bell of repeating the house-building segment of *pok bif* corresponds to the practice in 1984 of first building a "temporary" men's house and then constructing a "true" *bia* or *bif*. In the contemporary sequence, however, the scale of feasts increases rather than diminishes. The feast for reinterring the skull of the deceased no longer takes place nor does the practice of secondary burial. *En tura'n iu*, however, was reported in 1984 still to occur. The rafters of men's houses frequently contained a variety of personal effects of deceased lineage members, male and female, including purses (*tang*) blackened with age, bamboo pillows, sleeping beds, and walking sticks. At special feasts, these items might be burned or buried, thus eradicating the last material remnants of the deceased.

Given the cyclical nature of *pok bif*, occasions such as *en tura'n iu* may be thought of not only as postscripts to particular sequences but also as steps in a perpetually ongoing process. Such acts of finishing, which now include placing cement markers on graves, undoubtedly occur in the context of renewed cycles of men's house construction. For example, the graves of long-buried members of Solsol lineage were cemented in connection with building the temporary men's house that initiated the Solsol *pok bif*. Similarly, finishing the dead refers not merely to the physical destruction of the deceased's body and personal artifacts, but also to the memories that the living sustain of their dead. *Pok bif* provides a lineage with the means of controlling and regulating the process of forgetting (*sangkifeni*). The burdensome grief of the initial rites of death and burial, stimulated by a profusion of visible reminders, becomes progressively diminished as the *pok bif* sequence dissolves and makes invisible the image of death. At *morapup*, the corpse itself disappears; at subsequent feasts mourning taboos are abrogated and their visible tokens (*an asem* bands, black paint, etc.) are destroyed; at later feasts the last possessions of the deceased are destroyed. The progress is from memory to forgetting as the material substratum of memory slowly erodes.[45] As Munn says of Gawan

mortuary rites, they "involve the creation of a temporary memoriali-
zation so that, paradoxically, forgetting can be generated" (1986:166).

I suggest that Tangans regard these memories as being in any event
predestined to fade and perish along with their carriers. There is an
inevitability to forgetting, poignantly captured in one particular song
(*goigoi*):

Ohhhhhh me here, I'm going.
Ohhh me, I'm going.
Who will talk with me at this place?

My mother's brother/sister's son has died.
Has left me.
I'm going to forget him.

I'm going to forget him.
Great sorrow.
Siangu has died.
He will not confer with us about tomorrow's *kastam*.

It is control over, not the elimination of, this process of forgetting that is
crucial; forgetting must be made "official" (Battaglia 1990). Remembrance through *pok bif* incites another generation of Tangans to continue
the work of *kastam*. The realization of *pok bif* is its inculcation; the
fulfilment of *pok bif* is its prefigurement, and thus simultaneity extended
indefinitely. The rhythms of remembering and forgetting in this way
underpin the seemingly paradoxical combination of commemoration and
oblivion that constitutes Tangan mortuary rites.

5

Replacing the dead: identical exchange and lineage succession

Anthropological understanding has long accorded mortuary rites an instrumental role in the regeneration of life, the restoration of threatened social relations, the renewal of a generalized fecundity – in short, the reproduction of society (see Huntington and Metcalf 1979; Bloch and Parry 1982). Death, so the argument goes, quite tangibly challenges the permanence and integrity of the collectivity. Mortuary rites respond with a reallocation of the roles of the deceased which effectively reconstitutes the social order. As in any rite of passage, reintegration or rebirth follows the disintegration of death. Bloch and Parry summarize this position, strongly identified with Hertz and Van Gennep: "The rebirth which occurs at death is not only a denial of individual extinction, but also a reassertion of society and a renewal of life and creative power ..." (1982:5). Mortuary rites thus practically and inextricably relate death and social reproduction: the denial of contingent individual extinction comes about through the affirmation of timeless group continuity, that is, of the group's capacity to replenish its membership.

This essentially Durkheimian view suits well the image of lineage succession projected in Tangan mortuary rites: the ZS "replaces" a deceased MB. But it would be doubly wrong, I suggest, to attribute to Tangans a corresponding conception of "the social order" in which it is the survival of the collectivity or group *against* that of the individual that is regarded as problematic. For if Tangans can be at all said to represent "the social order" to themselves, then it would be in the form of relations that mediate the exchange of nurture (*fang*). The "problem of order," in this view, is one of activating these exchange relations over time (see Foster 1990a). A Durkheimian view of society, moreover, would posit death, in its association with individual physiological processes, as dis-

140

tinctively opposed to and even destructive of the collectivity. For Tangans, by contrast, I suggest that death is the reciprocal condition of human reproductive capacity, not external to human sociality but inevitably constitutive of it.[1] Indeed, the following myth depicts how death and sociality originated in each other.[2]

A middle-aged woman was clearing a garden patch when she caught her finger on a sharp piece of scrub and slit it so that it bled profusely. Shortly after this accident, rain began to fall, and the woman took shelter beneath a large *tau* tree. The blood from her finger dripped into a pool of water at the base of the *tau*, and, as it coagulated, formed a little red snake, known to the natives as *bumnafukfuk*. When the rain stopped, the woman went to her home.

The next day she returned, and on looking into the pool, she saw a small iguana (*gerem*). On the day following she paid another visit to the pool and in place of the *gerem* she found a brown frog (*gung*). The next day she visited the pool again and, lo and behold, two very small boys had taken the place of the *gung*. The woman did not take the children from the pool, but visited them from day to day. The boys grew rapidly, until at length, one morning, they spoke to the woman. However, not until they could walk did she take them out of the pool and bring them to her house. She fed and cared for them as if they were her own children, and the boys called her *tibung*, i.e., grandmother [MM]. It was not long before they were strong enough to help her with the work in the garden.

However, the day soon came when she could no longer accompany the boys to the garden, and she told them that she was going away. She warned them not to be surprised if they met a young woman on their return to the house. This young woman must be addressed as *tibung*, i.e., grandmother, and under no circumstances as *kek wok*, i.e., "my woman" or "wife."

When the boys returned home from their work in the garden, they saw a young woman coming towards the house. The bigger of the two boys – an adolescent – immediately forgot his grandmother's warning and called out to the girl, "*kek wok*," whilst the smaller lad – a pre-adolescent – called out, as his grandmother had told him, "*tibung*." The woman immediately began to upbraid the bigger of the two boys, explaining that she was really his aged "grandmother," who had sloughed her skin and cast it over the cliffs near Trewon [Tiriwan], a village on the south-east coast of Boieng [Boang]. If the boy had only heeded her warning, she, in company with all men, would have had the gift of eternal youth, but since he had disregarded her instructions, she and the rest of humanity were destined to suffer old age and death.

The woman then returned to the cliffs near Trewon, and retrieved her old skin, which had caught on a tree growing beneath the cliff. She tottered back to her house, and again upbraided the bigger boy for his conduct towards her.

The myth distinguishes between two methods of renewing life, asexual and sexual, the second of which supplants the first. Originally, people regenerated themselves by changing skins, a process involving no intercession – sexual or otherwise – on the part of others. Similarly, the two boys originate as the product of an accidental conjunction between the woman's blood and rainwater. Procreation is in this instance also overtly asexual.[3] Accordingly, the old woman and the boys live as grandmother and grandsons. Their particular relationship is signalled by the kin term that the boys use to address the woman; *tibung*, in Tangan terminology, designates "my mother's mother" but *not* "my father's mother" (*fengong*). The three comprise not a conjugal unit, but a kind of primordial and autonomous matrilineage.

This state of pure matriliny ends with the sexual advances of the precocious grandson. When the old grandmother returns as a presumably nubile young woman, the grandson greets her as "my wife" (*kek wok*). That is, the grandson transforms an enate into an affine, someone related by blood into someone related by marriage. The consequence of this action is twofold. First, the undifferentiated kin unit becomes differentiated, socially as well as sexually; the boy confronts the young woman as someone with a different matrilineal identity. Secondly, sexual reproduction replaces asexual regeneration; sexual intercourse between socially differentiated people supersedes individual skin changes as the means of continuous vitality. Because of the sexual precociousness of the grandson, the grandmother becomes mortal and dies. Because of the death of the grandmother, sexual reproduction becomes the method of attaining rebirth and sustaining life. Death and sex logically entail each other. The origin of death is the end of autoreproduction. But it is also the origin of sexuality and social differentiation, in short, the origin of human sociality – interdependence and relationality.

The Tangan myth of death suggests that affinal relations between lineages constitute the source of human reproduction. But this is not reflected in any simple way in Tangan ritual practice. As elsewhere in New Ireland, marriage does not circumscribe a discrete cultural focus marked by complex ceremony (cf. Clay 1977:105). Rather, mortuary rites provide the context in which reproductive concerns receive their most extended public attention. Indeed, by organizing a sequence of mortuary feasts, a matrilineage is said to "replace" as well as to "finish" its deceased members. (As I will subsequently make clearer, it is specifically the reproduction of matrilineages – collective individuals – and not individual human beings which is at stake in Tangan mortuary rites.) That is, mortuary ritual makes the lineage appear as an autoreproductive unit. Perhaps, then, the old grandmother's habit of asexual regeneration – and along with it, the conceit of an autonomous matriline – has not been entirely extinguished?

Yes, and no. Yes in the sense that an image of lineage autonomy and autoreproductivity is projected and enacted in mortuary feasting; no, in the sense that the very construction of this image implies the dependency of a lineage on the support of others, specifically, the support of a lineage's affinal/paternal relatives or *kinaf*. In other words, people related to each other as *kinaf* take turns or alternate in publicly constructing each other as lineages endowed with the capacity to effect their own succession (cf. Clay 1992). Mortuary feasting thus hinges on a paradox, the paradox of mutually constructed autonomy. It is this paradox, I argue, that lies at the core of the reproductive process accomplished in Tangan mortuary rites – the process that Tangans gloss as "replacement" – whereby living lineage members succeed or "take the place" (*kep tafu*) of deceased members.

I argue that through the performance of mortuary rites, a lineage periodically "changes its skin." By sponsoring a sequence of mortuary feasts and building a new men's house, lineages acquire a kind of continuity that derives not from bodily (sexual) reproduction, but from the capacity to convert consumables (cooked food and pigs) into durables (shell discs). Through such conversions, objectified in the central exchanges of the feast sequence, feast makers define themselves as permanent collective individuals (or matrilineages) and effective agents of their own regeneration. In other words, the *kinaf* relations that enable sexual reproduction and define the lineage as externally related are eclipsed by (or turned into) the collective uniformity of enatic relations (see M. Strathern 1988:257, 260). Mortuary feasting thus unfolds as the occasion for single lineages rather than related lineages to act visibly as the autonomous agents of reproduction – to act like the grandmother in the myth.

Nevertheless, this process is effected by exchanges themselves conceived of and organized as cooperative processes of "replacement." That is, the ideal structure of long-term exchange sequences is one in which two transacting units (lineages), related as *fat kinaf* ("bound cross-cousins"), alternately transfer identical amounts of resources (pigs, shell discs, paternal nurture) between each other. In the act of exchange, one lineage replaces resources previously received from the other lineage while committing the recipient lineage to replace these resources again in the future. It is such long-term transfers that alternately realize for the lineages involved the "self-replacement" of deceased members by structurally identical lineage counterparts. In their feasting activities and endeavors, lineages related as *kinaf* each serve as the "supportive witness" (Clay

1992:726) to the other's display of autonomy. Mortuary feasting is thus grounded in the interdependence and relationality that its imagery eclipses.

I begin this chapter with an attempt to formulate a specifically Tangan understanding of the exchanges associated with mortuary feasting. This involves articulating, as far as lexical analysis allows, a Tangan conception of identical exchange – the exchange of replicas, objects identical in several specifiable respects. I further define this conception of identical exchange by demonstrating how it organizes both the performance of mortuary rites and the *kinaf* relationship between intermarrying lineages. This latter endeavor necessarily resumes and revises the account of Tangan sociality presented in chapter 3; my immediate aim is to treat identical exchange as the framework of long-term lineage succession. In the next two chapters, I focus on the way in which an image of lineage succession is projected and enacted in the major feasts and exchanges that comprise any one instance of the mortuary sequence.

Exchange vocabulary: *senis* or "(ex)change"

Tangans use a variety of words to describe a variety of acts of exchange and categorically gloss many of these acts not with a Tangan word but with the Tok Pisin word *senis*.[4] The semantic domain of "*senis*" covers not only acts of exchange, but also the very process of change therein implied. That is, *senis* connotes both "change" and "exchange"; it reduces easily to neither connotation alone.[5] "*Senis*" frequently crops up in discussions of the kinds of changes which have occurred in Tanga over the last century (*ol kain senis i kamap*/"the various changes which have occurred"). Indeed, Tangans regularly use the word *senis* to talk about historical change in favor of constructions available in the Tangan language.[6] In this sense, "*senis*" primarily connotes transformation in outward appearance; for example, the word describes transformations in personal "looks" (*lukluk bilong en i senis pinis*/"his appearance has changed"). Somewhat related is the usage of "*senis*" familiar to American English speakers in asking for "change" of a dollar, that is, changing the form of a dollar from that of paper to coin.

Tangans also employ "*senis*" to describe a variety of exchange acts, including acts in which the principal connotation is one of substitution rather than transformation. Thus, for example, at *fasuigk*, the host who redistributes a pig to a man who contributed a pig "exchanges the pig" (*senisim pik/bili bo*) of the original donor with another pig of the same size or slightly larger. Likewise, a man who substitutes for another man at some task because of the latter's fatigue "(ex)changes" that man.

In these last two examples the emphasis of *"senis"* falls not so much on the equivalence of the two terms of the exchange, which for Tangans is axiomatic, but on the actual occurrence of the exchange. If one performs *bili bo* and exchanges a pig at the *fasuigk* distribution, it is taken for granted that the pigs exchanged will be of roughly identical size. By contrast, the other usages of *"senis"* stress the difference between the before and after status of the two terms of the change, that is, their formal non-identity (e.g., appearance before and appearance after). The distinction here between substitution and transformation, muted or masked by the Tok Pisin gloss of *senis*, emerges more sharply through an examination of Tangga words for exchange acts. Such an examination leads, I suggest, to the conclusion that notions of both substitution and transformation inform Tangan conceptions of ceremonial exchanges. However, I suggest that substitutive exchange acts, in which the identity and hence equivalence of the two terms related is taken axiomatically, illustrate the dominant or culturally privileged definition of Tangan exchange. With equivalence regarded as axiomatic, then, only the realization of the (ex)change remains problematic for Tangans. Such a definition inverts one prevalent anthropological understanding of exchange which, with its abiding concern for measuring reciprocity, takes the matter of equivalence as problematic rather than axiomatic, as the variable and therefore sociologically interesting aspect of exchange (see, for example, Sahlins 1972). Whereas such a concern is appropriate to the understanding of transformative exchanges, its usefulness in analyzing substitutive or identical exchange is limited.

Exchange vocabulary: *fil* and *kos* – "buy" and "repay"
Perhaps the paradigmatic act of transformative exchange for Tangans is barter (*fapik*). The word *fapik* describes the practice, rarely if ever engaged nowadays, of journeying to another district of the island(s) to barter local specialities. In the past, informants claimed, people from Taonsip would travel to Fonli to barter (*fapik*) mature coconuts for leafy greens (*tulip* [Gnetum gnemon]). Informants invariably stressed that *fapik* occurred in the times before Tangans used currency and that direct unmediated exchange epitomized *fapik*. One informant, moreover, pointed out that on some journeys an individual offering coconuts, for example, might depart with no advance idea of what form his or her barter would assume. In this respect, the informant likened *fapik* to shopping at a tradestore. The man said that he might know his wife to have some money and to intend to go to the store, but he cannot know

precisely what his wife might buy at the store. Similar transformative connotations of the word *fapik*, shorn of its causative prefix (*fa-*), inhere in the description of a person's radical change in appearance (e.g., as a result of illness): *par lo i sam la pik sigit* ("his appearance has gone [*la*] different [*pik*] altogether"). And, as in pidgin, the idea of historical change (*tel pik*) is conveyed with the same word, *pik*, used to indicate barter (*fapik*), a kind of exchange.

Tangans describe other acts of giving and taking that entail transformation with the word *fil*, the Tok Pisin gloss of which is not "*senis*" but "*baim*" ("to buy"). Transformation in these contexts also implies the act of exchanging one thing for a thing of another kind. *Fil fifin* ("to buy a young woman"), for example, denotes the payment that a groom's MB or F makes for a wife. The transaction involves, in part, the transfer of shell wealth and cash to the bride's parents and the reciprocal transfer of a woman to the household of her husband. Tangans regard the transactions as a payment for nurture (*fang*), and not for the woman *per se* (or her "fertility"), inasmuch as the woman is the product of her parent's nurture and "hard work." Thus payment goes to the bride's parents and not to her lineage alone.[7]

Similarly, *fil mal* ("to buy the barkcloth") denotes a payment most usually made from children to their father to acknowledge his care for and nurture of them. As in marriage payments, pigs, shell valuables, and cash constitute one term in an exchange in which the opposite term, "nurture" (*fang*), is of another species. *Fil* likewise does duty as the Tangan word describing cash transactions at a tradestore or indeed any cash transaction, such as paying taxes. Thus, the linking together of barter (*fapik*) and shopping in the informant's statement referred to above was not entirely fortuitous; both varieties of exchange are characterized by a transformation, perhaps unpredictable, in exchange objects.

The word *fil*, however, often implies more than simply a formal difference between the objects of an exchange. In effect, *fil* highlights the agency of "the buyer" as the instigator of the action, thereby suggesting an asymmetry generally absent from other exchanges (such as barter). The word also implies the construction of social relations in terms of debts and credits. In organizing support for mortuary rites, for example, a lineage leader "buys a leader" (*fil taufi*) by presenting a large cooked pig to another man, lineage mate or otherwise, who pledges assistance by raising a pig or pigs for the donor's upcoming feasts. The presentation of *fil taufi* obligates the recipient to work for the donor, thus temporarily making him an instrument and witness of the donor's agency.[8] Similarly, the assertiveness associated with "buying" (and hence *bisnis*) might be appropriated by a host lineage for metaphorical use in the context of recognizing mourning taboos. In one case, the brother of the deceased man referred to his brother's widow and her children, who assumed mourning taboos, as "workers" whom he was employing and whom he would pay a "fortnight" (salary) when the taboos were abrogated. Here, as in general, the affines temporarily acquiesced to the control of the deceased's enates, who ultimately determined the time at which mourning restrictions were lifted. But in this case, the implicit subordination and hierarchy were exaggerated by the host lineage's rejection of any initial prestations by its affines at the time the latter assumed the taboos (see chapter 4).

Marriage payments (*fil fifin*), timed to occur often long after the marriage, also frequently prompt people to talk about relationships in terms of debts (*dinau*, the pidgin word that Tangans use). Relatives of the couple to whom such payments are due may grumble about how outstanding obligations diminish the lineage's pool of shell wealth. Yet, the situation is reversed once payment has been made; for a woman and her children by residing on the husband/father's land incur a debt for the nurture provided them by the fruits of that land. These debts may of course later be acknowledged (though not repaid in kind) at a *fil mal* prestation to the father. Significantly, this prestation is alternatively called *kos fang* ("to repay care").

If the word *fil* implies hierarchy by stressing the agency of the giver, then the word *kos* (*bekim* in Tok Pisin) affirms the mutual equality of exchange relationships accomplished by a return gift or "backing" of the initial payment. *Kos*, which can be understood variously as "reciprocate," "repay," or "reply" (as in conversation: *kos wer*/"to reciprocate speech"), ideally suggests the return of an exact likeness. For instance, the phrase *kos fang* suggests the return of care to an elderly parent by his or her mature children. In the phrase *kos bo*, the word denotes the return of a pig for a pig given previously. The return of an exact likeness indicated by the word *kos* connotes cooperative reciprocity rather than competitive equality. A lineage meeting pig debts owed to a rival lineage aggressively describes the successful discharge of its obligations as *paket bo* ("to kill the pig") rather than *kos bo* (see Bell 1947a:56).

More generally, then, the words *fil* and *kos* connote respectively assertion and autonomy, cooperation and mutuality.[9] *Kos* transactions that follow upon *fil* transactions retroactively neutralize the hierarchical potential of the latter; they encompass autonomous action within a mutual relationship.[10] *Fil* and *kos* thus potentially refer to different aspects of a more inclusive reproductive or regenerative process which Tangans sometimes call *pilis* or *kilis*, words which connote "replacement." Many exchanges glossed with the terms *fil* and *kos* can be regarded as aspects or moments of this more encompassing process of "replacement." Accordingly, I propose that this encompassing process rather than its distinctive moments is the proper object of analysis in the study of Tangan exchanges. It is through examination of this process as a whole, moreover, that one can apprehend the instrumentality of exchange in Tangan social reproduction.

Exchange vocabulary: *pilis/kilis* – "Replace"

Pilis/kilis can be translated as "replace," but the words have two distinct connotations. In certain contexts, the gloss of "exchange" for *pilis/kilis* adequately conveys the sense of Tangan usage: *Negut i kilis pul kiang im porot*/"Negut exchanged my dog for a chicken." The words *pilis/kilis* most certainly refer to exchanges, both transformative like barter and substitutive like exchanges of identical pigs. More commonly, however, the words evoke an idea slightly different than that of "exchange." Thus the already mentioned usage of *senis* to describe one worker substituting for another (Tok Pisin: *Sapos yu les long katim ol diwai bai mi senisim yu*) translates the Tangga, *Le fom u main na popok tenak a ku kilis o* ("When you tire from chopping wood I will replace you"). Similarly, one uses the word *kilis* in the following context: "The battery for the radio is dead. I want to replace this battery."/*Battery na radio i sam kasa. A bet kilis battery ge*.

In these last two examples, *kilis* does not describe an act of giving and taking, a delimitable set of movements in which two parties transfer either objects or subjects. Instead, *kilis* reverberates with the connotations of "succession," the non-reciprocal, unilateral process whereby something or someone takes the place of something or someone else. That is, *kilis* conveys a sense of replacement *without* conveying a sense of exchange. The use of *pilis* in perhaps its definitive context also conveys this particular sense of replacement. Tangan men refer to their younger brothers or sisters' sons as their "replacements" (*pilis*) who upon the death of the elders will "take their place" (*kep tafu*). In this sense, "replacement" denotes the unilateral process of change whereby each generation succeeds its immediate predecessor.

Pilis and *kilis* seemingly designate two cognate processes, only one of which can be satisfactorily translated by the word "exchange" understood as a mutual act of giving and taking. The other process, that of "succession," in principle denies or eclipses one of the definitive qualities of the exchange process, namely, reciprocity. Substituting one thing or person for another in this sense requires no consideration of a return, no *quid pro quo*. Thus, the Tangan concept signified by *pilis* cannot be summarized by or reduced to the familiar notion of reciprocal exchange. For while the Tangan concept embraces the notion of reciprocal exchange, it couples that notion with a discernibly different concept of non-reciprocal substitution or succession. In other words, the notion of "replacement," like mortuary rites themselves, condenses two contradictory connotations.

The Tangan vocabulary for transactions thus discloses a set of conceptions underpinned by two related oppositions: transformation versus substitution and reciprocal change (exchange) versus non-reciprocal change. Together the two oppositions yield a fourfold classification within which various acts signified by the Tangan words can be located (see table 12). Non-reciprocal transformative change defines historical and developmental change (*tel pik*), while reciprocal transformative change includes barter (*fapik*), as well as transactions specified by the word *fil*. Coordinately, non-reciprocal substitutive change defines unilateral replacement (as of dead batteries: *kilis*), while reciprocal substitutive change denotes the exchange of identities implicit in the word *kos*. This latter sort of exchange equally describes a situation in which two men alternately replace each other at some task (*ru fakilis*/"the two replace each other"; reciprocity is denoted by attaching the prefix *fa-* to the word *kilis*).

With specific regard to exchange, then, the critical distinction is that between substitution and transformation. Substitutive or identical exchange involves the reciprocal transfer of replicas, of like or identical objects, while transformative exchange involves the transfer of objects unlike in kind or appearance.[11] This distinction recalls Meillassoux's contrast between the exchange of *identical* goods and the exchange of *equivalent* goods (1981:50). In the former exchanges, goods can only be "*substituted for one another*" (1981:65).[12] Consequently, the temporal dimension of the transaction (namely, its delayed character) rather than variation in the volume or content of the items transacted assumes greater importance in identical exchange.

For the remainder of this chapter I focus on how identical exchanges give structure to both mortuary rites and the social relations between *kinaf* that make the performance of mortuary rites possible. In the next

Table 12. *Schematic description of Tangan vocabulary for "change" and "exchange"*

	Reciprocal (exchange)	Non-reciprocal (change)
Transformative	*Fapik* (barter) *Fil, ting* ("buy")	*Pik, tel pik* (historical change)
Substitutive or identical	*Fakilis/fapilis* (identical exchange) *Bili, kos* (*bekim* in Tok Pisin) (reciprocate)	*Pilis/kilis* (substitution or succession)

chapter, I focus on transformative exchange as epitomized in the central transaction of mortuary rites, the exchange of cooked pigs for shell wealth (*lulu am bo*).

Identical exchange: *pok bif* and the *kinaf* relationship

Many of the exchange acts that accompany mortuary feasting appear to be instances of transformative exchange. When pigs are delivered at a hamlet, the host lineage "buys" (*tinge*) the baskets of yams and other food items with money (10-toea coins); and later at *fasuigk*, the pigs contributed by various supporters are "bought" (*tinge* or *sage*) with shell discs (*tintol*). Similarly, at *lulu am bo*, pig recipients "buy" (*lulu*) their pigs with shell valuables and/or cash.

Each of these instances of "buying" involves the transformative exchange of unlike objects, pigs and shell valuables, for example. Tangans, however, do not regard single occurrences of *tinge* or *lulu* as complete transactions. That is, the complete transaction requires the parties to the exchange to reverse roles. For example, a man who makes *tinge* payments at *fasuigk* must, in the future, receive such payments for a pig that he contributes to a feast sponsored by the man who first received *tinge*. Likewise, a man who presents five shell discs, a length of *kemetas*, and ten kina for a large pig at *lulu am bo* expects that at a future feast of his own sponsorship, he will receive the identical payment for a large pig distributed to his (former) creditor.[13] Of course, the axiomatic nature of exchanging like objects or replicas fails in itself to guarantee the *realization* of any particular exchange. Ideally, however, every transaction that takes place in the context of mortuary feasting repeats *and* foreshadows an identical transaction. Transformative exchanges thus appear to be identical exchanges when viewed over the long run.[14]

The overall organization of mortuary feasting is one of identical exchange: flows of assistance, conceived of as identically measured, move between lineages, especially lineages related as *kinaf*. *Kinaf* ideally provide each other with major support in all phases and aspects of *pok bif*, supplying each other with pigs, garden produce, and labor, including special skills such as those necessary for carving ridge posts or ensuring good weather. Indeed, all of the raw building materials for the Solsol men's house – ironwood, timber, bamboo, and sago palm leaves – originated from sources other than Solsol land. In this respect, the Solsol men's house almost achieved the ideal goal of extensive cooperation: the physical structure embodied and made visible both the multiple social relationships comprising the particular persons of Solsol lineage and the supportive quality of these relationships.

Kinaf relations, rather than brother relations, represent to Tangans the ideal of cooperation.[15] It is *kinaf* who provide each other with the "source/origin/base" (*an wara*) of the pile of food and pigs that a lineage distributes at mortuary feasts. Intralineage brother relations are themselves insufficient, however necessary, to support *pok bif*. The cooperative, reciprocal relations of *kinaf* and allies must be mobilized in order to ensure the success of mortuary rites. In some cases, individual men disgruntled with their own enatic relatives undertake *pok bif* and construct a new men's house almost entirely on the strength and resources of their sympathetic *kinaf* (see Foster 1988 for examples). Thus, the particular *kinaf* relations that enatic relatives sustain can provide the resources (and sometimes the proximate causes) for these enates to publicize themselves as a lineage.

The expectation of identical exchange also organizes the distribution of cooked pigs and pork pieces at particular mortuary feasts. Tangan men carved pigs, cooked whole, according to a method (*kumas*) that yields several named pieces used in pork exchanges. Of the named pieces, the rump (*butut*) is widely considered to be the choicest, closely followed in desirability by the two hind legs (*pao'm bo*). Recipients usually distribute only one of the front legs (*bong um pakalu'm bo*), cut so as to include an ample portion of the pig's thigh and head. The other front leg remains attached to the head of the pig (*pakalu'm bo*), which a pig recipient does not redistribute, but retains for consumption. In some instances, however, the second front leg may be distributed or cut into small pieces to make up a shortfall in individual portions. To this extent, then, it is not inaccurate to describe Tangan pig exchanges as the exchange of *cooked pig heads* rather than of whole pigs, live or cooked. Finally, large strips of fat (*kipti'm bo*) cut transversely from the flanks of the pig and meaty portions cut from the vertebrae of the pig enter into pork exchanges. The remainder of the pig, its ribs and fatty bits, are generally apportioned to women and children and require no reciprocation. A packet of the pig's internal organs (*mida na bo*), mixed with greens and baked with the pig, and sometimes of the pig's belly fat, may be kept or distributed at the discretion of the recipient. Similarly, the recipient, especially if a member of the host lineage, may cut into his own share of the pig's head to assure that all guests are provided with at least a token amount of pork or fat.

At almost all feasts in which the hosts distribute pork, including "eat everything"-style feasts, pork cuts are given to initiate or repay debts. Distribution generally follows several standard strategies and the demands of key social relationships. A pig recipient tends to distribute pork in recognition of paternal ties in both ascending and descending generations, that is, ties to both "fathers" and "children" (*kinaf*) of the lineage. Distributors also recognize affinal relations with pork pieces, giving *butut* and *pao'm bo* to WB and WF. WFs are often members of the distributor's clan or, less frequently, lineage. Such distributions are special instances of the common practice of engaging fellow clansmen in pork exchanges. Pork given to *kinaf*, however, is regarded as simply one aspect of a generalized relationship of identical exchange and so calculated less precisely than other pork prestations.

Pig recipients frequently manipulate pork exchanges as devices for influencing others (the Tok Pisin metaphor of "greasing" is apposite) to agree to provide support for feasting. In the months prior to the Solsol *pok bif*, for example, Partui received a pig on four separate occasions. In each ensuing distribution, he directed that the rump be given to one of the men (or one of their enates) who would be solicited to provide major support for the final feast. The timing of these distributions as well as their content *per se* communicates the intent of the giver; the choiceness of the pork indexes the significance of the relationship. Since the receiver frequently stands in a *kinaf* relation to the giver, the general nature of the gift requires no explication. Particular prestations at particular times, however, unambiguously refer to immediate and concrete projects for which the giver wishes to mobilize the relationship.

The exchange of *whole* pigs, both live and cooked, expresses even more clearly the principles of identical exchange. Cooked pigs require reciprocation with cooked pigs. Some informants claimed that debts for cooked pigs incurred in a particular context, for example at *moratineng*, must be settled within the same context, namely, at a future *moratineng*. My observations did not always confirm this prescription. For example, Partui once redistributed a cooked pig received as part of a marriage payment as explicit reciprocation for a pig received ten weeks earlier at a *moratineng* hosted by another lineage. Broadly speaking, however, debts related to *pok bif* normally entail reciprocation at other *pok bif* events. Tangans maintain in the practice of pig exchange the conceptual distinction between *pok bif* and the immediate feasts precipitated by death and burial.

Within the context of *pok bif*, moreover, the structure as well as content of reciprocated debts must be replicated. Frequently, as noted above, the contributor who delivers a pig at *so puek* will be designated at *fasuigk* as a recipient of a redistributed pig (*bili bo*). Reciprocation in this instance prefigures an act of double reciprocation for both parties. The original recipient of the live pig must present an identically sized and sexed pig at *so puek* and he must also receive at *fasuigk* a pig identical to the pig he originally redistributed. In other words, the complete transaction includes two discrete acts of giving and taking that may be schematized in the following way:

I. i A gives pig to B at *so puek*
    ii. B redistributes pig to A at *fasuigk*
II. i B gives pig to A at later *so puek*
    ii. A redistributes pig to B at later *fasuigk*

The number of discrete acts doubles, of course, if the "payments" of *tinge bo* and *lulu am bo* are interjected. These four discrete acts of giving and taking comprise a transactional unit that Tangans consider relatively complete in connection with participation in *pok bif*. In the Solsol *fasuigk*, two pig donors received in their turn a cooked pig as completion of the transactional unit. Two other donors, repaying debts for pigs at *so puek*, received cooked pigs that initiated *new* debts since the donors did not previously *bili bo* when Solsol lineage made the original prestation. Thus, *fasuigk* functions not simply as a redistributive mechanism for closing cycles of debt, but also as a forum for initiating new debts. Indeed, as in the famous *kula* exchange, the problem faced by parties to identical exchange in Tanga is not simply in meeting debts, but in accepting the potential consequences of meeting debts: a closed cycle represents a deactivated social relationship. *Fasuigk* provides one of several arena in which the skilled lineage leader balances the lineage's obligation to close debts with the necessity to open new debts and thereby infuse social relationships with renewed reproductive potential.[16]

Identical exchange: marriage and the *kinaf* relationship

Perhaps the most pronounced instance of identical exchange coalesces around the marriage payment (*fil fifin*), itself conducted under the auspices of a men's house feast. In addition to a transfer of shell valuables and cash from the groom's side to the bride's parents, each side exchanges prestations of food. Each party arranges its prestation in one of two compartments atop a specially built platform (*am borau na tinaule*). Generally, two or three cooked pigs, which are placed on top of layers of cooked *mangat* and drinking coconuts, make up each prestation. The groom's side determines in advance the number of pigs; the bride's side matches this number. Likewise, each side compiles identical amounts of *mangat* and drinking coconuts (*kuen*), clusters of betel nut (*fumbu*) and, if agreed upon, store-bought items such as rice, soap, cigarettes, and tinned fish. These latter items are hung from the branches of an upright length of bamboo.[17] In effect, each side of the platform should duplicate its opposite. After the payment of shells and cash has been completed, the bride's party, usually visitors at a men's house event of the groom's or groom's father's lineage, collects the prestation assembled by the groom's side. The bride's party then departs forthwith, carrying their pigs, baskets of food and betel nut, seemingly indifferent to the main men's house event. At their own men's house, the bride's party uses the prestation to conduct a small satellite feast in which the cooked pigs are redistributed to cancel or initiate debts in the name of the bride's lineage.

When Solsol lineage received marriage payment for one of Timir's sisters, the groom's contribution contained one more cooked pig than the bride's offering.[18] The pig, as well as 6 kina regarded as additional to the 50 kina cash component of the payment, served as a notice or announcement to the bride's lineage for a second child recently born to the bride. Neither the pig nor the additional cash, however, constituted a "penalty" for late payment. (One Solsol man had grumbled only half jokingly that pigs passed to the groom's side after the birth of a child should be sows which have littered once. Payments made after two children have been born should be acknowledged with sows that have littered twice. The suggestion reveals not only the Tangan sense of humor but also how the principle of exchanging replicas may be metaphorically extended.) Partui explained that the additional pig and money entailed a debt for Solsol lineage that would be repaid as acknowledgment for the "hard work" of the father in raising the child. The incident thus high-lights the position of marriage payments in an encompassing set of exchanges that amounts to nothing less than the activation of the *kinaf* relationship.

Male Tangan informants did not represent the *fat kinaf* relationship as an exchange of women (see chapter 3). Rather, men spoke explicitly of their marriage patterns as the product of "marrying back" into one's father's matrilineage or clan (*funmat*). This same expectation to follow the lines of *kinaf* relations, that is, to "marry back," holds for women as well. Given the moiety-like organization of the *kinaf* relationship, informants could have alternatively described the pattern in terms of marrying one's MBD. But, and this is my point, informants did not represent their expectations about marriage in strict genealogical terms, say as marriage with a specific relationship category. Instead, men conceived of marriage as facilitating an identical exchange between lineages of "hard work," the quintessential expression of which is paternal care (*fang*).

The medium of the *fat kinaf* relationship is *fang*, translatable into pidgin as "hard work," fairly rendered into English as "care" or "nurture." Maurer (1966) glosses the word in German as *aufziehen*, to breed, or *versongen*, to look after (hence *fangte*, "to adopt"). The word denotes the care bestowed upon a child by its father in the form of food, shelter, and money for educational fees.[19] Tangans regard *fang* as a variable, something that a father ideally offers and which merits acknowledgment on the part of grown children through prestations made in connection with mortuary feasting (*fil mal* or *kos fang*). Such prestations recognize paternal relations as optional, as created relationships in contrast to the relations given axiomatically by matrilineal identity.[20] The care bestowed upon members of a matrilineage by outsiders requires both reciprocation and constant renewal. Hence, Tangans regard various lineages as bound not through the exchange of women, but through the exchange of care provided by men. The pivotal relationship of this exchange is that between father and child, highlighted in Tangan relationship terminology by the restriction of the term *tema* to refer to men related to ego through affinal ties to ego's mother.[21] It is in this sense that a lineage defines its supporters either as *fat kinaf*, people to whom paternal care is given, or as *fat tualik* ("bound brothers"), people who receive paternal care from a shared source. While the former category by definition refers to members of other lineages, the latter – the obverse of *fat kinaf* – refers equally to members of other lineages *and* one's own matrilineage. In practice, patrilateral consanguinity rather than matrilineal descent defines both the lineage as a solidary unit and the relationships of the lineage to other such solidary units (chapter 3).

In broad (and synchronic) terms, the exchange of paternal nurture defines lineages related as *fat kinaf* as lineages that raise and care for the children of each other. This joint project of feeding and caring brings the child into being in the first place, or such is the implication of some versions of conception theory reported to me by senior Tangan women. Conception involves the joining together of the "blood" or "water" (both euphemisms for semen, *pekpeke*) of both the man and the woman; that is, both the semen of the man and the semen of the woman mix together. In mixing together, these fluids enclose or encase (*banisim* or *kalabusim* in Tok Pisin, "fencing" or "jailing") a dry (*mas*) clot of blood (*sun dediak*) in the woman's belly. Successful enclosure requires multiple acts of intercourse; unsuccessful enclosure results in the piece of blood exiting the woman's belly as menstrual blood (*bunbun*). Similarly, repeated acts of intercourse make the blood clot grow. The blood clot provides the environment in which the child spontaneously generates, a process likened to the evolution of larvae into frogs that occurs in the story of the primal grandmother. That is, the child develops inside the blood (the placenta or *dafngia*); it eats the blood and is nurtured by the blood (which the newborn defecates until its source of nurture becomes mother's milk; then the color of the newborn's feces changes from black to gold). In other words, the mother and the father together feed the developing child by forming the placenta, and it is this act of mutual feeding – rather than any separate contributions of mother and father to the fetal body – that defines the focus of local conception theory.[22]

Long term *kinaf* relations develop diachronically out of the intergenerational exchange of *fang* between children and their parents (cf. Fajans 1986). Specific transfers of pigs enter into this generalized flow of exchange, such as the transfer of a small live pig to the groom's lineage by the bride's in order to acknowledge the future provision of wife and children with food, coconuts, and betel nut grown on the land of the groom's lineage. Similarly, in their father's declining years, children may attempt to acknowledge received paternal care by arranging as part of *pok bif* (or, in some cases, actually initiating construction of a small men's house) the prestation called *kos fang*. One such observed occasion clarified the degree to which Tangans regard paternal care as optional rather than as axiomatic. The prestation began with an *am furis* in which an old man, flanked by two sons, entered the hamlet with a *laplap* slung around his neck, an obvious allusion to the barkcloth sling (*mal*) once used to carry children. In the sling the old man carried a concealed tape recorder emitting the sound of a crying infant. After some dialogue, one of the sons asked the man if he would be willing to give "the child" over to the care of clan Filimat. The man replied negatively, adding that he would look after (*fangte*) "the child." Those in attendance immediately understood the *am furis* as a staging of the man's decision years before to raise single-handedly his young daughter after the premature death of his wife. The son publicly thanked his father for the latter's "hard work" in looking after his sister who happily had already given birth to two children. There ensued a presentation in which the old man, overcome by tears, received from his children money (20 to 30 kina), a 20 kilogram bag of rice, new loincloths and bedsheets, and a large cooked pig.

Kos fang refers not only to the temporally restricted exchanges between children and their father, but also to exchanges which, regulated by the principles of identical exchange, span a potentially infinite number of generations.[23] The proper reciprocation of paternal nurture becomes, on this view, the paternal nurture rendered the father's sister's children, that is, rendered a man's own children when he "marries back" into the father's lineage. These children, whose replacement of their MBMB follows the principle of substituting like for like, are the replicas of their FF (see figure 3).[24] A man, for example, marries back into his father's lineage in order to reciprocate paternal nurture with his own "hard work"

Fig. 3   Reciprocating paternal nurture by "marrying back"

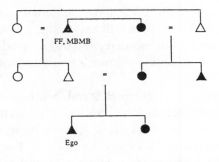

O, △   = Lineage X

●, ▲   = Lineage Y

in looking after his father's lineage replacements. Manilbau, fathered by a Tasik man but raised by a Solsol (Korofi) man married to Manilbau's classificatory MM, married his adoptive father's ZDD. The marriage was arranged not according to an automatic restricted transfer of women between lineages, in which case Manilbau should have taken a Tasik wife, but according to the demands of the identical exchange of paternal nurture. Manilbau's firstborn son in turn married back into Manilbau's lineage, thereby continuing the series of reciprocations. It is in this way that the identical exchange of paternal care over time, synonymous with the *kinaf* relation, produces the framework within which lineage succession, enacted in mortuary feasting, occurs.

One important implication of this processual view of the *kinaf* relationship concerns the position of women in exchange. Unlike men, women cannot reciprocate paternal care *in kind*. That is, even though women, like men, are expected to "marry back" into their fathers' lineages, they almost inevitably bestow parental care on members of their own lineage (adoption by women of children of other lineages is rare and certainly not a regular outcome of Tangan sociality). Thus the logic of identical exchange in the context of matriliny structurally defines women as permanent debtors; women receive paternal care which *their brothers* reciprocate. This logic accords with the residential situation of adult women, who often live on the land of their husbands and/or fathers and consume its produce. More generally, the logic at work here broadly identifies women with consumption and men with reciprocation (exchange), and hence the "replacement" of lineage personnel (cf. M. Strathern 1981). Significantly, the reciprocal "replacement" relationships of MB/ZS and MBMB/ZSZS have no female analogue in Tangan relationship terminology. And likewise, the public representation of lineage "replacement" in mortuary feasting is gender linked: only men (and boys) ascend the roof of the men's house and receive gifts of *lulu am bo*.[25]

Recent analyses of matrilineal social organizations in Papua New Guinea have recognized the importance of paternal nurture in entraining a number of exchanges, most often culminating in the context of mortuary ceremonies (Battaglia 1990; Clay 1977). In Tanga, paternal nurture functions as the medium for a number of exchanges throughout the lifecycle and beyond. That is, *pok bif* is not the context in which debts for paternal nurture are repaid in any final sense. The situation contrasts with the otherwise cognate practices of the Mandak of northern New Ireland who settle debts for "paternal substance" and "affinal nurture" primarily with payments made at mortuary feasts. The critical difference between these two systems for circulating nurture lies in the marriage patterning of the *kinaf* relationship. Unlike Tangans, Mandak "do not express any preferred or proscribed marriage categories" (Clay 1977:106). Debts initiated over the course of the father's lifetime therefore must be repaid at his death in transactions which potentially terminate future affinal exchanges of nurture. Clay refers here to the absence of preferred marriage categories defined in terms of lineages. Of course, the cross-moiety transfer of nurture continues *ad infinitum* (see Wagner 1986a for an explication of cross-moiety nurture relations in terms consistent with my own).[26] In the Tangan system, remarriage into the father's lineage continues affinal exchanges into the next generation and beyond. In both systems, however, marriage payments fall within the scope of nurture exchanges, a situation that accounts in part for the relatively little cultural emphasis accorded "bride-price" in New Ireland societies.[27]

Mandak marriage payments obligate those receiving a portion to contribute to death feasts in the groom's exogamous matriclan. Tangan marriage payments, inasmuch as they form part of a more generalized exchange relationship, entail similar obligations. More specifically, however, the ideal dualistic system of "marrying back" predicates that

Fig. 4   Balance of marriage payments as a result of "marrying back"

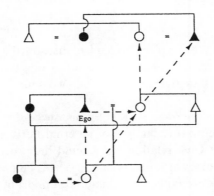

O, △   = Lineage X

●, ▲   = Lineage Y

− − ►   = Direction of marriage payments (*fil fifin*)

marriage payments made by ego are fully reciprocated on the marriage of ego's ZS. A marriage payment split between WF (ego's MB) and WM (ego's FZ) in recognition of their "hard work" sends only a portion of the payment outside of ego's lineage. This portion returns, of course, upon the marriage of ego's daughter to ego's ZS (see figure 4). Thus, marriage payments are not only contextualized within an overall circulation of paternal nurture – affinal nurture too, but Tangans use the idiom of paternity with its connotations of support to express the relationship – but also respond as well to the program of identical exchange. When the temporal perspective for viewing "bride-price" is expanded to embrace several generations, these apparently transformative exchanges become recognizable as elements of longer term identical exchanges. Meillassoux's (1981) characterization of marriage payments under conditions of identical exchange is apposite: marriage payments duplicate or ratify the primary circulation of productive and reproductive agents – in this case not nubile women, but nurturing men. The following letter, taken from a national daily newspaper, sums up the Tangan situation; not surprisingly, it was written by a New Ireland woman:

In my opinion I'd rather pay the groom's price because the man is going to look after my daughter's children and daughter . . . Looking at a married couple, it is clear to us that most of the income that is brought to the family is through the husband. Again when the bride's family are in need of money they will run to their daughter, poor girl if she's not working, do you know who's going to fulfil these requests?

(quoted in Filer 1985:176)

Here, as in Tanga, "bride price" is a misnomer, for the transfers of goods between lineages at marriage form part of a long term transfer of care (*fang*) and do not state the cost of a nubile woman.

Identical exchange: the framework of lineage succession
The long-term identical exchanges of paternal nurture which constitute and define the *fat kinaf* relationship ground the process of lineage succession. The temporary asymmetry of long-term commitments on the part of *kinaf* to provide each other with material support in mortuary feasting creates the context in which one lineage effects and publicizes the replacement of its dead. In other words, the coordination of delayed identical exchanges among lineages enables particular agents at certain times collectively to define themselves *as a lineage*. Exchanges in which a host lineage temporarily accumulates shell discs become the occasion for realizing succession within the lineage (chapter 6). Identical exchange, the

reciprocal replacement of replicas between lineages, is thus related functionally to the process of lineage succession, replacement within lineages.

Weiner's (1980) reanalysis of the Trobriand concept of *mapula*, on which she partly bases a critique of reciprocity-oriented approaches to exchange, reveals a similar relationship between exchange and succession in Trobriand social reproduction. *Mapula* implies a notion of replacement, according to Weiner, as when a man replaces (*mapula*) a coconut palm, destroyed by storm, that he previously gave (*mapula*) his son. On the death of the father, when his matrilineage (*dala*) attempts to reclaim (*sagali*) the palm, replacement (*mapula*) for the palm in some other form (i.e., male valuables such as stone axe blades or cash) must be offered to the son by his father's matrilineage. Likewise, both men and women may "take the place" (*kemapula*) of a deceased father by continuing to live on land belonging to the father's lineage and/or by contributing to mortuary distributions organized by the leader of the father's lineage. *Kemapula* connotes successorship within a lineage as well, specifically, succession to a chief's position by one of the possible brothers or sisters' sons a chief might designate.

Mapula thus denotes both replacement of things and replacement of persons. The two processes, moreover, stand in a determinate relationship to each other. The transfers (*mapula*) of things from father to son, for example, predicate the process of replacing persons (*kemapula*). *Kemapula*, in turn, implies a redirected flow of material objects. That is, an individual, by standing in the place of his/her deceased father in mortuary distributions sponsored by the father's lineage, reverses the flow of material resources initiated by his/her father's gifts (*mapula*). (Intralineage succession similarly hinges on the accomplishment of material transfers which, however, are called not *mapula* but *pokala* and which move from successor to incumbent.) In other words, intergenerational, interlineage material transfers make possible long-term continuity in social relationships in at least two ways. First, the obligation to reclaim (*sagali*) *dala* property devolves upon the lineage successors of the deceased: "individuals who had nothing to do with the original transaction" must bear the burden of reclamation (Weiner 1980:79). *Mapula* thus allows for continuity in social relations by contracting each new generation to circulate its resources in the service of obligations incurred by the preceding generation. Secondly, the obligation to "take the place" of a deceased father falls to his children, necessarily members of another lineage. Their contribution to the projects of their father's lineage adds to the pool of resources on which that lineage can draw. The contributions of children furnish their paternal lineage with an alternative supply of "elements of value" (Weiner 1980:81), that is, with labor and exchange wealth. In sum, the structure of material transfers enables the reproduction of a lineage through time by inseparably reproducing supportive interlineage relations. The process of "replacing" things is of a conceptual and practical whole with the process of "replacing" persons. Together, the two processes constitute the core of Trobriand social reproduction.

By locating acts of exchange within the larger context of individual life cycles and intergenerational transfers, Weiner argues that a "reproductive perspective" emerges from which the continuities in social relations and identities can be traced. The various exchanges making up the content of the Tangan mortuary sequence must be regarded in this fashion, not merely as isolated ceremonial events, but as public moments in a long-term process. This process, the transfer of paternal nurture between lineages related as *kinaf*, gives social relationships in Tanga their reproductive potential. The relations of reciprocal support among *kinaf* are the enabling conditions of lineage succession, not merely in the crude sense of biologically reproducing personnel, but in the local cultural sense of effecting replacement of the deceased MB through the successful achievement of mortuary feasting. Ongoing relations of identical exchange thus function as the framework for mortuary feasting and, together with mortuary feasting, as the wellspring of social reproduction.

Social reproduction of this sort, organized around identical exchanges and a notion of lineage succession, ideally functions in a conservative, homeostatic fashion – and it is a Tangan ideal that I now describe. Death removes individuals from the group, but their replacement engenders no alteration to the group other than the restoration of loss. "Taking my place" (*kep tafung*), the indigenous metaphor that describes lineage replacement, conveys well the image of conservation. *Tafu* implies a bounded empty space once filled and potentially filled again.[28] Thus, for example, *tafu* may refer to footprints that one finds on an empty stretch of beach. Footprints evidence the past presence of some individual, spaces once occupied in which someone walking behind may tread. Similarly, Tangans refer to a big man as *kaltu kep male* ("man who takes/holds the residential place/hamlet"). The big man succeeds to the residential site of the previous lineage leader, that is, the inheritor physically "takes the place" of the deceased big man. The actual men's house, periodically rebuilt at a limited number of different sites, likewise physically "takes the place" of previous men's houses.[29]

In reproductive terms, then, individuals succeed to the *tafu* vacated by the deceased. *Tafu* remain constant and fixed while the individuals passing through *tafu* vary. (The similarity between this idea and Radcliffe-Brown's views of social structure bears noting again.) Likewise, the continuous transfers of material resources (pigs, shell discs, yams) between lineages related as *kinaf* proceed as if according to some principle of conservation. The total amount of resources circulating in an exchange relationship remains ideally constant, subject only to the occasional rearrangements produced by asymmetrical transfers made at mortuary feasts. Of course, these "occasional rearrangements" possess a symbolism and logic that remain yet to be explicated (chapter 6). Here, the point to be made is simply that social reproduction in Tanga is a conservative process enabled by identical exchanges (themselves conservative) and by an ideal of filling or replacing the places the dead.

The net result of filling the places (*tafu*) of the dead is a *replica* of the premortem social organization. This replica duplicates in the first instance internal lineage relations with the replacement by the ZS of the MB or MBMB.[30] The circulation of names within a lineage neatly illustrates the idea. Partui organized *pok bif* to "finish" the memory of his deceased MBMB, Partui Matuk (Partui Sr.). Appropriately, Partui Lik (Partui Jr.),

Plate 9   Timir receives *lulu am bo* at Seber, 1985 with his classificatory ZS, Partui Lik (Andrew), and Kabisar (Eric), the actual ZS and namesake of an important ally of Solsol lineage

Partui's ZS, accompanied Timir in walking across the men's house, the performance of lineage replacement (Plate 9). More generally, MBs attempt to give lineage children the names of deceased lineage members, particularly members who died prematurely without either marrying or bearing children. Similarly, the feasts of death and burial, especially *moratineng*, provide opportunities for "replacing names" (*kilis asa*) in which the deceased's ZDS assumes his late MBMB's name. Names, like *tafu* and like the lineage itself, ideally perdure as fixed points through which passes the cyclical flux of lineage personnel.

The replica of premortem social organization effected by lineage replacement also duplicates interlineage *kinaf* relations. Tangans commonly refer to *kinaf* relations, as distinct from *kinaf* relatives, as *fat kinaf*. *Fat* is the Tangan word for "stone" or, adjectivally, for "held fast" (see chapter 6 for a discussion of the word *fat*). *Kinaf* relations ideally perdure in the manner of stones, that is, indestructibly. The interlineage exchanges of support both maintain and express this perdurance: a man replaces his father's care (*fang*) by caring for (*fangte*), in turn, children of his father's lineage. Like stone, moreover, the relationship is idealized as unchanging, as axiomatic as the relationship between MB and ZS. In practice, *kinaf* relations require maintenance lest they atrophy. *Kinaf* are related as "one blood," the justification given for banning marriage with the actual FZD/S or MBD/S, but the "one bloodedness" diminishes somewhat after the second generation. The FZDD/S is not only an eligible spouse but the preferred spouse. Although the *structure* of *kinaf* relations is given, the realization of these relations is often problematic rather than automatic.

Weiner concludes her argument for adopting the "reproductive perspective" with some remarks on how the need for matrilineages to reclaim property upon death constrains and limits the political possibilities of Trobriand lineage managers. Although property, including the body of the deceased, returns to a lineage at death, the reclamation process drains off "enormous amounts of personal wealth" in mortuary distributions (Weiner 1980:81). One consequence of this process is the definition of political and social hierarchy as weak by comparison with the situation of Polynesian chiefly status groups. Although the process of *kemapula* affords a lineage some access to the resources of children of lineage men (a not inconsiderable boon for polygynous chiefs), the maintenance of control over lineage resources requires of lineage managers:

constant individual attention to the demands of reclaiming, which in turn necessitates the equally constant accumulation and dispersal of resources. Internally, there is no way out of this system, which on the one hand has enormous

reproductive potential, and on the other hand contains equally impressive limitations.

(1980:81)

Weiner speculates that the need to reclaim one's position (even when
rightfully inherited) and the need to reclaim one's control of property
inhibits any possibility of individual chiefs establishing themselves in a
completely autonomous, hierarchical position. The exigencies of death
regulate a pump system of accumulation and dispersal that in many
respects recalls the cyclical career of a textbook Melanesian big man.
Indeed, cyclicity rather than linear expansion characterizes the system of
social reproduction as a whole.

The Tangan system of social reproduction – intralineage replacement
grounded in interlineage exchanges of nurture (*fang*) – shares certain
features with the Kiriwina system as outlined by Weiner. But if the
reproduction of social relations and identities in Tanga tends toward
stasis, it is not, as in the Kiriwina case, because of countervailing tendencies to accumulate and to disperse. Rather, Tangan ideals of social
relations as fixed and enduring, and of lineage succession as replacement
of vacated "slots" (*tafu*), predispose Tangan practice to create a sociality
that, paradoxically, Tangans represent as fixed. The dictates of identical
exchange do not prevent a lineage or lineage leader either from seeking
support outside existing relationships or from deploying the logic of
identical exchange to build new supportive relations. But neither do they
encourage such practices. As a result, the long-term continuities set up by
Tangan exchange relations are in principle continuities of replication
rather than multiplication, that is, products of stereotypic social reproduction. The phrase implies not that Tangans lack history or do not know
improvisation (as the actual practice of mortuary feasting attests), but
rather that replacement, the Tangan ideology of social reproduction, at
once limits and organizes social reproduction in definite ways. I return to
this issue in the conclusion.

6

Performing lineage succession: feast giving and value-creation

The prestation of shell wealth to the man who has just come down from the roof of a new men's house – the "replacement" of the "finished" dead – is one of the most compelling moments of the mortuary sequence. Shell discs silently accumulate at his feet as spectators crowd closer to see who gives what. But sometimes this picture does not develop as the recipient anticipates. For example, sometimes the recipient watches as a man or woman deposits a two-kina note at his feet instead of a shell disc. Most Tangans would insist that such a transaction does not "look good."[1] But their insistence would have nothing to do with some perceived non-equivalence between the two-kina note and the cooked pig that the note acknowledges. It would, however, have everything to do with a failure to enact the metaphor for which the occasion calls. In other words, the prestation must not be understood in terms of an exchange of equivalents, pig for shell, but rather in terms of the objectification of the image of lineage succession that the prestation enacts. This understanding requires first of all some revisioning of the concepts of exchange and exchange-value.

In this and the next chapter, I induce through ethnographic analysis values immanent in the exchange practices that figure in Tangan mortuary rites. I begin by rejecting the claim that the significance of identical exchanges can be wholly explained by noting how the transfer of like or unlike objects expresses or reiterates social relationships of "likeness" or "difference," that is, by emphasizing the social relations of exchange rather than the objects of exchange (see, for example, Clay 1977; Meillassoux 1981). Instead, I argue the necessity of analyzing the symbolism of specific exchange objects and the appropriateness of such objects to the contexts in which they circulate. I contrast this approach with exercises that attempt to deduce, in the absence of a generalized medium of exchange, the equivalence and hence quantitative value of qualitatively different exchange objects. In Tangan mortuary rites, the values implicated in both identical and transformative exchanges are not ratios of some shared feature of the objects (congealed labor or labor power, utility, etc.), but rather relations between attributes of exchange agents. These values specify the moral or social relations entangling exchange agents; exchange objects, in turn, tangibly signify these values.

I thus regard exchange objects as tokens of particular social relations that are produced and reproduced through the circulation of such tokens. That is, the circulation of objects – the act of exchange – effects a metaphorical juxtaposition between attributes of the exchangers that perforce specifies and qualifies the identities of the exchangers for each other (M. Strathern 1984). Munn (1986:15) refers to this process as evaluation, "the evaluative rendering of the self by significant others." Evaluation in this sense is an act of value-creation, a practical specification of significance.

My general aim in this chapter and the next is to demonstrate how in Tanga, as elsewhere in Melanesia, gift exchange is the prototypical act of value-creation, the privileged means for defining and making visible social relations and identities. My specific aim is to develop a theoretical approach to the feast giving and transformative exchanges central to Tangan mortuary rites, and thus to the image of lineage succession that these rites perform.

Exchange: commensuration or metaphor?

Identical exchange, the organizing activity of Tangan mortuary feasting, preempts questions about the equivalence of exchange objects: the "equivalent" of an exchange object is invariably a *replica* of that item – a pig for a pig, shell disc for shell disc, ten-kina note for ten-kina note.[2] That is, an object of exchange functions as the singular measure of its own value and requires for reciprocation a replica of itself (but, significantly, *not* itself). In this regard, exchange objects, particularly shell discs, are better thought of as tokens instead of as a currency. Put differently, no unitary, measurable quality, conceived as value-in-general, renders commensurable the diversity of value-forms given and received in exchange. Put less assertively, there is no necessity to presume such a conception of exchange-value in order to understand identical exchange. Equivalence is rendered axiomatic by the definition of exchange as a substitution of identical value-forms or replicas.

Transformative exchanges, at least in the context of Tangan mortuary rites, likewise obviate considerations of equivalence. The exchange of two kina for a large pig at *lulu am bo* frustrates attempts to deduce equivalencies from instances of exchange. Indeed, the radical asymmetry of the exchange (from the perspective of market prices) ought to make it plain that something other than equivalence is at stake. But, what? What understanding of value and exchange-value is appropriate to the practice of Tangan mortuary exchanges?

The question has two inseparably related components. First, we need to ask about the value of the objects exchanged and the determination of such value. Second, and perhaps less obviously, we need to ask about the value for the subjects (exchange agents) of the objects exchanged, especially since this value cannot be inferred from the "rational choices" that exchange agents make. Ceremonial exchange, and identical exchange in particular, ideally prescribe the specific objects which must be exchanged for each other (e.g., cooked pigs and shell discs; or identical shell discs). In other words, when the terms of exchange are axiomatic, value must be inferred not from choice, but from consideration of both the social context of the exchange *and* the symbolism of the exchange objects. Values thus inferred do not describe preferences. Rather these values stipulate the particular attributes of exchange agents who define themselves and their relationship in the very activity of exchange. Exchange, in other words, creates a context of action in which agents establish a relation between themselves in terms of attributes signified by the objects they transact. This relation, then, at once defines the value of the objects *and* the value of the agents for each other. Munn's observation about *kula* valuables is pertinent: "Although men appear to be the agents in defining [*kula*] shell value, in fact, without shells, men cannot define their own value; in this respect, shells and men are reciprocally agents of each other's value definition" (1983:283). It is to this double relation of persons and things as terms that define each other's significance that I refer by the word "value."

In order to get beyond an understanding of exchange as the affirmation of social relationships, exchange must be construed as activity that constructs a double relationship between objects and agents, that is, as an activity of value-creation or evaluation through which exchange agents construct and qualify identities for each other. This task of conceptualization is impeded by the notion that exchange is, above all, an act of commensuration. By contrast, this task is facilitated by the notion that exchange is a "symbolic process of metaphor building" (M. Strathern

1984).[3] I now differentiate these alternatives in a way consistent with the self-conscious Us/Them dichotomizing of the New Melanesian Ethnography.

In a capitalist commodity economy, the idea of exchange-value always implies commensurability, the register of which is price (or some analogue of price). Logically, commensurability implies a shared dimension of similarity along which the differences between particular items can be gauged. Anthropologists generally agree, however, that the possibility of *total* commensurability is a specific feature of the capitalist economic system. M. Strathern (1984:65), for example, claims that "mensuration based on intrinsic value is possible only in a commodity economy of the Western kind which symbolizes 'goods' in general as having intrinsic value." Similarly, Gregory (1982) proposes the opposition between cardinal and ordinal value as one of the dichotomies constitutive of an ideal typical contrast between Western capitalist and Melanesian gift economies.[4] Commensurability and cardinal value simultaneously enable and enshrine transfers of unlike commodities as the paradigm of exchange interaction.

The formal requirements of Tangan identical exchange seemingly deny the possibility of a *single* standard of evaluation and invalidate the assumption of mensuration in terms of "intrinsic value."[5] Gregory (1982) argues in this way that the exchange of like-for-like (what he calls "gift exchange," what I am calling identical exchange) cannot be understood in terms of "value" but rather must be understood in terms of "rank." That is, by reading "like for like" as "rank for rank," Gregory advocates use of the concept "spheres of exchange" (Bohannan 1955). Using the concept in the case of Tangan identical exchange, however, would lead to the demarcation of one sphere for every type of object exchanged, inasmuch as proper reciprocation entails the return of a replica. Since there would be an indefinite set of possibilities as to the definition of types, the concept of a "sphere" would lose any analytical potency which it might otherwise claim.

Incommensurability (or incomplete commensurability), however, disappears as "a problem" if we do not assume that the point of exchanging gifts or commodities is to establish equivalencies. M. Strathern (1984), for example, challenges this assumption in discussing the manifest asymmetry of Melanesian marriage exchanges. Strathern argues against the view that bridewealth payments substitute for women in some concrete way. She uncovers the fallacy of presuming the substitutability of exchange objects and thus of reading off the value of women in marriage exchanges "from what women 'are'" (1984:61) – biological reproducers, for instance. In order to determine the value of things or persons in exchange, it is necessary to consider "all the transactional elements in circulation" (1984:61). Her point, though, is to stress not the commensurability but rather the "partibility" of things and persons in exchange. That is, the co-occurrence of things and/or persons in a particular exchange implies not equivalence but rather a metaphorical juxtaposition of detachable attributes:[6] "Value is thus constructed in the identity of a thing or person with various sets of social relations in which it is embedded, and its simultaneous detachability from them" (Strathern 1987a:286; 1984:65). Things or persons circulated in exchange stand for their sources, the agents who circulate them; but in circulation, these things and persons become conceptually detachable or disjunct from their sources (Strathern 1987b:280). The metaphorical juxtaposition is double: both a relation between objects and agents and a relation between objects. This double relationship is the value of the exchange.

Strathern's position likens exchange to a "symbolic process of meta-phor building" (1984:65).[7] Exchange is a process in which agents con-struct *particular* differences (or similarities) relative to each other – instead of the equal value or equivalence of their objects – through the circulation of specific items in specific contexts. From this recognizably Maussian point of view, the circulation of exchange objects must be understood in terms of how these objects symbolize aspects of the persons of their exchangers, including the particular social relationship of the exchangers. Exchange objects thus function as the concrete embodiment of the relations that exchange creates between persons.

It follows from Strathern's argument that the terms of the metaphor constructed in exchange can be disclosed only through analysis of specifi-cities – the social relations of exchange *and* the significant properties and qualities of the objects of exchange (see Munn 1977). I begin with the latter as the first step in applying this New Melanesian Ethnographic perspective on exchange to Tangan mortuary feasting and ceremonial transactions.

En/fat: contrasted attributes and preeminent exchange objects
The central exchanges associated with men's house construction, *fasuigk* and *lulu am bo*, are manifestly transformative exchanges that invariably involve the transaction of pigs and shell valuables. This latter category includes small shell discs (ca. 1–2 cm.) strung in various ·lengths (*kemetas*), and the large grooved discs (*am fat*) restricted in use to Tanga

and Anir.[8] For Tangan men, *am fat* and not *kemetas* epitomize shell wealth, an integral feature of *kastam* and, in fact, a feature that visibly distinguishes *kastam* from the exclusively cash activities of *bisnis*.

Not being produced in 1985, a single *am fat* (*molot* in Tok Pisin) resulted from a laborious process estimated by Bell to require approximately six months to complete (Bell 1935d). Shell manufacturers, of whom there were only a few in 1933, were commissioned to make *am fat*. Their patrons supplied them with daily food during the production process and presented them with a large pig at a feast held upon completion of the disc. The procedure began by roughly trimming a valve of the giant clam (*Tridacna gigas*) into discoid shape "with the aid of a piece of water washed basalt held in the hand, *coup de poing* fashion" (Bell 1935d:101). Next, the surfaces of the roughly shaped valve were flattened by rubbing the shell back and forth across a flat volcanic rock sprinkled with gritty volcanic sand. When the shell achieved the appearance of a crudely fashioned slab of marble, the manufacturer proceeded to perfect its circular shape and to smooth the edges by rubbing the shell along the length of a hand-held piece of basalt. Piercing the shell to create a hole likewise involved rubbing the center of the disc in a circular movement around the top of a conically topped rod of basalt firmly set in the ground. Similar rods of larger size enabled the *am fat* maker to increase the diameter of the hole. Finally, the manufacturer incised grooves (*an dodo*) with a sharp stone knife (*an taltales*) around the edge of the disc. Bell claimed that no secrecy surrounded the manufacturing process; the *am fat* maker conducted all operations in a cleared space in front of his house (1935d:100).

Am fat come in an assortment of sizes and shapes, though two basic types can be identified. The first type, *am fat mil*, consists of tubes of varying length, some wide enough to be worn on the arm above the elbow, with thin bands incised around the outside. Long tubes of this type with as many as twenty five bands are called *puk sil*; shorter tubes are called *an malmal*. I saw only once a shell of this type circulate in exchange. Informants asserted that *am fat mil*, apparently very scarce, are heirlooms. Older female informants claimed that they wore similar but smaller tubes (*kelafat* or *am fat n'anima meriwen*) during dance performances for a new men's house.

The second type of *am fat* is called *tintol*. *Tintol* refers to single-grooved discs of varying diameter and breadth (or thickness). Medium-sized *tintol* are the standard tokens of marriage and mortuary exchanges.[9] Smaller varieties, called *kisi na witi* (*sutim long kok* in Tok Pisin, or "penis rings") never enter exchanges. Bell reported that women and children wore *kisi na witi* as armlets. I never saw such a specimen but informants claimed that they are plentiful. Larger varieties of *tintol* (*tintol dok* or "large *tintol*") are recognized by Tangans as rarer and more desirable than medium-sized *tintol*.[10]

Particularly fine specimens of *tintol dok* or *an simpendalu* might be called *kong kuen*, "coconut meat," on account of their whiteness.[11] Men also prefer discs without chips or cracks, that is, "without damage," as one man put it. White, perfectly formed, large specimens might also be called *am fat tengteng* ("*am fat* cries"), thus evoking the "cries" (*tengteng*) of the man who surrenders such a specimen in exchange. One man declared that true *am fat tengteng* never should be circulated but rather kept in one's storage box. Similarly, and most significantly, shells of the largest variety of *tintol*, called *warantang*, never circulate. The name *warantang* means "base of the basket," a reference to their place at the bottom of the special coiled baskets (*tang*) in which shell wealth was traditionally kept. Plate 10 shows examples of shell wealth.

Each lineage ideally holds one or more *warantang*, though informants reported that some lineages owned none. *Warantang* are individually named, and these names sometimes emphasize the immobility of the shell

Plate 10   Shell wealth in the possession of Partui Bonaventura, 1992: *an simpendalu* (lower right), *tintol dok* (top), and two *katalu'm bul* (center)

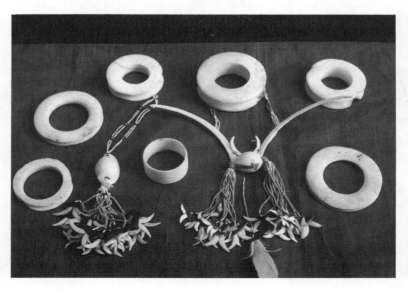

Table 13. *Some* warantang *names and their glosses*

Name	Gloss
Piliskis	"*Senisim sindaun*" in Tok Pisin; "change seats" – refers to the manner in which the shell remains in one place as its holders (those who sit on it) replace each other
Melala	"It stops, then goes" – refers to the shell's periodic movement in following the path of men's houses newly constructed at different origin/base sites (*waranmale*)
Lanaefef	"It arrives in the afternoon" – refers to how a lineage leader wordlessly shows the shell to another lineage member in the morning in order to request that a pig be tied up (*rerek bo*) for delivery to a feast in the afternoon
Ngalwakasak	"*Maus i nogut*" in Tok Pisin; "a taste or hunger for eating pigs"
Fasuse	"To make *suse*" – the shell sings out and persuades/compels lineage members to tie up pigs. *Suse* is a form of magic used to protect hamlets against intruders.
An uring	"Bamboo pillow" – refers to the bamboo pillows found in all men's houses. Like these pillows, the shell remains in one place and supports a man's head.
Kara	"Greedy for pork" – *Kara* is an extremely abusive term for a glutton. It refers to a *masalai* that assumes the form of a long red snake-like tail. The tail exits a man's or woman's anus in search of pork to eat. The man or woman is unaware of the tail; others see it but do not call attention to it.
Famatkarbun	"To awaken a desire for eating pig"

(table 13).[12] For example, one man reported the name of his lineage's *warantang* as "Ngangaten" or "it cannot go," while another woman reported the name of her lineage's shell as "Taupestang" or "it stays in the basket calling out for other shells to come." Lineage leaders cannot circulate such shells in mortuary or marriage payments. Such discs forever remain lineage heirlooms, displayed infrequently in the context of mortuary feasts and quickly returned to the security of their deposit boxes (chapter 7).

In addition to the large *warantang* (Plate 11), lineages often possess other heirlooms manufactured from Tridacna shells. These include *puk gem* (known in Tok Pisin as *kapkap*), smoothed, thin circles of shell overlaid with filigreed turtle shell; and *am pilak*, smoothed shells without the delicately worked overlay. Men, specifically big men, wear *puk gem* as medallions at important men's house feasts, while women likewise wear *am pilak*. Neither of these ornaments was being made in Tanga at the time of my fieldwork. A third type of ornamental heirloom, however, was now and then produced. Called *katalu'm bul* ("egg/testicle of the *bul*"), this valuable necklace consists of an egg cowrie (*am bilang*) from which depends several two to three inch pieces of red *kemetas*.[13] Each piece terminates in a brown, hemispherical seed case (*kotkot*) into which the teeth of dogs are inserted. The egg cowrie is fastened to a length of string. The representative sister's son typically wears a *katalu'm bul* ornament during his walk across the roof of the men's house at important mortuary feasts; sometimes a lineage leader will wear the ornament while supervising the proceedings at a mortuary feast.

Although *am fat* as a cover term refers to all varieties of Tridacna discs, the word *fat* commands a larger semantic domain. Substantively, *fat* denotes stones or rocks; as a modifier, the word evokes a range of related qualities including hardness, fastness, and durability. Thus, for example, one might describe anything firmly rooted as *fat*. Bell gives as illustrations of this usage references to "an old house pole, or a shrub in the bush which defies the efforts of a man to uproot it" (1935d:97). Similarly, the almost synonymous words *pirafat* and *tabafat* describe a man who remains calm amidst raging turmoil, as might an exceptional man aboard a storm-tossed canoe. Inflammable substances are described as *fat na if* ("impervious to fire"). *Fat* also connotes the idea of "fixation" as in the

Plate 11   Two *warantang* held by Kutbau Tarasinei in 1992: Lanaefef (left, *tintol*) and Ngalwakasak (*puk sil*)

sentence "*singagu i fat sing o*" ("he is fixated on you" or, literally, "his thought is stuck to you"), spoken in reference to a man's obsession with a particular woman.

Two very common and important terms also incorporate *fat* as a qualifier. *Parfat*, the word meaning "to know," suffixes *fat* to *par*, the word meaning "to see." *Parfat* identifies knowledge with "seeing securely," that is, perceiving and retaining images. Although other Austronesian languages exhibit the same equation of direct observation with knowledge, the Tangan usage is consistent with an encompassing epistemology based on vision rather than hearing, on images rather than words (see Wagner 1986a for a discussion of this phenomenon in another New Ireland society). This epistemology informs the nonverbal communications that comprise the mortuary sequence such that the significance of constructed images or revealed line dances appears as self-evident (see chapters 4 and 7).

Second, as previously indicated, the word *fat* in the phrases *fat kinaf* ("bound or fast cross-cousins") and *fat tualik* ("bound or fast brothers") qualifies the social relationship at issue as rooted and lasting. The analogy of *kinaf* relationships with stone, spontaneously volunteered by one man in the course of defending his position in a land dispute with his wife's lineage, thus likens the temporal durability of stones to the temporal continuity of relationships mediated by identical exchange.

The qualities of durability and permanence signified by the word *fat* endow shell discs with their value capacity. That is, these qualities are not simply fortuitous features of the object, as for example the color of paper money. Rather, they are precisely the properties that distinguish the objects as *significantly* different, and hence potential terms of a metaphorical juxtaposition. When asked hypothetically to choose among two large pigs, ten *tintol*, and one hundred kina, one man justified his selection of *tintol* on the grounds that cash would be used up (*en*) quickly and the pigs would be eaten (*en*).[14] The *tintol*, however, the man could place in his strongbox and know that they would not "stink" or "rot" (*mapu*) the next day. Although he would die, the man explained, someone else would inherit the *tintol* and someone else again afterwards. In other words, the distinctive feature of *am fat* is their *fat* quality, the quality which distinguishes them from pigs and cash in the reported example.[15]

The qualities of heaviness and permanence carry moral as well as physical connotations. Thus, for example, Partui commented upon a rash of deaths of senior Taonsip men by saying that "Taonsip is no longer heavy." That is, the aged men both iconically signified stability and durability and imparted these qualities to the social life of Taonsip. Similarly, a Muliama man offered as an antonym of the word *fat* the phrase *dang na sal*, which he glossed as "coming and going along the road." This sort of behavior, locally regarded as characteristic of promiscuous juveniles of both genders, contrasts with "sitting down in one place," the behavior appropriate of big men. In the same way, it is the *non-circulating*, individually named *mis* which make the clan "heavy" (*fat*).[16] Thus the transposable opposition between stability and movement establishes differences between circulating and non-circulating types of shell valuables, that is, within the category of shell wealth itself. Relative to the former, the latter are *fat* – "heavy" and fixed.

In the case of Tangan shell discs, *warantang* are *fat* relative to common *tintol*. Thus, for instance, Michael Tarangen, a local government councillor, remarked that *warantang* slept in the baskets like "kings" while *tintol* moved around in exchange like "workmen." Indeed, it is possible to distinguish *am fat* not only in terms of their size and shape, but also in terms of their relative mobility. *Kisi na witi*, the smallest shells, are also the most mobile. Men enjoyed telling me how the small hole of these shells was just large enough to accommodate a penis (*witi*, a slang word). In the past, when men wore no laplaps, a man would accordingly slip on one of the shells and expose himself to a woman; the woman would remove the shell for herself and the couple would then engage in sexual intercourse. In Tanga, as in Muliama, sexual promiscuity is associated with mobility, coming and going along the road; hence the local term for a child born with no recognized father, a "child of the road" (*sikwa'n saris*).

By contrast, *tintol* circulate at a lower velocity, mostly in marriage and mortuary payments, but also in the past in compensation payments (*poiem*, compensation payment for homicide). *Warantang* circulate at the lowest velocity, infrequently transmitted from a MB to his ZS. They are the ideal embodiment of stasis, and hence the sure foundation on which a big man stands or sits (*an waran keke'ng kaltu*, "base of a man's leg"). And, in fact, on the rare occasion of the public display of *warantang*, a big man will sit or stand on his lineage's shells as he receives a gift pig or speaks with a ZS on the roof of the men's house.[17]

Pigs and money, by contrast, are eminently consumable. Consumables, including vegetable food, are not "hard" but "soft" (*malmalum*); preferred consumables are often moist or juicy and not dry. For example, the most desirable betel nut is the young, "watery" kind (*am bu dan*) and not the overripe, hard and dry sort (*am bu fat*).[18] Consumption in general implies qualities and activities distinctly opposed to those connoted by the word *fat*. The word *en*, "to eat," condenses these connotations in a notion applicable to more than the epitomizing act of eating food. *En* refers equally to wasting money or to spending the money of others without their consent. The sharp blade of a bushknife is described simply as *pukfis i en* ("the knife eats"); thus the opposition between *en* and *fat* traditionally took the mundane material form of axes (*kompuki*) fitted with *Tridacna* shell blades. More obliquely, but no less commonly, *en* refers to sexual intercourse. One man might slyly ask another man in regard to a recent sexual encounter: "*O sam en?*" ("Have you eaten?").

The semantic domain of "consumption" (*en*) thus covers much the same area as the Umeda term *tadv*, to which Gell (1979) assigned three basic modalities: gastronomic, sexual, and aggressive. These modalities set up a *metaphorical* equation among the activities of eating, copulating, and killing. The Tangan term *en* establishes a similar metaphorical equation (the particular equation between eating and killing-cannibalizing is taken up in the following section). The "softness" and "mobility" of consumables leaves them vulnerable to consumption or loss through a number of processes that include most prominently ingestion (eating) and decay (as of a corpse or of rotting food). Similarly, physical work (*faim*) consumes strength (*mia*) which one must replenish, in turn, through the consumption of food. The vulnerability of the body to consumption (through decay, loss of strength) also extends, at least for men, to the activity of sexual intercourse. Frequent copulation, several male informants claimed, results in illness (*kwatar*) characterized by lethargy, weakness, and "loose skin" (*fo i main/fo i molmet*). Such sexual overindulgence earns a man a reputation for selfishness: "the man eats very badly" (*kaltu i en saksak*).

In its most common usage the word *en* means eating food or, as a noun, a feast. And feasts, in turn, generally imply the consumption of pork. Tangans in 1984–85 rarely exchanged live pigs and never to my knowledge exchanged live mature adult pigs (or, for that matter, uncooked food not destined for immediate cooking). Unlike *am fat*, which survive the context of their display or transfer (that is, the feast), pigs (pork) enter into exchanges only as a prelude to their consumption. Just as shell discs epitomize the qualities that constitute their value capacity, exchange pigs signify "consumability," an attribute inseparable from their recognition as valuables.[19]

Consumability, however, must be taken to mean not only the actual edibility of the pig in the context of feasts, but also the expenditure of "hard work" (*fang*) necessitated by raising pigs. Tangans, unlike mainland New Irelanders, do not purchase pigs with cash for use in *kastam*. Pigs used in *kastam*, especially those given to recipients of *warangus* baskets, are "home-grown" either by members of the host lineage or by their supporters. In 1933, according to Bell (1947b:40), women almost exclusively cared for the pigs of a household, feeding the pigs cooked yams and "kaukau tubers" on the assumption that pigs fed raw tubers would be more apt to break into gardens; in 1985, both men and women fed an evening meal of coconut meat to the pigs domiciled at their household.[20] Women as well as men also possess knowledge about herbal infusions for pigs that induce rapid growth and development of a fat and glossy skin. Accordingly, pigs exhibit in themselves the "care" (*fang*) of their owners, a connection that goes some way toward making sense of the routine practice of joining the prestation of a pig to the prestation of other items, such as carved houseposts (*tutor*) or taboo markers (*an ulau*). The transfer of the pig supports or complements the transfer of other items; without the pig, Partui once explained, he would be ashamed (*mai-e*) to deliver a housepost to another lineage's men's house. Similarly, at the final mortuary feast, recipients of *warangus* baskets supplement their gifts of large pigs with gifts of smaller pigs rendered as assistance or support to the host lineage.

Pigs and *am fat*, the pre-eminent objects of Tangan exchanges, thus iconically signify conventionally recognized qualities (e.g., durability, edibility, "hard work"). *Am fat* provide an almost paradigmatic example of iconicity in their tangible embodiment of permanence and heaviness, coterminous qualities of the shell (or elements of the icon) inseparable from their apprehension as value-forms.[21] Likewise, pigs testify bodily to the (past) accumulated expenditure of their owners and the potential (future) consumption of their recipients. In exchange, pigs and *am fat* establish and signify a relationship between the qualities they sensuously embody, on the one hand, and the agents who give and receive these objects in exchange, on the other. For example, the durable shell discs signify the durability of the ZS that receives them at *lulu am bo*, that is, the capacity of the matrilineage continually to "replace" itself. Reciprocally, the fat pigs distributed by this lineage materialize its productive expenditure or "hard work." Unlike a generalized and abstract money, these pigs and *am fat* neither express nor facilitate the comparison of *all* things. Instead, they qualitatively and immediately state a specific comparison, that is, a specific set of relations between persons and between persons and things.

Consumption, non-consumption, and giving in Tanga

The contrast between *en* and *fat* is plain enough. Indeed, it corresponds neatly to the familiar distinction between durables and consumables. Shell valuables and land fall into the class of *fat*; food, pigs, and cash typify the class of *en*. But precisely how is this contrast implicated in Tangan mortuary rites?

I suggest that the opposition between *en* and *fat* amounts to nothing less than the central axis of a conceptual scheme that orients mortuary rites. The opposition underpins both the key exchanges of mortuary feasting and the process of lineage succession effected by these exchanges. Munn's notion of a generative schema is apposite: "... a guiding, generative formula that underlies and organizes significance in different overt symbolic formations or processes, and that is available as an implicit constructive form for the handling of experience" (1986:121).[22] *En* and *fat* each stand for a range of acts that can be glossed as consumption and non-consumption respectively, the first epitomized in the activity of eating food and the second epitomized by abstention from eating. The opposition between these two kinds of actions, both in idea and in practice, is mediated by the activity of "giving" (*fen*), itself defined causatively as "making [others] eat" (*fa-en*). *Fen* is the means whereby Tangans, acting collectively in hosting feasts, transform consumption into non-consumption, impermanence into durability. Collective agents (lineages) create values, regarded as preconditions for future action, through transfers of symbolic media (*am fat*, pigs, food) that exhibit in themselves attributes of their transactors. That is, *en*, *fen*, and *fat* together abbreviate a set of normatively defined and organized activities that enable exchange agents to construct themselves as relatively impervious (*fat*) to the exigencies of consumption (*en*). In the remainder of this chapter and the whole of the next, my object of analysis is the single mortuary sequence conceived as a matrix of such normatively defined activities. I begin by explicating the activity of feast giving, that is, the activity of creating an occasion in which to feed others publicly; in the next chapter I explicate the important transformative exchange of *lulu am bo*.

In her analysis of Gawan value transformations, Munn (1986) contrasts acts of consumption ("negative" value transformations) and acts of transmission ("positive" value transformations). In the Gawan view, for example, eating food rather than giving it to visitors destroys for the consumer the positively valued capacity to extend his influence and to build his good name. To some extent, the same opposition informs

Tangan morality. Tangans label the selfish man as one who "eats badly" (*en sak*) and contrast him to the ideally generous man who "causes reciprocal giving" (*kaltu fafafen*). As in Gawa, selfishness implies close handedness or retention while generosity means giving with two hands. Thus Tangan children sometimes play a game in which one child determines the generosity of another by tossing two hemispherically shaped seed pods in the manner of throwing dice. Should both pods land with their flat side downward, the child is deemed selfish. When one pod lands in this way while the other pod rests on its curved side, the child is said to give with one hand. Both pods resting on their curved backs designate the child as *kaltu fafafen*, the man who gives with both hands.[23]

In daily interaction, moreover, transmission is in fact the practical alternative to eating. Tangans recognize an obligation to offer food to others in whose presence they eat (cf. Kahn 1986). To a lesser extent this obligation applies to the consumption of betel nut and tobacco where individuals may protest but rarely refuse the demanding request (*sising*) of "*lak t'am bu*" or "*la brus*" ("Let a betel nut come" or "Tobacco come"). This generalized recognition coordinates a repertoire of tacitly respected strategies for consumption that recall Kahn's report of one Wamiran's attitudes toward sharing:

Our custom is that if we have food we have to give it to all the people who see it or know about it. If we have food and don't give it to them, they will be jealous and angry. It is our custom to be jealous and angry about food.

(Kahn 1980:259)

Thus, the afternoon main meal is eaten out of sight either indoors or, if eaten on open-air verandahs, in the shadows of dusk. Passersby act appropriately by never intruding upon these meals, always listening for the sound of clinking enamel plates before making their presence known. Similarly, I observed on at least one occasion a family delaying its already prepared afternoon meal until the voluntary departure of an unexpected visitor.

Tangans regulate both the presence of others and the publicity or visibility of consumables. This latter kind of strategy emerges most clearly in regard to the personal baskets or purses (*tang*) that all adults carry with them.[24] Men typically keep their purses clutched securely under their left arms or held by the handles before them. In this way, the contents of the purse remain hidden to others (unattended baskets are fair game for prying eyes and hands). Women achieve the same effect with their differently designed baskets (*guruk*) by draping a piece of folded cloth over the top of the contents. By denying visual access to the contents of the purse an individual partially fends off requests for betel nut and tobacco. A man may oblige a request by carefully opening his basket such that only he can look inside and apportion the requested amount of tobacco or betel nut. In cases where a man actually has no betel or tobacco in his purse, requests precipitate animated performances in which the importuned man swears his destitution while emptying the contents of his basket for all to see: "*Sing Deo! Tu Iat!*" ("In the name of God! Truly!"). Such displays, however, do not guarantee that the man retains no personal supply (*kibal*) of tobacco or betel nut secreted in his house or elsewhere from which he periodically replenishes his basket (one close friend hid betel nuts in a kitchen garden).

The dynamics of eating and transmitting, sometimes palpably tense, thus often hinge upon the visibility of cooked food and other consumables. It is in this context that the massive exhibition of food at feasts becomes understandable as an almost bold assertion of the recognition that to view cooked food entitles the viewer to partake. Conversely, *warantang*, the supreme lineage heirlooms that rarely gain public exposure, become understandable as negations of the ideal of transmission. The hidden existence of these shells implies the secret consumption of their owners. (I develop this point below and in the next chapter.)

In slight contrast to the Gawan case, Tangans do not locate the negative aspects of eating in the act itself, but rather in *excessive* eating or in the inability to control eating.[25] (Indeed, to the extent that consumption implies nurture received or commensality, eating has a potential positive aspect.) The etiquette of non-"eat everything" feasts is revealing in this sense, especially as observed by those men invited to receive their share of the distribution inside the men's house. Each man sits silently, often stoically, as the hosts and their helpers disassemble the food pile (*gus*) and distribute (*ti*) the food into individual portions. Men seated inside the men's house receive either larger quantities and/or choicer selections of the betel nut and food supply than the men and women seated outside. These men, moreover, often receive the choicest cuts of pork; this is the reason for their being invited to sit inside the men's house. As one of the hosts enters with a huge rump, the guests stare forward unblinkingly, sometimes expecting reciprocation of a previous gift, sometimes anticipating indebtedness. Once the portions have been distributed, a prayer and the symbolic "first bite" mark the commencement of eating. In most cases, however, guests generally nibble at their food, perhaps sampling a banana or slicing a modest piece of pork to eat in complement with a yam. After an interval of several minutes, each portion, in some instances amounting to more than ten pounds of cooked tubers, is collected into plaited baskets and carried off in all directions by the various recipients.

Several considerations enter here. First, guests maintain a high degree of self-consciousness about their demeanor in the eyes of each other. Partui once answered my question as to why guests eat so little at feasts by pointing out that it would not look good if a guest choked, that is, ate without restraint. The distribution of food into individual portions thus facilitates not only the presentation of choice cuts to particular individuals, but also the public exercise of self control on the part of *each* guest. Moreover, recipients of better cuts may offer pieces to their less fortunate neighbors, thereby partially turning consumption into an act of transmission.

Secondly, the recipient of a choice, debt-generating cut of pork receives the meat as a representative of his lineage (*matambia*) and therefore remains obliged to return the piece to his own men's house (*bia*) and not to his familial cook house (*felungkur*). At his own men's house, the cut of pork may be pooled for redistribution with other pieces of meat received by other lineage members who attended the feast. (Consistent with the ethic of restraint on eating, a leader generally attempts to limit the number of his fellow lineage members attending a feast to no more than two or three.) Men who disregard this convention expose themselves to the disapprobrious charge of being selfish. More seriously, however, a lineage leader may decline to recognize the debts initiated by pieces of pork disposed of in this way and deny the consumer the privilege of using pieces of pigs presented to the lineage in order to repay *the consumer's* debts. That is, a lineage leader might respond to the privatization of consumption by privatizing debts.

Alternatively, lineage members may assemble to consume together the collected portion(s) of pork and vegetable food inside the men's house. On most of these occasions, women will be excluded, though women do partake when either collected portions are large enough to provide them with a share after the men have eaten or when women themselves contribute to the pool of portions. (This latter instance is less frequent since, in general, men attend more feasts in more parts of the island than women. Women who are not associated with the host lineage in some way primarily attend only those feasts designated as *moratineng* and even then they attend only local *moratineng*.) Eating within one's own men's house among one's lineage mates (and sometimes invited friends) requires much less attention to self-presentation. Men often exhorted me to eat at my own, invariably slower pace, reminding me that I was under no obligation to stop eating when everyone else had (a habit attributed to Europeans but, I suggest, equally characteristic of formal feasting etiquette[26]). In the men's house, feasting etiquette resembles more closely the expectations for behaviour at "eat everything" feasts (see below). Thus, the men's house functions as the site of communal consumption for lineage members, the protected site at which the public demands of self-restraint yield to indulging the pleasures of a full stomach (*balang i sam dik/*"my belly is like a full basket").

It is important to note that Tangan feast givers give their guests an opportunity to exercise restraint as consumers, that is, to display public control over consumption (Clay 1992). Similarly, feast givers give their guests, or at least some of them, the opportunity to become givers in their own right by redistributing pigs and pork pieces to others. But these opportunities are overshadowed, I want to suggest now, by the way in which feast givers actively construct their guests not only as consumers, but also as consumable.

Nea: the image of excessive consumption

The image of excessive eating, of gluttony, inhabits the Tangan imagination in the form of Nea, the trickster become tricked figure of several Tangan stories (*pansoksok*). Nea is variously depicted as a stupid, greedy, ugly man and more generally as the paradigm of boorishness (see Bell 1941:64). Stories often describe in this vein several Nea, related as brothers, all exemplars of disapproved behavior. These stories frequently map the dynamics of uncontrolled consumption on to kin relations, particularly reciprocal relations between affines/*kinaf*, in a fashion exemplified by the story of Nea and the clam shells:[27]

There was a man all of whose sisters were married to Neas. These sisters and Neas spent most of their time in the bush working on their gardens every day. Their *tambu* [brother-in-law] was skilled at getting meat. He would take his canoe and bring back fish and other things. All his *tambu* would then come and eat with him. In the afternoon they would go into the men's house and eat the fish that their *tambu* caught. Every day this would happen. The next day the man would say "You go to the bush and I'll go the beach and find some meat [*arbus*] for us." He would say this to his wife. His wife would go to the bush and get some taro, yams, and *mami*. She would come back and prepare the food and the man would return with the fish. He would cook the fish and when it was done he would call all his *tambu* and they would go into the men's house and eat. Every day this would happen.

One day the man went fishing and saw a clamshell in the water. He dove down and speared the clam, removing the meat and leaving the shell in the water. He came back and told his wife to prepare the clam meat, to cover it up in leaves and to bake it. She baked it and in the afternoon the man called his children and told them to go tell all the *tambu* to come and have a little something to eat. He had told his wife to go get some food. In the afternoon, the *tambu* all came and filled up the men's house. The man took the clam meat out of its leaf covering and told his *tambu* to distribute it to everyone in the men's house. They dealt out all the yams and *mami* and taro and they ate. Afterwards, they conversed. One man inquired "Hey, *tambu*, where did you find this meat?" His *tambu* replied "Hey, *tambu*, do you think this stuff is difficult to find? I just found it in the sea." "Hey, *tambu*, I think that tomorrow we'll return and go to the sea and you can teach us these things." The man replied "All right. Tomorrow you all come and we'll go out in a canoe and I'll find some and show you. You can get some for yourselves."

The man woke up early the next morning and went first to the beach. He readied the fruit of a special kind of large-leafed tree called *fut*. He filled up his basket with the same number of fruit as there were Nea. When he had enough in the basket, he put the basket in the canoe. He turned around and saw all his *tambu* coming. "Hey, *tambu*, what's happening, you ran away from us and came first."

"Yes, I came to wait for you here."

They got the canoe and put it on the water. All the Nea climbed in first and their *tambu* sat down last in the bow with his basket of *fut*. They paddled and paddled until they were in deep waters. The man said "You musn't paddle strongly now. Paddle gently and let's look down into the water." They all looked down and saw a clam shell. "There's one – a clam shell."

"Hey, *tambu*, if I dive down what am I supposed to do?"

"*Tambu*, go down but don't grab it. Just put your head inside the shell, lift it up, walk with it in the water and go ashore with your clam shell."

"All right. I'll try it" said the Nea. He stood up, held in his breath and went down. He planted his head in the clam shell and the shell snapped closed on him. The Nea struggled under the water while the others paddled away. The man took one of the fruits out of his basket and threw it away under the canoe while it pulled away. He looked behind him and saw the fruit bobbing up and down on the water. He said "Hey, look, there – he's drifting ashore with his *am fat* now."

His *tambu* all replied "Oooeey. That's not to go to the men's house, that's for the cook house [*felungkur*]." But it wasn't the man they saw bobbing, only the fruit. The man was stuck in the clam shell. They paddled on and spotted another shell.

"Here's one!"

"Hey, *tambu*, what am I supposed to do with it?"

"How many times do I have to explain? I just showed that other man. Go down, put your head in the shell, carry it to the surface and go ashore with your shell."

The Nea went down and put his head in the shell. The shell shut closed on his head and he began to struggle. His *tambu* yelled out "Paddle on! Paddle on!" As they pulled away, he took out another fruit and threw it away behind him. They paddled away and when they looked back they said "There's his head, he's got the shell. He's not going to eat it in the men's house, he'll take it to his own cook house." They paddled on and found another shell. The man counted the remaining Nea and marked a fruit for each of them. One *tambu* asked him "What should I do?"

"Ah, *tambu*, I told you already. How many times do I have to tell you all? Go down, put your head inside, lift up the shell and take it ashore."

The Nea held his breath, went down, put his head inside and began to struggle. The others paddled away. The man took another fruit and threw it behind him.

They paddled on and found other shells until all the fruits in the basket were gone and all the Nea were finished. The man alone paddled ashore. The wives of all the Nea saw the man coming back ashore. (His name was Soi.)

"Hey, where are our husbands? Where are your *tambu*?"

"Who knows where they are? I don't know where your husbands are?"

The women realized that Soi had taken their husbands to go find clam shells to spear. They asked him: "Do you know this man who tricked our husbands? We think they've all died."

All the Nea were stuck inside the shells under the water. Only Soi came ashore. The women went [tape garbled] What were they to do? Their husbands were dead inside the clam shells.

The story represents the gluttony of Nea in two distinct but related respects. First, the Neas voice their intention to deliver their catch not to the men's house but to the cook house, that is, not to the site of collective consumption but to the private domain of restricted consumption. Each Nea intends to violate the prevailing expectation that large catches of fish, tortoise or wild pig are brought to the men's house for distribution to lineage men and other guests. This opposition between restricted consumption and collective consumption, physically manifest in the distinction between *felungkur* (women's cookhouse) and *bia* (men's house), is the same practical and conceptual antinomy to which the opposition between *bisnis* and *kastam* is coordinated (chapters 2 and 3).

Secondly, the Nea persistently abuse the hospitality of their *tambu*, always appearing for their share of the catch and never reciprocating in kind. This incapacity to reciprocate signals not only the breach of proper etiquette between *kinaf*, but also the relative unproductivity of Nea. Unproductivity implies the incapacity to maintain relations of nurture (*fang*). In the case of Soi, the Nea were unable to sustain relations of reciprocal nurture with their *ifalik* (ZH/WB or *tambu*).

The story of Nea and Nepirpir illustrates the same inability of Nea to provide nurture but in this case the relations emphasized are those between Nea and his wife and child.[28]

The sister of Nepirpir married Nea. She stayed with Nea. The woman became pregnant. She was pregnant and gave birth. Nea would leave the woman to stay with his son and go off to work. Work, work, work and he would come back. They would cook for themselves and the three would sleep. The next day, Nea would leave the two alone again.

One day, Nepirpir came upon his sister and the child alone during the day. "Hey, you two, you sit here and what do you eat?"

"Oh, your brother-in-law goes to the bush and leaves us two for a long time. In the afternoon he'll show up."

"Put the child over there and go collect firewood."

All right. She gave the child to his uncle and the woman left. She collected firewood and returned.

"Fetch some pieces of ironwood and some pieces of the *mit* tree here. And some branches of *patma*." She came with them.

"Throw them down. All right. Prepare an oven and make a fire." She built a fire and lit it. The fire consumed the wood.

"All right. Take away the stones from atop the fire." She removed the stones.

He said "When you hear the horizon rumble with thunder and lightning, take apart the oven." He then got down and stretched out in the middle of the fire. His sister then placed the stones on top of him. She piled all the stones until there were no more, then covered the stones with leaves and put pandanus palm leaves atop the other leaves. She came back, picked up her child, washed him and sat down to wait for the oven to be done.

She heard the lightning and thunder and the horizon rumbling. The two took apart the oven now. They removed the leaves. A layer of unpeeled yams was on top. The two continued to take apart the oven. A layer of peeled yams covered up another layer beneath. The two dug deeper below into the oven: *mangat*. The two went further below: large yams. They filled up baskets and put them to one side. The three of them ate. Nepirpir went to the beach and bathed, decorated his hair with lime, put a feather in his hair and came back. He approached "Has your father come?"

"Oh, no."

"What are you two doing then? The child's things are here. Go ahead, eat." He left.

Nea came. "Hey, mama, where did this stuff come from?"

"It's the child's stuff from his uncle."

"Oh really? You say it's stuff for you two only from your brother-in-law." All the time Nea would act like this.

One day, Nea thought to himself "I'll try it like my brother-in-law." Nea spoke to his wife one day "Hey, wife, put the child here and go collect firewood."

"What for, Nea?"

"Do you think that group [teknonym for brother-in-law] there didn't inform me? I'll do to myself just like that group does it. Leave me be and I'll roast myself in the oven. Put my purse over there." She gave the child to Nea and went out. She chopped some ironwood, pieces of *mit*, and large branches of *patma*, and returned with them. She built a fire, putting large stones on top of it.

"Hey, mama, why is the fire so large?"

"Oh, really, do you think the boy's uncle talks like that?"

"Yes, you say, yes, you say does your *tambu* talk like that?"

"Your *tambu* sits quietly."

The fire smoked and burned. Nea sat there thoroughly petrified by the fire. The fire burned brightly.

"Hey, mama, why is this fire burning like that?"

"Oh, really, you think that your *tambu* talks like that? The fire can burn red hot and he won't talk like that."

"Yes, you talk, your *tambu* talks like that, your *tambu* sits down quietly."

The fire consumed all the wood. The heat was intense. Nea broke out in a sweat. He was afraid of the fire. She took away the stones.

"Hey, mama, these stones are red hot and the fire is glowing."

"Oh, really, do you think that the boy's uncle speaks like that? When it's red hot, he does it."

"Yes, you say, he does everything quietly."

She finished removing the stones. "All right, Nea, lie down there."

"Wowowowo, wait, you two, until the fire is a little cooler."

"What are you doing? My boy's uncle doesn't do it like that. When the fire is like this, he bends down and lays himself out."

"Really, yes, you say he does it."

Nea got down and laid himself out inside the oven. He sizzled in the heat. He squirmed to one place and the wife piled the stones there. He squirmed to another place and she piled the stones there. He stammered "wititititi" and she put stones there. The woman piled up the oven until it was completely covered with stones. Nea evacuated his bowels in the oven and died. She then put on some leaves and covered them with pandanus leaves. She then returned to the child and washed him. The two of them waited.

Nea had told them that when they heard the horizon rumble they were to open up the oven. They waited, waited, waited until the right time had passed. The horizon didn't rumble. "What now, I think the man is dead here. I'll try to open the oven." She began to take apart the oven, first the pandanus leaves, then the layer of leaves down to what they were covering. There was nothing being covered. She went down farther to the peeled *mami*. There were no peeled *mami*. She went down farther into the oven. *Mangat*, there were no *mangat*.

She removed the stones and saw Nea, his mouth char-broiled. "Weee, Nea, you failed to imitate your *tambu*. You yourself have done yourself wrong. Your mouth is cooked!" The two of them rolled Nea out of the fire [like a cooked pig] and stretched him out. The two cried for him.

Nepirpir came. "What are you two crying for?"

"Oh, look at your *tambu* there. He imitated you. We collected firewood and made an oven. Now his mouth is fried and we're crying for him."

"This group misunderstands these things. They think that they are able to work these things just the same. They look and deceive themselves. They think that they are able to work this thing. They themselves did themselves wrong. Now their mouth is cooked and they've defecated in the middle of the oven. Who can remedy this?" Nepirpir left. Nea was dead.

Nepirpir clearly embodies both the productivity and correct behavior that together comprise the ability to realize nurture obligations to his sister's son in view of the father's failure to discharge the same basic obligations. Nea's unproductivity takes the form of bungled imitation or repetition, a parody of Tangan procedures of mimetic education, first of his wife's words and then, fatally, of Nepirpir's food production. Nepirpir pointedly designates his largesse as the "personal things of the boy" (*tonsu ang kaik*; the personal possessive form is used), thereby provoking Nea likewise to provide food. Nea's failure to produce food for his wife and child eventuates instead in Nea making food of himself. The story thus posits a definite relationship between food production and food consumption, namely, that the inability to produce food leaves one vulnerable to the possibility of becoming food. In the first story, the unproductive and overconsumptive Nea become, at the hands of their *tambu*, the food of the clamshells that the Nea originally intended to eat. Put otherwise, and in terms more recognizable as aspects of everyday practice, the story equates consuming the food of others with the consumption of one's self by others; or, again, the act of giving food *to* others with the act of making food *of* others. Indeed, many Nea tales end with Nea being tricked by the protagonists who then kill and eat Nea himself.

These implicit premises emerge clearly in the following story. The story, recorded by the missionary Maurer (1975) and translated into German, is here rendered in close translation of Maurer's Tangga text: [29]

In one village, the adults went off to their work. They left their children to stay behind and look after the village. One day, the children were there during the day when they heard a rooster calling in the bush. They spoke: "Hey, brother, listen to the rooster cackling somewhere. Our roosters don't cackle like that." They stopped playing and everyone listened. They listened and heard the rooster cackle again. They spoke: "Yes, another kind of rooster – it doesn't sound like our roosters." They then discussed a plan: "Let's chase and kill it for ourselves, all of us, no one can stay behind."

They all went to the bush. The young girls put the infants in carrying slings – they were still very small – and they too followed. They walked toward the sound of the rooster until they found it. They shouted at it and chased it. The rooster ran and the children followed it. When it hid somewhere in the bush, they stood up in a circle to trap it. They tightened the circle until they found it. No one of them was lazy, because the bigger children had said: "Whoever stays behind and does not chase the rooster – we will not give any to him." Every one of them did not tire in defeating the rooster and trying to kill it.

The owner of the rooster was Nea. Nea saw the children running towards him. He greeted them and was happy, thinking "little snacks for me." The children paid no attention to Nea and thought only of killing the rooster. Nea watched them go inside of a cave. Nea then spoke "*tiri* close." The cave closed and trapped the children. The children were taken by surprise when the cave closed. They did not know how to get themselves out. There was no way, the cave was sealed completely. The children ran out of ideas. They sat down and cried. Brothers and sisters sat together in little groups.

Nea came and began to console them. "You mustn't cry. I'm your grand-father, stop crying. You can play here inside our house. I'll go look for food inside the garden." He turned and walked away from them. He spoke: "*tiri* open." The cave opened. Nea went out and stood in his yard. He reversed his speech: "*tiri* close." The cave shut again. Nea left and the children inside the cave cried to themselves. They knew that they were going to be killed. They felt sorry for their mothers and fathers. Their parents would not see them and they would be killed in a faraway place by Nea.

One small child, whose parents had died, did not feel frightened and he alone did not cry. He felt calm and admonished the children. "You must stop crying all the time. Stop crying and let's think of a way to save ourselves." He then asked them "What did Nea say when the cave opened and he left?" The children answered him "We didn't hear well what Nea said." The little orphan said "Pay attention. Nea spoke like this: '*tiri* open'." The boy said this and the cave opened. All the children were overjoyed. They got up, went outside and stood in the yard. The child then asked them "Hey, children, what did Nea say when the cave trapped us?" The children replied "We didn't hear what he said very well because we were crying." The child said "Nea spoke like this: '*tiri* close'." The cave closed. The children went back to their village.

The children told their story about Nea to their fathers. Their fathers asked them, "Do you still know where this cave is?" The children replied, "Yes, we still know." All the fathers spoke, "Tomorrow you will show it to us so that we can get rid of him altogether lest he hide you and kill you."

The next day, they all grabbed axes and clubs and they went to Nea. They found him at his cave and asked him "So, you want to eat our children?" Nea replied "No, no, no, no, no. I don't want to kill them. I left them to stay in the cave until I found food for them. Because they are just ignorant children, they were afraid of me and ran away. And now they have spoken no good of me to you." The fathers did not accept Nea's explanation. They entered the cave and killed Nea. They threw him outside and there they chopped him up with their axes. They scattered his remains and returned to their village. They said to each other "Everything is good now. We killed him so that our children can live happily without anything to harm them." Like lightning it is finished, my story to you.

Unlike Nea in the last story, the orphan here successfully imitates or mimics the actions necessary to liberate the children from Nea's hidea-way. When the avenging parents confront Nea with the question "So, you want to eat our children?", Nea replies that he intended to get food *for* the children. Indeed, Nea protests that the ignorant children misun-derstood his intentions. Yet the misunderstanding, I suggest, is unmistakably motivated by the force of metaphorical equations. Being eaten and eating the food of others are cognate modalities of a single proposition. The gastronomic modality of "eating" (*en*) shades into the

aggressive modality: being fed is metaphorically equal to being canni-
balized.

Mortuary feasting and force-feeding

During the *am furis* of one particular mortuary feast, the hosts (An Siko
lineage of clan Korofi) enacted a sequence from the story of Nea and the
children. The feast announced the host lineage's plan to remove a restriction on feasting and consuming pork inside their men's house that had
been initiated nearly a year before and signalled by the erection of a
forked branch (*paluk*) in front of the men's house. In order to communicate to the seated guests that the feast was to be "eat everything" (*en tike*),
one of the host men placed the branch squarely in the middle of the front
entranceway to the men's house. A second man almost simultaneously
hung from the center of the lintel of the rear entrance a shell necklace with
an egg cowrie pendant (*katalu'm bul*). The practical effect of symbolically
blocking the entranceways was to lock (*kut*) the guests inside the men's
house. Egression thereby became construable as aggression and technically punishable by a fine in the form of a shell valuable like the egg
cowrie pendant.

After the distribution of food and "locking" of the guests inside, the An
Siko lineage leader approached the front of the men's house and spoke
"*tiri par, tiri kut*." Two other members of the host lineage joined the
"locked" guests inside the men's house. These two men sat quietly on
bamboo pillows at the base of the central ridge post, surrounded by men
eating their individual portions. The two men did not eat. After a period
of several minutes, one man turned to the other and asked if he had heard
the words that Nea had used to lock the door. As in the story, his
companion replied that he did not know. The first man then stood up and,
in successful imitation of Nea, spoke the words "*tiri par, tiri kut*" in order
to remove the *paluk* and thereby allow the remainder of the male guests to
pour into the men's house from outside.

At a similar "eat everything" feast, after the guests had been seated
within the men's house (recall how guests must often be mock-forcibly led
to their seats), two groups of youths from the host lineage emerged
yelping from some nearby bush. Each group ran into the hamlet
shouldering a long, straight wooden pole (*bakut*), painted with red and
black rings and reddened tips. One group headed for the front entranceway, the other for the rear, and each at the same time lowered the poles
into the crotches of forked poles planted on either side of the entranceways. The principal feast organizer then stood a small stem of bamboo

before each pole and draped strands of red shells (*kemetas*) from the bamboo. The *bakut* thus more than figuratively blocked the exit of the guests.

Such recurrent symbolic practice indicates that, from the point of view of the hosts, "eat everything" feasts are in some respects a form of *enforced eating*. The hosts ensure that their guests not only partake of but entirely consume their proffered distribution by confining the guests to the men's house. Later on, after the various shell valuables have been removed and a second sitting of men allowed into the men's house, the host's injunction still applies to the food itself. Guests must return the following day to finish their unconsumed portions. On some occasions, guests may forego this obligation by making small money payments to the host lineage. On one occasion, a recipient lineage presented the host lineage with a shell disc (*tintol*), remarked upon by the hosts as the correct form of compensation in this context, in order to remove their portion from the host men's house for consumption at their own men's house.

For the duration of their enforced eating, then, the guests are likened to Nea's "guests"; that is, the guests are constructed as potential food themselves. Both the guests inside the locked men's house and the children inside Nea's cave forfeited their autonomy, especially, control over their own movement. While the children were almost eaten by force, the guests were forced to eat. Guests, moreover, temporarily take on the features of gluttons inasmuch as enforced eating, like gluttony, is a type of consumption in which the eater exercises no restraint or control. Enforced eaters thereby become identified with the very idea of unrestrained consumption for which Nea himself stands. The "eat everything" feast thus constructs the guests as both eaters and eaten, active consumers and passive consumables.

Conclusion: feast giving and value-creation

The Nea stories provide insight into the meaning and moral complexity of feast giving, of food transmission as "making others eat" (*fa + en*). Giving here functions, however, not as the negation of eating (consumption), but rather as the activity that practically mediates the opposition between eating (consumption) and not eating (non-consumption). In this sense, "making others eat" reciprocally implies and dialectically constructs noneaters as well as eaters. In the context of certain feasts, for example, the transmission of food to others coordinates public abstention from eating on the part of the host lineage. Members of the host lineage distribute the food to guests and then retire to another part of the feast site either to supervise the event or to perform the *am furis* (plate 12).

Abstention in the context of feasting recalls the powerful image of the *kaiwabu* described in Young's classic account of how Goodenough islanders "fight with food" (1971). During the climactic distributions of competitive festivals, a representative of the food-distributing clan, called the *kaiwabu* occupies a:

chest-high sitting platform which has been constructed to one side of the hamlet, and from which can be viewed the other platforms piled high with food and butchered pigs. From the moment of seating himself cross-legged on the platform at mid-morning to the time of the departure of the final guests at dusk, the *kaiwabu* should not be seen to move, speak, eat, drink or do anything except gaze fixedly at the crowd and vigorously chew betel.

(Young 1971:248–9)

The *kaiwabu* embodies the culturally valued attributes of abstention, self-restraint, and control. Though in less dramatic form, Tangan feast sponsors engage in the same kind of behavior by delaying consumption of their share of feast food until after the departure of their guests. In effect, feast givers display themselves as nonconsumers. Their abstention from consumption performs "durability," that is, resistance to consumption.

Plate 12   Women being "made to eat" by receiving cuts of pork during a mortuary feast at Bulam, 1984

Feast giving, in other words, is an act of evaluation or value-creation. Hosts and guests define their relation to each other in terms of the attributes and qualities associated with their respective actions – eating and not eating. The ceremonial exchange of cooked pigs and shell discs, performed in the context of feasts, objectifies this relationship in the material form of the items that the exchange juxtaposes. In the next chapter, I retrace the entire sequence of mortuary feasts and exchanges in order to demonstrate how this process of value-creation unfolds in the wake of death. I also demonstrate how the aggressive and almost anti-social character of feast giving as force-feeding in fact disguises social relations of complementarity and dependency, social relations presupposed by the very performance of mortuary feasts.

7

Performing lineage succession: transformative exchange and the power of mortuary rites

Looking backwards, the entire sequence of mortuary feasting and exchange comes into view as a set of evaluations effected through the practico-symbolic mediation of giving (*fen*). Adopting such a perspective allows me to show how the mortuary sequence redefines the host lineage as enduring and transcendent (*fat*), autonomous relative to other lineages and to deceased lineage members. Mortuary rites and transformative exchanges, in particular, constitute the lineage *as a lineage*, that is, as a self-replacing bounded group of homologous individuals – what Louis Dumont (1970) would call a "collective individual." This effect is a salient and integral aspect of "finishing" the dead.

But mortuary feasting and exchange are also exercises in the manipulation of power (*mui*). That is, the process of reevaluation entailed in the mortuary sequence makes power visible in three distinct but interlocking ways:

1. The evaluation of the host lineage as enduring (*fat*) implies control over processes of growth (life and fertility) and decay (death and destruction) associated with the three modalities of consumption (*en*).
2. The practice of mortuary feasting as a process of gradually disclosed revelations implies control over public knowledge, on the one hand, and the capacity to fix the form of social relations by evincing or objectifying them, on the other.
3. The construction of the lineage as a collective individual implies a denial or eclipse of a form of sociality that privileges dependency and relationality, and the affirmation of a form of sociality that privileges autonomy and self-sufficiency.

In making these claims, I suggest in this chapter that the mortuary sequence be conceived as a cyclical and reciprocal evaluative process whereby agents alternately assume the values of *en* and *fat* towards each other. It is through this process that agents take turns at mutually constructing each other's autonomy – the paradox of Tangan mortuary rites. The process thus models the complementarity of *en* and *fat* as value-terms, and the two forms of sociality for which they respectively stand. This complementarity, in turn, organizes social reproduction as a regulated oscillation between life and death.

The mortuary sequence as evaluative process
If we reconsider the mortuary sequence synoptically, as completed rather than contingent action, the sequence appears as a syntagm of evaluations.[1] Over the length of this syntagm, the agents who initiate the action of feasting and exchange reevaluate themselves with reference to the social relationships constitutive of their identity. That is, the enatic relatives of the deceased reevaluate themselves from consumers (*en*) to non-consumers or endurers (*fat*) through the mediation of giving (*fen*), of causing others to eat. This process begins during the first phase of the mortuary sequence, in the rites of burial and mourning, and culminates at the final feast (*arer sigit*) in the culminating exchange of cooked pigs and shell discs (*lulu am bo*). Reevaluations of this sort are intrinsic to the process of social reproduction or, in the Tangan view, the process of "replacement."

Throughout the immediate rites of burial and mourning, the identification of the host lineage with death is unambiguous. The lineage of the deceased assumes the status of consumers/consumed relative to other lineages. This becomes clear in two important respects. First, only members of the lineage of the deceased officially receive pigs at the feast held for waking the corpse (*kis fakut*, "sit down in silence"). These pigs are not given to representatives of other lineages as tokens in a gift exchange. Rather, a male lineage mate of the deceased eats the pig cooked for the occasion, that is, the rump of a whole cooked pig will be put to the mouth of this man for the official first bite. Similarly, only lineage men receive pigs at the feast made three days after burial. The name of this feast, *en mapu'ng kinit* ("eating the stink of the corpse"), metaphorically relates the cooked pigs and the putrefaction of the corpse. The obligation of consuming the corpse/pork falls primarily to the deceased's own lineage mates; affinal and patrilateral relatives have by this time undertaken restrictions on eating pork (see below). In this way the lineage of the deceased both feeds and eats itself, and thereby exhibits itself as the preeminent consumer. It is in this sense that the lineage of the deceased identifies itself not only with a particular death, but with the consumptive connotations of death in general.

Secondly, the institution of mourning taboos, which occurs around the time of burial, also dialectically constructs the host lineage as consumers. Affinal and paternal relatives (*kinaf*) of the deceased's lineage, who usually make up the bulk of the mourners, generally assume dietary restrictions (*tam en*); don black clothing and face paint; let their hair grow; and curtail both their productive activities, such as gardening, and their physical mobility. In the case of mourning widow/ers, strict confinement to the men's house of the deceased spouse might be sustained for up to several weeks following the death. Mourners publicly advertise their "sacrifices" by wearing tight wrist and ankle bands (*pan tam en*), one band per "sacrifice." These bands are made of the tough lygodium creepers (*an asem*) once used to lash together the planks of ocean-going canoes.

In one sense, the mourners themselves determine and initiate these observances by making prestations of various kinds to the deceased's lineage: small amounts of cash for dietary restrictions, small live pigs or even shell discs for more stringent taboos such as confinement. Mourners thus define themselves through gift-giving as non-consumers relative to the lineage of the deceased. Indeed, the mourners physically embody the qualities of "fastness" (*fat*) in their confinement and immobility, and the qualities of "resistance to consumption" in their self-imposed dietary restrictions (or fasting – signified by the bands fastened around their joints). Those who assume mourning taboos thus enact a bodily image of "not eating."

But in another sense, it is the lineage of the deceased that enables (or causes) the mourners to construct themselves as non-consumers and, perforce, the lineage of the deceased as consumers. That is, by undertaking the project of hosting feasts for the deceased (as opposed to "rubbishing" the deceased), the lineage of the deceased elicits from mourners the gifts that dialectically construct donor and recipient as non-consumer and consumer. These gifts, like the cooked pigs that the lineage presents to itself at *kis fakut* and *en mapu'ng kinit*, publicly qualify the lineage with the attributes of consumption.

Having eaten the putrefying corpse, the lineage of the deceased initiates a series of feasts which effectively divests it of its recently acquired attributes. That is, the lineage of the deceased now acts as giver, and hence as non-consumer, rather than as recipient and consumer/

consumed. For example, a feast might be made in order to "call out the widow/er" from his or her confinement. The lineage of the deceased will formally and precisely reciprocate to the lineage of the widow/er the gifts originally received when the mourning taboos were instituted. Over time, at one or more separate feasts, restrictions on confinement, diet, dress, and coiffure will be lifted for all mourners. In short, the visible reminders of death – ankle and wrist bracelets, black clothes and face paint, uncut hair – are all progressively dispelled by the active feast giving of the lineage of the deceased. The visible markers of the relations comprising the person of the deceased are rendered invisible and thus "finished." This first phase of the mortuary sequence ends with a feast (*moratineng*) at which the host lineage compensates with gifts of pork the women who wailed and keened over the corpse. The distribution partially restores exchange relations between the host lineage and its various relatives to the configuration prevailing before the death occurred. The visible signs of death and the gift debts which originated with these signs thus disappear together.

The feast of *moratineng* introduces the second phase of the mortuary sequence in which the lineage of the deceased both continues to construct itself as durable relative to other lineages and begins to redefine its value as "consumers" relative to its own ancestral members (*tumlang*). For usually during this particular feast, the host lineage reveals its intentions to build a memorial men's house and "finish" the dead. This project at once acknowledges and dissolves the debt owed to the ancestors for their "hard work" or "care" (*fang*) in clearing matrilineal land, planting fruit-bearing trees, and managing the resources of the present generation. In this sense, commemoration of the dead is an enatic version of the repayment of paternal nurture (*kos fang*) achieved in patrilateral cross-cousin marriage.[2] The culmination of this phase of the mortuary sequence thus constitutes the lineage as durable relative to the two sources of its sustenance: living affinal and patrilateral relatives (*kinaf*, the principal mourners), and dead matrilineal forebears.

The task of building a new men's house involves above all a demonstration of the host lineage's productive capacity: the cultivation of large gardens on the part of lineage members and their supporters; the husbandry of many pigs; the acquisition of scarce building materials (bamboo, sago leaf thatching, timber); and the coordination and deployment of an adequate workforce. During the numerous feasts which mark the progress of construction, the host lineage displays signs (*finai-lim*) of this capacity. That is, the host lineage produces signs of its viability instead of as before erasing signs of its vulnerability (to death). One of the most prominent of these signs, all of which foreshadow the climactic final feast (*arer sigit*) of the sequence, is the basket of cooked food known as *warangus* or "base of the food heap." Throughout the second phase of the mortuary cycle, the host lineage presents these baskets to men designated to receive large pigs at the final feast. Each basket contains a selection of the vegetable food, betel nut and fruits (for example, bananas, breadfruit, drinking coconuts) distributed at the feast at which the baskets are presented. Acceptance of a basket by a man from another lineage obligates that lineage to contribute a large pig (*waram pan sinol*) and a smaller pig (*so keke'm bo*) as well as a substantial amount of garden produce to the final feast.[3] This garden produce will form part of the food heap (*gus*) prominently displayed prior to distribution in the center of the newly constructed men's house.

At the earlier feasts of phase two (for example, the feast that marks the dibbling of the gardens made to supply future feasts), the baskets presented are both small in size and few in number.[4] In proportion to the progress of feasting, the number of baskets increases. More and more people are drawn into the project and "caused to eat" by the host lineage. Each basket signifies an additional link in the host lineage's network of support relations and anticipates the augmentation of the main food pile distributed at the final feast. Likewise, the size of the baskets grows over the course of the feasts associated with steps in the building process; the portions of food comprising the basket become larger and larger. Changes in the material form of the baskets thus model the increasing capacity of the host lineage to give feasts, that is, to elicit from others the food and pigs necessary to satiate the consumptive needs of a large audience. This capacity, and the concomitant construction of the host lineage as permanent and transcendent, is realized most thoroughly in the central transformative exchange of the final feast of the mortuary sequence.

Lulu am bo

Lulu am bo refers to the payment for pigs made twice during the mortuary sequence, once at the feast following the thatching of the roof (*en bala'm bia*) and again at the final feast. On both occasions a ZS or ZSZS of the deceased man or men commemorated by the feast sequence climbs on to the roof of the men's house (plate 13). There he stands, ornamented with one or more of the host lineage's shell valuables: the perennial ZS – the embodiment of lineage succession.[5] Frequently, the ZS or the ZSZS

Plate 13   Alois Negat stands on the roof of the men's house made at Bulam in
1984 to commemorate his recently deceased MB, Taurai

mounts the men's house along with his own actual ZS, physically (and, of course, iconically) demonstrating the continuity of the lineage across two generations. A chorus of lineage members gathered before the front of the men's house sing specially composed verses and engage the ZS in a dramatic dialogue (*am furis*) (plate 14). During the course of the performance, the ZS traverses the ridgepole until he stands at the end closest to the chorus. On command, the ZS steps down a colorfully festooned bamboo ladder and then sits facing the area in front of the men's house. Various men, sometimes women, each designated the previous day as a pig recipient, come forward to "buy" (*lulu*) the pigs. The scene transpires without commentary, individuals depositing shell discs (specifically, *tintol*) at the feet of the ZS. Spectators quietly absorb themselves in this the preeminent image of Tangan social life.

The entire scene of *lulu am bo* – the walk of the ZS, the *am furis* and, especially, the transfer of *tintol* – comprises a singularly condensed image of "replacement" (*pilis*), of the ZS "taking the place" (*kep tafu*) of the deceased MB. "Replacement," as I argued in chapter 5, synthesizes in its connotations the notions of reciprocal and non-reciprocal substitution. *Lulu am bo* is the enactment of this synthesis. The ZS who receives the shell discs is identical to his MB in their identity as *lineage* members; the ZS fits into the "slot" (*tafu*) vacated by the deceased MB. The transaction

Plate 14   Partui leads the chorus in an *am furis*

itself is one in a series of identical exchanges, for every *lulu* either reciprocates a previous *lulu* or engenders a debt for future *lulu*. A double process of substitution, of one thing taking the place of something else, is thus advanced: the reciprocal transfer of replicas and the non-reciprocal replacement of dead matrilineage members. Put differently, the long-term exchange of like objects makes possible the replacement of lineage members *who are likenesses of each other*.

The relationship of the asymmetrical transfer – shells for cooked pigs – to the process of lineage replacement that it effects depends upon the iconicity of the very objects of exchange. Shell discs, the durable qualities of which iconically signify intergenerational continuity, flow into the hands of the host lineage in the person of the replacing ZS. Cooked pigs, icons of consumption, flow out from the lineage to those who offer *lulu*. In this sense, *lulu* constitutes the definitive act of giving (*fen*) whereby givers of food materially realize their status as *fat* by the inflow of actual *am fat*. *Lulu* culminates the mortuary sequence not in the magnitude of the transaction, but in the degree to which the transaction *objectifies* all that otherwise remains implicit in the act of making others eat.[6] In *lulu*, the host lineage converts the consumable products of its work (*faim*) and care (*fang*), food and pigs, into the durable, iconic *am fat*. Making others eat elicits, as gifts to the host lineage, the *am fat* with which the lineage becomes identified; the host lineage appropriates as part of its collective identity the qualities of the iconic exchange media taken in at *lulu*. Thus, the temporary asymmetry of *lulu am bo* facilitates the projection of the image of one lineage's successful replacement process, the realized conversion of death and the ultimate consumption represented by death into the perdurance and longevity embodied by shell discs.

This conversion was articulated in one of the *am furis* surrounding *lulu am bo* at a final feast which I attended. Due to a dispute within the host lineage, the largest pig was presented to the mother of the nominal feast organizers instead of to a classificatory MB, that is, to a male lineage leader. At the moment when other pig recipients deposited shell discs at the feet of the ZS (or, in this case, the S, since the absence of the MB was heavily emphasized), the mother of the man accepting the shells stepped forward with a younger son and daughter (viz., the man's siblings). Pointing to the younger son she said "Here is your *kemetas*." Likewise indicating the daughter, she spoke "Here is your *am fat*." In other words, the mother offered to her son the son's own siblings as *lulu* for the large pig. The *am furis* thus metaphorically equated the durable icons of lineage continuity with the physical embodiments of the lineage, the women's children.

Power: control over consumption

The reevaluation of the host lineage as *fat* accomplished through mortuary practices is an exercise in power manipulation. Like other New Irelanders, Tangans regard power (*mui*) as a diffuse force permeating the world that is susceptible to the manipulation of certain individuals for a variety of purposes (cf. Clay 1986, Wagner 1986a). Somanil Funil described power as follows:

Power is in everything – in man, the sea, the bush and everything else. Men can manipulate power. A man can take ginger or lime powder or bush plants and bespell them (give them power) and then give them to you to eat. Afterwards, whoever wants to fight with you, you'll be able to kill or bodily injure him. It's as I said. Everything has power. But man can acquire a little extra power. Power and strength are truly the same. There is no difference. It's not like with other words – these two are truly the same.

Power, as Wagner notes for the Barok, is *sui generis*, put there by its creators and hence a legacy of the ancestors. Leo Netang thus observed one day, when a gathering of men at an "eat everything" feast was unable to consume two small pigs, that people die but nonetheless leave their "strength" (*mia*) or "power" (*mui*) from which the living draw help. Such power is manifest as a men's house that visitors respect (*pepe*); the ability to make lightning; and the fact that many hungry men failed to finish eating two small pigs. Netang denied that people know the ultimate source of such power and he opined that perhaps it was best simply to call power "God" and leave it at that. He noted, however, that the "power of the ancestors" (*ingiat*) remained in the ground even if contemporary men knew not how to manipulate it.

Although Somanil's and Netang's statements equate power (*mui*) with physical strength (*mia*), I suggest that a useful analytical distinction can be made between them. While physical strength is both depletable and replenishable (through the intake of food), power proper is transcendent and constant, there, as Netang said, whether or not men know how to work it.[7] Alternatively, one might say that *mia* is a manifestation of *mui* in human form, a particular and temporary token of the abstract permanent type; additional *mui* can result in increased physical strength. I propose that power, with its connotations of immunity to dissipation, is of a conceptual whole with the value-term *fat*. This unity is immanent in power usages that depend upon the control of consumption for their efficacy.

Tangans employ power manipulations (*ate*) in regard to a number of concerns including sickness, gardening, weather conditions, sexual attraction and various aspects of the performance of *kastam* (protecting line dancers from distraction, ensuring sufficient food by controlling the appetite of guests, attracting many visitors to a men's house). Often, abstention from drink and certain foods is part of the procedures of empowerment. For example, one man claimed that in making love magic, a man neither can drink nor ingest juicy/fatty foods such as papaya, leafy greens and, especially, pork. These foods are considered "heavy" and capable of "weighing down" the power inside a man (my informant, Emil Fumpas, likened the effect to an overloaded ship that cannot go very fast). Water is considered to reduce the "heat/power" of a man's blood and skin and hence reduce the effectiveness of the magic. Similarly, men called *ingiat* who embody, in Wagner's (1986a:142) felicitous phrase, "the most puissant degree of power," are subject to a life-long taboo on the consumption of pork.[8] In one sense, then, the person who epitomizes the presence of power also epitomizes the negation of consumption through the avoidance of that preeminent comestible, pork. The parallel with mourning taboos and feast giving is clear: abstention from pork constructs the *ingiat* as one who is *fat* relative to others. In the case of the *ingiat*, however, this status is permanent and irreversible; hence the *ingiat*'s threatening autonomy, an autonomy unencompassed within the alternating asymmetries of an exchange relationship.

The same kind of control over consumption evident in abstention characterizes one of the recognized procedures for making rain. Therein, a rainmaker (*waranfat*) mixes a solution of bark scrapings and water inside a large clam shell (*am fat*) (cf. Clay 1986:144). The solution is covered with leaves and left to rot in a secret place. As the solution blackens and begins to stink, black clouds form and rain falls. To end the rain, the rainmaker removes the rotting potion from the shell container. Besides exemplifying the sort of practical analogy involved in power usages, the technique stresses how control over (or containment of) the process of consumptive decay is itself a manifestation of power. That this process of controlling decay is synonymous with the construction of oneself as *fat* (that is, appropriating as part of one's identity the qualisigns of the value-term *fat*) is clear from the title of the rainmaker. *Waranfat* means "base/origin/master of the stones." The stones to which the title refers are the smooth, round pieces of basalt that rainmakers handle to create rain or sun.[9]

Perhaps the most dramatic instances of power use in Tanga are the enactments of two men's secret societies, *tumbuan* and Sokopana. The mode of distributing pork to the initiated men at a *tumbuan* meeting indicates how control over consumption is intrinsic to the manipulation of power. *Tumbuan* sponsors divide the cooked pigs, brought by representatives of "visiting" *tumbuan* groups and by prospective members as part of their initiation fee, into numerous small bits instead of the usual partition into named and unnamed cuts. The pieces, together with yams and taro also cooked within the "meeting place" (*taraiu*), are spread atop banana leaves laid out in the center of the meeting grounds where the *tumbuan* dances. Men come forward and squat before the food, eating in a manner referred to as "bush style," that is, eating together from a central collective supply instead of individually from private portions.[10] During the eating, the masked figure of the *tumbuan* silently supervises the men, kneeling at one end of the food pile and observing the quiet, almost circumspect scene. "Eat everything" is the rule; food never leaves the confines of the meeting place.

The operative division of personnel opposes the *tumbuan* (and by extension the owner/sponsor [*ain pindik*] of the *tumbuan*) to the members, themselves undistinguished with regard to the apportionment of food. Emphatically, the *tumbuan* does not eat, but instead causes or enforces food consumption on the part of the society members. The *tumbuan* here recalls the shell valuables which "lock" guests inside a men's house as part of other "eat everything" events. More generally, participants in meetings strictly observe a code of etiquette that punishes with fines breaches of order such as arguing, shouting or singing *tumbuan* verses outside of the meeting place. The value-term of non-consumption (*fat*) embodied by the *tumbuan* thus connotes more than abstention from eating. Rather, the *tumbuan*, with its capacity to exact compliance to an ideal of social behavior, indexes a power (*mui*) that defines the limits of autonomous action. As in interlineage gift relations, enforced eaters assume a subordinate status relative to food givers. But unlike these relations, the relationship between the *tumbuan* and its society members is not reversible: the *tumbuan*, like the *ingiat*, never eats. The value-term of non-consumption incarnated by the *tumbuan* possesses an axiomatic, transcendent quality denied to ordinary feast givers. In a sense, the value-term of *fat* in this context defines the constraints of applied power on human sociality (see Errington 1977 for an interpretation of Karavar *tumbuan* along these same lines).[11]

What remains implicit in *tumbuan* performances, as in Nea stories, was once made explicit in the meetings of another secret society called Sokopana (Bell:1935b). To wit, relative to Sokopana, men, women, and children were potential food. Sokopana expresses in a similar medium the same conceptual opposition enacted in *tumbuan* performances. Instead of making others eat, however, Sokopana simply eats others, achieving in a direct fashion the end envisioned in giving (*fa + en*) unto others. Bell (1935b:317 ff.) describes Sokopana as "the devouring ghost [*kinit*]" known and feared by the uninitiated as an all-consuming demon. Novices suffer stories of how the ghost "will eat them up and vomit them forth"; the numerous incisions razored into the backs of the initiates confirm them as bearers of "the tooth-marks of the devouring ghost." Any initiate who died in the course of the rites had his death attributed to being eaten by Sokopana. During Sokopana meetings, moreover, the ghost allegedly "feasted upon, in the company of the initiated, a huge quantity of rich food" (Bell 1935b:333). In short, the common representation of Sokopana was one of *en* incarnate, the realization of almost indiscriminate consumption.[12]

The organization and content of Sokopana ceremonies suggest that control over Sokopana is contingent upon the construction of Sokopana adepts as *fat*. As part of the scarification procedure, many of the society members as well as the novices (*merio*) step forward to receive a whipping at the hands of the chief *kabin pindik* or highest ranking member of the graded secret society. The *kabin pindik* administers with a thin brown cane (*mala-mala*; *mala* means "lightweight"), or sometimes with a thorny vine ("the ghost's teeth"), vertical or horizontal switches depending upon the status of the victim. Bell (1935b:327) remarks of one such occurrence:

As each man, i.e., with the exception of the *merio*, came forward to be whipped, the operator [chief *kabin pindik*, in this case, Ngamnabo], brought from a basket at his feet a present of an *am fat* or a string or several strings of *kemetas* which he handed to his victim, the size of the present varying with the standing of the man in the secret society. In the case of other *kabin pindik*, the size of the present would be prohibitive, so that it is not often that these men are whipped. Someone asked Namnabo for permission to whip him, i.e. Namnabo, with the *mala-mala*. Namnabo scornfully replied that there was not a man on Boieng with valuables sufficient to buy such an honour.

The scenario suggests not only that *kabin pindik* take on the features of the all-devouring ghost, but also that their capacity to do so implies control over consumption. This control is the cause and consequence of an adept's command of shell valuables. Ngamnabo's payment (called *si'ng kinit*) demonstrates that a man's standing in the society was directly *representable* in terms of greater or lesser amounts of *am fat* and *kemetas*, that is, of *fat* objects. Ngamnabo himself, moreover, as paramount *kabin pindik* and administrator of whippings, claimed that no single man commanded enough *am fat* and *kemetas* to represent his standing properly.

Ngamnabo's boast illustrates the degree of rank and stratification in Tangan social life once enabled by the society. The distinction between initiated and uninitiated members rested on the hierarchical opposition of the latter to the former as *en* to *fat*.[13] This same overarching opposition of initiated (as *fat*) to uninitiated (as *en*, the "food" of Sokopana) also ordered the hierarchy of grades, of which there were four. Accordingly, the grades of the Sokopana society were tangibly represented by the greater or lesser amounts of *am fat/kemetas* received at *si'ng kinit*.[14] Progress in the society amounted to the transition from relatively *en* statuses to relatively *fat* statuses, each passage effected by attendance at a society meeting and submission to the whippings meted out by the *kabin pindik*. An original evaluation of an initiate as *"en"* undergoes operation to produce a reevaluation of the initiate as, relatively, *"fat."* Transition in this sense is an evaluative process, indeed, precisely the same sort of evaluative process that transpires over the course of a sequence of mortuary rites.

But Ngamnabo's boast also says something about the logical complementarity of the value-terms *en* and *fat*, a subject to which I will return in the conclusion of this chapter. The control of *am fat* by the chief *kabin pindik*, for example, both enables and grounds his control over the administration of Sokopana's consuming capacity.[15] From a different perspective, however, this appropriated status of all-consumer predicates the control of the *kabin pindik* over *fat* objects. Thus Bell reports that at the end of the Sokopana rites, men from various parts of the island exact a levy or tribute from the uninitiated men and women of their districts. The fee consists in strings of *kemetas* and several *am fat* hung on a bamboo stick (*an'gaf ang kinit*) presented to the chief *kabin pindik*. In addition, the *kabin pindik* organizing the rites (not always the same man as the chief *kabin pindik*) collects the initiation fees of newly inducted members, fees payable in *am fat* and *kemetas*. The figure of the *kabin pindik* thus merges or totalizes the value-terms of *en* and *fat*. On the one hand it incarnates the consuming ghost, the power (*mui*) of unrestrained consumption, Sokopana as the *kinit rokai* or "wild ghost from the bush." On the other it indexes large quantities of *fat* objects, tokens of the power (*mui*) evinced in the control over consumption. This mutual entailment of *en* and *fat*, I will argue below, is not merely expressed but repeatedly constituted in the cyclical, evaluative processes of mortuary feasting and ceremonial exchange.

Power: control of knowledge

The reevaluation that feast givers achieve for themselves manifests power not only through the control of consumption, but also through the control of knowledge. I have already emphasized how the sequence of mortuary events unfolds as a process of gradual revelation. A host lineage periodically publicizes its plans or intentions in the form of signs (*finailim*) such as the *warangus* baskets (see above). The cumulative effect of these displays is the foreshadowing of the final feast of the mortuary sequence, such that the eventual realization of that feast constitutes a retrospective validation of previous predictions (or, more precisely, omens). Here I want to argue that a dialectic of concealment and revelation, underpinned by an epistemology rooted in vision, is intrinsic to Tangan mortuary practices, including ceremonial exchange. By mastering this dialectic, feast givers exercise control over how they make themselves known by other people.

The following story of Nea can be read as a lesson both in the dynamics of concealment and revelation conditioning the circulation of shells and in the dangers that these dynamics generate:[16]

Ni-a shambled into a settlement empty of all people except five little boys who were playing on the dancing square. He asked them where all the men and women were and was told that they were all working in the gardens about a mile away. He then asked where they had hidden all their necklaces and arm rings and other ornaments. Four of the little boys feigned ignorance but the fifth, a little boy with sores around his mouth and between the cheeks of his behind came forward and with one hand in his mouth and the other scratching his bottom, said that they were hidden under the wood heap.

Ni-a then went over to the wood heap, and finding the ornaments decorated himself with them and sang the following ditty:

> *Pilak nak un turing.* (Repeated *ad lib.*)
> (The shell disks will come back. Don't worry.)

He then assured the little boys that he would only walk around for a short time and then return to the settlement and give them back the ornaments. He went off singing his song, and true to his promise returned in a little while and handed back the ornaments to the boys. The valuables were replaced in their hiding place but the women, on their return from the gardens, noticed that they had been disturbed. They asked the boys who had been touching their ornaments and they were told about the visit of Ni-a. The women then changed the hiding place.

The next day Ni-a came again and asked the same questions of the same five little boys and received the same answers. When the little boy suffering from yaws told Ni-a where the jewels were, the old man said: "You are a good little boy. You have a face just like mine." He decked himself out with the ornaments and went off, but did not return as on the previous day.

When the women returned from the gardens the little boys told them that Ni-a had stolen all their ornaments. The women then went to the place where Ni-a lived and began to dance before him in a most lascivious manner. They pushed to one side their *fung-fung* (traditional leaf girdles), bent their knees and opened them and shut them, singing all the while the ditty which Ni-a sang when he stole the ornaments, with the addition of the phrase *La-li*, which, freely translated, means Hey, come on, hand them over.

Ni-a, being an old man, wore no pubic covering. He had made a small fire on the dancing square and was lying down beside it, watching the dance. As the line of women advanced towards him, Ni-a could not avoid being sexually aroused. At last he had an erection and out tumbled all the *am pilak* (shell disks) and other ornaments which he had stuffed beneath his foreskin. (Every action of Ni-a is mimicked at this stage. His pop-eyed look at the dancers – his holding down of his rising penis and his last scurried departure.)

If one goes to the island of Malendok, one may see there the erect penis of Ni-a, turned into stone. It is called *li n'am pilak*, or the cave of the *pilak*. Rising from its floor there stands a huge stalagmite.

The story, I suggest, depicts exchange transactions as specific instances of revelatory display through which agents constitute and communicate knowledge about themselves to others. That is, it imagines the circulation of valuables as a process of making unseen things visible. Nea first succeeds in removing the shells from their hiding place under the wood pile and then in decorating himself with the shells. After displaying himself in this fashion, Nea returns the shells to the boys who restore them to their hiding place. The women, however, discover the disturbance and hide the shells anew. Nea again succeeds in removing the shells from their hiding place, only this time to hide them himself beneath his foreskin. The shells move, in short, from one hiding place to another – just as shell discs move in exchange from the storage box of the giver to that of the receiver. Circulation takes the dialectical form of appearance and disappearance.

In order to coax the shells from their new hiding place, the women themselves make visible what normally remains hidden: first their own genitalia, and then Nea's penis. Dancing provocatively, the women open and shut their legs, thereby exposing to Nea's view the means for exposing the hidden shells (a reversal of the exposure of "penis rings" [*kisi na witi*] by men to women). Nea's irrepressible sexual arousal, in turn, reveals the stolen shells (*am pilak*) and relieves him of control over the shells. The incident renders an exchange transaction as the aggressive attempt of one agent to publicize the hidden valuables of another. Publicity, moreover, implies visibility and openness to inspection. The story thus suggests that the cultural logic impelling the exchange is less one of Maussian obligations and more one of coercive display and exhibition. From this perspective, Tangan sociality assumes the general form of eliciting revelations from others *and* making revelations in response to the elicitations of others. Only through and in display – of which exchange, the transfer of objects, is a privileged instance – do persons and things become definitely intertwined and, hence, social identities valorized.[17]

Display and exhibition as realized in exchange serve two purposes. First, they verify the resources of giver and receiver, unequivocally so inasmuch as Tangan epistemology identifies visual perception as the only source of reliable knowledge (see below). Objects and object qualities become definitely associated with particular persons. Secondly, they demonstrate the extent to which control over the dynamics of making hidden things seen indexes control over the objects seen or shown. These dynamics, however, underlie more practices than the circulation of shell valuables. They condition mundane social intercourse and even the overall organization of the mortuary sequence itself. Accordingly, as I will indicate, agents communicate knowledge about themselves in a variety of contexts by means of exercising control over what others see. This insistence upon vision characterizes the culturally specific terms in which exchange practices must be interpreted.

In discussing the emphasis that his Barok informants placed on directly witnessing rather than speaking about images, Roy Wagner (1986a:xiv) wondered if New Irelanders were not after all "from Missouri" (the "show-me" state). Tangans likewise emphasize the relationship between visual apprehension and knowledge. The verb "to know" (*parfat*) combines the word for seeing (*par*) with the modifier for "rootedness" (*fat*). To know is to grasp firmly with the eyes. This kind of knowing contrasts with the kind suggested by the verb "to understand" (*ong*) or, literally, "to hear." A Tangan uses this latter word to inquire if someone understands what he or she is *saying*. Thus, for example, an admonishing mother interrogates her disobedient child: "*O sam ong?*" ("Do you hear/understand me?").

Knowledge acquired by direct observation is more certain than that acquired by other means. Only knowledge of this sort, for example, can be admitted in local courts as the basis of accusations. Visual apprehension or witnessing, moreover, often entails a proprietary relationship between the viewer and the object viewed, such that the viewer achieves a degree of mastery over the object observed. Wagner has argued that such an attitude orients the practice of lodgelike cults or mysteries (such as Sokopana and *tumbuan*) among the Barok. Initiation into such mysteries (*pindik*, which can also be glossed as "revelation" [Wagner 1986a:123]) might involve the revelation that the presence of menacing spirits is actually the sound of certain instruments being played. The effect is not to debunk the spirits, but rather to confer upon the initiate the power to sustain and control the illusion. Revelation leads to a reconstitution of the initiate's social identity as a person who can control the mystery.[18]

In Tanga, the prerogatives that seeing confer upon the seer affect the conduct of exchange, even in the most mundane situations. I have already mentioned how adults shield the contents of their purse from the view of others, a strategy that effectively reduces unwelcome requests for betel nut. For seeing that another person possesses betel ideally obliges that person to surrender some to the observer. Keeping one's supply hidden thus enables one to deny requests ("Sorry, I don't have any") and thus to control one's responses to the solicitations of others. Every man's purse (*tang*) therefore recalls the basket (*tang*) that contains the valuable shell discs. It is symbolic of a personal capacity to enter into exchange, a capacity paradoxically preserved by its own negation, the refusal to give.

Seeing, in other words, constitutes not only knowledge but also control; seeing performatively asserts proprietary rights. But the practical consequences of this for Tangans are twofold. On the one hand, people attempt to conceal certain items – betel nut, food, tobacco – from the demanding inspection of others. On the other hand, however, people sometimes use the deliberate revelation of these items in order to engender a degree of control over the person or persons to whom they are shown. This latter strategy lies behind mortuary feasts, the context of all major exchanges. Feast sponsors display heaps of food and cooked pigs as challenges to the proprietary rights of spectating guests. That is, feast sponsors preempt the proprietary assertion of the spectators by boldly revealing to them an accumulation of food which the spectators become obliged to eat. Similarly, it is the revelation by the women of their genitalia that compels Nea to surrender the shells. The same practical dynamic of concealing and revealing thus underpins both elaborate mortuary feasts and ordinary requests for a leaf of tobacco or a betel nut. It is also this dynamic that organizes the performative sequence of mortuary rites. Briefly, here's how.

The sequence of mortuary feasts undertaken by the lineage of the deceased comprises a series of communications, predominantly but not exclusively nonverbal, that publicize the intentions or "plans" (*enfinawer*) of the hosts. Feast organizers shroud their plans in secrecy for two different reasons, one strategic, the other aesthetic. First, the pig distributions ideally involve holding some pigs in reserve in the event that someone unexpectedly contributes a large pig to a feast that must be matched with a pig of the same size. To advertise one's resources early in the feast sequence might invite other big men to challenge a host lineage by contributing large, not easily matched pigs.

Second, as one informant explained, *kastam* displays a particular lineage's competence ("style") in mangement. Outsiders should not be privy to a lineage's plans lest they copy them; guests merely "come to eat" and to observe if things are running properly. Running a feast properly means running it in an orderly, controlled fashion (*ris*), one thing after another, in much the same way as mourning restrictions are lifted one by one. Thus, the image for "planning" in Tangga is "stacking words one on top of the other" (*fagate niwer*), an image contrasted with that of "sloppy talk" (*gongon falek*) in which discussants speak out of turn or jump (*kalap* in Tok Pisin) from one topic to another. (Many Tangan men associated orderly discussions with European efficiency, and accordingly attempted to adopt parliamentary procedures of record keeping and public speaking in holding their own meetings.) Secrecy thus enables feast organizers to publicize their plans in a measured and regulated manner.

Foreshadowing, itself a sort of gradual revelation, is the master trope of this process of "budgeted revelation" (Lindstrom 1991b). Each feast involves a display of "signs" (*finailim*) that indicate both the progress of preparations for and the scale of the climactic final feast (*arer sigit*) at which numerous shell valuables change hands. Over the course of the feast sequence, then, the hosts prefigure and revise an image of the final feast by rearranging the display of "signs."[19]

Perhaps the most salient example of these "signs" is the *am furis*. *Furis* are word pictures, dialogues or soliloquies which often contain a number of metaphorical allusions to the circumstances of the feasting. Tangans regard *furis* as instances of figurative speech, the word for which in Tangga is *pokta niwer* or "edge talk" (*baksait tok* or *tok piksa* in Tok Pisin). "Edge talk" reveals to people the outside or surface of one's intentions, but not the inside (*bala*) or meaning of these intentions. Hosts perform an *am furis* during the course of mortuary feasts and guests seek to discover the true intentions of the hosts in the words of the performers. But *furis* do not always state the intentions of their performers in a way open to only one interpretation. Nor do the performers ever provide an exegesis for their audience. *Furis* are either self-evidently significant or self-evidently ambiguous. In other words, *furis* are partial revelations; they conjure images that are very much elements in the overall process of revealing plans, such as indicating where a men's house is to be built or whether there is dissension among the hosts, but they do not state plans unambiguously (for example, see Foster 1990a).

Appropriately, then, *furis* can serve not only to presage future feasts, but also to qualify the likelihood of such events coming to pass. For example, actors sometimes refer to or even physically mimic the attempt of a canoe to come ashore while rough seas pound the reef. The search for a safe landing allegorizes the uncertain attempt of the lineage to host the sequence of necessary feasts. In some circumstances, moreover, these allegories refer to conflicts such as disputes over land which ordinarily never receive public airing outside of local court hearings. Such *furis* also introduce an element of contingency into the proceedings, distancing the host lineage from boastful assertions about the certainty of their plans. *Furis* thus effectively, though elliptically, make unseen or hidden things – plans, disputes, accusations, intentions – visible and known. At the same time though, the *am furis* leaves a residue of uncertainty about the ultimate realization in practice of these partial revelations. This uncertainty over whether or not men's houses will be built and final feasts hosted is at once uncertainty over the circulation of shell valuables. For the return of the shells to their donors presupposes the successful realization of the mortuary sequence itself.

Conceived as such, the successful sequence culminates in the coming to pass of previous foreshadowing, in an event that effectively performs its own prefigured image and thereby retrospectively validates past projections of itself. The process moves from partial to absolute revelation, toward the event which conceals (and foreshadows) nothing. This final feast demonstrates the capacity of the host lineage to realize its plans. And a major part of that capacity involves coercing others into displaying and transferring shell valuables. Through such coercion, the host lineage constitutes itself as socially potent, potent enough to extend itself and its projects into the future, to produce the preconditions of future action (see Munn 1983). The qualities of the shells – persistence, durability, and rootedness – become appropriated as aspects of the host lineage. Through the logic of revelatory display, exchange thus operates as the privileged means for constructing knowable and valued social identities.

Power: the eclipse of relationality, the intimation of autonomy

The manifestation of power through either control over consumption or control over knowledge is never innocent. Power for Tangans, as for the Barok, seems in its very conception to have a competitive aspect (cf. the definition offered by Somanil; Wagner 1986a:139). Power usages such as love magic and weather magic, for instance, assert control over the behavior of others. Rainmaking and sunmaking assume their importance in the context of feasting. Those people working *kastam* seek to ensure the success of their plans by making sun, while those wishing to "show their strength" (*soim strong* in Tok Pisin) secretly challenge the feast organizers with rain magic of their own. Love magic constitutes nothing less than a forcible attempt to direct the thoughts (*singagu*) of someone else to oneself, to make oneself someone else's obsession. Power usage (*ate*) thus provides Tangans with a means for realizing autonomous action (Clay 1986). The result of such usages (made mostly by men) is to turn others into the witnesses of one's own capacity to act, to make them see and thus know one's own agency (Clay 1992).

As vehicles for autonomy, power uses potentially bring about the same result as uncontrolled consumption, the dominant forms of which are gluttony and hoarding. Nea, for example, in his unbridled drive to consume, behaves much like the Gawan witch: his actions constitute both a radical assertion of his autonomy and the effective "destruction of relationality" (Munn 1986:418). Nea's disregard of affinal/paternal obligations detaches himself from the alternation of roles as feeder/fed that defines *kinaf* relations as continuous identical exchange. Nea is thus the archetypal figure of destructive consumption – consumption that exceeds the legitimate constraints of the social relations of food transmission.

Likewise, hoarding is a form of destructive consumption. Hoarding derives its negative valence through its denial of consumption for others. The hoarder, although in one sense a non-consumer or abstainer, asserts his autonomy in the same way as Nea: through a denial of sociality, specifically, the "relationality" of identical exchange.[20] In this sense, the connotations of hoarding shade into those of gluttony: self-indulgence precipitates social deprivation. Appropriately, Tangans use the phrase "to eat badly" (*en sak*), the label of a glutton, as interchangeable with the idiomatic expression, "hard nut" (*am pao fat*). *Pao* is the name of a variety of delicate nut with an outer casing of varying degrees of hardness (*fat*). *Am pao fat* refers to a nut with a shell so hard that one cannot tear away the outer casing with one's teeth but must instead use a sharp knife to extract the meat. *Fat* here connotes extreme "fastness" – the retentiveness of the greedy man symbolized by a closed fist (recall the child's game). Thus, extreme "fastness" or *fat* merges in its connotations with excessive (or hyper-) consumption (*en sak*). Significantly, the hard and fast shell conceals the edible nut; hoarding, like restricted consumption (chapter 6), implies hiding. Both miserliness and gluttony, forms of self assertion detached from the social relations of food transmission, constitute immoral behavior. Their immorality as expressions of greed lies precisely in the denial of the sociality constructed in repeated acts of identical exchange.

But this equation of autonomy with immorality poses a problem for understanding Tangan mortuary rites as an evaluative process. For, as I have been arguing, the construction of the host lineage as *fat* is in many ways an exercise of power manipulation, a manifestly unambiguous attempt to assert autonomy. Here I want to emphasize how in acting together in mortuary rites agents construct themselves as a collective individual – bounded, autonomous, and composed of essentially homologous individuals; in short, a lineage. In so doing, these agents deny or eclipse, at least temporarily, their dependency upon and relations with "external" others, especially affinal/paternal relatives (*kinaf*). This denial or eclipse manifests power as much as does control over consumption and knowledge. It is also what gives an edge to the experience of mortuary practices – their status as a form of public aggression.

Tangan mortuary feasting clearly requires and practically engenders alliances established through reciprocal exchanges of support and nurture (*fang*). Without the labor, pigs, and food of its various affinal/patrilateral relatives, no lineage could host a sequence of impressive mortuary feasts. And this fact is given tacit recognition at almost every mortuary feast in the distribution of pork to the guests: it is the *kinaf* of host lineage members who typically receive the choicest (named) cuts of pork. The reception of a desirable item of consumption thus marks a special relationship with the donor. That is, pork distribution hierarchizes the consumers into an order based on relative closeness – in both the genealogical and moral sense – to the donors. Consumers of more pork (*kinaf*, other lineage leaders, honored guests) stand near the top of this order; consumers of less pork (everyone else, and especially women), stand near the bottom.

Looked at this way, the consumption of pork pieces indicates an exchange of nurture and distinguishes recipients from non-recipients on the basis of legitimate claims to nurture. Keep in mind that pork cuts are intended for consumption in a way that cooked whole pigs, also given at feasts, are not. Prestations of pork cuts provide recipients with the means of consumption whereas prestations of whole pigs also furnish recipients with the means of further redistribution. In other words, pork cuts are given as food, the consumption of which – and this is the point – is *positively* valenced.[21] Pork moves back and forth at feasts as part of the reciprocal relationship whereby *kinaf* nurture each other (chapters 3 and 5).

Despite such gestures, however, feast givers provoke their guests to perceive gifts of food not as reciprocal nurturing but rather as unilateral force-feeding. Over the course of the feast sequence, host lineages construct themselves as permanent and transcendent (*fat*) by constructing their guests as "edible" (*en*). On the night before the final feast, members of the host lineage singe the scalps of people who will receive pigs the next day: "Tonight we cook you, tomorrow we cook your pigs!" The process as a whole, epitomized in *lulu am bo*, symbolically renders the host lineage as enduring and unconsumable. Or, to resume an earlier discussion, the process likens the lineage to the primordial grandmother of myth, capable of regenerating herself infinitely without the intercession of others. How are we to understand this apparent paradox of mortuary feasting – the contradiction between nurture and force-feeding?

By means, I suggest, of the New Melanesian Ethnography's model of personhood and agency. I do so, however, in order to soften rather than harden the model's Us/Them oppositon, to demonstrate how Our conventional sociality can be seen as the contingent innovation of Their sociality. That is, I associate the two actions of nurture and force-feeding with two different forms of sociality. Nurturing and force-feeding make social relations visible in two different forms, each of which presupposes a particular definition of personhood and agency. The form of sociality engendered through reciprocal nurturing presupposes a world in which persons are not individuals but rather "dividuals," "the plural and composite site of the relations that produced them" (Strathern 1988:13). In other words, social relations – and hence interdependency and difference – are taken for granted, and persons "naturally" incorporate the fact of connection or relation (Strathern 1988:92–3). In such a world, an "agent acts in the knowledge of his or her own constitution as a person in the regard of others" (Strathern 1988:275, emphasis removed). That is, persons impinge upon each other such that agents do not cause their own actions. Rather, the agent is a person who acts because of or in view of his or her constitutive relations. As Strathern puts it, "To act as one's own cause becomes an innovation on this convention" (1988:273).

It is precisely this innovation that is accomplished through the action of force-feeding. For force-feeding makes social relations appear in a form that presupposes (and precipitates) the definition of persons as individuals. Individuals are not composite but singular, irreducible and

autonomous entities that preexist and potentially stand outside the relations connecting them. (It is these secondary inter-relations that comprise
"society.") Hence, independence and similarity are made to appear as
"natural" conditions. Agency, moreover, is vested in the individual. That
is, the agent acts as his or her own cause; to be made to act or caused to
act by another is to capitulate to an act of domination, a denigration of
personhood.

Tangan mortuary feasting is a collective action that gathers together a
number of particular composite persons, persons differentiated from each
other in terms of their particular constitutive relations. (In fact, it is these
multiple and variable relations that are recognized in gifts of pork cuts.)
In so doing, this action temporarily eliminates what differentiates these
persons, thereby creating for them a unitary identity; or, differently put,
thereby creating out of them a collective individual. Individual members
of this collectivity replicate in singular form (one enate) what they have
created in collective form – the *matambia* or *matrilineage* initiating the
action. The establishment of this unitary identity is a precondition for
lineage replacement: the substitution of dead matrilineage members by
living ones, the succession of new lineage leaders to the "places" (*tafu*) of
old ones. In other words, what in an "individualistic universe" is taken to
be the normal and given form of sociality – a collection of individuals
making up a collective individual ("group") – is in Tanga the product of
mortuary feasting (Dumont 1970).

The construction of the lineage as a collective individual eliminates
differences among persons and perforce posits the moral basis of their
interactions as one of shared, essential identity. This construction of
similarity entails a contrast – the construction of difference between the
lineage and a categorically different "other." The action of force-feeding
accomplishes both constructions, for force-feeding (unlike nurture)
creates an agent acting in his or her cause *against* the cause of the other.
That is, force-feeding involves action taken not in view of relations or
connections but in pursuit of autonomy. This autonomy is achieved for
the lineage in qualifying itself as *fat* – even if only temporarily, and even if
only by virtue of the acquiescence of the lineage's supporters, specifically,
its *kinaf*.

Force-feeding therefore manifests power in two senses. The first sense
is consistent with indigenous understandings of power (*mui*), for the
collective individuality created through force-feeding is a transcendence
of relationality, an escape from a world in which relations define
persons rather than vice versa. Collective individuals are autonomous,

unencompassed by relations and hence – like power itself – outside of sociality.

The second sense in which force-feeding manifests power is more consistent with Western sociological understandings. Strathern has noted that the achievement of unitary identity works "by overcoming or resisting the moral basis of heterogeneous domestic dependencies" (1988:285). Accordingly, the collective events that engender such identity "have as much an amoral, antisocial character to them as do autonomous persons who go their own way" (1988:13). In transcending the relationality of exchanges among *kinaf*, then, feast givers, like misers and Gawan witches, go their own way at the expense of others. The denial of dependency amounts to an act of subordination, the denial of autonomy for others.

It should not be surprising that both forms of sociality appear in the same context of mortuary feasting; for both are the product of the same kind of action – giving. Indeed, Tangans use the same gesture to evince either form. At feasts, the pig offered for "first bite" might be playfully pressed in the laughing face of an honored recipient (say, at certain "eat everything" feasts) or solemnly proffered to a recipient whose credits are being "killed" (*paket bo*).[22] Perhaps more to the point, Tangans can evince both forms of sociality simultaneously in a single gesture. A man who offers a betel nut to a companion often poises the nut in his fingers and holds it close to his own body. He might say "*Bu li*" ("Take it"). But it is not entirely clear whether he is extending something to a friend or inviting the friend to indebt himself by grasping the nut on display. All acts of give and take are likewise inherently ambiguous, charged with the potential to express and assert nurture or enforced eating. The public deployment of this ambiguity is what gives the collective action of mortuary feasting its compellingness – its force as heightened experience.

Social reproduction and the complementarity of *en* and *fat*

The denial of dependency (and equality) implicit in the practice of mortuary feasting is ultimately premised upon the strength of ongoing relations of reciprocal (identical) exchange. The guests (*kinaf*) who acquiesce in the host lineage's project of self-constitution do so with the expectation that the hosts will acquiesce, in turn, in a similar project. This expectation is legitimated in practice by the past performance of the host lineage, the action of the host lineage in constructing *other* collective individuals as relatively durable (*fat*). The extent to which a lineage has allowed itself to be made consumable and to stand as the source of another's durability thus measures the extent to which it can similarly reconstitute itself in the future. In other words, when relationality can be taken for granted (conventional), its periodic denial (innovation) is then made possible. The eclipse of relationality is just that, an eclipse – perhaps even a mirage – neither an irreversible negation nor a total destruction.

In effect, reciprocal force-feeding affords agents with an acceptable instrument for asserting relative autonomy without denying consumption for others. Feast givers construct themselves as autonomous non-consumers within a social relationship that ensures the reversibility of such autonomy. Acts of force-feeding become, over time, acts of succor; single prestations take their place in the long-term transfer of care between lineages. Periodic manifestations of power remain encompassed and domesticated within the limits of sociality.

I suggest that this view of reciprocity, in which agents alternately act toward each other as consumers and non-consumers, defines an ideal of social reproduction. The staged threat of Tangan mortuary practices is that the relative construction of food recipients as "consumable" might become absolute and unalterable. Delayed identical exchange obviates this threat. Reciprocal feasting constructs pairs of lineages as alternately eating and feeding each other, and thereby defines an enduring relationality in which agents stand as the source and product of each other's (paternal) nurture. Though not always successful in practice, such relationships of nurturant paternity ideally reconcile the transcendent identity of the lineage as an autonomous collective individual with its periodic need to become the subordinate "food" of another lineage. Long-term cycles of mortuary feasting and ceremonial exchange thus enable agents to sustain a sociality that strips both death and gift giving of their contingency and uncontrollable nature (cf. de Coppet 1982; Weiner 1980).

Social reproduction thus takes the form of a controlled alternation between consumption and non-consumption, relationality and autonomy. Tangan sociality hinges on the transformation of one into the other, as in *lulu am bo*: the overcoming of consumption through the conversion of consumables (cooked pigs and cooked vegetables) into durables (Tridacna shell valuables). This theme of domesticating consumption pervades Tangan folklore, particularly the corpus of Nea stories. In one story, the domestication of consumption is associated with the origin of sustained sociality. A Boang man related a story (found elsewhere in island Melanesia; see Battaglia 1990) about a huge pig (*bo angwang*) that terrorized the island, destroying hamlets and devouring people. The entire population fled, except for an old woman who could find no space in any of the departing canoes. Subsequently, this old woman gave birth to two boys (here the story contains elements of the myth of the origin of death examined in chapter 5). The boys grew up to slay the pig, the enormous jawbone of which they placed on a raft and set adrift. When the jawbone came ashore at the abode of the refugees, the people realized that *bo angwang* had been vanquished and they happily returned to Tanga.

If the slaying of a man-eating pig reconstituted human sociality, the slaying of a man-eating man (who combines all three modalities of consumption) conversely gave rise to pigs.[23]

A warrior had killed all of the men. All the men were finished (*rop*) and only two women were left – two sisters. Only these two remained in the empty place. The two lived there and worked for themselves. Both of them were without husbands. Only the two of them worked in the garden.

The garden came into bearing and the two sisters harvested. One morning, after it had rained during the night, the two sisters awoke very early. They got up and went to harvest. There was a big puddle in the path. A small boy sat in the puddle splashing. The two sisters came and saw him splashing in the puddle. One of the sisters came first and said "Sister, there's a child for us here. Our small boy is splashing in a puddle down here in the road."

They took him and all three went to the garden. The three of them went, the smaller, younger sister sitting with the child while the bigger, elder sister weeded the garden. She finished weeding, came back and took the child. The big sister stayed with the child and the little sister harvested. She finished harvesting and put a pile of seed yams in the garden storehouse.

The three returned. One of the sisters held the child and the other peeled yams. She peeled enough for the three of them to eat. The two sisters cooked some on top of the fire. When cooked, the three of them made an oven. They took the child and the three of them ate sitting on one of the benches. The two sisters chewed the food and gave it to the child (*meme*). The three of them ate everything. The oven was ready and the three removed the rest of the food. The sisters filled up their baskets with food, one for the little sister and another for the big sister. The three of them ate and the sisters chewed the child's food. The sisters hung up the baskets and all three laid down on the beds. They stretched out and fell asleep.

It was night. The three slept and the night passed on. In the depths of the night, suddenly, the child awoke and grew in size. He grew right between the two women. He grew and grew and grew into a big man. He then climbed over one of the sisters at the edge of the bed and spoke, "Alung, you two want to look after (*fang*) me? And just what man do you two think has finished all the men and women of your district? You two didn't see that it was only me? And now you two want to take care of me?"

He stood up and removed one of the baskets of yams. He ate and ate and finished everything. He hung up the empty basket, took the other basket and ate from it too. He ate everything and put back the empty basket. He then climbed again over one of the sisters at the edge of the bed, the same as before. He laid down between the two and became small again. He grew very small and began to whimper between the two sisters. The two awoke and watched over him (*par tura*). The three of them stayed awake until dawn.

At daybreak, the big sister said "Hey, get the two baskets with our food. Let's eat and go to work." The little sister got up and held one of the baskets. It had nothing in it – an empty basket. She then checked her big sister's basket. It too held nothing – it was finished (*rop*). The two sisters looked at each other. The little sister said, "Hey, there's nothing in the baskets." The two looked at each other. Then all three got up and went to work again, to harvest.

They went off. The little sister stayed with the child and her big sister weeded. She finished weeding and the little sister went to harvest. She finished harvesting and the three of them placed a pile of seed yams in the storehouse. They took some food for themselves and went back. They returned and the little sister stayed with the child while the big sister peeled the yams. She peeled, made a fire and oven, and cooked some food on top of the fire. They finished cooking, collected some food and ate. The two of them fed (*fenfen*) the child. They chewed the food for him.

The two sisters spoke to each other. "Tonight, I will pretend to sleep first," the big sister told her little sister. "And I will watch. Then I'll sleep and you will keep watch." The three removed the food from the oven, ate everything and went to sleep.

In the depths of the night, the child grew large and expanded in size. The big sister heard the child. She heard him growing larger and larger and she thought, "Hey, I think that this child ate everything of ours. He grows bigger."

He grew large, climbed over the other woman to the edge of the bed. He spoke, "Hey, why do you two want to take care of me? What man do you two think has finished all your men and women here in this area? It was me. And you two want to take care of me?" The woman heard him as she secretly kept watch during the night.

He took one of the baskets and ate everything inside. He ate everything and the woman observed him unseen. He replaced (*tuf mile*) the basket and took the other one and ate everything inside. He hung it up again, climbed back over the woman and lowered himself between them. He shrank again, getting smaller and smaller until he became a child. He started to cry and the sisters awoke.

"Get up, little sister. Get up. Collect our things and let's eat and go off to work." She checked one of the baskets; it was empty. There was nothing to eat there. She checked the other basket; it was empty. The two sisters looked at each other. They took the child and put him outside. He crawled around while the two sisters talked. "Hey, you think that we're not taking care of something else altogether? This child here eats everything of ours. At night he climbs over me, he stands up close to me and says, 'Hey, you two women, you want to look after me? Now who do you think finished all your relatives – men and women – here at this place? Me. And now you two want to take care of me?'" The big sister told her little sister. They talked "What shall we do with him? Shall we run away?"

They took a length of bamboo and bore a hole through its center down to its base. The base of the bamboo was itself also pierced. The big sister seized the bamboo and tossing it outside said, "Hey, child, take this bamboo tube to the beach and fill it up with saltwater for cooking our yams and leafy greens."

The child crawled to her and pushed along the bamboo with the back of his hand. He crawled along and pushed the bamboo ahead. He went forward a ways and stood up when he reached the path to the beach. He looked behind. He was already out of sight (*patep*). He became a big man, grabbed the bamboo container and sped away with it.

The two women worked quickly to collect pandanus leaves, and needles and thread, which they put inside the leaves. They ran away.

The man went to the beach and filled up the tube. He returned with it and it emptied out along the way. He ran back and filled it up again. He ascended the path with it, but the tube emptied out. He looked at the base of the bamboo. "Hey, have those two women tricked me? Yes! I'll eat them as snacks! (*Ak un demdem*) I'll look at their butts today! [i.e., I'll fight them]" He shattered the bamboo tube and ran back to the house as a grown man.

When he arrived he didn't see the two women. They had run away. They ran away and climbed a chestnut tree. They had taken a rope with them.

The man sniffed around for the two women. He smelled their scent and followed their trail. He smelled their trail and finally smelled them in the tree. He looked up and saw the two women. They had sat down at the very top of the chestnut tree. "Abelung, here you are. I'll see to you two today." "Oh no, our child, you climb up here to us. Let's rest up here."

They lowered the rope to him. He began to climb and tried to hold on to a branch of the tree. The two sisters cut the rope and he fell down and fractured one of his legs. They lowered the rope again. "Hey, no, no. Take this rope." He replied "Alung, one of my legs is broken, but I have another side and my two hands are still here. I'll climb up to you two!"

They gave him the rope and pulled him up, up, up. He tried to grab a branch of the tree and they cut the rope. He fell down and broke one of his arms. "One hand and one leg still remain!" The two lowered the rope. He climbed on to it. When he tried to latch on to a branch, they cut the rope. He fell down and broke his other leg. "My other hand is here. I'm still able to climb up to you two." They lowered the rope to him. He hung on to it and ascended. When he tried to hold on to a branch, they cut the rope. He fell down and broke his other arm.

"My mouth is still here. I can climb up to you." They lowered the rope. He clenched the rope in his teeth and the two pulled, pulled, pulled. He tried to rest his chin on a branch in order to grab on tightly. They cut the rope. He fell down and broke his neck.

He laid still at the base of the chestnut tree. "Ah, he's dead." The two women sat and sewed. They sewed with needle and thread. The little sister fumbled her needle and it fell from her hand. It fell close to the dead man down below. "Hey, sister, my needle fell down. I'll go down." "If you go down there what will you do? There are needles here. Can't you sew with them. If you go down, whatever that thing is, its spirit (*malafua*) will attack you." "Come on, he's not dead yet? Where is there a spirit?" The two argued and argued.

The big sister tired. Her little sister's desire was fixed on getting her needle. So, she descended. She dangled from the branches that the two sisters had climbed and stood up down below. She looked for the needle. She asked her big sister "Where did it land?" "It fell down over there, close to that thing/monster (*sukuku*)." She combed the grass looking. The spirit of the man flew up and penetrated the woman, forcing her to the ground with a loud noise. She was no longer a woman of the place (i.e., human; *fifin na male*). She became a female pig.

She had become a pig. Her sister sitting down at the top of the tree heard a different language come up from her sister. Her sister squealed like a pig at the foot of the chestnut tree. She cried "Weeeek, weeeeek."

"Alung, what did I say to you! I told you so! I said that if you go down to fetch your needle the spirit of that thing would go inside of you. Now what are you going to do? Now you've turned into something else."

The pig cried circling the foot of the tree. The sister descended and the two left. They returned to their place. They went into their house. The pig dug up the inside of the house, upset all of the beds and destroyed the inside of the house. Its sister shouted, "Go! Leave!" The pig did not obey.

The two went inside the garden to find leafy greens. The sister climbed over the stile and the female pig smashed the fence. Smashed the fence, climbed over – leafy greens were pulled down, bananas, yams and *mami*. The female pig rooted and destroyed them.

The big sister grew angry, very angry. So she grabbed one of their digging sticks and whacked the pig in the middle of the head. The sister pig felt pain, picked itself up, broke through the other side of the fence and went bush. It ran away altogether and became utterly wild (*rokai*) in the bush.

After a while, it became pregnant. The female pig became pregnant in the bush. It gave birth. Some men still inhabited this district. They heard the cries of the litter. The piglets cried "ngekngekngek" as they followed behind their mother. The men collected the piglets and took care (*fangte*) of them. They took care of them and the piglets became pigs.

The pigs all came from that woman, the woman who became a pig. Her sister returned home and cried and cried and cried until she withered away (*mak la an ut mapek*) and died herself inside their house. *Ka pil ma ka ret.* The end.

In this story, pigs originate through a double act of domestication. First, the sisters attempt to domesticate (*fang*, "nurture") the boy. Eventually, they achieve domestication not through nurture, but through radical aggression – the homicide of the man-eater. The same process then unfolds around the pig-sister, herself the product of domestication by aggression. Unresponsive to nurture, the pig-sister incurs the wrath of her sibling, who wallops the animal on the head and drives it into the bush. There, the now "wild" (*rokai*) pig-sister gives birth to a litter which a group of men gathers up and brings home to look after (*fangte*). In the end, the nurture of the men tames the offspring of the "wild" pig-sister. Uncontrolled consumption (recall here the characterization of Sokopana as *kinit rokai*, the "wild ghost from the bush") again yields to the demands of domestication. The apparently final victory of men (and not women?) over the breeding process of the pigs signals both their triumph over unrestrained consumption and the conversion of unrestrained consumption into a resource of reproduction.

The stories of *bo angwang* and the origin of pigs superficially express the creation of relatively enduring, self-replacing realities ("society" on the one hand, domesticated pigs on the other) out of the defeat of consumption. In Tangan value-terms, the elimination of *en* apparently generates *fat*. This, however, is not always the case. In the story of the origin of death presented in chapter 5, unrestrained consumption (in a sexual rather than gastronomic modality) triumphed over the enduring, self-replacing capacity of the eternal grandmother. The result of this victory was death, the introduction of the most potent form of consumption into society. But death manifestly was not the end of life. That is, the termination of immortality meant the operation of a new method for perpetuating life: sexual and hence interlineage reproduction. As in the stories of *bo angwang* and the origin of pigs, the resolution to the threat of consumption is domestication, the integration of consumption into a set of practices that enable the conversion of "wild" consumption – marauding pigs, ferocious man-eaters, sexually aroused boys, and death itself – into domesticated perpetuity.

It is in this sense that the narratives of the origin of pigs and the origin of death can be read as variations on a theme. In the former, two young women adopt a child who as an adult has killed all of the island's inhabitants; in the latter, an old woman adopts/generates two boys who grow to kill the pig that caused all of the island's inhabitants to depart. In the former, the impetuosity of the younger sister precipitates her transformation into a pig whose offspring eventually become domesticated at the hands of human nurture (*fang*); in the latter, the impetuosity of the older brother changes him from grandson to husband and thus establishes the relations of affinity/paternity (*kinaf*) or reciprocal nurture between lineages which regulate sexuality. In both origin stories, the final product is not the eradication of consumption, but the control of consumption. "Eating," in its modalities of food consumption and sexuality, becomes part of a set of relations which promote reproduction. Piglets develop into tamed animals that eat regularly and do not attack gardens; as adults they reproduce for their tamers and enter into the exchanges which replace lineage personnel. Likewise, sexuality, regulated by affinity, enlists in the service of lineage replacement; promiscuous and mobile sexuality is contained within the bounds of cross-cousinship (*fat kinaf*). The practice of *kinaf* relations defines certain lineages as the paternal nurturers of each other; regular transfers of *fang* ("nurture") ensure the continuity of discrete lineages.

Over the course of a single mortuary sequence, one episode in a cyclical process of conversion is enacted: the reevaluation of the host lineage from *en* to *fat*, from a lineage imposed upon by death, the ultimate form of consumption, to a lineage reconstituted and publicly validated as momentarily autonomous and transcendent. In the long run of mortuary sequences, identical exchange (or, more precisely, reciprocity) functions as the operator that makes such alternations possible; for a lineage reconstitutes itself as *fat* by renewing obligations to assume the status of *en* toward other lineages. Identical exchange thus implies a paired totality: the complementary and dialectically related value-terms of *en* and *fat*. As paired terms, the images of ultimate consumption (death) and absolute perdurance (lineage immortality) reciprocally imply each other. Mortuary feasting, then, idealized as the perpetual oscillation of *en* and *fat*, is nothing less than the alternation of life and death, the transformation of one into the other.

III

TOWARD COMPARATIVE
HISTORICAL ETHNOGRAPHY

8

Social reproduction and *kastam* in comparative perspective

I began this book by treating mortuary rites as *kastam*, an exercise that required me to trace a history of changes out of which *kastam* emerged as an explicit cultural category – a word and label self-consciously used by Tangans to describe mortuary feasting and exchange as well as to differentiate these activities as a domain distinct from other domains: *gavman*, *lotu*, and *bisnis*. I then treated mortuary rites in terms of their equally indigenous apprehension as the means for "finishing" and "replacing" the dead, an exercise that required me to conceptualize feasting and exchange as the practical vehicle for producing a kind of sociality predicated upon culturally specific assumptions about relationality and autonomy. While the first task illustrates the concerns of the New Melanesian History, the second illustrates those of the New Melanesian Ethnography. I have argued that if there is to be a New Melanesian Anthropology, then these two tasks – so easily separable from each other – *must* be carried out side by side. What, then, does their juxtaposition yield in this case? What sort of questions does each task pose when put in the context of the other? I explore these issues in this conclusion by way of suggesting a basis for the comparative historical analysis of *kastam* and social reproduction in Melanesian societies. That is, in lieu of a dramatic manifesto or charter for a New Melanesian Anthropology, I offer a preliminary example of the kinds of questions and analyses such an anthropology would engage.

Social reproduction, as accomplished in Tangan mortuary rites, can be taken to exemplify a type of social reproduction that I call replication in contradistinction to multiplication. In developing an ideal typical distinction between replication and multiplication, I focus specifically on the ways in which agents produce sociality through the circulation of valued objects. I argue that whereas replication involves a logic of "keeping-

227

while-giving," an emphasis on securing the return of valuables put into circulation, multiplication involves a logic of dispersal, of strategies intended to increase the quantity of valuables put into circulation. My intention in drawing this contrast is first of all to highlight the specificity of Tangan social reproduction and, secondarily, to recapitulate some of the themes of earlier chapters by explicating the cultural assumptions behind Tangan exchange. In so doing, I point to differences in the social practice of exchange and thereby identify one dimension (albeit an important one) of a comparative analysis of social reproduction in Melanesian societies.

In the final section, I return to the issue of continuity and change raised in Part I – the paradoxical issue of *kastam* as new and old, invention and convention. I use the contrast between replication and multiplication to think about differences in how Melanesians have engaged the historical encounter with forms of commodity production and exchange. I suggest that in Tanga the exigencies of replication have conditioned the historical process of commoditization. This conditioning encouraged the separation of *kastam* and *bisnis* as practically distinct domains. This separation, in turn, has contributed to the continuity of the symbolic forms and practices of mortuary rites.

By contrast, multiplication has appeared to condition a conjunction of *bisnis* and *kastam* in at least some Highlands New Guinea societies. This conjunction has given exchange practices a dynamic and synthetic cast, and thus the appearance of a "fit" between indigenous forms of ceremonial gift giving and introduced forms of commodity circulation.

Replication: the containment of sociality

Now it is evident that the circuit M–C–M would be absurd and without meaning if the intention were to exchange by this means two equal sums of money, $100 for $100. The miser's plan would be far simpler and surer; he sticks to his $100 instead of exposing it to the dangers of circulation.

Marx, Capital I, Part II, Chapter IV

Exchange always presents dangers to the agents involved. The story of Nea discussed in chapter 7 makes this point particularly well. Nea overcomes the initial efforts of the four boys to retain the shells by appealing to the youngster most akin to himself. To some extent, this "affinity" or "kinship" makes possible the surrender of the shells which Nea promises to return. Nea's song simultaneously voices and allays the worry of the boys: the shells might not come back. (This concern, of course, is the underside of the identity all givers construct for themselves relative to receivers.) And, it so happens, after just one complete circuit of the shells, Nea disavows the obligation to return the shells and absconds with them.

The story links together through the character of Nea the ideas of hyperconsumption and unrealized reciprocity or aborted exchange. As in the other stories, Nea fails to fulfil his "affinal" responsibilities by perverting the circulation of the shells. Nea hoards the shells beneath his foreskin, his behavior here parallel to the consumption of clamshell meat in the cookhouse (chapter 6). As previously argued, hoarding and gluttony are two facets of a single concept – the abuse of consumption. By this logic, consumption conceptually opposes not only production (recall that Nea visits the children while the other adults work in the gardens), but also exchange. Consumption squanders the possibility of exchange and hence sociality. Hence the description of a man who commits incest (*mumu*) as "a man who eats his own food pile" (*kaltu i en gus aia*) rather than, as he ought, distribute it to others.

The dangers of circulation dramatized in the story of Nea apply to all forms of circulation based on delayed exchange, such as the identical exchange that organizes Tangan mortuary rites. For the agents involved, the dangers increase in proportion to the importance of the circulated objects in value-creation. In Tanga, given the symbolic and instrumental significance of shell valuables, the total supply of which is not increasing, their circulation proves particularly vulnerable to the threat represented by Nea. The conventional response to this situation takes the ambivalent form of denying reciprocity, that is, of behaving like Nea himself. Weiner, exploring more generally strategies to counter "potential loss and the constant need to give away what is most valued," refers to this response as "keeping-while-giving" (1985:211; cf. Munn 1983). Keeping-while-giving, Weiner argues, focuses specifically upon objects intrinsically bound up with the identity and history of their transactors. Through keeping-while-giving, agents effect a degree of control over objects such as Tangan *am fat*, Maori *taonga* (nephrite axeblades), and Kwakiutl coppers that symbolically condense aspects of the relational personhood of the actors themselves. The circulation of these objects invariably traces a path leading back to the person or persons identified with the objects.

Weiner (1985:212) identifies two kinds of objects that correspond respectively to strong and weak forms of keeping: "those that should never circulate and those that under certain circumstances may be given to others either on loan, as copies, or in return for another object of the same kind." This latter kind of object includes, for example, the variety of shell discs (*tintol*) used in Tangan identical exchanges. These objects, always transferred with the expectation of receiving replicas in the future, iconically signify the perdurance of the lineage while serving as instruments of that perdurance. This is the weak form of keeping, keeping-while-giving.

Weiner's first type of object, non-circulating heirlooms, describes a different variety of shell valuable.[1] The archetype of this category is the disc called *warantang* ("base of the basket"), the very name of which articulates the ambivalence of keeping in any form. On the one hand, "base of the basket" denotes the resting place of this disc at the bottom of the *tang*, the receptacle used for storing all *am fat*, *kemetas*, and other shell valuables. Therein shell valuables remain both hidden from the view of others and removed from circulation. On the other, the name equally connotes the "origin" or "foundation" of the *tang*. In this sense, *warantang* provide the basis for the *tang*, the repository of all circulating shell discs and hence the symbol of a lineage's capacity to partake in identical exchange (just as one's personal purse [*tang*] symbolizes the capacity to meet the mundane obligations of giving and taking betel nut, lime, tobacco, etc.). The denial of reciprocity thus paradoxically predicates or grounds reciprocity itself; keeping allows giving. Yet, "giving" is also a form of keeping since all *tintol* put in circulation publicize the promise of *tintol* returned. Thus, Tangans handle shell discs in both of the ways identified by Weiner, either by limiting circulation to the transfer of replicas or by declining to circulate the discs at all.

This undercurrent of retention, this pervasive keeping-while-giving, characterizes replication as a specific form of social reproduction. Both keeping and keeping-while-giving work as strategies to control the social identities and relationships iconically signified by *warantang* and *tintol* respectively. Consider again the *warantang*. *Warantang*, according to Bell, are the largest type of *tintol* (1935d:110). *Warantang* exceed ordinary *tintol* in both diameter and thickness; if dropped, they hit the ground with a dull thud that Tangans render onomatopoetically as "*paldin!*" The diameter of the aperture of the *warantang*, however, is noticeably smaller than that of *tintol*. Overall, the effect of *warantang* is one of "more *fat*": there is simply more shell than in the case of *tintol* used in *lulu* and in other transactions. It is this material quality of being more *fat*, I suggest, that suits *warantang* to their function of symbolizing the lineage as a perdurable, self-replacing reality. Being more *fat*, moreover, entails a greater degree of fixity or fastness for *warantang*, in short, their non-circulation. Thus Somanil described a display of *warantang* as follows:

Suppose Nemalaf gave Ngamnabo a cooked pig. Ngamnabo would take a *warantang* disc and put it on the ground and sit down on top of it. He would also place one foot on another *warantang* disc and the other foot on a third *warantang* disc. Then Nemalaf would place the pig to Ngamnabo's mouth. When they have finished placing the pig thus ["first bite"], the discs would be collected and put inside their storage box. That's all.

Nemalaf, the lineage leader of Solsol lineage, presents a pig to his MB, Ngamnabo, the leader whom Nemalaf succeeded or replaced. Nemalaf's succession, and by extension the continuity of the lineage, is depicted as literally based on *warantang*, the discs upon which the lineage (represented by its preeminent MB, Ngamnabo) sits or, alternatively, the objects which anchor and stabilize enatic identities.

Keeping *warantang* out of circulation involves a kind of hoarding, a strategy by which the continuity between MB and ZS that defines lineage replacement is safeguarded. The preeminent *am fat* that symbolize the lineage remain always in the hands of lineage members, insulated even from the demands of fathers and children (*kinaf*). *Warantang*, like land, become the fixed material objects around which lineage replacement revolves. New members succeed to control over the *warantang* as old members succeeded previously; the net result is a replica of the original situation. The denial of circulation (and, of necessity, reciprocity) ensures some measure of control over the process of social reproduction. Keeping *warantang* provides a minimal definition, as it were, of the matrilineage, a "base" (*an wara*) from which lineage members can operate in the more dangerous arena of identical exchange. The keeping of *warantang* within the lineage and their devolution from MB to ZS thus encodes and recuperates the asexual and antisocial method of reproduction displaced by the origin of death (chapter 4). Keeping, in other words, is the form of (non-)circulation associated with lineage autonomy: the lineage replaces itself as if unaided by the actions of other agents (*kinaf*).

But even this form of non-circulation is fraught with danger inasmuch as the ZS cannot assume that the MB will automatically transmit *warantang* (and, of course, particular ZSs might compete among themselves for the inheritance of their MB in a manner that recalls the solicitations of men competing in *kula* for a famous shell that has come into a mutual partner's hands). Bell (1935d:105) comments on the habit of big men who bury large discs and later reveal their location to a favored nephew/heir. But many men told me apocalyptic tales of dying lineage elders who secretly bury their shells (*kafngi am fat*) without disclosing their location to their surviving heirs or sisters' sons. Accordingly, ZSs who aspire to replace or succeed their MB as lineage leaders will present their old uncle with large pigs at mortuary feasts. These presentations work in precisely the same way as the presentations of pigs made at *fasuigk* distributions. That is, they serve to elicit and make visible shell valuables hidden away in the strongboxes of others. In other words, a ZS uses the same mechanism of coercive force-feeding on his lineage elders as he does on his affines/ children (*kinaf*) in order to turn these elders too into the witnesses and means of his self-construction as their successor.

Identical exchange, the circulation of shell valuables within a network of non-enatic relations, is perhaps even less predictable and therefore fraught with more danger; consequently, it works according to a different logic: not keeping, but keeping-while-giving. In identical exchange, hoarding (as the Nea story warns) is out of place. The hoarder might disengage from public sociality and so avoid the reevaluation brought about by another's acts of giving, but this attempt to evade the relativity and relationship of exchange ultimately results in social sterility. Bell put the case well:

> Hoarding means that the hoarder has cut himself off from the social life; that he has failed to carry out certain obligations which are due from all adult male members of the community. By refusing to attend feasts and aid his own clan or his wife's clan in communal activities – all of which involve the use of many *am fat* – he avoids incurring a load of debt, but at the same time he becomes what the natives term a *khaltu wut* – i.e., a social outcast.
>
> *(1935d:105)*

Thus, whereas keeping as a strategy is appropriate with respect to some *am fat*, such as the *warantang*, keeping does not by itself achieve social reproduction. Just as the value-terms *fat* and *en* imply each other, keeping and keeping-while-giving form a single unit of Tangan social practice.[2] Each makes the other possible and each contributes to the same end – lineage succession.

Replication, then, as a specific form of social reproduction, is recognizable by its various provisions for limiting the circulation of objects and thereby containing the flow of sociality, that is, putting a halt to the proliferation of relations (and risks) engendered through exchange. Put otherwise, replication is recognizable by the non-use of reciprocity in multiplying social relations. Tangan replication thus consists in the interrelated practices of identical exchange (keeping-while-giving) and keeping pure and simple (keeping heirlooms within the lineage). The figure of the ZS in *lulu am bo* summarizes in potent symbolic form both of these elements of replication. Decorated with non-circulating lineage heirlooms, the ZS recalls the predecessors that he directly succeeds; given circulating *tintol*, the ZS accepts the instruments that allow future participation in the replacement of other (*kinaf*) lineages – the shells kept while given. Accordingly, the ZS descends from the roof of the new men's house as the present replacement of the maternal uncles whom his performance "finishes."

Multiplication: the expansion of sociality

The features that make replication a distinctive type of social reproductive activity emerge more clearly through contrast with a type that I propose to call multiplication. This contrast is limited: it focuses solely on exchange practices (mostly ceremonial exchanges) and their consequences for the creation and ensuing shape of social relations. Exchange practices, of course, are but one aspect of social reproduction; my preoccupation with them here is an introduction to the question raised at the end of this chapter: how can we begin to discuss Tangan replication from an historical perspective? Or, to paraphrase Sahlins (1981, 1985), how did a particular type of social reproduction condition its own transformation under definite historical circumstances?

As an ideal type, multiplication can be delineated through a contrast with replication that isolates four features of exchange practices: (1) the degree to which the norms of exchange prescribe or proscribe incremental transactions; (2) the degree to which the logic of circulation enjoins accumulation or dispersal; (3) the degree to which the circulation of valuables is "enchained," that is, the extent of the social relations implicated by the circulation process; and (4) the degree to which the circulation of material wealth creates and sustains alliances (affinal and military).[3] My use of the word "degree" suggests that the kinds of contrasts that I draw will remain somewhat blurred at the edges. Each of the four features implies a continuum of possibilities, though any empirical combination of possibilities will comprise a singular configuration.[4] The features chosen, I repeat, focus on exchange at the expense of not only production but also other practices that engender sociality (ritual, warfare, parenting). This bias mimics the biases of Melanesian social practice – or at least of Melanesianist anthropologists – in which the dictates of exchange often organize all other action and interaction. Consequently, these features provide only the beginnings of a comparative approach to social reproduction within Melanesia. My immediate goal is much more modest: simply, to define the specificity of the Tangan case by embedding it in a comparative context.

The type of social reproduction that I call multiplication is generally associated with Highlands New Guinea societies.[5] Three such societies, each with its distinctively dominant component of circulation or exchange, illustrate the type: Melpa society with its *moka* exchanges; Enga society with *tee* exchanges; and Mendi society with its *twem* and *sem* exchanges.[6]

Among these three instances of exchange, Melpa *moka* remains the paradigmatic example of incremental giving. In the ideal transaction, X gives Y two pearlshells and one pig as an initiatory gift; Y in return makes *moka* to X by giving eight pearlshells. A. Strathern emphasizes that a mode of obtaining "profit" or of prescribing incremental giving actually defines *moka*:

It is only if Y's total *moka* gift is *worth more than* the initiatory gift, and preferably worth more by a standard margin, that Y is said to be 'making true *moka*' or 'giving on the back of' the initiatory gift. Otherwise he is just 'repaying debts' and not making *moka* at all.

(1975:373)

Strathern notes that a future transaction in which X and Y reverse roles *could* generate a long-term equilibrium not unlike that characteristic of identical exchange. In fact, however, this does *not* occur; for in the next sequence:

Y will attempt to initiate more exchanges and try to give X more than 8 shells, in order to gain prestige and to stimulate X into stepping up exchanges in the future.

(A. Strathern 1975:373–4)

Strathern concludes that because of the drive for prestige created by individual ambition and inter-group rivalry "there is an inherent trend towards expansion in *moka* transactions" (1975:374). Undoubtedly, this trend has been exacerbated by the cessation of warfare and by the inflation of pearlshells, but the point is that the prescription for incremental giving defined *moka* prior to European intervention. The consequences of European involvement in Melpa political economy must be appreciated in this light.

Explicitly referring to *moka*, Lederman argues that the incremental repayment of debts similarly characterizes both public ceremonial transactions (*sem*) and informal daily exchanges (*twem*) in Mendi:

A principle of 'generosity,' whereby one tends to repay more than one has previously borrowed, underlies *all* contexts of exchange in Mendi, and is the means by which individuals and groups attain political standing.

(1986b:14)

Indeed, some Mendi exchanges, such as postmarital affinal transactions, are *symmetrically asymmetrical,* allowing no opportunity for a reversal of roles between giver and taker. Similarly, Enga *tee* transactions use incremental giving as a measure of individual political standing. In the *tee,* however, the locus of competition is not the exchange partnership *per se,* but the respective clan units of the partners.[7] The displays of pigs on *tee* parade grounds unambiguously identify the clan member who passes along to his partner the greatest number of pigs. Each man, moreover, competes with his deceased father(s) by attempting to extend his line of staked pigs beyond the mark achieved by his father. The principle of incremental giving thus informs competition both among living clansmen and between living clansmen and their deceased agnates.

The immediate effect of incremental giving is to focus the attention of the transactors on the amount transacted as much as on the transaction itself. Whereas in identical exchange the amount of the transaction is given axiomatically, in incremental giving the amount usually varies. Lederman says of Mendi transactions that "the amount of increment is not customary or fixed, but involves strategizing and situational plays on the rules of exchange" (1986b:14). Tangan identical exchange also involves "strategizing and situational plays," especially with regard to timing and scale. But even with respect to scale, a host lineage can increase only the number of recipients, not the amount owed to previous givers. The *realization* of the transaction rather than its relative size absorbs the attention of the actors involved.

Incremental giving is fueled not only by circumstances of competition for prestige and political standing, but also by an exchange logic manifestly different from that of keeping-while-giving. *Moka* and *twem/sem* exchanges in particular enjoin the dispersal of wealth as opposed to its retention. Lederman claims that:

First and very generally, social relationships (whether between clans or *twem* partners) and both individual and corporate political status are made through the dispersal of wealth, not its accumulation. Individuals are not supposed to hold on to wealth for long ... Unless one is planning and preparing to make a specific gift, one cannot legitimately hoard or accumulate valuables.

(1986b:13–14)

Similarly, Strathern notes that hoarding is no virtue in *moka*. The big men who make *moka*:

... are more likely to claim prestige, and to be accorded it, either because they have given away a large number of pigs and/or shells by themselves in a *moka* or because they have given a private *moka* and do *not* claim back a return sequence from their partner.

(1975:374)

Unlike the little boys in the story of Nea, Melpa big men do not worry about the return of their pigs *per se.*[8] Instead, they aim to accumulate large numbers of debts and credits. Compare the situation in Tanga where a lineage disperses pigs in order to accumulate shell discs. The renown of the lineage derives from its association with the exchange objects themselves, not from the stockpiling of debts and credits entailed in the transaction. Actors in expansive systems of circulation are motivated not to keep but to give, to exceed and surpass previous performances. These systems lack the *ambivalent* alternation of retention and dispersal characteristic of identical exchange and of replication in general. Indeed, the structural organization of the Enga *tee* actually precludes accumulating the objects of exchange – live pigs and, subsequently, pork. No one man (or, rather, his wife or wives) would be capable either of sustaining a large pig population for long or of consuming the huge amounts of pork passed along the *tee* chain. The systemic logic is clear and imperative; dispersal (and disbursal) triumphs over accumulation. Instead of the cyclical, equilibrated patterns engendered by keeping-while-giving, expansive systems of circulation produce ever-imbalanced sequences of incremental giving in which return implies not control by the recipient over the objects of exchange but instead subordination in the exchange relationship.

The combined demands of incremental giving and of the pressure to disperse wealth encourage exchange agents to expand and cultivate networks of exchange partnerships. This aspect of expansive systems of circulation has been examined most often with regard to the question of how big men build followings and finance their activities. A. Strathern, in a comparison of several Highlands cases, notes how both Melpa and Enga big men in particular rely on financial arrangements to realize their goals in exchange. That is, big men "make numerous links through outside partnerships with men of a range of clans around them, either via kin and affinal ties or simply by contracting friendships" (Strathern 1978:74). Likewise, Enga big men attempt to diversify their partnerships in order to increase both the total number of pigs given away at a *tee* prestation *and* the total number of recipients involved. This diversity, according to one account (Elkin 1953:185), receives public symbolic recognition in the display of staked pigs on the *tee* grounds:

He [an individual donor] ties a piece of bark or fibre around certain pegs, to mark the number of pigs which he has for individuals in different groups. Thus if the sixth and fifteenth pegs are marked, it means that six and nine pigs are to be handed over to individuals from two distinct places.

Both Enga and Melpa big men need not depend solely on the assistance of group-mates to make a prestation. In Andrew Strathern's terms, they need not rely on a strategy of "production," the labor of their own settlements provided by women, bachelors, and landless clients, as their only source of exchange goods (i.e., pigs). This situation contrasts with the Tangan case in which the largest pigs presented at the final feast of the mortuary sequence are ideally "home-grown," that is, raised by members of the host matrilineage. Of course, Tangan big men exploit financial arrangements somewhat: both *kinaf* and allies ("brothers") furnish pigs for the construction of the men's house. Yet, the heaviest burden of pig and vegetable production falls to the host matrilineage. The difference with the Highlands cases is therefore one of degree, just as there are differences of degree among Highlands societies themselves.

Lederman has demonstrated for the Mendi that "financial arrangements" are exclusive neither to the projects of big men nor to large-scale inter-group exchanges. In Mendi society, *twem* relationships, in which men, women, widows, and bachelors all participate, operate according to the same logic as clan pig kills. *Twem* or personal exchange relationships grow out of mundane, ego-centered transfers of wealth (pigs, pearlshells, and money) marked by a high velocity of circulation (Lederman 1986a:67). Although *twem* exchanges might occur in the context of clan pig festivals, they constitute a distinct cultural reality and stand as "a creative achievement and reflection of a person's active engagement in social life as an autonomous person" (Lederman 1986b:21). Thus, in Mendi society, the twin compulsions to expand exchange relationships and to circulate wealth incrementally organize not only interclan relations and big man/client relations but also an extensive range of personal relations as well.

The pervasiveness of financial arrangements and of proliferating debt/ credit relationships in the multiplicative system of circulation has the effect of "enchaining" any one transaction in a much larger nexus of transactions. *Moka* and, of course, *tee* exchanges are the clearest examples of such enchainment. Not only does any one exchange mobilize a multiplicity of social relationships through the creation and discharge of debts and credits, each exchange also forms part of a sequence of exchanges the timing and achievement of which require massive coordination. These sequences extend in space as well as in time and comprehend the wholesale movement of hundreds of pigs through the valley systems of the Western Highlands. In both *moka* and *tee*, then, the relative sequencing of events acquires paramount significance since each exchange finances the proceeding exchange. The extension of exchange relationships in time and space implied by any one transaction far exceeds that achieved in the case of Tangan exchanges. To some extent, the very objects of exchange augment this potential for expansion. *Moka*, *tee*, and *twem* involve the circulation of live pigs instead of or as well as pork with the obvious but very real consequence that a single object of exchange generates more than a single debt/credit relationship.

Tangans achieve the same effect on a greatly reduced scale through transfers of whole cooked pigs at mortuary feasts. The distributor of a cooked pig might have received the pig from a supporter (perhaps even the supporter received the pig from another supporter). In turn, the recipient of a cooked pig retains the head and distributes the various pieces to representatives of other lineages thereby creating another set of debt/credit relationships. Therewith, however, the chain of debts and credits called into being abruptly ends. The consumption of pork, so intrinsic to the meaning of Tangan gifts, effectively destroys the means of circulation. Presentation of *cooked* pigs makes sense in Tangan cultural terms; the gift of pork implies only consumption (*en*) and fails to furnish recipients with the means of further production, namely, fertile sows.

Furthermore, the repayment of debts in Tanga for whole cooked pigs rarely retraces all of the "links" in the original chain. Each debt remains distinct from every other debt, implying an independent dyadic relationship rather than a recognized "chain" of such relationships. The overall effect is an explicit reduction in the scale of exchange events. This reduction affects not only the total number of pigs amassed at any one distribution, but also the extent of the social relationships activated by any one distribution. Whereas the emphasis of multiplication on dispersal and increment exerts pressure to elaborate social relationships, the tacit emphasis of replication on *recovering* the objects in circulation produces no such effect. The organizers of a Tangan mortuary sequence might solicit contributions of pigs with *warangus* prestations, for example, in order to increase the size of their pig distribution.[9] But the distribution itself does not shift the whole burden of reciprocity onto the shoulders of the recipients. Each pig given implies shell valuables received with the obligation to reciprocate (and thus to receive a cooked pig) at some future distribution. In other words, every credit established by the distribution of a pig simultaneously establishes a debt for the shell valuables received. This contingency tends to limit the size of distributions, for the larger the dispersal, the greater the number of debts as well as credits that a host lineage contracts. (And this is the case regardless of the distributed pigs being "produced" or "financed.") Large numbers of outstanding debts potentially present difficulties. Should the debts fall due all at once, a lineage might find itself unable to meet its obligations, especially if the lineage were in the midst of hosting its own mortuary feasts (hence the importance of timing). The result would be a serious diminution in the capacity of the lineage to assert its autonomy; indeed, a signal failure to eclipse "relationality."

The question of enchainment raises the related question of the degree to which the circulation of wealth practically constitutes and sustains alliances. Godelier, in a comparison of Highlands societies that bears some resemblance to the present exercise, argues that in "big men societies" such as Enga, Melpa, and Mendi:

The reproduction of life and the production of relations of kinship are entirely dependent on the exchange of women for wealth and, in another sphere, all inter-tribal political relations imply "economic" exchanges, the circulation and redistribution of wealth. The very nature of social relations, the logic underpinning the workings of these societies, calls forth and stimulates the production and circulation of material wealth for the sake of their social reproduction.

(1986:177)

Although his immediate aim is to contrast the bridewealth practices of "big men societies" with the sister-exchange customs of the Baruya (a "great man society"), Godelier suggests a more comprehensive feature of multiplication and its expansive exchange practices. To wit, the circulation of material wealth more than anything else constitutes and defines alliances, particularly affinal alliances. Godelier cites A. Strathern to illustrate how in Melpa society bridewealth is bound up with *moka* exchanges to the extent that "a marriage is fully established when the affines make *moka* with the breeding pigs a young couple have been endowed with" (1986:179).[10] A bride's parents likewise attempts to increase the size of the bridewealth under pressure of the "general competitive context of *moka* exchange arrangements" (1986:178). Similarly, among the Tombema Enga, bridewealth works as the means for kinsmen of the groom to expand their network of *tee* partnerships by contributing to the payment. In both Melpa and Enga societies, the circulation of wealth not only creates affinal alliances but also subsumes such alliances within the organization of competitive exchange.

Bulmer's (1960) account of *maku (tee)* exchange among the Kyaka Enga, leads Godelier to argue further that:

Generally speaking, the establishment of relations of exchange has a profound effect on the relative importance of various categories of the kin to a given individual. The less directly related one is, the more the relation of Maku exchange becomes the predominant factor in relations between kin and it tends to devalue 'genealogically calculated agnatic kinship outside the expanded family or lineage.'

(1986:179)

This devaluation is consistent with the familiar (but much criticized) characterization of Highlands societies as "loose structures" within which individuals develop and consolidate group affiliation with either the mother's group or father's group through active exchange relationships.[11] LiPuma (1988) has aptly termed this process in Maring society "the gift of kinship." In similar fashion, the practical efficacy of exchange establishes group affiliation for war refugees, adoptees, and those seeking land rights. Exchange thus becomes the way to expand the population of local groupings, a necessity dictated by the demand for intensified production dictated, in turn, by the demands of intensified exchange. Exchange, in short, both works and becomes culturally conceived of as the means for shifting old alliances and creating new alliances.[12] Exchange interjects flexibility, flux, and realignment into social relations.

In Tanga, by contrast, identical exchange in its ideal form between *kinaf* (patrilateral/affinal relatives) is conceived to be as enduring and fixed *(fat)* as the lineage itself. Both the identity of the matrilineage and its enduring relationship with other lineages comprise a single conceptual package. Affinity is regarded to be as "given" as descent inasmuch as affinity equally implies paternity. Clan identity, moreover, is non-negotiable. Individuals acquire clan identity through their mothers and never lose that membership however much they might decline to act upon it. Nor can an individual acquire new lineage affiliation by residing with and supporting the projects of another matrilineage (e.g., the lineage of a man's children). Exchange, then, does not primarily interject flux into social relations, but rather perpetuates kin relations through transfers of care and feeding *(fang)* mediated by repeated intermarriage. As in the Highlands cases, the circulation of wealth in bridewealth and at mortuary feasts evinces and revitalizes social relationships. But the circulation of wealth in Tanga neither exclusively grounds nor regularly innovates affinal alliances. On the contrary, the circulation of wealth mainly occurs and acquires meaning within a context of already instituted relationships, namely, the context of *kinaf* relations.

In sum, the contrast between replication and multiplication can be put in (admittedly) stark terms. Multiplication describes a type of social reproduction that privileges the proliferation and expansion of social relationships, and that achieves such an end through the circulation of wealth. By contrast, replication is conservative, a type of social reproduction in which agents relatively underexploit the potential of exchange in expanding and transforming sociality.

Replication, multiplication, *kastam*, and *bisnis*: a concluding hypothesis
How does the ideal typical distinction between replication and multiplication further an understanding of contemporary changes in social reproduction? I suggest that the distinction can help elucidate how the process of commoditization sketched in chapter 2 has taken different trajectories in different societies within Papua New Guinea and perhaps all of Melanesia. In this final section I briefly sketch the relationship between indigenous exchange practices, commodity exchange, and the categories of *bisnis* and *kastam* in Tanga and two Highlands societies. My aim is to suggest how different exchange practices, characteristic of different types of social reproduction, have become articulated with commodity exchange and how these articulations have conditioned different understandings of "custom" or "tradition." These differences are most easily appreciated in taxonomic terms, especially in terms of the taxonomic relationship between the newly emergent cultural categories of *kastam* and *bisnis*.

I have argued that it was only the emergence of *bisnis* as a category of lived practice that crystallized the taxonomic definition of Tangan *kastam*. Looked at this way, the Tangan case suggests that the meaning of *kastam* always depends upon its location in a set of various relational contrasts: *kastam/bisnis*; *kastam/lotu*; *lotu/bisnis*; and so forth. Significantly, the literature on *kastam* in the western Pacific suggests that different relational contrasts have more or less salience in different societies. Indeed, the salience of particular relational contrasts also varies historically and contextually within a society, inasmuch as the very definition of the terms of these contrasts is an intrinsic feature of ongoing political practice and debate. For instance, Lindstrom (1982) and Tonkinson (1982) have demonstrated how the positive revaluation of *kastom* by nationalist politicians in Vanuatu has refigured in many ways the contrast between *lotu* and *kastom*. Earlier associations of *kastom* with ignorance and immorality, and *lotu* (Christianity) with knowledge and propriety, have given way to a more complicated evaluative relationship. Political contests accordingly have taken shape as arguments over whether or not *kastam* and *lotu* are complementary or antithetical categories (cf. Latukefu 1988).

It is also relevant to note that not only the salience of relational contrasts, but also the relational contrasts themselves might vary from society to society. Ton Otto (1990) has recently argued that Baluan islanders in Manus Province, Papua New Guinea, do not generally recognize *bisnis* as a separate sphere or category of experience. Instead, Baluan people conceptually subdivide their social experience into the three domains of *kastam*, *lotu*, and *gavman*. Otto speculates that the absence of *bisnis* from this scheme might reflect the basis of the Baluan cash economy in remittances from migrant workers rather than in local commerce and petty commodity production.

Nonetheless, it seems fair to say that a broad contrast between *bisnis* and *kastam* is central in many western Pacific societies. This contrast often seizes upon money and monetary transactions as privileged markers of collective identity. In Fiji, for example, the contrast between the "way of the land" and the "path of money" provides rural or village Fijians with an idiom for differentiating themselves from urban Fijians, Fiji-Indians, and Europeans (Kaplan 1988; Thomas 1992a). That is, the self-conscious representation of exchange practices – giving and sharing versus buying and selling – has become a standard part of the project of defining a distinctive cultural identity (e.g., Linnekin 1983). (This, of course, should come as no surprise, for Pacific anthropologists from Malinowski onwards have been engaged in virtually the same task [see Thomas 1992a].) What Lindstrom said about the perceptions of his Tannese interlocutors has much wider application:

People recognize two distinct economic modes: one of customary, balanced reciprocal exchange which occurs within long-term relationships; the second the cash economy of single, isolated transactions which are bounded and presume no continuing rights and duties between the transactors.

(1982:326)

It is as if the Tannese concur with the Maussian distinction between "gifts" and "commodities" so often invoked in the comparative exercises of the New Melanesian Ethnography (Strathern 1988) and criticized in the polemics of the New Melanesian History (Thomas 1991; Carrier 1992a). In the Tangan case, I suggest, recognition of a cognate distinction is part of an overall perception of *kastam* and *bisnis* as antithetical forms of activity.

Perhaps the distinctive feature of Tangan *kastam*, which primarily denotes mortuary feasting and exchange, is its detachment from and opposition to *bisnis* or active involvement in commodity production and exchange (chapter 2). The recent history of the islands suggests, however, that this practical and conceptual dichotomy fully emerged only during the 1960s. What appears to have precipitated the formulation of *bisnis* and *kastam* as distinct, disjunct spheres of activity was the attempt by several big men to exert control over the production and marketing of copra. Their effort recalled the more successful attempt of big men during the 1920s and 1930s to control the trade goods and cash entering the island with returning indentured laborers. In this latter case, big men apparently were able to use this control as a resource for increasing their participation in the exchanges associated with mortuary feasting. Bell's ethnography implies that overtly competitive exchange effloresced. Large transfers of live pigs occurred in which lineage leaders challenged each other in quasi-potlatch style. Exchanges involved not a reciprocal transfer of replicas, but the institution of hierarchical social relations by means of expanding the size and scale of prestations. No such efflorescence, by contrast, accompanied the later accumulation of copra proceeds by an elite group of big men. Rather, big men apparently consumed the cash proceeds directly in raising their own standard of living or indirectly by investing in the ill-fated project of acquiring a copra boat.

It is tempting to interpret these two episodes in the history of Tangan political economy as attempts to eclipse relationality, that is, to circumvent the morality of identical exchange by means of exploiting relations of commodity production and exchange. In the first case, big men such as Kiapsel and Sumsuma acted as intermediaries who converted cash and commodities into pigs, and deployed these pigs in competitive exchanges. In the second case, big men directly employed their lineage mates and allies in commodity production and accumulated the meager proceeds of commodity exchange mainly by dispensing with wages. Each strategy effectively insinuated a previously absent degree of autonomy (and hence hierarchy) into social relations, whether between seniors and juniors, men and women, or one lineage and another. By drawing upon and creating a set of social relations *outside the bounds of identical exchange*, big men sidestepped the constraining obligation to reciprocate contributions to their projects *in kind*, that is, to transfer replicas.

Both of these maneuvers ultimately failed in the face of specific historical circumstances, notably, the end of indenture and the increase in ease of access to copra markets. But historical circumstances alone insufficiently account for the resulting disengagement of *kastam* and *bisnis*. Commodity relations continued to refigure local social relations

244 Toward comparative historical ethnography

and to engender hierarchy, *but not in the context of kastam*. With the redefinition of the role of big men, *kastam* evolved into the forum *par excellence* for identical exchange, for the long-term reciprocal transfer of replicas. Overtly competitive feasting and the assertion of authority by big men over cash cropping declined rapidly. The reinstatement of identical exchange as the organizing framework of mortuary feasting and big man politics entailed the insulation of *kastam* from *bisnis*. And this insulation, in turn, has affected the practice of mortuary rites. That is, insulation has worked to conserve the symbolic form and performative sequence of mortuary events, such that they appear to have changed little since the time of Bell's fieldwork in 1933. Indeed, mortuary rites in 1984–85 were conducted self-consciously as *kastam*, as activities that were both indigenous and ancestral.

Yet, and this is my point, what appears to be a remarkable example of persistence is in fact the precipitate of a radical change in the political economic context of everyday life (see Carrier and Carrier 1989). The emergence of *kastam* as a separate domain of activity – a domain that is more and more becoming self-consciously identified by Tangans with a local Tangan identity and, as a result, perhaps deliberately conserved in a way hitherto unimagined – was premised upon a process of commoditization that has transformed Tangan matriliny and created new forms of household social organization (chapters 2 and 3). As a result of this process, *kastam* now denotes for Tangans a form of sociality that differs from that associated with the domain of *bisnis* (a domain itself associated with Europeans). Indeed, the dichotomy between relationality and autonomy implicit within the practice of *kastam* describes the opposition between *kastam* and *bisnis*; the image of the autonomous collective individual (or matrilineage) constructed in mortuary rites recalls the image of the autonomous and threatening (European) businessman – The Individual in the the Western model of personhood. The difference is that in the practice of *kastam*, relationality and autonomy are continuously turned the one into the other by means of long-term identical exchanges; autonomy is thus encompassed within relationality. In the practice of *bisnis*, however, there are no such means for encompassment; the threat of absolute and irreversible autonomy – of subordination within a relationship of unequal exchange, such as that entailed in simple commodity production or wage labor – is omnipresent and immovable.

Is one of the conditions for the maintenance of a form of social reproduction grounded in identical exchange a sealing off of key social relations (in the Tangan case, *kinaf* relations) from the hierarchizing effects of commodity exchange? Is the disjunction between *kastam* and *bisnis* a feature of replicative social reproduction? A comparative approach to these questions is useful if not mandatory. A. Strathern has commented that "there is no doubt that the Highlands systems of prestige gift-giving do map themselves on to an introduced capitalist system in a remarkable fashion" (1982c:551; cited in Feil 1987:286). Can we account for this mapping without characterizing either Highlands societies or Highlands big men as somehow ethically predisposed to the practices of commodity production and exchange (Finney 1973)?

The penetration of commodity production and exchange into New Guinea Highlands societies presents several contrasts with the Tangan case. Among the Melpa, for example, men have abandoned pearl shells and adopted cash for use in *moka* prestations since the end of the 1960s. The use of cash and other commodities in *moka* occurs on an impressive scale. Strathern (1979) described one prestation in which the Kawelka clan group transferred a Toyota Land Cruiser, dozens of commercially raised pigs, and approximately $A10,000 to the Tipuka clan group in 1974. "Money-*moka*," Strathern argues, represents the attempt of big men, and men in general, to control women's cash proceeds from the sale of coffee beans. Although female labor is critical for the production of coffee beans, men claim rights of disposal over coffee money on the grounds that they planted the trees on their own clan land (Strathern 1979, 1982d). The point here is that Melpa big men, unlike their Tangan counterparts, thus far have been able to integrate forms of commodity production and exchange into the flexible, pre-existing structure of *moka*. Despite the ensuing conflicts between husbands and wives, younger men and older men, *moka* continues to incorporate and encompass commodity relations in the same way that it absorbs money. *Moka* entails a complex and dynamic relationship with the commodity economy, not a withdrawal from it. This relationship, of course, has meant the transformation of *moka* itself (for example, women apparently now make prestations in their own names; see Nihill 1991), but not its disengagement from commodity production and exchange.

Similarly, Boyd recently argued that "profit and prestige are firmly linked in the contemporary Highlands political economy" (1985:336). That is, at least in the Okapa District of the Eastern Highlands, indigenous pig slaughters and distributions have been transformed into commercialized dance festivals called *singsing bisnis*. *Singsing bisnis* combine elements of commodity transactions with features of longstanding intergroup competitive exchanges. On the one hand, sponsors collect admission and concession fees; on the other hand, sponsors distribute gifts of pork, beer, and money to prominent guests and thereby create for themselves credits and prestige. Boyd recognizes the continuity of *singsing bisnis* with traditional pig festivals and so, perhaps inadvertently, do local people:

> A current sponsor summed up the prevailing view of *singsing bisnis*: "This is the new *pasin* [custom] here. It is good and we will keep it. The pig festivals are gone and now all we think about is money."
>
> *(1985:336)*

Although the author of this quote clearly registers the difference between pig festivals and *singsing bisnis*, the definition of the latter as a "new custom" suggests that *bisnis* is not regarded, as it is in Tanga, as antagonistic to custom. Rather, *singsing bisnis*, like money-*moka*, dynamically synthesizes indigenous forms of sociality with introduced forms of commodity relations. Grossman (1984:32) describes a similar strategy for Kapanara villagers in the Eastern Highlands who never question whether *bisnis* is a good thing:

> People do not accumulate money for hoarding or purchasing substantial amounts of material goods for themselves. They channel much of their income, either as cash or goods purchased with money, into the system of reciprocal exchange, in which generosity is highly valued. The more money an individual has, the greater is his potential to give to others. Contributing to another's bridewealth payment, helping a relative with a feast for his affines, giving generously in exchanges, and providing plentiful food to guests are manifestations of such valued behavior.

The idea of a "new custom" expresses well this practical interpenetration of old and new forms of sociality, this conjunction between commodity relations and local forms of evincing social relationships (see Warry 1987 for another Eastern Highlands example).

It is tempting to correlate such synthetic innovations as money-*moka* and *singsing bisnis* with multiplicative social reproduction. The pressures generated by expansive exchange practices to disperse valuables continually in ever increasing quantities presumably make money a much sought after resource. Money potentially enables individuals to expand their participation in exchange; money might be converted into pigs (or beer) for prestations or circulated as a valuable itself. Pumping ever greater amounts of money into circulation does not mean an increase in the danger of circulation, but an augmentation of the name of the donor. In an enchained system of exchanges, moreover, the material form of money allows it to travel through an indefinitely extensive set of transactions. Consequently, commodity production and exchange, the source and locus of money, become potentially useful for the development of indigenous forms of circulation (see Nihill 1989). Commodity relations are put in the service of the indigenous mode of producing sociality – what Sahlins (1992, 1993) is pleased to call "develop-man," the way in which They use Our things to become more like Themselves. Instead, then, of bracketing *bisnis* as a sphere of activity disjunct from *kastam*, the requirements of expansive social reproduction seemingly encourage their marriage.

The long-term viability of such a marriage is another question, one that exposes the limits of the static taxonomic association that I am suggesting here. For it is possible to read the situation in the Highlands as a repetition, with variations, of developments that occurred earlier in Tanga. The project of "develop-man" spawns its own contradictions. Lederman's (1986a) discussion of the Mendi situation is relevant in this regard.[13] Although Mendi apparently reject the notion of commercializing pig festivals in the manner of Boyd's informants, they do not object to the circulation of money in *twem* networks. Indeed, Mendi regard both money and *bisnis* or being desirable precisely because of their involvement in gift exchanges (Lederman 1986a:231). This much is consistent with my hypothesis about expansive forms of reproduction.

But Mendi are not unaware of the problems associated with incorporating money into gift exchanges. Wage-earners and urban businessmen often regard the use of money in personal and clan exchanges as unprofitable (see Grossman 1984:243); reciprocally, people committed to traditional social relations regard *bisnis* as withdrawal from exchange and hence antagonistic to the social ethic of *twem* and *sem*. From this perspective, the commodity relations of *bisnis* appear as not properly social, as engendering hierarchical relations not through reciprocal redistributions, but through accumulation (Lederman 1986a:263). Mendi thus confront a choice between two kinds of sociality:

Both commercial and gift exchange projects are talked about these days as ways of "making money," but they are thought to differ in their effects on intergroup and interpersonal relationships and, particularly, in their schemes of social morality and personal responsibility.

(Lederman 1986b:23)

It is possible to infer from this that an explicit distinction between *bisnis* and *kastam* is emerging in Mendi society.[14] (Grossman's [1984:245] observation in Kapanara of an "ideological separation of subsistence and *bisnis*, with each domain having its own system of morality" is surely not unique.) Whether or not the practical concomitant of this distinction will be the insulation of *twem* and *sem* exchanges from money, in particular, and from commodity relations, in general, remains to be seen.

The disjunction between *kastam* and *bisnis* in Tanga was the result of a confluence of specific historical factors. But it was also the result of a perceived incompatibility of commodity production and exchange with local exchange practices and the processes of social reproduction they underpin. Similarly, the integration of *bisnis* and *kastam* characteristic of at least some Highlands societies appears to have resulted from a perceived compatibility – at least initially, and at least by men – between local and introduced ways. Ultimately, any comparison of these processes will have to consider the internal complexity and specific histories of particular societies. That is, any comparison will have to acknowledge the concerns and techniques of both the New Melanesian Ethnography and the New Melanesian History. I end here by proposing that the distinction between replication and multiplication as two types of social reproduction provides the preliminary basis for such a comparative analysis, and that such a comparative analysis is the proper subject matter of a New Melanesian Anthropology.

Notes

1 Introduction: history, alterity, and a new (Melanesian) anthropology

1 I emphasize the word "heightened" in order to avoid implying that there was once a world inhabited by people without any degree of cultural self-consciousness.

2 Wagner 1974 is an early and lucid attempt at such a reconceptualization. Other exemplary texts of the New Melanesian Ethnography include: Battaglia 1990, 1992; Clay 1986, 1992; Iteanu 1990; Mosko 1992; Strathern 1988, 1990; Wagner 1986a, 1991a; J. Weiner 1988.

3 The New Melanesian Ethnography thus partakes of the larger and more disparate efforts of anthropologists to rethink the nature of Melanesian social formations in terms of "structure" and "process" (see Carrier and Carrier 1991; LiPuma 1988; Merlan and Rumsey 1991).

4 It might well be the case that such a conjunction *precludes* the emergence of *kastam* as an explicit category. Note in this regard that very little of the vast recent literature on *kastam* in Melanesia is based on Highlands ethnography.

2 Commoditization and the emergence of *kastam*

1 I am unaware of any reference to the word *kastam* or to its use by Tangans in any of the numerous publications resulting from Bell's fieldwork in 1933.

2 The division of social life into conceptually and practically discrete domains has been described for other parts of island Melanesia (see Lindstrom 1982; Otto 1990; Neumann 1992).

3 The argument in this chapter employs the theoretical framework proposed by Bernstein (1979) for African peasantries. For an example of Bernstein's approach applied to a Papua New Guinea case study see the work of Fahey (1984, 1986) on the "proletarianization" of a peri-urban village near Madang.

4 In rural Melanesia, such commodity relations usually take the form of cash cropping and/or the exchange of labor power for wages. The opposition between "use-values" and "commodities" comes from Bernstein (1979). In Marx's terms, a society dominated by the production and exchange of *concrete* use-values increasingly comes to reproduce itself through the production and exchange of *abstract* exchange-values or "Values" – "congelation[s] of homogenous human labor, of labor power expended" (Marx 1979[1867]:38).

5 It is perhaps unnecessary to point out that Bernstein's materialist understanding of "social reproduction" differs from my own sketched in the Introduction. I see our views as complementary rather than contradictory; they focus on different aspects of people's attempts to create the conditions for future action.

6 Nor is there any logical necessity to assume that this result is the inevitable end point of a world-historical teleology – as perhaps suggested by the famous assertion of Marx and Engels in the *Communist Manifesto* about the bourgeoisie creating a world after its own image.

7 PR NAM 8 = Patrol Report Number 8, Namatanai Subdistrict. Copies of patrol reports dating back to 1945 were examined in the National Archives and Public Records of Papua New Guinea, Waigani. I thank Mr. V. Dairi, Research Officer, for arranging access to these materials.

8 In 1991, Islands Aviation began a service that connected the offshore islands of Anir, Tanga, Lihir, and Tabar both to each other and to the towns of Rabaul, Namatanai, and Kavieng.

9 Informants were generally unable to gloss the word. Bell (1977:vi) recorded the claim of Temaliflif that Tangga is a Lihir word for the group of islands as a whole. Tangans themselves refer to (their) language as *niwer*. A "strip of language" (*sun niwer*) is a monologue or speech. I follow the convention of current practice on Tanga in spelling the name of the island group with only one "g."

10 Beaumont (1976:388) estimates a cognate percentage of 42 for the Tangga and Lihir languages. Tangans do not in general regard their relationship with Lihir islanders as being as close as that with Anir/Feni people.

11 Although *tumbuan* originated in coastal southern New Ireland, the association of Tolai and *tumbuan* is a strong one. Lak speakers in southern New Ireland recognize a Tolai type of *tumbuan* (*koropo*) distinct from the local variety (*kambentuktuk*) (see Albert 1987b).

12 A 1969 patrol report estimates that 5,120 acres of Boang are arable (PR NAM 12/1968–69).

13 See, for example, the account by Mrs. William Kent of the brief encounter between the H.M.S. *Buffalo* and some Tangan canoes in 1803 (Whittaker, Gash, Hookey, and Lacey 1975:293), as well as Beale's (1839:319–22) account of an extended session of bartering hoop iron for vegetable tubers with some St. John's (Anir) islanders in 1832.

14 Deutsche Handels- und Plantagen-Gesselschaft der Sudsee-Inseln zu Hamburg.

15 The practice of shipping New Guinea laborers to Samoa, a proximate cause of German annexation in 1884, continued until the end of German control of the colony. Bell mentions a conversation with one Tangan man who had lived in Samoa for twenty years (1953:29).

16 The figure of 368 Tangans is taken from Price and Baker (1976). Thirty-seven Anir islanders and 649 Lihir islanders also entered Queensland from 1883–84. The relatively low number for Anir fits well with accounts of recruiting there cited in this chapter.

17 Wawn gives the number as ninety-four, sixty-three males and thirty-one

females "all from the smaller islands lying near the eastern coast of New Ireland," and "nearly half" from Tanga (Kaen Is.) (1973:333).

18 Indeed, one could interpret the responses of the Nissan elders and the Anir islanders as strategies intended to drive up the price of labor paid by the recruiters. Such an interpretation, suggested to me by Scott MacWilliam, would argue that commodity relations and practices had become regularized over the course of the labor trade.

19 It is important not to forget that some islanders might have controlled this relationship at the expense of others: senior men at the expense of juniors, men in general at the expense of women.

20 The Australian administration imposed in 1921 an annual head tax of 10s in all areas declared taxable districts. In 1926, all territory under government control was so declared. Rowley points out that on odd patrols to outlying areas during the 1914–21 period: "taxes were collected . . . from villages which had little or no other contact with government" (1958:176). It is quite possible that patrol officers collected taxes in the Tanga Islands from the beginning of Australian civil rule in 1922.

21 One older man (Kiaptes of clan Tasik) told me that Kiapsel maintained his own jailhouse for the punishment of those who disobeyed him. It is difficult to assess the degree of Kiapsel's authority, though the abuse of the *luluai* position by local despots was by no means uncommon in New Guinea. For the classic example see Hogbin (1963).

22 Rowley wrote that the origin of the system of paramount *luluai*, officials with authority over other *luluai*, is obscure. But the Australians recognized the German practice in Regulations made under the Native Administration Ordinance (1921–22) (Rowley 1958:223). On Tanga, the position effectively disappeared after World War II, during which Ngamnabo was relieved of the position by the Japanese allegedly at the instigation of another man, Bitlik, Bell's former servant and principal informant.

23 The society was dormant on Tanga in 1984–85, though still operating in Muliama where perhaps some Tangan men had encountered it.

24 Timanmale also suggested that the custom of *dafal* came from Muliama in southern New Ireland. Brown (1972:105) observed the practice on the west coast of southern New Ireland in 1876.

25 I say "less commoditized" (in Bernstein's sense) because pig production involved, though indirectly, the use of commodity items (e.g., knives and axes to clear gardens in which food for pigs was cultivated, and in some cases European boars; see footnote 27). Clearly, however, the use of commodities in pig production does not preclude the exchange of pigs according to the precepts of a local cultural reason.

26 This is by no means a complete accounting for the individuals involved. Names appear in odd contexts throughout postwar patrol reports and no definitive list of *luluai* during Bell's fieldwork is available.

27 Bell tended to relegate such information, if he reported it at all, to footnotes. For example, he noted that in November 1933: ". . . two important chieftains, who had had experience on a mainland plantation, were using six European type boars for breeding purposes" (1947b:37).

28 A small Japanese platoon occupied Boang for part of the war in order to monitor shipping lanes. In a dramatic raid on the island, an Allied patrol led by the coastwatcher Murray killed several Japanese soldiers before escaping by submarine (Murray 1973:132–81).

29 For instance, Schlaginhaufen (1908) claims to have visited Tanga in 1908 aboard the vessel of a Chinese merchant from the west coast of Southern New Mecklenburg. The text is unclear as to whether the merchant was trading on Tanga or if Schlaginhaufen had chartered the vessel for his visit.

30 It is certain, however, that Chinese recruiters did visit the islands. For example, Gammage (1975) reports that Sumsuma left the islands in 1913 with Ah Mok, a prosperous Namatanai agent for the New Guinea Company (Biskup 1970:100). Similarly, Nerong, a former *luluai* and big man, claimed that prior to 1933 Tangans occasionally bartered sun-dried copra for trade goods supplied by a Muliama-based merchant named Lem Sing (?).

31 Bell (1934) mentioned the arrival of a Chinese planter on Boang, probably Chin Pak, at the beginning of 1933. Chin Pak's brother, Chin Him, captained the boat (*Kwong Chow*) that brought Bell to Tanga. Chin Him also attempted to lease land while Bell was on Boang (Bell 1953).

32 Although Bell's fieldnotes suggest that a Carpenter plantation was already in operation on Malendok in 1933.

33 Interestingly, the earliest extant patrol report for Tanga mentions the officer's intervention in a minor dispute over work hours and task work on Sunmiul plantation in 1934 (PR NAM 1/1934–35).

34 The Tangan case, as will be seen, contrasts markedly with that of the development of smallholder coffee production in the Highlands where the colonial state actively extended agricultural services to promote production (Grossman 1984; MacWilliam 1986). In the absence of state services, Tangans themselves orchestrated the transition from labor reserve to entrenched simple commodity production. The Tangan case makes ironic the argument of Snowden (1981?) and others that the colonial state often used cooperative societies as instruments for regulating native leaders and collective activity.

35 Schooling had been provided by Catholic Mission catechists from before the war. By 1959, the Amfar school gave instruction through standard four. Secondary education was completed on the New Ireland mainland or in the Rabaul area, as was the case in 1984. For an account of a similar intergenerational struggle see Clay 1986:258ff.

36 Fingleton quotes a 1964 World Bank report on Papua New Guinea which asserted that: "... traditional land tenure systems imposed 'grave limitations' on agricultural development, and were 'quite unsuited to the rapidly emerging commercial farming scene which needs the assurance of permanent use rights by individuals to specific areas of larger size than needed for subsistence gardens'" (1984:158).

37 Maurer was the first permanent European missionary posted to the island. He arrived in 1933, eight years after Neuhaus had installed Tolai catechists in the group. Maurer stayed until 1937. He resumed residence after the war.

38 For instance, Fr. Hager began construction of an airstrip at Amfar which, however, does not appear to have been brought into regular use until the 1970s.

39 Fr. Hager's successor, Fr. Vavro, continued these undertakings, as did Fr. Leon Wiessenberger, the missionary resident at Amfar during 1984–85.

40 By 1992, the Mission had applied this criticism to itself and had withdrawn from the copra business.

41 Admittedly, in 1984 copra prices reached record heights on the world market, producing a welcome windfall for smallholders.

42 Possibly, the statistics reflect not increased production, but rather increased sales to the Mission. I cannot make a strong case for interpreting the figures in this way.

43 By 1992, the outlook was bleaker. The copra market had collapsed, and Tangans found themselves more than ever before dependent upon remittances. The civil war in Bougainville, moreover, had caused many Tangan migrant workers to return home, sometimes with their families, thus straining the already limited supplies of land for gardening as well as closing off an important avenue for remittance income.

3 *Kastam, bisnis,* and matriliny

1 I use the slightly unconventional terms "enate" and "enatic" to denote relatives and relationships traced through females; I intend to evoke associations with the terms "agnate" and "agnatic" familiar from classic discussions of unilineal descent groups. I also use the terminological abbreviations of MBMB and ZSZS instead of MMB and ZDS in order to underscore the image of lineage succession projected in Tangan mortuary rites.

2 This gloss is hardly definitive. *Fakausi* can mean "to make beautiful"; *matam funbaratam* can mean "eye of the family groups (lineages)," but it might also refer to *matamfunmat* ("eye of the clan"), the name of places on lineage land associated with the presence of non-human power (*mui*).

3 The exception to this generalization is the sea eagle (*kosor*), totem of clan Tasik. Several clan Tasik people said that they do not eat this animal. If a dead sea eagle is discovered, it will be given burial by clan members.

4 I am unsure of the exact disposition of clan Eski. One Eski lineage has a men's house near the Mission station at Amfar and, in general, clan members seem to reside on the western end of the island and to marry predominantly into clan Filimat.

5 This relationship is one commonly mobilized to gather support for hosting feasts. In one case that I have described elsewhere (Foster 1988), the host lineage of clan Korofi received material assistance from lineages of clans Fasambo and Ku on the basis of such longstanding relations.

6 Note that the totem of clan Tasik is the sea eagle (*kosor*) while the totem of clan Tulafaleng is the sea hawk (*tagau*). On the mainland of New Ireland, these are the totems of exogamous moieties (*bik pisin* and *smol pisin*, respectively); on Tanga, the close relationship of the two birds is sometimes given as a reason for why clans Tasik and Tulafaleng *cannot* intermarry. One informant also claimed that there was a prohibition on intermarriage between clans Tasik and Tunaman, and clans Fale and Tunaman. Genealogies show rare instances of such marriages.

7 In addition, Tangans visiting mainland New Ireland, especially Muliama,

apparently have no difficulty slotting themselves into the moiety system operative there. One Muliama man claimed that the word *funmat* meant "moiety" and that "clans" are called *birbiranmat*.

8 Genealogies collected by W. J. Read for the Land Titles Commission suggest that smaller non-Boang-based clans (Pen, Tulefaleng, Firfir) contain smaller lineages. I am unable to corroborate this with my own data.

9 "Line" is my gloss for the Tok Pisin term *lain* used by Tangans. I prefer this term to both segment and sublineage, but it too unhappily implies a segmentary definition for what is a non-segmentary concept. The comments of Merlan and Rumsey (1991:36) about the Ku Waru term *talapi* are apposite: "The most literal sense of the term *talapi* is something like 'line', 'row', or 'column' ... Suggestive as this image might be for descent theorists, in Ku Waru discourse the point of contact between the more and less literal senses of the term *talapi* is not – as they might assume – in some notion of a line of descent by which each member of a group is linked to its apical ancestor. What is locally relevant is not a vertical genealogical line, but a horizontal, tactical one: the line of men who form a single flank on the battlefield and dance as a single row at ceremonial exchange events." What is locally relevant in Tanga is that a "line" is a cluster of co-resident enates who potentially form the core of a new lineage.

10 The exercise also recalls Wagner's effort to translate the Barok word for clan (1986a:xiv). Wagner argues that the word is a verbal image which at once contains and elicits numerous possible glosses.

11 This describes the situation in 1984–85, by which time men's houses had taken on the functions of funeral houses (*fel*) described by Bell (1949b). In the past, it is possible that while funeral houses – temporary structures in any event – were built at various sites, men's houses remained associated with a single site. Bell (1949b:345) noted a reluctance to move men's houses to a new site because the ground underneath was used as a grave for corpses awaiting secondary burial. This burial practice was discontinued under administrative pressure in the 1930s, after which corpses were buried permanently either nearby the men's house or in new "neighborhood" cemeteries (see chapter 4).

12 When I initially asked for the names of big men associated with particular lineages, I sometimes was given the names of men eighty years old or older. This identification expresses indirectly the conception of big man as the eldest lineage male (rather than a presently active feast maker), as physical mediator between the living and dead of a lineage.

13 Again, both women and men are members of this pool. I defer discussion of the *fat kinaf* relationship as a specific kind of exchange relationship to chapter 5.

14 The decline of polygynous marriages after World War II removed from the field of social practice one of the most effective means of creating dense patrilateral relatedness not only within the lineage, but also within and between clans. I suggest that this is one factor contributing to a perceived trend toward lineage atomism, that is, an increase in the number of men's houses being built with a simultaneous reduction in the scale of the associated feasting.

15 Actual WB/ZH relatives use not the euphemistic paternal terms, but another

set of teknonyms (e.g., *an sieng* – "platoon"). Classificatory in-laws, however, use the paternal/filial term *kaik* (inasmuch as each is the child of the other).

16 It is relevant in this regard to note that Kamdamut was without any actual sisters of his own. Kamdamut's MB, Sikel, married Partui's elderly M, Funkorofi. Sikel was not the genitor of Funkorofi's offspring; the marriage seems to have taken place after Partui and his siblings were fully mature. Nonetheless, the implied ties of patrilateral relationship ideally should have been recognized as part of the relationship between Kamdamut and Partui (see Clay 1977:40 for a similar example).

17 Bachelors occasionally have their own sleeping quarters, which often function as crash pads for their peers. Teenage boys on the whole enjoy a very mobile lifestyle, dependent upon their mothers, brothers (including FB), and sometimes casual employers for cooked food (see footnote 24).

18 I qualify "returned" because it is quite possible that a woman moves to her matrilineal land for the first time upon the death of her husband. Born on the land of her father (or her HF), relocated upon marriage to the land of her husband (which could be the land of her father if she marries into her father's lineage), a woman conceivably can live the whole of her life on land of a lineage other than her own.

19 The idea is captured in certain place names, such as Mokatilistunglo, which various men told me was once a bush (*mok*) site for gardens that supported feasts at the base/origin place of Solsol lineage.

20 However, another man claimed that *tara* referred to "the power of the ground" while *madas* referred to "the power that men give to things." I take this statement to reflect the sometimes articulated view that *madas* is more amenable to the manipulations (*suse*) of men than *tara*.

21 Such a protected place is sometimes called *male suse*. *Suse* refers at once to the magic for protecting the place, the bespelled Cordyline plants (*ang gaf*) which signify such protection, and the *masalai bilong ples* ("domestic spirits," as opposed to *masalai bilong bus*, "bush spirits" or *tara* proper) which protect the hamlet.

22 Jessep argues convincingly that the activity of Barok Demarcation Committees encouraged cash dealings in land during the late sixties (1980a:124). This was probably also the case on Tanga.

23 Neungteng of the Tefa line of clan Firfir gave me a similar account and mentioned that a young Firfir girl bore the name "Binnamale" ("destitute of a place") to commemorate the consequence of Pasam's actions.

24 Men with extensive holdings sometimes hire ("charter") groups of teenagers to process copra for them at a fixed daily cash wage which might or might not include an afternoon meal.

25 Since only men plant and thus technically own coconuts, I discuss rights to the trees from a male perspective. Women, however, with their husbands, can harvest palms under the control of their brothers in the name of their children.

26 Certain other large fruit-bearing trees (e.g., breadfruit and canarium almond) growing on lineage land might be used collectively following a first-fruits feast (see chapter 4). I am uncertain whether the trees that I saw used in this manner were cultivated or wild.

27 Moreover, since most of this income is spent on imported food items that rarely enter into feast distributions, cash income does not circulate outside the household in the form of cooked food. Contrast Albert's (1987a) description of inter-household food transfers among the Lak of mainland New Ireland.

28 This argument can be traced back at least as far as the late fifties/early sixties. One officer observed in 1961: "The patrol was informed that it was the peoples' wish to change from matrilineal to patrilineal inheritance rights. They were most definite, that as from the beginning of 1962, all new plantings of coconuts would come under patrilineal inheritance rights on the death of the owner ... It is therefore felt that these people have taken an important step, by changing their inheritance rights, in attaining increased economic prosperity" (PR NAM 8/1961–62). In general, patrol officers and low-level administrators responded favorably to signs of patrilineality on the then generally accepted grounds that such tenure was necessary to promote individual entrepreneurial enterprise (see Fingleton 1984). At least one informant told me that the Australians mandated patrilineal inheritance.

29 Once a man suggested to me that *kastam* ought to be monetized by charging fees for pork at feasts in order to stimulate *kastam* as a form of "economic development" (*kirapim ples* in Tok Pisin). Most Tangan men, I submit, would find this idea unacceptable and thus far Tangans have resisted the commercialization of *kastam* (see chapter 8). One man in fact distinguished Tangan *kastam* from *kastam* on nearby Lihir on the grounds that people were required to buy their pork at feasts on Lihir. Another man similarly contrasted Tangans with Tolai on the grounds that Tolai had lost their *kastam* in the greedy pursuit of *bisnis*.

30 The dialectics of consumption and non-consumption, eating and making others eat, are constructed in subsequent chapters.

31 The Tangan view of this matter recalls Fortes's classic statement (1953) on unilineal descent groups. This view is not at all uncommon in island Melanesia (see Thune 1980; Fortune 1932). For another pertinent Austronesian example see Bloch (1985).

4 Finishing the dead: an outline of Tangan mortuary feasts and exchanges

1 Blumer, following George Herbert Mead, describes joint action as follows: "One, joint actions have to be initiated – and they may not be. Two, once started a joint action may be interrupted, abandoned, or transformed. Three, the participants may not make a common definition of the joint action into which they are thrown and hence may orient their acts on different premises. Four, a common definition of a joint action may still allow wide differences in the direction of the separate lines of action and hence in the course taken by the joint action ..." (1966:541).

2 Bell (1937) also identified "burial rites" and "funeral-house building rites" as distinct stages in the mortuary sequence. For a discussion of the differences between Bell's account and my own see Foster 1988.

3 *Fa-rop*: *rop* means "to come to an end," as in "my speech is finished" (*kek sun i wer i sam rop*). Disputes, coconuts full of juice, and horseplay might all similarly "come to an end." Finishing the dead is a common idiom in New

Ireland. Compare the Tangan word *farop* with its cognates in Barok (*korop*) and Lak (*kirop*) (Wagner 1986a; Albert 1987a).

4 However, Tangans sometimes differentiate between *kinaf*, relatives of "one blood," and affines or relatives by marriage, referred to generally by the Tok Pisin term *tambu*. The distinction is invoked in various contexts, "*kinaf*" being used to signify togetherness, "*tambu*" being used to signify separation.

5 Bell (1937:319) wrote: "In these days some District Officers, in ignorance of the consequences of their orders, instruct the *luluai* to see that all men of his 'line' [census unit] are buried in the one cemetery. A 'line' often comprises representatives of half a dozen different clans, whilst the cemetery belongs to only one clan. Whenever a man of an alien clan is buried in that cemetery, the clan upon whose land the cemetery is situated claims and is paid compensation for opening their land to the bones of a 'foreigner.' Besides creating ill-will between the clans, such a practice interferes with the smooth operations of all the many subsequent rites which centre about the bones of the dead man." It is possible, based on the argument made in chapter 2, to speculate that *luluai* themselves exploited this situation to exercise influence over the mortuary feasting of other lineages (Bell's "clans").

6 For instance, on one occasion a young aspiring lineage leader's MB died unexpectedly within weeks of the deaths of the man's son and father. Feasting for the MB was postponed until the man could replenish his stocks of vegetable food and pigs.

7 At all Tangan feasts, individuals are served their own portions which are placed before them atop a banana leaf placemat. Individuals receiving certain prime cuts (rump, legs, or large back sections) will have to reciprocate them at a future distribution. These distributions are discussed in chapter 6.

8 One man called this meal *morawas*, a reference to the hardwood (*was*) of digging sticks once used to dig the grave and still used to break ground in new gardens.

9 In general, *mor* are feasts or small meals given in compensation for some service performed (wailing, assisting in garden work or housebuilding, etc.) while *en* denotes feasts unassociated with any such services.

10 I attended *en turan* a few days before the death of Marasus in 1992, and *pam bi* a few days afterwards. Both gatherings convened the same group of people, at the same evening hour, in the same place.

11 This rite allowed Tabunima's MBD to return to her job on the New Ireland mainland.

12 This kind of presentation is referred to as *sing paklun minet* ("for the skull/ head of the corpse/deceased"), perhaps an allusion to the display of the skull once made during the final feast of *pok bif*.

13 These *an u-a* were recorded at Angkamu hamlet in the eastern end of Boang at the men's house of a lineage of clan Tunaman, in April 1984. The singers were practicing in preparation for a trip to Anir, where their performance would be part of a mortuary feast sequence. For Tangga language versions see Foster 1988.

14 Ngamnabo was not a member of Tabunima's lineage though he married two women of Tabunima's clan.

15 Compare Wagner's remarks about Barok (central New Ireland) sociality: "...
Barok public life is a drama of self-evident [visible] signs of gestures, phrases,
and sequences that are immediately recognizable in their public import and
inseparable, in their outward form, from the intentionality of the actor"
(1987:173).
16 My use of the term "iconic," as the above examples make clear, does not imply
a theory of representation based on ideas of "natural" resemblance (for a
critique of such theory see Mitchell 1987). Icons are conventional signs, as
Pierce himself recognized. By the use of the term icon, I emphasize the
qualitative immediacy of the icon and not any necessary resemblance to its
referent (see Rochberg-Halton 1986 for a similar argument and see Munn 1986
for a related concept of iconicity).
17 The procedure of *fil taufi* lends its name to the temporary *am fimfil*, which is a
euphonic rendering of the reduplication, *filfil*. *Taufia* is an epithet of respect.
Kaltu taufi may be used interchangeably with *kaltu dok* (big man), though Bell
(1955:283) suggests that there was once a recognized distinction in rank
implied by the two terms. Brothers-in-law, real and classificatory, sometimes
use the term *taufia* as a respectful form of address. *Fil taufi* might also be
performed at *moratineng* (see footnote 12). See Wagner (1986a:199) for a
similar kind of payment to secure participation in mortuary feasting.
18 In this respect, it makes sense to consider the *am fimfil* itself as a "sign"
(*finailim*) of the true men's house which stands as an "emblem" (*do*) of the
matrilineage.
19 If a woman's brothers or MB solicits her support for an upcoming feast, she
will offer yams from her supply. Her husband might also contribute yams from
his supply.
20 Tangans, unlike many mainland New Irelanders, train (*pipse ang kubun er*) the
vines of their yams to climb poles (*tenak*) up to nine feet tall. Trained yams
indicate a garden's progress, communicating by their height the approximate
size of the growing yams and by their color (green or brown) the time to begin
harvesting. These signs are eminently public. Gardens thereby become particularly potent means of advertising the agency, potential and realized, of the
gardener.
21 See Foster 1988 for further discussion of garden layouts, garden work, garden
magic, and garden locations.
22 Maurer (1966) translates *gus* as *haupen*, "pile" or "heap." Hence the meaning
of *warangus* as "base of the food heap."
23 *Fawit* is an indigenous metaphor that likens pulling someone into the preparations for a feast to the use of a special rope (*fefel*) and basket (*gul*) employed
to reach and avoid bruising ripe delicate fruits (such as *tau*) growing at the end
of long branches.
24 Among mainland New Ireland groups, the construction of men's houses
apparently is an affair distinct from mortuary rites and feasting (Albert 1987a;
Wagner 1986a).
25 But not entirely. During the fieldwork period, one small *fel* was erected at
Funiautaraukalo hamlet, near Warankeng in the Lop district of Boang island,
and another was planned. The sponsor of the *fel* at Warankeng, Nesua, and his

brother, Tasmale, explained that too many men's houses were being constructed presently. Unlike men's houses, *fel* are disassembled after their commemorative feasts are held. The erection of a *fel*, moreover, does not require
succeeding generations to erect *fel* at the same site.

26 Promissory men's houses are generally smaller than "true" men's houses (*bia*
or *bif*).

27 However, the use of bamboo as a building material has declined. No longer are
the side walls (*balo*) constructed of "rods of bamboo lashed horizontally to a
number of upright bamboo poles" (Bell 1949b:322). Instead, long bamboo
rods are split to form 18-inch wide panels that are nailed to upright timber wall
posts. Crossties (*tatus*) also tend to be timber rather than bamboo, even in
smaller men's houses. Tangans explain the switch to this style of construction,
reportedly imported from mainland central New Ireland, as the product of a
severe bamboo shortage. Although a few women's residences/cookhouses
(*felungkur*) with old-style rod walls could be observed in 1984, all other
structures employed the panelling method.

28 This kind of play is commonly associated with moiety interaction (see for
example Powdermaker 1971), but the two groups were not related to each
other in any way obvious to me.

29 *Aiang* is the possessive form used in relation to edibles, kin, and other aspects
of personal identity. The other form for the first person possessive, used for
detachable objects, is *kiang* or *kek*. The distinction is both common and
significant in Austronesian languages (see Damon 1978 for an extended discussion).

30 The same restriction on stepping over things applies to certain physical
interactions between men and women. Bell noted that: "A sign that the closest
intimacy exists between a man and a woman is expressed by their stepping over
each other's outstretched legs" (1935c:180). More generally, the protocol of
relative elevation prohibits women from climbing trees (at least in the presence
of men) and from walking past a newly built men's house with baskets on their
heads. Male informants disagreed about whether it was appropriate for
women to sit in pickup trucks driving by such men's houses or whether women
ought to alight, walk past the men's house, and then remount the truck at some
point farther along the road. Male informants in favor of such an observance
justified their position by arguing that women must show deference (*ninatke*)
for the deceased commemorated by the men's house.

31 In such cases, *fasuigk* coincides with the preparation of *mangat* packets that
always takes place the day before a feast and often issues in a combination
feast/*mor* called *en fafas* (see table 11). A cooked pig sometimes supplements
the *mangat* packets that provide the mainstay of *en fafas*.

32 This image of a man at *fasuigk* is central to men's house *kastam*. It was in fact
instantiated by the carved post (*tutor*) that stood in the Solsol men's house, a
life-size figure with a spear and a (wooden) shell disc held in its outstretched
arms.

33 Encircling people or things denotes proprietary rights in the same way as
stepping over (*kau*) things. During the course of men's house feasting, pigs,
guests, and the men's house itself (filled with food and pigs) are all encircled by

representatives of the host lineage. Likewise, the ZS steps over the food and pigs amassed within the men's house as he traverses the ridgepole.

34 Clay (1986:216) makes similar observations about Mandak songs: "The communicating features of song composition are in the sounds of the words and their fit to music, for this is what determines the social acceptance and approval of a song, not its content." *Bot* compositions communicate not primarily as lyrics, but as words that, in the context of song, evoke commonly shared and strongly felt images. Translation of such songs often proved fruitless; for their significance lay not in the words themselves but in the images conjured and experienced only in the act of singing them. Indeed, in order to transcribe and translate some songs (*walau*) once connected with building ocean-going canoes, Kiapun, who assisted me, found it impossible simply to "say" the words. The only way of recalling and reciting the verbal content of the songs for transcription involved singing them slowly, again and again, phrase by phrase, with a small group of singers expressly brought along for the purpose. It is as if the songs enjoy no existence (say, as Tangga language texts of the sort I've made of them in Foster 1988) apart from their being sung.

35 Wagner's (1986a:127) experience learning Barok *tinie* (line dances) nicely makes this point while suggesting that the Tangan situation is more general in New Ireland: "... I was instructed in how to hold the ... drum, how to brace it against my knee, and how to hold my fingers in striking it. I was not, however, given any instruction in anything relating to the substantive 'content' of the *tinie*, either in terms of rhythmic or melodic patterns, or in those of its 'meaningful' verbal or mimetic intent ... My task was simply to begin drumming along with the others ... trying to keep their rhythm and figuration, stopping or changing when they did, and hoping not to be 'caught out' when the whole barrage came to a halt."

36 Peeling tubers is a quintessentially female task. The word for vulva, *konsipin*, can be translated as "peeled yam."

37 The absence of public oratory as the accompaniment of ceremonial exchange contrasts markedly with the extended speechmaking typically associated with ceremonial exchange in the New Guinea Highlands (see, for example, Merlan and Rumsey 1991).

38 Two of the three final feasts that I observed were accompanied by *singsing*. The leader of a group charged with delivering a *singsing* may, in turn, seek out a *buai* man for help in organizing an innovative dance (cf. Nachman 1978). *Buai* means "betel nut" in Tok Pisin and Kuanua. *Buai* men are adepts of a variety of power usages (see chapter 7) that for the most part concern the innovation and execution of song and dance performances. At least three Taonsip men were considered *buai* men in 1985; each had been initiated into the secrets of *buai* by men from the Duke of York Islands or southern New Ireland. *Buai* is regarded by Tangans as Tolai in origin (cf. Nachman 1978; Wagner 1986a).

39 In this, they differed markedly from the *arel sigit* described in detail by Bell (1947b) which featured a massive competitive exchange of live pigs (chapter 2).

40 For the Solsol final feast, Partui constructed an *an sup* that resembled a step ladder in some respects but also sported the pendulous tapered tip from which

hung the flower (*lom*) of a banana tree. Partui described the *an sup* as unique ("*i no gat wanpela an sup long Tanga i olsem*"; "there is no other *an sup* like this") but at the same time as customary ("*em i an sup bilong tumbuna iet*"; "it is a traditional *an sup*"). His remark captures well the mix of innovation and appeal to convention connoted by the idea of *kastam*.

41 The word *arer* ("to inspect") denotes a feast with a *singsing*; *en* denotes a feast without a *singsing*. See Nachman (1978) for a description of dances and a catalogue of the names of dances common in the Gazelle–New Ireland–North Solomons area.

42 Christmas is a popular time for feasts. High school students who board off island and urban workers return to the islands for holiday.

43 This gesture epitomizes the idea of controlled revelation as an index of power (chapter 7). For a discussion of similar tricks or mysteries (*pindik*) see Wagner 1986a.

44 The formation and decoration of the dancers marked the *singsing* as *limbung*, a reportedly Tolai import associated with the famous *tumbuan* masked dancers. The headdresses of the dancers bore a geometrical design associated with the "eye" of a *tumbuan* mask (see Albert 1987b for illustrations).

45 In the past, the progress of both forgetting and making invisible the material signifiers of death paralleled somewhat the deterioration and disposal of the corpse. From this point of view, cementing graves might be understood not as final acts of commemoration, but as final acts of "hiding" the deceased.

5 Replacing the dead: identical exchange and lineage succession

1 Of course, certain actual deaths (e.g., the sudden death of a young adult by accident, violence or unexpected illness) upset this representation, but by exposing not the degree to which *death* threatens sociality, but rather the degree to which certain people (sorcerers, homicides) or spirits (*masalai*, God) threaten the sociality from which they are detached.

2 This version of the myth was published by Bell (1935c). I did not elicit a similar version of the myth during my own fieldwork, though at least one other myth I heard (see chapter 8) contains the story of the old woman and the spontaneously generated grandsons. As Bell noted, this myth enjoys wide distribution throughout island Melanesia. Significantly, Fortune (1932:186) recorded one version among the Dobu Islanders. The matrilineal social organizations and developed mortuary rites of the Massim bear strong resemblances to those of Tanga (cf. Thune 1980; Young 1987; Damon and Wagner 1989).

3 I say "overtly" inasmuch as the myth resonates with Tangan notions of conception described below.

4 Given the enormous literature on exchange in Papua New Guinea societies, accounts of the indigenous vocabulary of exchange are relatively rare. For one sustained account see Barraud *et al.* (1984). For a non-Melanesian example of the fruitfulness of such accounts see Benveniste (1971).

5 In Tangga, *fa-* may be prefixed to words meaning "change" to indicate reciprocal action or "exchange." See text below.

6 For example, the sentence *A bet o peteng in an tonsu ri tel pik in male Tanga an wara fanu murmur ri la wa ge lo* can be translated as "I would like you to tell me

about the things that changed [*tel pik*] in Tanga as a result of white men coming here."

7 See chapter 3 and below for further discussion of marriage payments and the exchange of nurture.

8 Likewise, the acceptance of a *warangus* basket obligates the recipient to work for the lineage of the donor. Informants explained to me that once a man earmarks a pig for a recipient at *pok bif*, as for example Timir earmarked one of his pigs for Partui, he becomes beholden to the wishes of the designated recipient. The pig cannot be withdrawn and given elsewhere; it is irrevocably committed.

9 In a similar fashion, affinal and paternal kin terms refer to different dimensions of the same social relationship. Over time, however, the negative connotations of affinity give way to the positive connotations of paternity. A terminological shift accompanies the process by which affines are "converted" into paternal relatives via the conventions of the *kinaf* relationship. The assertion implicit in marriage payments (*fil fifin*) yields in the next generation to the cooperation connoted by the recognition of paternal care (*kos fang*).

10 By contrast, the word *fil* denotes a discrete (unencompassed) act of giving and taking when used to depict a purchase at the store: money is given, a commodity taken. That *fil* in this case lacks a coordinate return transaction or "backing" (*kos*) speaks of the morally ambiguous nature of store purchases.

11 I use the terms substitutive exchange and identical exchange more or less interchangeably. However, I use the term identical exchange more frequently in keeping with usage already established in the literature on exchange.

12 For Meillassoux, the association of these kinds of exchanges with the concept of spheres of values follows accordingly. I am equally critical of this formulation as a satisfactory explication of identical exchange and of Meillassoux's contention that goods in identical exchange have "no value" (see chapter 6).

13 Expectation, of course, is not a guarantee. Numerous factors always render uncertain the probability of reciprocation at any given time. Feast sponsors organize distributions according to their own immediate considerations; it might be more important to distribute a pig as solicitation for future assistance than to reciprocate (*kos*) a past gift.

14 Immediate and direct identical exchanges do occur. For example, the exchange of equal amounts of money or of cooked pigs at a court hearing announces the resolution of grievances between two disputants, appropriately referred to by Tangans as "shaking hands," the gesture *par excellence* of identical exchange.

15 Consistent with this ideal, the most likely targets of sorcery accusations are the lineage mates of the suspected victim.

16 *Fasuigk* distributions thus constitute another mechanism for constructing social time, foreshadowing the future at the same time as it draws the past into the present. For a discussion both of the construction of time and of strategies for keeping exchange relationships alive see Munn 1983.

17 Both older informants and Bell (1948:53) reported a previously common practice of infant betrothal in which the groom's mother makes gifts of food to the bride's mother and thereby effectively nurtures and grows the body of the bride herself through the medium of breast milk. Marriage alliance was thus

subsumed under the heading of exchanges of generalized nurture (*fang*) (see below). The use of *am borau na tinaule*, and especially the exchange of tradestore items, was said to be a recent phenomenon. Transfers of shell valuables to the bride's parents, however, seem to have been a longstanding feature of marriage arrangements. Bell (1935d) mentions that at marriage "several" *am fat* were given by the husband to his wife's father. Parkinson (n.d.:266) recorded as the standard "brideprice": 20 meters of *kemetas*, four to six shell discs, and one or two pigs which, together with taro and drinking coconuts, furnished a feast for the relatives of the young couple. Most of my male informants agreed that standard payment in 1984–85 was: ten shell discs, one strand of *kemetas*, a small amount of cash (rarely exceeding 50 kina), and the pigs and food necessary for the *am borau*. Significantly, the payment seems not to have changed greatly since the turn of the century.

18 In this instance the father of the bride was deceased and the total payment went to her mother, Tingkausi, and through Tingkausi into a lineage supply that furnished most of the shells used at the Solsol *fasuigk*. Significantly, however, Tingkausi, offered three of the shell discs to her deceased husband's ZS (*kewalik*), that is, to her husband's "replacement." If both the mother and father of the bride have died, it is expected that the bride's lineage will receive the entire payment.

19 See Clay 1977 for a comprehensive discussion of the notion of nurture among the Mandak. Whereas Clay identifies three aspects of nurture (maternal, paternal, and affinal), I suggest that Tangans associate the idea of nurture particularly with the father/child relationship.

20 Thune (1980:79) contends that Normanby islanders similarly regard matrilateral relatedness as "natural" in contrast to the "created" ties of affinity and paternity.

21 This feature distinguishes the Tangan terminology from mainland two-line systems in which the F and FB are categorically identical. In the Tangan system, the FB is addressed as "my brother" (*tuaklik*).

22 When I leadingly suggested to one man that the father's semen was alone responsible for forming the child, as Clay (1977) reports for the Mandak, he denied this on the ground that semen alone would simply dry up. The idea of blood mixture, similar to Barok ideas about conception (Wagner 1983), does supply a logic for a taboo on marriage with actual cross-cousins – relatives of *wan blut* ("one blood") – that gives way to a preference for marriage in the next generation.

23 For example, for the Solsol men's house *bot*, Kiapun organized the performance of songs (*walau*) associated with the construction and launching of ocean-going canoes. Kiapun learned these songs from his maternal grandfather, Ngamnabo, one of the men being "finished" in the Solsol mortuary rites. Kiapun described the *walau* performances to me as an instance of *kos fang*, returning to Ngamnabo's matrilineal descendants the care their MB had bestowed upon Kiapun. He assured me that he would not have organized *walau* performances for just any *bot*; it was his connection to Ngamnabo that was being displayed.

24 The *kinaf* relationship is conceived in less egocentric terms; a particular man

might not "marry back," but a lineage brother might. The lineage, not the individual, is the relevant unit for exchanges of nurture. Similarly, figure 4 represents the categorical principle involved in marrying back, not an actual case, since marriage with the actual FZD is prohibited. Note too that Tangan relationship terminology does *not* equate FF with MBMB.

25 Nevertheless, in early 1992, Partui was considering hosting a mortuary sequence in which women would not only sit inside the funeral house (*fel*) – Partui was planning to build a *fel* instead of a *bia* (men's house) – and consume the choicest pork, but also walk across the ridgepole during the *am furis*.

26 Battaglia (1985), however, describes the Sabarl system for circulating paternal nurture through death exchanges as constructing long-term continuities in the absence of cross-cousin marriage.

27 I suggest that this deemphasis on "bride-price" is consistent as well with a self-conscious effort to insulate *kastam* from *bisnis*, that is, to legislate limits on the amount of cash allowed to circulate in marriage transactions. Such strategies have removed marriage payments from the influence of inflation.

28 *Tafu* may be rendered in Tok Pisin not only as "*ples bilong samting*" but also as "*mak bilong samting*"/"the mark of something." Similarly, the word *tafu* can be glossed as "role," as in Somanil's comment that he "played the role" (*kep tafu; kisim ples* in Tok Pisin) of Jesus in a dramatization of the crucifixion sponsored by the parish.

29 Maurer (1966) explains how the interrogative phrase *tafu se*? might mean "who has been sitting/standing/working here (that is, in this place [*stelle*])." He then gives as an example of a response to the interrogative *tafu sa*? ("what is this the place of?") *tafum fel* ("place of the house"), which he translates as: *da hat fruher mal ein Haus gestanden.*

30 Recall that Tangan relationship terminology does not merge the MBMB into the same classification as FF or MF as in a standard two-line terminology. The MB/ZS tie is highlighted across two generations rather than one.

6 Performing lineage succession: feast giving and value-creation

1 One man similarly suggested to me that dropping paper currency on a pig at a *fasuigk* distribution would not look good (*par lo i ti guam*) because the pig would not grunt as it does when a shell disc strikes its flank.

2 Replicas are defined in accordance with certain criteria. For example, for pigs, the relevant criteria are size, sex, and number; for shell discs (*am fat*), size, number, and type (see below and Bell 1935d for discussion of *am fat* types).

3 Clay's observation is pertinent: "The significance of exchanging – pigs, shell valuables, money – derives from the exchanging contexts. The metaphorical meaning assumed by such objects is used to communicate and change social relationships" (1977:125).

4 For a discussion of how anthropologists have dealt with the question of incommensurability see Foster 1990b.

5 But see Munn (1986) who treats value as the relative potency of actions with respect to some broad parameter of culturally defined significance. The possibility thereby exists of identifying a single dimension, such as capacity to

extend space–time, along which all exchanges and exchange objects can be evaluated.

6 Strathern's position, of course, entails the particular view of Melanesian personhood set out in the New Melanesian Ethnography (see Introduction). I take up this view in the next chapter.

7 This conceptualization of exchange derives from the work of Roy Wagner, who has restated his thesis in his most recent publications (esp. 1986b).

8 *Kemetas* (*mis* in Tok Pisin) is used widely in transactions throughout central and northern mainland New Ireland and the offshore islands, where it is the preeminent shell valuable. Lihir is the major center of *kemetas* production in south-central New Ireland (see Filer and Jackson 1988). The shells (perhaps *Chrysostoma paradoxum* of the family Trochidae [Wagner 1986a:81]) are worked into small discs, bored and then strung in various lengths on locally made twine or store-bought fishing line. Although Tangan men were aware of different named categories of *kemetas*, they used only the small red variety in prestations. For descriptions of *mis* and *mis* categories see Clay 1986:192 ff.; Wagner 1986a:80 ff.; Lewis 1929.

Bell reported the declining use of locally produced "small-diameter black, brown and white shell disks strung on fibre string" called *an ai-o-mil* (1950:95). He correctly speculated that *kemetas* imported from Lihir was ousting the home product. For more on the varieties of New Ireland shell wealth see Albert 1987a; Foster 1988.

9 See Bell 1935d for measurements of the different varieties of *am fat*.

10 There is perhaps a third type of *am fat* called *an simpendalu*. *An simpendalu* are thinner or flatter as well as greater in diameter than ordinary *tintol*; the groove around the outside edge is incised less deeply. A small variety of *an simpendalu* is called *an tu am fat*.

11 It is entirely relevant to my argument about evaluation to note that *am fat* are often cleaned before their public display in exchange transactions. The shells are washed with soap and water and sometimes bleached with Omo, a commercial laundry detergent.

12 The identification of the lineage with *warantang* is discussed subsequently. In Muliama, one informant similarly explained to me that every clan possesses *individually* named lengths of *mis*. These named shell valuables (after one of which the informant had named his daughter) do not circulate but rather remain in a "clan bank" (*lum na warankomo*/"hole of the base/origin of the banana/clan") managed by the clan leader. A leader succeeds his predecessor and "sits down on top of the *lum*."

13 This ornament is called *bun* by the Barok of central New Ireland who regard it as the "basis of the clan" (see the dust jacket of Wagner 1986a for a photo).

14 I asked this question as part of what appears in retrospect as a misdirected attempt to determine equivalencies.

15 Ben Topikol, an articulate and influential big man in Muliama, told me that his priorities were *kemetas*, money, and pigs, in that order. *Kemetas* and money, he pointed out, could be stored in the house. Because pigs must remain outside, however, they are liable to run away.

16 One man explained inflation to me in similar terms in noting that the PNG kina was no longer as "heavy" as it had been.

17 Several men claimed that *warantang* were displayed much less frequently now than in the past out of fear of retaliations for boastful exhibitions.

18 In other words, there are a number of oppositions (wet/dry, soft/hard, and possibly cool-sweet [*mir*]/hot [*pos*]) that, if not practically interchangeable with the *en/fat* dichotomy, are "more or less closely interrelated" (cf. Bourdieu 1977). I am concerned mainly with the *en/fat* dichotomy, however, as the economical contrast which summarizes the rest.

19 This observation is relevant to making sense of the metaphor built in the exchange of shell discs and whole cooked pigs at major mortuary feasts. The durability of the shell discs is defined contrastively in relation to the edibility of cooked pigs – not live pigs with the capacity to reproduce themselves physically (see Macintyre 1984; cf. Kahn 1986 for a similar point in regard to gifts of taro from which the corms have been removed).

20 Polygynous marriages thus enabled big men to increase their production of pigs. The substitution of coconut meat for cooked food clearly changed the social relations of pig production (cf. Clay 1986:164–5). Women were relieved of the burden of caring for the beasts (recall that only young men climb coconut palms). Big men possibly lost some of their control over the pig population as a new means for raising the animals became available.

21 In Pierce's terms, *am fat*, as embodied qualities, are "qualisigns" as well as icons: "Since a quality is whatever it is positively in itself, a quality can only denote an object by virtue of some common ingredient or similarity; so that a Qualisign is necessarily an Icon" (1955:115; see Munn 1986 for a related analysis of value in terms of icons and qualisigns).

22 So too is Bourdieu's notion of "a conceptual scheme immanent in practice" (1977:118; see also Sahlins 1981). Such schemes provide the terms which organize practice in diverse contexts according to an economical logic. The value-term *en* ("consumption"), for example, interrelates the distinct activities of eating, copulating, and killing. At the same time, these schemes are themselves the products of the concrete activity that they organize. That is, for example, the pragmatic content of the value-term *en* is the activity of eating, copulating, and killing through which agents create and acquire the value attribute of "consumption." Accordingly, the practical efficacy of conceptual schemes does not depend necessarily upon action *self-consciously* conceived in the terms of these schemes. Rather, contexts of action are themselves structured by those terms and thus predispose (but do not constrain) agents to acquiesce to the immanence of the scheme.

23 The game comprises, in Bourdieu's words, a "structural exercise" or "pedagogic action" that transmits practical mastery of the conceptual schemes that guide practice (1977:87–8).

24 The connection of these baskets with personal identity is comically demonstrated by the huge baskets that teenage boys carry about. Older men generally carry smaller, finely woven purses. A common jibe directed at basketless boys or men who request not only betel nut or tobacco but also the various paraphernalia necessary for chewing or smoking (lime, paper,

matches, etc.) is that they are like girls or young women, who often travel without baskets.

25 Different forms of "eating" (*en*) are subject to same logic. For example, the phrase *Kaltu i en si* describes a man who eats well from the hand of another man and who thinks all the time of this other man. The phrase also is applied to an adulterous couple whose illicit sex leads to their divorces and subsequent remarriage to each other. Such inability to control one's consumptive desires is likened to the behavior of dogs.

26 One man similarly remarked to me that the European habit of stocking a pantry was preferable to the Tangan method of trudging daily to the garden, even in inclement weather, as a way of regulating consumption. He, and others, credited Europeans with the capacity to regulate their food intake precisely, eating measured amounts of food at predetermined hours instead of eating whatever one can eat whenever, a self-deprecating but revealing Tangan self-caricature.

27 This story was recorded in Tok Pisin at Am Putput hamlet near Amfar, Boang Island, on December 15, 1984. The story was told by Nemet of clan Filimat.

28 This story was recorded on March 27, 1985 in the Tangga language at Balantaltal hamlet, Lif Island. The story was told by August Paptabil of clan Korofi. A similar version of this story in which the origin of coconuts is explained was recorded by Bell (1949c). Nepirpir, possibly the yellow honey-eater or some species of sunbird (*pirpir* denotes the color "yellow"), is something of an extraordinary character in Tangan folklore, capable of miraculous feats. The male bird is renowned among Tangans for the elaborate nests that it builds for the female to incubate eggs. These nests, I was told, have a door that when open functions as an awning to prevent rain from coming in and when closed completely seals the nest. Tangan men who find the nests take them home as prized treasures. The description of the nests recalled for me Bell's description of the baskets in which young girls (*dafal*) once were secluded as part of a process of making them beautiful (Bell 1936).

29 I thank Somanil Funil for his help in translating this and the other Nea stories. Coincidentally, it was Somanil's father, Funil, a former Head Catechist, who told the story to Maurer.

7 Performing lineage succession: transformative exchange and the power of mortuary rites

1 It might be helpful to consult tables 11 and 12 while reading this section.

2 Hence the common practice whereby the host lineage presents a large cooked pig to a senior matrilineage member, typically an aged lineage leader – the prototypical MBMB.

3 Most baskets are presented to representatives of other lineages. Exceptions include the prestations mentioned in footnote 2.

4 I have seen *warangus* presentations early on in a *pok bif* sequence which consisted simply of a modest portion of yams, *mangat* or the like (no pork) laid out atop a dish ready made from the sheath of a betel palm leaf (*piok*).

5 In the past, the ZS carried with him the skull of a deceased MB in a barkcloth sling of the sort once used by mothers to transport their infants (Bell 1937).

The act perhaps signified a reversal in the relations of dependence entailed in parental care inasmuch as the living (junior) ZS seems to nurture the dead (senior) MB. In 1985, the ZS carried or wore ceremonial axes and other lineage heirlooms.

6 The effect is analogous to that achieved by hosts of "eat everything" feasts who take in *tintol* as compensation for allowing the consumption of pork outside the confines of the men's house. (In fact, this is the only other context I know in which *am fat* are exchanged directly against pork.)

7 For example, to deplete one's strength in hard work is to *fapos miam* ("make hot your strength"). Partui used this expression to describe a father who wastes his energies and resources on children who fail to acknowledge his efforts. There are other contexts in which heat is connected with the depletion of strength: sexual intercourse with young women supposedly is avoided by older men because young women are "too hot." Similarly, excessive sexual intercourse is thought to sap a man's strength and cause illness. By this logic, heat is not only a cause of sapped strength, but a sign of the presence of manifest power. Hence the technique of making oneself hot/dry in love magic (see below).

8 Tangan informants claimed that only one man, an elderly resident of Anir, was an acknowledged *ingiat*. *Ingiat* are thought to be able to change their form, that is, to transform themselves into sharks and travel to other islands where they transform themselves into dogs or other terrestrial creatures, including human beings (cf. Bell 1947a:324). *Ingiat*, in other words, attain the highest form of control over *mui*: the control over form itself (see Wagner 1986a).

9 See Bell 1950. Nachman (1978) also discusses the similar but more elaborate rainmaking practices of Nissan islanders.

10 The scene recalls other "eat everything" feasts at which the members of a lineage together squat around their pork sections while members of other lineages eat separately from their respective portions.

11 *Tumbuan*, like shell discs, can be passed on and inherited. Unlike their owners, then, *tumbuan* possess a degree of immortality. Nonetheless, the parallel between the *tumbuan*, on the one hand, and the *ingiat* and *tumbuan* owner (*ain pindik*), on the other, is clear; all effect a degree of superordination through the regulation of consumption.

12 In Muliama, where Sokopana flourished in 1985, the ghost's consumption included the destruction of old men's houses preparatory to their reconstruction as part of a mortuary sequence. In Bell's account (1935b), Sokopana was responsible for the destruction of a ceremonial food container and the consumption of its contents as part of an ongoing mortuary sequence (a procedure associated by my informants with mainland New Ireland techniques). For other accounts of Sokopana (*sogopana, talun*) see Wagner 1986a and Albert 1987a, 1989).

13 The initiated have, as it were, overcome the threat of consumption. Certain adepts, such as *kabin pindik*, possess further the capacity to control the hyperconsuming ghost.

14 Significantly, the *merio* received from the chief *kabin pindik* a small stone,

waterwashed basalt, as a token of the silence or secrecy which they pledged. Such stones are part of the paraphernalia of rain makers (*waranfat*).

15 See Clay (1986:285) for a similar interpretation of Errington's description of Karavar *tumbuan* that emphasizes a big man's control of the "enduring power of the *tumbuan*."

16 This version of the story is taken from Bell (1941). The story was current on Tanga during my fieldwork.

17 The story can also be read as another instance of manifesting power through control over consumption. In the story, the women offer Nea not pork but themselves in order to recover the *am fat*. That is, the women proffer "edibles" (*en*), but in a sexual rather than gastronomic modality. Reciprocally, the *am fat* assume or exhibit a sexual aspect in their identification with Nea's penis. First, Nea's penis becomes the storehouse of the *am fat* hidden beneath his foreskin. Secondly, at the end of the story, Nea's erect penis itself turns into stone, the primary connotation of the word *fat*. The solicitations of the women overcome Nea's retentiveness: he involuntarily surrenders the shells. Nea thus suffers, and hence demonstrates, the danger that circulation poses for recipients: coercion by the unsolicited presentations of others into relinquishing objects preferably kept for oneself.

18 See Young's (1987: 249–50) discussion of "disguise and revelation" as the mechanisms of a technology of power found in many Melanesian societies, especially those of the Massim area of southeast Papua New Guinea.

19 The progress of the feasting therefore takes on the same form of continual revelation and revision that characterizes initiation sequences among the Baktaman (Barth 1975) and Telefolmin (Jorgensen 1980).

20 Although the hoarder retains control over the objects he hoards, his retention ultimately denies him the only culturally recognized means for attaching the qualities of those objects to his person, namely, display. The hoarder is unsociable (*kaltu wut*) because his lack of generosity implies a refusal to enter into a reciprocal process of identity construction that demands periodic displays of objects. Reciprocity, in this view, connotes not so much an obligation to repay as a willingness to become the instrument of another person's self-definition.

21 Eating carries a potential positive valence in other contexts. Eating, for example, realizes male sociality in potent fashion. *En tike*, the "eat everything" feasts associated with, among other things, various stages in men's house construction, furnish the context for often raucous conviviality. Men and boys excitedly anticipate and enjoy pork consumption; women and girls complain about their exclusion. Pork, more than fish or fowl, satisfies the desire that leaves people otherwise "hungry for meat" (*kabut*). *En tike* gather together men and male youths for the relatively unrestrained consumption of pork, a kind of gastronomic effervescence. On these occasions, men abandon the etiquette of controlled consumption and adopt the ethic of eating until it's all gone that distinguishes *en tike* as a special kind of feast. More generally, commensality within a men's house as part of a "satellite feast" (see above) defines lineage solidarity: a lineage is in at least one sense a group that eats pork collectively.

22 In addition, the actual timing of gifts in practice further ambiguates the matter. A prestation of a piece of pork might in one sense appear aggressive, yet when reciprocated, the original prestation might be retroactively constructed as nurturant (*fang*).

23 This story was recorded in the Tangga language on February 25, 1985 in Mokatilistunglo hamlet in the Taonsip area of Boang. The story was told by Kuriang, the leader of Sukeobom lineage of clan Korofi.

8 Social reproduction and *kastam* in comparative perspective

1 The category includes the shell heirlooms previously mentioned and described: *puk gem, katalu'm bul, am pilak*.

2 Accordingly, it is possible to regard circulating *am fat* as "*en*" relative to the non-circulating *warantang*. That is, the opposition between *en* and *fat* hierarchizes or ranks the different kinds of *am fat*, the more ideally "*fat*" shells circulating less frequently or, in the most extreme case, not at all.

3 My selection of criteria has been guided as well by the work of Andrew Strathern, not only by his ethnography of a paradigmatic expansive system (Melpa society/*moka* exchange), but also by his significant comparative analyses of *moka* and other exchange systems in Papua New Guinea societies (1969, 1975, 1978, 1983).

4 Most of the comparisons within the Highlands make use of this idea of a continuum (e.g., A. Strathern 1969). The comparison here proposes to extend, as it were, the length of such a continuum.

5 This is not to say that there is no differentiation among Highlands societies in forms of social reproduction (see, for example, Feil 1987). Nor do I seek to suggest yet another Islands/Highlands opposition. The scale of my contrast fits somewhere between the monolithic Us/Them dichotomy of the New Melanesian Ethnography and the intra-regional comparisons of A. Strathern (1969) and Lederman (1986a). It is perhaps closest in scale to Strathern's comparisons of *moka* with non-Highlands exchange systems such as *kula* (1983).

6 I include Mendi society for two reasons. First, Mendi *sem* exchanges take the form of pig kills, common throughout the Highlands, rather than that of the chained exchanges of live pigs characteristic of Melpa *moka* and Enga *tee*. I want to demonstrate how multiplication need not be exclusively associated with the kind of exchanges found in the latter two cases. Second, many of Lederman's goals in pursuing an historically based comparative political economy of Papua New Guinea societies are similar to my own (cf. Lederman 1986b).

7 I follow in this regard the recent interpretations of D. Feil (1980) whose view differs somewhat from that of Meggitt (1974). Meggitt regards *tee* prestations as the focus for interclan rivalry rather than intraclan rivalry. For a perspective that dissolves this difference see Merlan and Rumsey 1991. For a more extended analysis of *tee* exchanges see Foster (1985).

8 It is at this point that a detailed analysis of the relationship of exchange to production is required. Melpa big men depend for their security in part on a productive base of female labor that promises to provide them with new pigs to replace pigs given in *moka*. The situation in Tanga, for example, is radically

different. Shells could not in 1985 be procured or replaced with newly manufactured specimens. Likewise, the production of pigs in Tanga does not rest on
a base of female labor. Pigs consume coconuts not sweet potatoes and
coconuts are much more the affair of men than of women. This simple
difference itself needs much more investigation, for in the Tangan situation
raising a large pig herd means to some extent a reduction in cash income since
pigs feed on the source of that income in copra sales. In the Highlands
societies, the relationship among female labor, pig herding, and coffee production is both different and more complicated (see for example Strathern
1979).

9 Note, too, that the size of a gift to any one individual/lineage at a major pig
distribution (*fasuigk*) was usually fixed at one. Only the size of the pigs, not the
number, varied. This has the effect of spreading a small number of pigs over a
wider range of relationships. But it also has the "non-effect" of not impelling
host lineages to increase as much as possible the size of each individual
prestation (the opposite of *moka*).

10 The same can be said of Melpa death payments which frequently develop into
moka exchanges (Strathern 1982a).

11 Melpa and Mendi are like this. The Enga case is less clear. Meggitt claims a
strictly agnatic organization for the Mae Enga; Feil claims a much more
flexible situation for the Tombema Enga.

12 Lederman notes, for example, how Mendi distinguish between *twem* (personal
exchange) networks and clans (*sem onda*): "While *twem* networks are conceptualized by the Mendi as ephemeral, ego-centered creations – as the temporary
products of individual initiative – clans are conceptualized as enduring col-
lectivities" (1986b:19; cf. Feil 1984; Forge 1972).

13 See in this regard Strathern's comments about emerging contradictory trends
within the money-*moka* (1982d:315) and Warry's comments about the dilem-
mas of Chuave *bisnismen* (1987:139ff).

14 Nihill makes a similar observation for the nearby Anganen: "*Bisnis* is now
very popular, especially among younger men. In some respects it and exchange
[i.e., 'traditional' exchange] now rival each other as the major objects of men's
wealth, with a small but growing proportion of men arguing that exchange is
wasteful and *bisnis* productive, financially and for prestige" (1991:62). Nihill
goes on to note that the growing shift of men into *bisnis* is accompanied by a
move of women into exchange. This observation raises the possibility of an
emergent opposition between *bisnis* and *kastam* that is gender linked, that is,
the emergence of a feminized domain of *kastam*.

References

Albert, Steven M. 1986. "Completely by accident I discovered its meaning": the iconography of New Ireland *malagan. Journal of the Polynesian Society* 95: 239–52.

1987a. The Work of Marriage and Death: Ritual and Political Process Among the Lak, Southern New Ireland, Papua New Guinea. Ph.D. dissertation, Anthropology Department, University of Chicago.

1987b. *Tubuan:* masks and men in Southern New Ireland, Papua New Guinea. *Expedition* 29(1):17–26.

1989. Cultural implication: representing the domain of devils among the Lak. *Man* (N.S.) 24:273–88.

Anderson, Benedict. 1983. *Imagined Communities: Reflections on the Origin and Spread of Nationalism.* London: Verso.

Australia. 1914/21–1940. Prime Minister's Dept. Report to the Council of the League of Nations on the Administration of the Territory of New Guinea.

Babadzan, Alain. 1988. *Kastom* and nation building in the South Pacific. In R. Guidieri, F. Pellizi, and S. Tambiah, eds., *Ethnicities and Nations* (Austin: University of Texas Press), pp. 199–228.

Barraud, Cécile, Daniel de Coppet, André Iteanu, and Roger Jamous. 1984. Des relations et des mortes: quatres sociétés vues sous l'angle des échanges. In J. Galey, ed., *Différences, Valeurs, Hiérarchie: Textes Offerts à Louis Dumont* (Paris: Editions de l'Ecole des Hautes Etudes en Sciences Sociales), pp. 421–520.

Barth, Frederik. 1975. *Ritual and Knowledge among the Baktaman of New Guinea.* New Haven: Yale University Press.

Battaglia, Debbora. 1985. "We feed our father": paternal nurture among the Sabarl of Papua New Guinea. *American Ethnologist* 12:427–41.

1990. *On the Bones of the Serpent: Person, Memory, and Mortality in Sabarl Island Society.* Chicago: University of Chicago Press.

1992. The body in the gift: memory and forgetting in Sabarl mortuary exchange. *American Ethnologist* 19:3–18.

Beale, Thomas. 1839. *Natural History of the Sperm Whale.* London.

Beaumont, C. H. 1976. Austronesian languages: New Ireland. In S. A. Wurm, ed.,

New Guinea Area Language Study, Vol. 2. Australian National University, Pacific Linguistic Series C, No. 39, pp. 387–97.

Bell, F. L. S. 1934. A report on field work in Tanga. *Oceania* 4:290–309.

1935a. Warfare among the Tanga. *Oceania* 5:253–79.

1935b. Sokopana: a Melanesian secret society. *Journal of the Royal Anthropological Institute* 65:311–41.

1935c. The avoidance situation in Tanga, part I. *Oceania* 6:175–96.

1935d. The social significance of *Amfat* among the Tanga of New Ireland. *Journal of the Polynesian Society* 44:97–111.

1935e. A myth of the origin of death. *Mankind* 1:261–2.

1936. Dafal. *The Journal of the Polynesian Society* 45:83–98.

1937. Death in Tanga. *Oceania* 7:316–39.

1941. The narrative in Tanga, part I. *Mankind* 3:57–67.

1946. The place of food in the social life of the Tanga, part I. *Oceania* 17:139–62.

1947a. The place of food in the social life of the Tanga, part II. *Oceania* 17:310–26.

1947b. The place of food in the social life of the Tanga, part III. *Oceania* 18:36–59.

1948. The place of food in the social life of the Tanga, part V. *Oceania* 19:51–74.

1949a. The industrial arts in Tanga. *Oceania* 19:206–33.

1949b. The industrial arts in Tanga, part II. *Oceania* 19:320–48.

1949c. The narrative in Tanga, part VI. *Mankind* 4:99–101.

1950. Travel and communication in Tanga. *Oceania* 21:81–106.

1953. Land tenure in Tanga. *Oceania* 24:28–56.

1955. The role of the individual in Tangan society. *Journal of the Polynesian Society* 64:281–91.

1977. *Tanga–English, English–Tanga Dictionary.* Oceania Linguistic Monographs, No. 21.

Benveniste, Emile. 1971. Gift and exchange in the Indo-European vocabulary. In *Problems in General Linguistics.* Mary E. Meek, transl. (Coral Gables: University of Miami Press), pp. 271–80.

Bernstein, Henry. 1979. African peasantries: a theoretical framework. *Journal of Peasant Studies* 6:421–43.

Billings, Dorothy and Nicolas Peterson. 1967. *Malanggan* and *memai* in New Ireland. *Oceania* 38:24–32.

Biskup, Peter. 1970. Foreign coloured labour in German New Guinea: a study in economic development. *Journal of Pacific History* 5:85–107.

Bloch, Maurice. 1985. Almost eating the ancestors. *Man* (N.S.) 20:631–46.

Bloch, Maurice and Jonathan Parry, eds. 1982. *Death and the Regeneration of Life.* Cambridge: Cambridge University Press.

Blumer, Herbert. 1966. Sociological implications of the thought of G. H. Mead. *American Journal of Sociology* 71:535–44.

Bohannan, Paul. 1955. Some principles of exchange and investment among the Tiv. *American Anthropologist* 57:60–70.

Bourdieu, Pierre. 1977. *Outline of a Theory of Practice.* Richard Nice, transl. Cambridge: Cambridge University Press.

Boyd, David J. 1985. The commercialisation of ritual in the Eastern Highlands of Papua New Guinea. *Man* (N.S.) 20:325–40.

Brown, George. 1972[1910]. *Melanesians and Polynesians: Their Life-Histories Described and Compared.* New York: Benjamin Blom.

Bulmer, R. N. H. 1960. Political aspects of the Moka ceremonial exchange system among the Kyaka. *Oceania* 31:1–13.

Capell, A. 1977. Introduction. In F. L. S. Bell, *Dictionary*, pp. i–xxx.

Carrier, Achsah, and James Carrier. 1991. *Structure and Process in a Melanesian Society: Ponam's Progress in the Twentieth Century.* Philadelphia: Harwood.

Carrier, James. 1992a. Occidentalism: the world turned upside-down. *American Ethnologist* 19:195–212.

    1992b. Introduction. In J. Carrier, ed., *History and Tradition in Melanesian Anthropology* (Berkeley: University of California Press), pp. 1–37.

Carrier, James, and Achsah Carrier. 1989. *Wage, Trade, and Exchange: A Manus Society in the Modern State.* Berkeley: University of California Press.

Clay, Brenda. 1977. *Pinikindu: Maternal Nurture, Paternal Substance.* Chicago: University of Chicago Press.

    1986. *Mandak Realities: Person and Power in Central New Ireland.* New Brunswick: Rutgers University Press.

    1992. Other times, other places: agency and the big man in Central New Ireland. *Man* (N.S.) 27:719–33.

Cohn, Bernard S. 1981. History and anthropology: towards a rapprochement. *Journal of Interdisciplinary History* 12:227–52.

Coppet, Daniel de. 1982. The life-giving death. In S. C. Humphreys and H. King, eds., *Mortality and Immortality: The Anthropology and Archaeology of Death* (New York: Academic Press), pp. 175–204.

Corris, Peter. 1968. "Blackbirding" in New Guinea waters, 1883–84. *Journal of Pacific History* 3:85–105.

Damon, Frederick H. 1978. Modes of Production and the Circulation of Value on the Other Side of the Kula Ring. Ph.D. dissertation, Anthropology Department, Princeton University.

Damon, Frederick, and Roy Wagner, eds. 1989. *Death Rituals and Life in the Societies of the Kula Ring.* DeKalb, Illinois: Northern Illinois University Press.

Dampier, William. 1906. *Dampier's Voyages. 2 vols.* John Masefield, ed. London: E. Grant Richards.

Docker, Edward W. 1970. *The Blackbirders: The Recruiting of South Seas Labour for Queensland, 1863–1907.* Sydney: Angus and Robertson.

Dumont, Louis. 1970. Religion, politics and society in the individualistic universe. *Proceedings of the Royal Anthropological Institute of Great Britain and Ireland,* pp. 31–41.

Elkin, A. P. 1953. Delayed exchange in Wabag sub-district, Central Highlands of New Guinea, with notes on the social organization. *Oceania* 23:161–201.

Epstein, A. L. 1979. *Tambu*: the shell money of the Tolai. In R. H. Hook, ed., *Fantasy and Symbol: Studies in Anthropological Interpretation* (New York: Academic Press), pp. 149–205.

Errington, Frederick. 1974. *Karavar: Masks and Power in a Melanesian Ritual.* Ithaca: Cornell University Press.

Errington, Shelly. 1977. Order and power in Karavar. In Raymond D. Fogelson and Richard N. Adams, eds., *The Anthropology of Power* (New York: Academic Press), pp. 23–44.

Fahey, Stephanie. 1984. Proletarianization and changing gender relations among the peri-urban villagers of Madang, Papua New Guinea. In R. J. May, ed., *Social Stratification in Papua New Guinea*. Working Paper (Australian National University, Department of Political and Social Change), No. 5, pp. 219–55.

  1986. Development, labour relations and gender in Papua New Guinea. *Mankind* 16:118–31.

Fajans, Jane. 1986. Exchange, reciprocity and reproduction among the Baining. Paper presented at the annual meeting of the American Anthropological Association, Philadelphia.

Feil, D. K. 1980. Symmetry and complementarity: patterns of competition and exchange in the Enga *tee*. *Oceania* 51:20–39.

  1984. *Ways of Exchange: The Enga Tee of Papua New Guinea*. St. Lucia: University of Queensland Press.

  1987. *The Evolution of Highland Papua New Guinea Societies*. Cambridge: Cambridge University Press.

Filer, Colin. 1985. What is this thing called "brideprice"? In Don Gardner and Nicolas Modjeska, eds., *Recent Studies in the Political Economy of Papua New Guinea Societies*, Special Issue, *Mankind* 15:163–83.

Filer, Colin, and Richard Jackson. 1988[1986]. *The Social and Economic Impact of a Gold Mine on Lihir*. Port Moresby: University of Papua New Guinea.

Fingleton, Jim. 1984. Land tenure conversion: the privileged reserve of an elite. In R. J. May, ed., *Social Stratification in Papua New Guinea*. Working Paper (Australian National University, Department of Political and Social Change), No. 5, pp. 152–73.

Finney, Ben. 1973. *Big-Men and Business: Entrepreneurship and Economic Growth in the New Guinea Highlands*. Honolulu: University of Hawaii Press.

Firth, Stewart. 1976. The transformation of the labour trade in German New Guinea, 1899–1914. *Journal of Pacific History* 11:51–65.

  1982. *New Guinea Under the Germans*. Melbourne: Melbourne University Press.

Forge, Anthony. 1972. The golden fleece. *Man* (N.S.) 7:527–40.

Fortes, Meyer. 1953. The structure of unilineal descent groups. *American Anthropologist* 55:17–41.

Fortune, R. F. 1932. *Sorcerers of Dobu: The Social Anthropology of the Dobu Islanders of the Western Pacific*. New York: E. P. Dutton.

Foster, Robert J. 1985. Production and value in the Enga *tee*. *Oceania* 55:182–96.

  1987. Komine and Tanga: a note on writing the history of German New Guinea. *Journal of Pacific History* 22:56–64.

  1988. Social Reproduction and Value in a New Ireland Society, Tanga Islands, Papua New Guinea. Ph.D. dissertation, Anthropology Department, University of Chicago.

  1990a. Value without equivalence: exchange and replacement in a Melanesian society. *Man* (N.S.) 25:54–69.

  1990b. Nurture and force-feeding: mortuary feasting and the construction of collective individuals in a New Ireland society. *American Ethnologist* 17:431–48.

Gammage, Bill. 1975. The Rabaul strike, 1929. *Journal of Pacific History* 10:3–29.

Gardner, Don and Nicholas Modjeska, eds. 1985. *Recent Studies in the Political Economy of Papua New Guinea Societies.* Special Issue, *Mankind* 15:81–203.

Gell, Alfred. 1979. Reflections on a cut finger: taboo in the Umeda conception of the self. In R. H. Hook, ed., *Fantasy and Symbol: Studies in Anthropological Interpretation* (New York: Academic Press), pp. 133–48.

Gewertz, Deborah and Frederick Errington. 1991a. *Twisted Histories, Altered Contexts: Representing the Chambri in a World System.* Cambridge: Cambridge University Press.

1991b. We think, therefore they are? – On occidentalizing the world. *Anthropological Quarterly* 64:80–91.

Godelier, Maurice. 1978. "Salt money" and the circulation of commodities among the Baruya of New Guinea. In *Perspectives in Marxist Anthropology.* Cambridge: Cambridge University Press, pp. 127–51.

1986. *The Making of Great Men: Male Domination and Power among the New Guinea Baruya.* Rupert Swyer, transl. Cambridge: Cambridge University Press.

Godelier, Maurice, and Marilyn Strathern, eds. 1991. *Big Men and Great Men: Personifications of Power in Melanesia.* Cambridge: Cambridge University Press.

Gregory, Christopher A. 1980. Gifts to men and gifts to God: gift exchange and capital accumulation in contemporary Papua New Guinea. *Man* (N.S.) 15:626–52.

1982. *Gifts and Commodities.* New York: Academic Press.

Grossman, Lawrence. 1984. *Peasants, Subsistence Ecology, and Development in the Highlands of Papua New Guinea.* Princeton: Princeton University Press.

Herskovits, Melville J. 1956. On some modes of ethnographic comparison. *Bijdragen Tot De Taal-, Land en Volkenkunde* 112:129–48.

Hogbin, H. Ian. 1963. Government chiefs in New Guinea. In Meyer Fortes, ed., *Social Structure: Studies Presented to A. R. Radcliffe-Brown* (New York: Russell and Russell), pp. 189–206.

Huntington, Richard and Peter Metcalf. 1979. *Celebrations of Death: The Anthropology of Mortuary Ritual.* Cambridge: Cambridge University Press.

Iteanu, André. 1990. The concept of the person and the ritual system: an Orokaiva view. *Man* (N.S.) 25:35–53.

Jack-Hinton, C. 1972. Discovery. In *Encyclopedia of Papua New Guinea.* Melbourne: Melbourne University Press.

Jessep, Owen. 1980a. Land demarcation in New Ireland. *Melanesian Law Journal* 8:112–33.

1980b. Land and spirits in a New Ireland village. *Mankind* 12:300–10.

1987. *Pigs, Children and Land among the Barok of New Ireland.* Land Studies Centre Occasional Paper 87/1. University of Papua New Guinea.

Jorgensen, Dan. 1980. What's in a name: the meaning of meaninglessness in Telefolmin. *Ethos* 8:344–66.

Josephides, Lisette. 1985. *The Production of Inequality: Gender and Exchange among the Kewa*. London: Tavistock.

1991. Metaphors, metathemes, and the construction of sociality: a critique of the new Melanesian ethnography. *Man* (N.S.) 26:145–61.

Kahn, Miriam. 1980. Always in Hunger: Food as Metaphor for Social Identity in Wamira, Papua New Guinea. Ph.D. dissertation, Anthropology Department, Bryn Mawr College.

1986. *Always Hungry, Never Greedy: Food and the Expression of Gender in a Melanesian Society*. Cambridge: Cambridge University Press.

Kaplan, Martha. 1988. The coups in Fiji: colonial contradictions and the post-colonial crisis. *Critique of Anthropology* 8:93–116.

Kaplan, Susan. 1976. Ethnological and biogeographical significance of pottery sherds from Nissan Island, Papua New Guinea. *Fieldiana: Anthropology* Vol. 66:35–89.

Keesing, Roger. 1989. Creating the past: custom and identity in the contemporary Pacific. *Contemporary Pacific* 1:19–42.

1992. *Custom and Confrontation: The Kwaio Struggle for Cultural Autonomy*. Chicago: University of Chicago Press.

Keesing, Roger, and Margaret Jolly. 1992. Epilogue. In J. Carrier, ed., *History and Tradition in Melanesian Anthropology* (Berkeley: University of California Press), pp. 224–47.

Keesing, Roger M. and Robert Tonkinson, eds. 1982. *Reinventing Traditional Culture: The Politics of Kastom in Island Melanesia*. Special Issue, *Mankind* 13:297–399.

Kelly, Raymond C. 1977. *Etoro Social Structure: A Study in Structural Contradiction*. Ann Arbor: University of Michigan Press.

King, David and Stephen Ranck, eds. 1982. *Papua New Guinea Atlas: A Nation in Transition*. Bathurst, N.S.W.: Robert Brown and Associates (Australia) in conjunction with the University of Papua New Guinea.

Küchler, Susanne. 1983. The *Malangan* of Nombowai. *Oral History* 11(2):65–98.

1987. *Malangan*: art and memory in a Melanesian society. *Man* (N.S.) 22:238–55.

1988. Malangan: objects, sacrifice, and the production of memory. *American Ethnologist* 14:625–37.

Latukefu, Sione. 1988. Noble traditions and Christian principles as national ideology in Papua New Guinea: do their philosophies complement or contradict each other? *Pacific Studies* 11:83–96.

Lederman, Rena. 1986a. *What Gifts Engender: Social Relations and Politics in Mendi, Highland Papua New Guinea*. Cambridge: Cambridge University Press.

1986b. Changing times in Mendi: notes towards writing Highland New Guinea history. *Ethnohistory* 33:1–30.

Lewis, Albert. 1929. *Melanesian Shell Money in Field Museum Collections*. *Fieldiana: Anthropology* Vol. 19.

Lewis, Phillip H. 1969. *The Social Context of Art in Northern New Ireland*. *Fieldiana: Anthropology* Vol. 58.

Lindstrom, Lamont. 1982. *Leftamop kastom*: the political history of tradition on Tanna (Vanuatu). In Keesing and Tonkinson, eds., pp. 313–29.

1990a. *Pasin tumbuna*: cultural traditions and national identity in Papua New Guinea. Paper presented at Association for Social Anthropology in Oceania meeting, Kauai, Hawaii.

1990b. *Knowledge and Power in a South Pacific Society*. Washington, D.C.: Smithsonian Institution Press.

Linnekin, Jocelyn. 1983. Defining tradition: variations on the Hawaiian identity. *American Ethnologist* 10:241–52.

1990. The politics of culture in the Pacific. In J. Linnekin and L. Poyer, eds., *Cultural Identity and Ethnicity in the Pacific* (Honolulu: University of Hawaii Press), pp. 149–73.

LiPuma, Edward. 1988. *The Gift of Kinship: Structure and Practice in Maring Social Organization*. Cambridge: Cambridge University Press.

LiPuma, Edward and Sarah Meltzoff. 1990. Ceremonies of Independence and public culture in the Solomon Islands. *Public Culture* 3:77–92.

MacClancy, Jeremy. 1982. Vanuatu and *Kastom*: A Study of Cultural Symbols in the Inception of a Nation-State in the South Pacific. Ph.D. Thesis, Department of Social Anthropology, University of Oxford.

Macintyre, Martha. 1984. The problem of the semi-alienable pig. *Canberra Anthropology* 7:109–21.

MacWilliam, Scott. 1986. International capital, indigenous accumulation and the state in Papua New Guinea: the case of the Development Bank. *Capital and Class* No. 29, Summer, pp. 150–81.

Mair, Lucy P. 1970. *Australia in New Guinea*. Melbourne: Melbourne University Press.

Malinowski, Bronislaw. 1961[1922]. *Argonauts of the Western Pacific: An Account of Native Enterprise and Adventure in the Archipelagoes of Melanesian New Guinea*. New York: E. P. Dutton.

Marcus, George and Dick Cushman. 1982. Ethnographies as texts. *Annual Review of Anthropology* 11:25–69.

Marx, Karl. 1979[1867]. *Capital, Vol. 1: A Critical Analysis of Capitalist Production*. Samuel Moore and Edward Aveling, transls. New York: International Publishers.

Maurer, Heinrich. 1966. *Grammatik der Tangga-Sprache* (Melanesian). Micro-Bibliotheca Anthropos, Vol. 39.

1975. Drei marchen von den Tangga-Inseln, New Ireland. In H. Janssen, J. Sterly, and K. Wittkemper, eds., *Carl Laufer MSC: Missionar und Ethnologe auf Neu-Guinea: Eine Gedenkschrift fur P. Carl Laufer MSC gewidmet von seinen Freunden* (Freiburg im Breisgau: Herder.), pp. 107–38.

Mauss, Marcel. 1967[1925]. *The Gift: Forms and Functions of Exchange in Archaic Societies*. Ian Cunnison, transl. New York: Norton.

Meggitt, Mervyn. 1974. "Pigs are our hearts!": the Te exchange cycle among the Mae Enga. *Oceania* 44:165–203.

Meillassoux, Claude. 1981. *Maidens, Meal and Money: Capitalism and the Domestic Community*. Cambridge: Cambridge University Press.

Merlan, Francesca and Alan Rumsey. 1991. *Ku Waru: Language and Segmentary*

Politics in the Western Nebilyer Valley, Papua New Guinea. Cambridge: Cambridge University Press.

Mihalic, F. 1971. *The Jacaranda Dictionary and Grammar of Melanesian Pidgin.* Milton, Queensland: Jacaranda Press.

Mitchell, W. J. T. 1987. *Iconology: Image, Text, Ideology.* Chicago: University of Chicago Press.

Modjeska, Nicholas. 1982. Production and inequality: perspectives from Central New Guinea. In Andrew Strathern, ed., *Inequality in New Guinea Highlands Societies* (Cambridge: Cambridge University Press), pp. 50–108.

1985. Exchange value and Melanesian trade reconsidered. In Don Gardner and Nicholas Modjeska, eds., *Recent Studies in the Political Economy of Papua New Guinea Societies,* Special Issue, *Mankind* 15:145–62.

Moore, Sally Falk. 1986. *Social Facts and Fabrications: "Customary" Law on Kilimanjaro, 1880–1980.* Cambridge: Cambridge University Press.

Morauta, Louise. 1984. *Left Behind in the Village: Economic and Social Conditions in an Area of High Outmigration.* Boroko: Institute of Applied Social and Economic Research.

Mosko, Mark. 1992. Motherless sons: 'divine kings' and 'partible persons' in Melanesia and Polynesia. *Man* (N.S.) 27:693–717.

Munn, Nancy D. 1977. Spatiotemporal transformations of Gawa canoes. *Journal de la Société des Océanistes* 33:39–53.

1983. Gawan kula: Spatiotemporal control and the symbolism of influence. In Edmund Leach and Jerry Leach, eds., *The Kula: New Perspectives on Massim Exchange* (Cambridge: Cambridge University Press), pp. 277–308.

1986. *The Fame of Gawa: A Symbolic Study of Value Transformation in a Massim (Papua New Guinea) Society.* Cambridge: Cambridge University Press.

Murray, Mary. 1967. *Hunted: A Coastwatcher's Story.* Sydney: Rigby, Ltd.

Nachman, Steven R. 1978. In Honor of the Dead, In Defiance of the Living: An Analysis of the Nissan Mortuary Feast. Ph.D. dissertation, Anthropology Department, Yale University.

Neuhaus, P. K. 1925. Die neue Mission auf den Tanga-Inseln. *Hiltruper Monatshefte* 42:327–30.

Neumann, Klaus. 1992. Tradition and identity in Papua New Guinea: some observations regarding Tami and Tolai. *Oceania* 62:295–316.

Nihill, Michael. 1989. The new pearlshells: aspects of money and meaning in Anganen exchange. *Canberra Anthropology* 12:144–60.

1991. Money and "moka": men, women, and change in Anganen mortuary exchange. *Journal of the Polynesian Society* 100:45–69.

Otto, Ton. 1990. The Politics of Tradition in Baluan: Social Change and the Appropriation of the Past in a Manus Society. Ph.D. Thesis, Anthropology Department, Research School of Pacific Studies, The Australian National University.

Papua New Guinea. 1983. National Statistics Office. Provincial Data System, Rural Community Register: New Ireland Province.

Parkinson, Richard. n.d. Thirty Years in the South Seas. N. C. Barry, ed. and transl. Typescript. New Guinea Collection, University of Papua New Guinea. (Original: *Dreissig Jahre in der Sudsee,* Stuttgart, 1907.)

Parry, Jonathan. 1986. *The Gift*, the Indian gift, and the "Indian gift." *Man* (N.S.) 21:453–73.

Philibert, Jean-Marc. 1986. The politics of tradition: toward a generic culture in Vanuatu. *Mankind* 16:1–12.

Pierce, Charles S. 1955. *Philosophical Writings of Pierce*. Justus Buchler, ed. New York: Dover.

Powdermaker, Hortense. 1971[1933]. *Life in Lesu: The Study of a Melanesian Society in New Ireland*. New York: Norton.

Price, Charles A. with Elizabeth Baker. 1976. Origins of Pacific Island labourers in Queensland, 1863–1904: a research note. *Journal of Pacific History* 11:106–21.

Rannie, Douglas. 1912. *My Adventures Among South Seas Cannibals*. London: Seeley, Service and Company.

Rochberg-Halton, Eugene. 1986. *Meaning and Modernity: Social Theory in the Pragmatic Attitude*. Chicago: University of Chicago Press.

Rowley, C. D. 1958. *The Australians in German New Guinea, 1914–1921*. Melbourne: Melbourne University Press.

Sack, Peter and Dymphna Clark, eds. and transls. 1979. *German New Guinea: The Annual Reports*. Canberra: Australian National University Press.

Sahlins, Marshall D. 1963. Poor man, rich man, big man, chief: political types in Melanesia and Polynesia. *Comparative Studies in Society and History* 5:285–300.

1972. *Stone Age Economics*. Chicago: Aldine.

1981. *Historical Metaphors and Mythical Realities: Structure in the Early History of the Sandwich Islands Kingdom*. Ann Arbor: University of Michigan Press.

1985. *Islands of History*. Chicago: University of Chicago Press.

1988. Cosmologies of capitalism: the trans-Pacific sector of the 'world system.' *Proceedings of the British Academy for 1988*, pp. 1–51.

1992. The economics of develop-man in the Pacific. *Res* 21:13–25.

1993. Goodbye to *Tristes Tropes*: ethnography in the context of modern world history. *Journal of Modern History* 65:1–25.

Said, Edward. 1978. *Orientalism*. New York: Vintage Books.

Salisbury, Richard. 1962. *From Stone to Steel: Economic Consequences of a Technological Change in New Guinea*. New York: Cambridge University Press.

Scarr, Deryck. 1967. *Fragments of Empire: A History of the Western Pacific High Commission, 1877–1914*. Canberra: Australian National University Press.

Schlaginhaufen, Otto. 1908. Ein besuch auf den Tanga-Inseln. *Globus* 94:165–9.

Shineberg, Dorothy. 1967. *They Came for Sandalwood: A Study of the Sandalwood Trade in the South-West Pacific*. Carlton, Victoria: Melbourne University Press.

Snowden, Catherine. 1980? Copra co-operatives. In Donald Denoon and Catherine Snowden, eds., *A History of Agriculture in Papua New Guinea: A Time to Plant, A Time to Uproot* (Boroko: Institute of Papua New Guinea Studies), pp. 185–204.

Strathern, Andrew. 1969. Finance and production: two strategies in New Guinea Highlands exchange systems. *Oceania* 40:42–67.

1971. *The Rope of Moka: Big-Men and Ceremonial Exchange in Mount Hagen, New Guinea.* Cambridge: Cambridge University Press.

1975. By toil or guile?: the use of coils and crescents by Tolai and Hagen big-men. *Journal de Société des Océanistes* 31:363–78.

1978. "Finance and Production" revisited: in pursuit of a comparison. *Research in Economic Anthropology* 1:73–104.

1979. Gender, ideology and money in Mount Hagen. *Man* (N.S.) 14:530–48.

1982a. Death as exchange: two Melanesian cases. In S. C. Humphreys and H. King, eds., *Mortality and Immortality: The Anthropology and Archaeology of Death* (New York: Academic Press), pp. 175–204.

1982b. Witchcraft, greed, cannibalism and death: some related themes from the New Guinea Highlands. In Maurice Bloch and Jonathan Parry, eds., *Death and the Regeneration of Life* (Cambridge: Cambridge University Press), pp. 111–33.

1982c. Alienating the inalienable (Correspondence). *Man* (N.S.) 17:548–51.

1982d. The division of labor and processes of social change in Mount Hagen. *American Ethnologist* 9:307–19.

1983. The kula in comparative perspective. In J. Leach and E. Leach, eds., *The Kula: New Perspectives on Massim Exchange* (Cambridge: Cambridge University Press), pp. 73–88.

Strathern, Marilyn. 1972. *Women in Between: Female Roles in a Male World, Mt. Hagen, New Guinea.* London: (Academic) Seminar Press.

1981. Self-interest and the social good: some implications of Hagen gender imagery. In S. B. Ortner and H. Whitehead, eds., *Sexual Meanings: The Cultural Construction of Gender and Sexuality* (New York: Cambridge University Press), pp. 166–91.

1984. Marriage exchanges: a Melanesian comment. *Annual Review of Anthropology* 13:41–73.

1987a. Conclusion. In M. Strathern, ed., *Dealing with Inequality: Analysing Gender Relations in Melanesia and Beyond* (Cambridge: Cambridge University Press), pp. 278–302.

1987b. Producing difference: connections and disconnections in two New Guinea Highland kinship systems. In J. Collier and S. Yanagisako, eds., *Gender and Kinship: Essays towards Unified Analysis* (Stanford: Stanford University Press), pp. 271–300.

1988. *The Gender of the Gift: Problems with Women and Problems with Society in Melanesia.* Berkeley: University of California Press.

1990. Artefacts of history: events and the interpretation of images. In J. Siikala, ed., *Culture and History in the Pacific* (Helsinki: The Finnish Anthropological Society), pp. 25–44.

1991. One man and many men. In M. Godelier and M. Strathern, eds., pp. 197–214.

1993. Entangled objects: detached metaphors. *Social Analysis* 34:88–101.

Territory of Papua and New Guinea. 1944–74. Department of Native Affairs. New Ireland District, Namatanai Sub-District. Patrol Reports. National Archives of Papua New Guinea.

1963. Native Land Commission and Land Titles Commission. Exhibits A through M, Tanga Land Investigation. Files of the Author.

Thomas, Nicholas. 1991. *Entangled Objects: Exchange, Material Culture, and Colonialism in the Pacific*. Cambridge, MA: Harvard University Press.

1992a. Substantivization and anthropological discourse: the transformation of practices into institutions in neotraditional Pacific societies. In J. Carrier, ed., *History and Tradition in Melanesian Anthropology* (Berkeley: University of California Press), pp. 64–85.

1992b. The inversion of tradition. *American Ethnologist* 19:213–32.

Thompson, Herb and Scott MacWilliam. 1992. *The Political Economy of Papua New Guinea: Critical Essays*. Manila: Journal of Contemporary Asia Publishers.

Thune, Carl E. 1980. The Rhetoric of Remembrance: Collective Life and Personal Tragedy in Loboda Village. Ph.D. dissertation, Anthropology Department, Princeton University.

Tonkinson, Robert. 1982. National identity and the problem of *kastom* in Vanuatu. In Keesing and Tonkinson, eds., pp. 306–15.

Wagner, Roy. 1974. Are there social groups in the New Guinea Highlands? In M. Leaf, ed., *Frontiers of Anthropology* (New York: Nostrand), pp. 95–122.

1981 (1975). *The Invention of Culture*. Chicago: University of Chicago Press.

1983. The ends of innocence: conception and seduction among the Daribi of Karimui and the Barok of New Ireland. *Mankind* 14:75–83.

1986a. *Asiwinarong: Image, Ethos and Social Power among the Usen Barok of New Ireland*. Princeton: Princeton University Press.

1986b. *Symbols that Stand for Themselves*. Chicago: University of Chicago Press.

1987. Daribi and Barok images of public man: a comparison. In L. Langness and T. Hays, eds., *Anthropology in the High Valleys: Essays on the New Guinea Highlands in Honor of Kenneth E. Read* (Novato, California: Chandler and Sharp), pp. 163–84.

1991a. The fractal person. In M. Godelier and M. Strathern, eds., pp. 159–73.

1991b. New Ireland is shaped like a rifle and we are at the trigger: the power of digestion in cultural reproduction. In A. Biersack, ed., *Clio in Oceania: Toward a Historical Anthropology* (Washington, D.C.: Smithsonian Institution Press), pp. 329–46.

Warry, Wayne. 1987. *Chuave Politics: Changing Patterns of Leadership in the Papua New Guinea Highlands*. Political and Social Change Monograph 4. Canberra: Research School of Pacific Studies, Australian National University.

Wawn, William T. 1973[1893]. *The South Sea Islanders and the Queensland Labour Trade*. Peter Corris, ed. Honolulu: University Press of Hawaii.

Weiner, Annette B. 1976. *Women of Value, Men of Renown: New Perspectives in Trobriand Exchange*. Austin: University of Texas Press.

1980. Reproduction: a replacement for reciprocity. *American Ethnologist* 7:71–85.

1985. Inalienable wealth. *American Ethnologist* 12:210–27.

1992. *Inalienable Possessions: The Paradox of Keeping-While-Giving.* Berkeley: University of California Press.

Weiner, James W. 1988. *The Heart of the Pearlshell: The Mythological Dimension of Foi Sociality.* Berkeley: University of California Press.

Whittaker, J. L., N. G. Gash, J. F. Hookey, and R. J. Lacey. 1975. *Documents and Readings in New Guinea History: Prehistory to 1889.* Milton, Queensland: The Jacaranda Press.

White, Geoffrey. 1991. *Identity Through History: Living Stories in a Solomon Islands Society.* Cambridge: Cambridge University Press.

Wolf, Eric R. 1982. *Europe and the People Without History.* Berkeley: University of California Press.

Young, Michael W. 1971. *Fighting with Food: Leadership, Values and Social Control in a Massim Society.* Cambridge: Cambridge University Press.

1987. The tusk, the flute and the serpent: disguise and revelation in Goodenough mythology. In M. Strathern, ed., *Dealing With Inequality: Analysing Gender Relations in Melanesia and Beyond* (Cambridge: Cambridge University Press), pp. 229–54.

Index

Cambridge Studies in Social and Cultural Anthroplogy

Editors: ERNEST GELLNER, JACK GOODY, STEPHEN GUDEMAN, MICHAEL HERZFELD, JONATHAN PARRY

* available in paperback